THE
BRIEF ENGLISH
HANDBOOK

THE

BRIEF ENGLISH

HANDBOOK

Fifth Edition

EDWARD A. DORNAN
Orange Coast College

CHARLES W. DAWE
Orange Coast College

HarperCollins*CollegePublishers*

Acquisitions Editor: Ellen Schatz
Developmental Editor: Sarah Helyar Smith Editorial Services
Project Editor: Lois Lombardo
Design Manager: Sandra Watanabe
Cover Designer: Sandra Watanabe
Electronic Production Manager: Valerie A. Sawyer
Manufacturing Manager: Helene G. Landers
Electronic Page Makeup: Dorothy Bungert/EriBen Graphics
Printer and Binder: RR Donnelley & Sons Company
Cover Printer: The Lehigh Press, Inc.

The Brief English Handbook, Fifth Edition

Library of Congress Cataloging-in-Publication Data

Dornan, Edward A.
        The brief English handbook/Edward A. Dornan, Charles W. Dawe.—
    5th ed.
            p.   cm.
        Includes index.
        ISBN 0-673-52488-4 (student edition)
        ISBN 0-673-52519-8 (instructor's edition)
        1.   English language—Grammar—Handbooks, manuals, etc.   2.   English
    language—Rhetoric—Handbooks, manuals, etc.   I. Dawe, Charles W.
    II. Title.
    PE1112.D67   1996
    428.2—dc20   95-32726
                                                                  CIP

        98 9 8 7 6 5

Contents

11 Verb Forms and Verb Tense 64

12 Subjunctive Mood 76

13 Active and Passive Voice 78

14 Adjectives and Adverbs 82

24 Unnecessary Commas 167

25 The Semicolon 173

26 The Colon 178

27 The Dash 181

28 Quotation Marks 183

29 The Ellipsis Mark 190

30 Parentheses 192

31 Brackets 194

46   Writing the Argument Essay and Critical Thinking 346

47   Writing an Analytical Essay about Literature 373

Preface

This fifth edition of *The Brief English Handbook* is still a compact, easy-to-use guide to standard American English and college writing. The organization remains straightforward, the design clear, the rules prominent and carefully indexed, and the coverage thorough.

While revising this edition, we concentrated on integrating recent changes in Modern Language Association and American Psychological Association documentation styles in the three chapters devoted to research-based writing—chapter 48, "Researching a Paper"; chapter 49, "Writing a Research Paper"; and chapter 50, "A Documentation Guide." We also reinforced the information on using computers for word processing and for conducting research.

Distinguishing Features

Chapter 45, "Writing the Essay," integrates modes of thought and the composing process. This chapter begins with an explanation of the writer-reader relationship and then presents an analytical student essay, "Subtle Persuasion," that reflects dominant academic standards and a variety of paragraph modes. After examining the essay, students will be ready to *retrace* the course of its development. Throughout the discussion, which proceeds step by step from finding a subject to proofreading the final draft, we emphasize the interplay of associational and analytical thinking. The chapter ends with "Guidelines for Peer Review," which is designed either to reinforce the instructor's current peer review procedures or to introduce students to independent peer review sessions.

Chapter 46, "Writing the Argument Essay and Critical Thinking," integrates critical thinking concepts with argumentation. Throughout the chapter, we emphasize the role of analysis, synthesis, and evaluation in critical thinking. We also discuss the evaluation of fact and opinion, the varieties and uses of evidence, the nature of inductive and deductive reasoning, and types of fallacious reasoning—all covered as they relate to the composition of a sound argument.

Chapter 49, "Writing a Research Paper," models a student paper on the timely subject of home education. Students can follow detailed examples in several stages of development, from forming a thesis and making an outline, through the drafting stages, and finally to the final research paper, which is fully annotated.

Chapter 15, "Reminders for ESL Writers," is designed for second-language students who have learned English but still need to consciously review their essays for common ESL mistakes. From an ESL perspective we review such recurring problems as sentence completeness, verb combinations, faulty repetitions, and misused participles and coordinators.

Organization

The handbook follows the logical arrangement of moving from small to large. We begin with a review of the essentials of grammar before presenting sentence structure and punctuation. We also list grammatical terms alphabetically in a glossary and meticulously cross-reference terms to their definitions throughout the text. Following the grammar review, we present several chapters on sentence errors, sentence clarity, and sentence variety, where we emphasize the common faults that plague student essays.

Our approach is necessarily prescriptive in matters of standard English but more relaxed in matters of style. In the chapters on punctuation and mechanics, we include more detail and more examples than other textbooks of comparable length. We saw no good reason to take shortcuts here; students should refer to punctuation rules, especially those on comma usage, with the assurance that the text can answer their queries succinctly and directly.

In the chapters on diction, we cover a wide range of topics, including guidelines for avoiding sexist language. Common usage problems, especially matters of diction, are also listed alphabetically in a glossary.

The next seven chapters concentrate on composition. Chapter 44, "Writing Paragraphs," offers more than twenty models of student and professional paragraphs to illustrate unity, coherence, and methods of development. Chapter 45, "Writing the Essay," in addition to linking associational and analytical thinking to the writing, integrates current research on composing and revision. Chapter 46, "Writing the Argument Essay and Critical Thinking," embodies the application of critical thought to argumentation. Chapter 47, "Writing an Analytical Essay about Literature," defines literary analysis and offers brief models for composing an analytical essay.

The three chapters on the research paper simplify the process of researching a subject and composing a documented paper. Chapter 48, "Researching a Paper," presents a clear explanation of research techniques, beginning with finding a topic and ending with questions that students typically ask about research. Chapter 49, "Writing a Research Paper," follows one student's writing process from thesis to final paper. And chapter 50, "A Documentation Guide," concludes the sequence with a handy reference guide for MLA, APA, and CBE styles.

Special Features

Other features of *The Brief English Handbook,* fifth edition, deserve special mention. Rules and advice are indexed by page tabs in the corners and by a thorough system of cross-referencing; in addition, of course, there is a complete subject index. Exercises reinforce rules and examples in every part of the book. Most of the exercises concentrate on a single theme or topic rather than on five or ten unrelated ideas and include sentence combining and controlled composition. For handy reference, the instructor's annotated edition includes the answers to exercises with the exercises themselves.

When revising *The Brief English Handbook,* we committed ourselves to keeping the tone lively and encouraging. We hope you and your students will find this tone refreshing.

Ancillaries and Software

Available with this new edition of *The Brief English Handbook* is *The Writer's Workshop,* an interactive software program developed by the Daedalus Group. It surpasses any existing commercial word processing program (IBM or Mac) in providing writing prompts—invention heuristics, revision strategies, and writing techniques—for students while they compose their papers. It includes the *Documentor* program to help students put their reference citations into correct MLA or APA format, as well as reference material from *The Brief English Handbook, Fifth Edition* to provide grammar help on-line.

A variety of print supplements, including a workbook of exercises called *The Brief English Workbook,* are also available to adopters. For more details, please contact your local HarperCollins sales representative.

Acknowledgments

We have had the good fortune to receive helpful suggestions from many students and instructors throughout the country: Jennifer Bradley, University of California, Los Angeles; Barbara Carson, University of Georgia; Reginald Clarke, Citrus College; Terrence A. Dalyrimple, Angelo State University; Patty Emmons, Northern Virginia Community College; Norma Engberry, University of Nevada, Las Vegas; Joan Fitch, Mississippi Gulf Coast Community

College; Adelaide Frazier, University of New Orleans; Stephen Goldman, University of Kansas; Rosanna Grassi, Syracuse University; Michael Grimwood, North Carolina State University; Lin Humphrey, Citrus College; Elizabeth Jordan, University of California, San Diego; Melinda Kramer, Purdue University; Joyce Lipkis, Santa Monica College; Lisa Martin, Cape Cod Community College; Michael Meyer, University of Connecticut; Janet Minc, Wayne General and Technical College; Elizabeth Mitchell, Ocean County College; Jeannette Morgan, University of Houston; Robert Mueller, Illinois Valley Community College; Janice Neulieb, Illinois State University; Jack Oruch, University of Kansas; Charles Reinhardt, Vincennes University; William Reynolds, Hope College; Maureen Ryan, University of Southern Mississippi; Alan Schwartz, Queensborough Community College; Robert A. Schwegler, University of Rhode Island; Anne B. Slater, Frederick Community College; John Stewart, Utah State University; Linda Tiemann, Blinn College; Virginia Wagner, Mendocino College; Carroll Wilson, Raritan Valley Community College; Nancy Yee, Fitchburg State College; and William Zehringer, Bloomsburg State College. We offer a special thanks to Robert Dees for his work on the research chapters and to Sarah E. Cummings for her assistance with the chapter on English as a second language. We also wish to express our gratitude to our HarperCollins editors—Ellen Schatz, Sarah Helyar Smith, and Lois Lombardo.

Edward A. Dornan
Charles W. Dawe

To the Student

We wrote *The Brief English Handbook* as a concise guide to grammatical accuracy, effective sentences, correct punctuation, word selection, and sound development of paragraphs, essays, and research papers. *The Brief English Handbook*'s primary use will probably be in a composition class, where the teacher might assign chapters and exercises for class discussion or refer you to the book to correct your written work. We hope you will also see its value as a companion to any course that requires writing.

We have kept the structure of *The Brief English Handbook* simple and direct. We begin with the essentials of grammar. The first part presents parts of speech, parts of sentences, phrases, clauses, and kinds of sentences. Your instructor might ask you to review these first five chapters; indeed, if you feel apprehensive about such terms as *noun, verb, subject, predicate, clause,* and *phrase,* we also recommend that you do so.

In the second part, "Sentence Errors," we cover common mistakes writers make when expressing their thoughts in writing—fragments, comma splices and fused sentences, failure to establish the correct relations between subjects and verbs as well as between pronouns and antecedents—the kinds of errors that hinder clear communication. In the third part, "Sentence Clarity and Variety," we continue the discussion of sentences, but we emphasize ways to write clear and accurate sentences while keeping a reader interested in what you have to say. Some of the techniques we explain are varying sentences patterns, using modifiers, arranging words for emphasis, and enhancing the impact of sentences through parallel structure.

In the fourth and fifth parts, "Punctuation" and "Mechanics," we give rules for using commas, semicolons, colons, dashes, capitalization, abbreviations, and the like. In the sixth part, "Diction," we concentrate on words and urge you to select words that are appropriate, exact, and concise.

In the seventh part, "Paragraphs, Essays, and Research Papers," we present the kinds of writing you will be required to do in college and in your professional life. We begin with paragraphs, stressing the importance of clear topic sentences, paragraph unity, and paragraph coherence. We then discuss the whole essay and guide you through the process of selecting a topic, generating ideas, organizing a paper, completing a rough draft, revising the draft, and writing a final draft. The last three chapters trace the process of writing and documenting a research paper, perhaps the most important learning activity you will undertake in your first year of college writing.

Finally, at the end of the book we have included two glossaries. The glossary of usage explains many of the words and phrases writers find troublesome and confusing. The glossary of grammatical terms defines the specialized words we use throughout the text.

Revising Your Papers

Sometimes your instructor might write comments in the margins of your paper suggesting that you refer to *The Brief English Handbook* for certain information. You can best find the information first by deciphering the key terms in the teacher's comments and then by looking them up in the index, which lists every important term we have used, or by scanning the table of contents, which lists the book's main parts, chapters, and chapter sections.

At other times your instructor might write numbers or symbols in the margins of your paper. Numbers refer to chapters, and if a letter is used with a number, the letters refer to a chapter section (for instance, 19g refers to section g in chapter 19). The numbers and letters are printed in the table of contents and on tabs on the upper outside corners of the pages where you can find the information they refer to. You can find out what symbols such as *frag* or // indicate—

frag indicates fragment and [//] indicates parallelism—by referring to the inside front cover, where the words the symbols represent are listed alphabetically. They also appear next to the tabs on each page and at the beginning of each chapter.

If your instructor uses numbers to indicate needed corrections and to suggest revisions, your returned papers might look like the following example, which is the introductory paragraph of a student essay.

28b   "Time to Slow Down"

          When I first returned to the city after ten months in a

38g   forestry camp, I was not ready to reenter the pace of daily life.

      For a few uncomfortable days, I had the feeling I was living

      within the frenetic action of an old silent movie. People around

6a   me rushing as though they were late for an appointment.

7a   At first this activity made me nervous, my experience in the

      forestry camp had given me a more leisurely approach to daily

      activities.

If instead of numbers your instructor uses symbols, your returned papers might look like the following, which is the continuation of the paragraph in the student essay.

      In the months that followed, I began to understand that the

      speed of daily living, which had upset me when I returned, was

      only the most obvious part of a deeper attitude. We are so busy
                       vb
      when rushed from one experience to another, developing new

      interests and dropping old ones, that we seldom take the time
                                  ref
      to do anything well. This shows in our responses to public

affairs, in our educational programs, and in our relationships with each other.

After your instructor returns your paper, use the text to look up the notations; in a different color ink, make the necessary corrections in your paper before beginning the revised draft.

Your instructor's notations can be a valuable aid in learning the rules and guidelines for clear writing. We suggest you use the notations as a study guide, carefully reading the information they refer to and completing the exercises that accompany the information. We also suggest you keep a record of the notations so that you can return to *The Brief English Handbook* before each new assignment to review the rules and guidelines that have given you trouble. By following these two procedures, you will gain as much as possible from the experience of having your instructor, who is a professionally trained reader, evaluate your written work.

THE

BRIEF ENGLISH

HANDBOOK

Grammar

Why study grammar? If you understand the parts of a sentence and how they function, you will be able to arrange them to convey a complete thought clearly and effectively.

You have probably studied grammar before, and many of its terms may already be familiar to you. This section of the handbook offers a review that will refresh your understanding of grammar and increase your confidence when writing.

1 Parts of Speech

There are eight **parts of speech** in English: nouns, pronouns, verbs, adjectives, adverbs, prepositions, conjunctions, and interjections. The same word can function as more than one part of speech. To identify a word's part of speech, determine how the word is used in a sentence. The word *coach,* for instance, may function as a noun in one sentence and as a verb in another.

> The *coach* has a gentle way with players. [Noun]
> I *coach* my daughter's softball team. [Verb]

1a Nouns name persons, places, things, or ideas.

Nouns may be classified as proper, common, abstract, concrete, and collective.

Proper nouns name particular persons, places, things, or events and are capitalized: *Charles Dickens, London, Christmas.*

Common nouns do not name particular persons, places, things, or events; therefore, they are not capitalized: *writer, city, holiday.*

Abstract nouns name intangible qualities, ideas, or characteristics: *love, democracy, courage.*

Concrete nouns name tangible things that can be perceived through the senses: *wind, rain, pencil, nose, knife, needle.*

Collective nouns name groups of individuals: *audience, family, army, herd, jury, squad.* (See agreement of collective nouns and verbs, 8f; of collective nouns and pronouns, 9d.)

NOTE: A **compound noun,** which may be a common or proper noun, is composed of more than one word: *high school, crosswalk, sister-in-law, Labor Day.* (See hyphen, 38b; forming the possessive case, 35a; forming plurals, 40j.) A dictionary will list a compound noun as a single entry. Referring to a dictionary is especially important for determining capitalization of compound nouns. (See capitals, 34f.)

1b Pronouns take the place of nouns.

In the following sentence, the pronoun *him* substitutes for *John Franklin,* and the pronoun *them* substitutes for *fans.*

> John Franklin ran eighty yards for a touchdown. Six fans ran onto the field to greet *him* before officials chased *them* back to the stands.

The word that a pronoun replaces is called the **antecedent** of the pronoun. *John Franklin* is the antecedent of *him,* and *fans* is the antecedent of *them.*

Pronouns are classified as personal, possessive, reflexive, relative, interrogative, demonstrative, and indefinite.

Personal pronouns refer to a person or a thing. They have plural and singular forms.

	SINGULAR	PLURAL
FIRST PERSON	I, me	we, us
SECOND PERSON	you	you
THIRD PERSON	he, she, him, her, it	they, them

Possessive pronouns are forms of personal pronouns that show ownership or relation. (See case, chapter 10.)

my, mine	his	its	their, theirs
your, yours	her, hers	our, ours	

Reflexive pronouns are formed by combining personal pronouns with *-self* and *-selves.*

myself	ourselves
yourself	yourselves
himself, herself, itself	themselves

A reflexive pronoun indicates that someone or something named in a sentence acts (or reflects) upon itself.

Leo treated *himself* to shrimp scampi.

Reflexive pronouns that are used to emphasize a noun or pronoun are sometimes called intensive pronouns.

Leo *himself* will eat the shrimp scampi.

Relative pronouns introduce adjective clauses. (See dependent clauses, 4b.)

who	whom	whose	that	which

The couple *who performed the tango* won first prize.

Interrogative pronouns are used in questions.

who	whom	whose	which	what

Whom did you call?

Demonstrative pronouns point to or identify a noun. (See pronoun reference, 18a.)

this	that	these	those

That is your problem.
This is the question: How will we raise the money?

Indefinite pronouns function as nouns in a sentence but do not take the place of a specific person or thing. Following are some common indefinite pronouns.

all	any	anyone	each
another	anybody	anything	either

everybody	most	nobody	some
everyone	one	none	somebody
many	neither	several	something

Somebody will reap the benefits.

1c Verbs express action or a state of being.

A **verb** may express physical action (*dance, walk, jump*), mental action (*dream, guess, trust*), or state of being (*is, are, were*). A noun or pronoun must have a verb to form a complete sentence. (See sentence, 2b; sentence fragments, 6b.)

Action Verbs

Action verbs are classified by whether or not they must be followed by an object—a noun or pronoun that completes the action of the verb by showing who or what is acted upon.

A **transitive verb** expresses action that has an object. (See direct object, 2g; indirect object, 2h.)

> The pitcher *tossed* the ball. [Tossed what? The *ball,* the object of *tossed*]
>
> The voters *believed* the politician. [Believed whom? The *politician,* the object of *believed*]

An **intransitive verb** expresses action that has no object.

> The pitcher *smiled.*
> The stream *runs* through the canyon.

Although some verbs are transitive only (*destroy, send, forbid*) and others are intransitive only (*tremble, chuckle, happen*), most verbs can function as either transitive or intransitive.

> The guide *explained* the danger. [Transitive]
> The guide never *explained.* [Intransitive]

Linking Verbs

Linking verbs express a state of being or a condition rather than an action. The most common linking verbs are forms of *be,* such as *am, is, are, was,* and *were.* Words such as *appear, become, feel, grow, look, smell,* and *taste* function as both linking verbs and action verbs. These verbs link the subject of a sentence with a predicate nominative or predicate adjective—a noun, pronoun, or adjective that identifies or modifies the subject. (See subject, 2a; predicate nominative, 2j; predicate adjective, 2i.)

> The butler *is* the killer. [The predicate nominative *killer* identifies the subject *butler.*]
>
> The silence *became* frightening. [The predicate adjective *frightening* modifies the subject *silence.*]

Many linking verbs also function as transitive as well as intransitive verbs.

> The butler *looked* gloomy. [Linking verb]
> The butler *looked* for an escape. [Intransitive verb]
> Carmen's hair *grew* gray from shock. [Linking verb]
> Mr. Higgins *grew* plums. [Transitive verb]

Helping Verbs and Verb Phrases

A verb often includes one or more **helping verbs,** sometimes called **auxiliary verbs.**

COMMON HELPING VERBS

am	has	can (may) have
are	had	could (would, should) be
is	can	could (would, should) have
was	may	will (shall) have been
were	will (shall) be	might have
do	will (shall) have	might have been
did	has (had) been	must

| have | can (may) be | must have |
| | | must have been |

The verb and its helping verb form a **verb phrase.**

> The comet *has been approaching* earth for two years. [*Has* and *been* are helping verbs for the verb *approaching.*]

In some sentences the verb and its helping verb are separated.

> The day *has* finally *arrived.*
> *Did* they *reach* Georgia?

(See tense, chapter 11; passive voice, chapter 13.)

1d Adjectives modify nouns and pronouns.

To *modify* a word means to *limit*—that is, to make its meaning more definite. **Adjectives** limit in three ways.

By describing:

> A *tall* woman stepped from the *curious* crowd.
> The *white* and *black* car won the race.

By pointing out which one:

> *That* man is my brother.

By telling how many:

> *Twelve* children and *several* parents attended.

Adjectives normally are placed directly before the words they modify, but sometimes a writer places descriptive adjectives after the words they modify.

> The stallion, *long* and *lean,* galloped past us.

Predicate adjectives generally follow linking verbs and modify the subject of a sentence. (See predicate adjective, 2i.)

The runners were *tired* and *thirsty*. [*Tired* and *thirsty* modify the subject *runners*.]

Adjectives or Pronouns?

A word may be used as more than one part of speech. This is especially true of the words listed below, which may serve as adjectives or pronouns depending on the way they function in a sentence.

all	either	one	these
another	few	other	this
any	many	several	those
both	more	some	what
each	neither	that	which

This book is overdue. *Those* books are on reserve. [Adjectives]
This is the overdue book. *Those* are the books on reserve.
[Pronouns]

The definite article *the* and the indefinite articles *a* (used before words beginning with a consonant sound) and *an* (used before words beginning with a vowel sound) are also classified as adjectives.

1e Adverbs modify verbs, adjectives, other adverbs, and groups of words.

Adverbs most commonly modify verbs by telling how, when, where, or to what extent.

He reads *carefully*. [How]
He reads *late*. [When]
He reads *everywhere*. [Where]
He reads *widely*. [To what extent]

Adverbs sometimes modify adjectives and other adverbs.

She is *truly* dedicated. [Modifies the adjective *dedicated*]
She studies *terribly* hard. [Modifies the adverb *hard*]

Adverbs sometimes modify groups of words.

> *Unfortunately,* I cannot attend the wedding. [Modifies the whole sentence]

Many adverbs end in *-ly,* but not all words that end in *-ly* are adverbs.

> The day was *chilly,* but the group jogged *briskly* through the park. [*Chilly* is an adjective; *briskly* is an adverb.]

1f A preposition shows the relation of a noun or pronoun to some other word in a sentence.

Prepositions usually introduce a word group called a **prepositional phrase,** which always consists of the preposition and an **object of the preposition**—a noun or pronoun that relates to another word in the sentence.

> The effect *of pesticides* threatens wildlife *in marshes.*

Pesticides is related to *effect* because it indicates which effect. *Marshes* is related to *wildlife* because it indicates where wildlife is threatened. The prepositions *of* and *in* indicate the relations between these words. (See prepositional phrases, 3a.)

Prepositions usually show direction or position. The following words are among the most common prepositions.

above	at	beyond	into	under
across	before	by	of	up
after	behind	down	on	upon
against	below	during	out	with
along	beneath	for	over	within
among	beside	from	through	without
around	between	in	to	

> *Around* the corner and *beyond* the tracks the road turns.

Groups of words, such as *along with, according to,* and *in spite of,* sometimes serve as prepositions. (See idioms, 42c.)

According to the latest report, the company is nearly bankrupt.

1g Conjunctions join words, phrases, or clauses.

Conjunctions are usually classified into three categories: coordinating conjunctions, correlative conjunctions, and subordinating conjunctions.

There are seven **coordinating conjunctions:** *and, but, or, yet, for, nor,* and *so.* (See subject and predicate, 2a–2f; main clauses, 4a; compound sentences, 5b.)

Oranges, lemons, *and* limes are citrus fruits. [Joining words]

The fish bite in the morning *or* after sundown. [Joining prepositional phrases]

The comet hit, *but* no one saw it. [Joining the clauses of a compound sentence]

Correlative conjunctions are always used in pairs: *both . . . and; not only . . . but also; either . . . or;* and *neither . . . nor.*

Both the California condor *and* the Maryland darter are struggling to survive.

Neither animal *nor* plant species are safe from human encroachment.

Subordinating conjunctions begin dependent clauses. Some common subordinating conjunctions, several of which also function as prepositions, are *after, although, because, before, if, since, so that, though, unless, until, when, where,* and *while.* (See dependent clauses, 4b.)

Humans must uncover their fears *before* they can uncover their courage.

When psychology develops a model of human nature, it will not be based solely on neuroses and character disorders.

NOTE: **Conjunctive adverbs** join main, or independent, clauses. Words such as *consequently, furthermore, hence, however, indeed, moreover, nevertheless, subsequently, therefore,* and *thus* are conjunctive adverbs. (See main clauses, 4a; semicolon, 25b.)

> Paralysis was President Franklin Delano Roosevelt's only experience with defeat; *consequently,* he never revealed the extent of his handicap.

> Statistics show that advertising generates sales; manufacturers, *therefore,* will continue to support Madison Avenue copywriters.

1h Interjections express surprise or strong emotion and have no grammatical relation to sentences.

Examples of interjections are *Oh! Wow! Ah! Ouch! Hey! My goodness!*

> *Ouch!* It bit my finger.

Exercise 1: Review

Name the part of speech of each italicized word in the following paragraph, using the abbreviations *N* for noun, *PRO* for pronoun, *V* for verb, *ADJ* for adjective, *ADV* for adverb, *PREP* for preposition, *C* for conjunction, and *I* for interjection.

Medical-school instructors *believe* that good care *begins* with a record of a patient's medical history; *therefore,* the *skill* of *diagnosis* rests on the simple act of talking with a patient. The doctor must listen, ask important questions, and *not only* hear what the patient says *but also* hear what the patient does not say. *This* discussion will enable the doctor to create a diagnosis and a *treatment* plan.

Although medical interviewing has been part of the *diagnostic* process since medicine began, authorities are *officially* recognizing that *it* is the foundation of any successful treatment. The next time your doctor begins *with* a discussion of your medical history, do not protest with an "*Oh no,*" not again," *but* instead appreciate the importance of this process.

2 Parts of Sentences

Effective writing starts with clear, grammatical sentences. A **sentence** is a group of words that contains a **subject** and a **predicate** and is not dependent on another group of words to complete its meaning. (See subordinating conjunctions, 1g; main clauses and dependent clauses, chapter 4.)

> *Although the celebration ended with a fireworks display* [Not a sentence because its meaning is not complete]
>
> *The celebration ended with a fireworks display.* [Complete sentence]
>
> *How did the celebration end?* [Complete sentence]

Subject and Predicate

2a The simple subject is the word or words that act, are acted upon, or are described.

> *Quail Hill* rises at the end of University Drive.

Birds have been nesting among the rocks and shrubs.
Bundled in coats, *students* stroll to the peak each evening.

NOTE: Sometimes the subject *you* is implied.

Speak to us! [Meaning *You speak to us.*]

2b **The simple predicate, sometimes referred to as the *verb*, is the word or words that tell what the subject did or how it was acted upon.**

Quail Hill *rises* at the end of University Drive.
Birds *have been nesting* among the rocks and shrubs.
Bundled in coats, students *stroll* to the peak each evening.

2c **The complete subject is the group of words that includes the simple subject and its modifiers.**

The student rally began at noon. [*Rally* is the simple subject. *The student rally* is the complete subject.]

The candidate from Benton Hall will speak at two o'clock. [*Candidate* is the simple subject. *The candidate from Benton Hall* is the complete subject.]

2d **The complete predicate is the group of words that includes the simple predicate and its modifiers.**

The student rally *began at noon.* [*Began* is the simple predicate. *Began at noon* is the complete predicate.]

The candidate from Benton Hall *will speak at two o'clock.* [*Will speak* is the simple predicate (note that it includes the helping verb *will*). *Will speak at two o'clock* is the complete predicate.]

2e **A compound subject consists of two or more subjects that are joined by a conjunction and that have the same predicate.**

Samuel King and *William Black* took the first aerial photographs.

Either *he* or *she* will fly the balloon.

2f **A compound predicate consists of two or more verbs that are joined by a conjunction and that have the same subject.**

The rumble of the train *echoes* through the valley and *rolls* over the hills.

Space shuttles *will fly* to the moon and *return* with payloads of minerals.

Complements

Some sentences express the writer's thought by means of a subject and predicate only: *He worked. She arrived.* Most sentences, however, have within the complete predicate one or more words that add to the meaning of the subject and simple predicate.

They appointed *a new president.*
He is *an engineer.*

These elements are called **complements,** and they function as direct and indirect objects and as predicate adjectives and predicate nominatives. (See verbs, 1c.)

2g **A direct object is a word or word group that receives the action of a transitive verb.**

A direct object answers the question What? or Whom?

The Civic League invited *Julio* to speak. [*Julio* is the direct object of the transitive verb *invited.*]

She teaches *fifth grade.* [*Fifth grade* is the direct object of the transitive verb *teaches.*]

2h **An indirect object of a verb precedes the direct object and usually indicates to whom or for whom the action is done.**

The caretaker gave *Kim* the key. [*Kim* is the indirect object (*key* is the direct object) of the transitive verb *gave.*]

To identify an indirect object, reconstruct the sentence by using the preposition *to* or *for.*

The caretaker gave the key *to Kim.* [Now *Kim* no longer functions as the indirect object but as the object of the preposition *to.*]

2i **A predicate adjective is an adjective that follows a linking verb and modifies the subject of the verb.**

The animals seem *restless.* [The predicate adjective *restless* follows the linking verb *seem* and modifies the subject *animals;* the restless animals.]

2j **A predicate nominative is a noun or pronoun that follows a linking verb and renames or identifies the subject of the verb.**

(See subjective case, 10a.)

The man with gray hair is *Mr. Sumato.* [The predicate nominative *Mr. Sumato* follows the linking verb *is* and identifies the subject *man.*]

Exercise 2

Underline and identify the direct objects (*DO*), indirect objects (*IO*), predicate adjectives (*PA*), and predicate nominatives (*PN*) in the following sentences.

1. Metaphors create vivid images in people's minds.

2. Highly charged images can become trademarks or handicaps for politicians.

3. Lincoln's "a house divided" won him success, but Hoover's "a chicken in every pot" brought him scorn.

4. In fear of vivid language, many politicians give us empty phrases.

5. This vague use of language often sounds dull.

3   Phrases

Words in sentences function not only individually but also in groups. The most common word group is the **phrase.** A phrase may be used as a noun, verb, adjective, or adverb.

Prepositional Phrases

3a   Prepositional phrases begin with a preposition and end with a noun or pronoun.

Prepositional phrases function as adjectives or adverbs. (See prepositions, 1f.)

The fibula *of the left leg* is broken. [Adjective: modifies the noun *fibula*]

As she turned, her mask fell *to the floor.* [Adverb: modifies the verb *fell*]

Appositives

3b An appositive is a noun or pronoun—often with modifiers—placed near another noun or pronoun to explain, describe, or identify it.

The Wolves' Den, *a hangout for college intellectuals,* caught fire. [A *hangout for college intellectuals* describes *Wolves' Den.*]
My brother *David* works nights. [*David* identifies *brother.*]

Usually an appositive follows the word it refers to, but it may also precede the word. (See comma, 23c.)

A thrilling love story, John and Marsha's romance would make a wonderful film. [A *thrilling love story* describes *romance.*]

Exercise 3

Combine each group of sentences into one sentence by using prepositional phrases and appositives. You may need to revise wording and exclude some words to make the new sentences read correctly. For example:

The purpose is to enrich a person's life. This is the purpose of a college education. A college education is the best investment anyone can make.

The purpose *of a college education, the best investment anyone can make,* is to enrich a person's life.

1. History is the foundation of any liberal arts education. It is a basic subject. History is in most curricula.

2. Sigmund Freud visited the United States. Freud is the father of psychoanalysis. He came to the United States in August and September. The year was 1909.

3. Bodybuilders seem dedicated. They are both male and female. The dedication is self-torture.

4. Personal forgiveness can be granted only by victims, not by observers. Forgiveness is a kind of moral embrace. The embrace is between two people.

5. Upton Sinclair wrote radical novels. Most of his novels are about corruption of the capitalistic system. He was a California candidate for governor in 1934.

Verbals and Verbal Phrases

A **verbal** is a verb that does not function as the simple predicate of a clause. Instead, verbals (which include infinitives, present participles, and past participles) function as nouns, adjectives, and adverbs.

3c Infinitives and infinitive phrases function as nouns, adjectives, and adverbs.

An **infinitive phrase** includes the **infinitive**—the plain form of a verb preceded by *to*—as well as its complements or modifiers. (See verb forms, chapter 11.)

Her favorite pastime is *to dance.* [Noun: predicate nominative]

I have three choices *to offer you.* [Adjective: modifies *choices*]

He seems eager *to gain knowledge.* [Adverb: modifies *eager*]

3d Participles and participial phrases are verb forms that function as adjectives.

Present participles end in *-ing* (*running, laughing, flying*). **Past participles** usually end in *-ed* (*flopped, jumped, dangled*), but a few end in *-en* (*beaten*), and some change entirely (*begun, swum, brought*). (See note on gerunds, 3e; verb forms, chapter 11.)

Tired, the runner slumped to the ground. [Past participle: modifies *runner*]

The *developing* crisis dominated the news. [Present participle: modifies *crisis*]

Participial phrases consist of a participle and its complements or modifiers.

The cat *howling through the night* belongs to Cesar.

Glutted with inexpensive imports, the automobile market has declined.

Beaten by Lady Luck, the gambler quit the game.

Exercise 4

Combine each group of sentences by using infinitive and participial phrases. Follow the directions in brackets after each group. You may need to add words, delete words, and/or change tenses. Example:

> Time ticks away in relentless beats. It is a major preoccupation of most Americans. [Use a present participial phrase.]
>
> *Ticking away in relentless beats,* time is a major occupation of most Americans.

1. The Navy keeps accurate world time. This is the Navy's tremendous responsibility. [Use an infinitive phrase as the subject.]

2. Atomic clocks outstrip the performance of the solar system. Every two years atomic clocks must be reset. [Use a present participial phrase.]

3. The Naval Observatory operates about fifty atomic clocks. They are stored in climate-controlled vaults. [Use a past participial phrase.]

4. Navigation satellites are accurate. They are accurate enough to locate an oil well. They are even accurate enough to guide a battleship through fog. [Use two infinitive phrases joined by *or.*]

5. Our lives are conditioned by a steady television diet. Our lives are measured in increments as regular as television commercials. [Use a past participial phrase.]

3e Gerunds and gerund phrases function as nouns.

A **gerund** is the present participle of a verb—formed by adding -*ing* to the infinitive—and is used as a noun.

> *Dreaming* leads to creation. [Gerund as subject]

A **gerund phrase** consists of a gerund and its complements or modifiers. Like the gerund, the gerund phrase is used as a noun.

> I love *dancing until dawn.* [Gerund phrase as direct object]
> *Flying to Rome* is costly. [Gerund phrase as subject]

NOTE: Since both gerunds and present participles end in -*ing,* they are sometimes confused. You can avoid confusing them by determining their function in a sentence. Gerunds function as nouns. Present participles, when not serving as part of the predicate, function as adjectives.

> *Running* keeps me fit for tennis. [*Running* is the subject of the sentence; therefore, it is a gerund.]

> The water *running* in the kitchen is a nuisance. [*Running* modifies *water;* therefore, it is a participle.]

Exercise 5

Write two sentences for each of the following words, using the word in a gerund phrase and a present participial phrase. For example:

> *diving*
> *Diving from the ten-meter board* is thrilling. [Gerund phrase]
> *Diving beneath the surface,* he saw a world of splendid color. [Participial phrase]

1. hoping
2. drifting
3. flinging
4. washing
5. speaking

Absolute Phrases

3f An absolute phrase consists of a noun and usually a participle, plus modifiers, that add to the meaning of a sentence but have no grammatical relation to it.

An **absolute phrase** differs from other phrases because it does not modify a particular word but instead modifies an entire sentence. An absolute phrase may appear almost anywhere in a sentence.

> The palm tree swayed, *its slick leaves shimmering with light.*

> *A magnifying glass raised to his eye,* Sherlock Holmes examined the weapon.

> The two of us worked the entire night—*Barbara at the computer and I at the tape recorder*—transcribing our field notes.

Exercise 6

Combine each group of sentences using absolute phrases. You may need to add or omit words and change tenses. For example:

> The players were leaning over their cards. They were chatting softly.
>
> The poker game continued for hours.
>
> *The players leaning over their cards and chatting softly,* the poker game continued for hours.

1. Her novel was finished. Renée decided to vacation in Paris.

2. The Mercedes skidded to a stop in the rain. Its brakes were squealing. Its taillights were glowing.

3. The horses rounded the turn. Their nostrils were flaring. Their necks were stretching toward the finish line.

4. The mysteries of the earth have been explored. The 1990s adventurer will turn to the secrets of the mind.

5. The lifeguard sat on the sand. Suntan lotion was glistening on her back, and the wind was gently lifting her hair.

4 Clauses

A **clause** is a group of words that has a subject and a predicate. There are two kinds of clauses: main clauses (sometimes called *independent clauses*) and dependent clauses (sometimes called *subordinate clauses*).

4a Main clauses form grammatically complete sentences.

Main clauses may stand alone or be joined by coordinating conjunctions (see 1g), conjunctive adverbs (see note, 1g), or semicolons (see 25a–25c). (Also see comma, 23a.)

> The cobra is a poisonous snake. Its bite is often fatal. [Two main clauses standing alone, separated by a period]
>
> The cobra is a poisonous snake, and its bite is often fatal. [Two main clauses joined by a comma and the coordinating conjunction *and*]
>
> The cobra is a poisonous snake; indeed, its bite is often fatal. [Two main clauses joined by a semicolon and the conjunctive adverb *indeed*]
>
> The cobra is a poisonous snake; its bite is often fatal. [Two main clauses joined by a semicolon]

4b Dependent clauses do not form grammatically complete sentences.

Dependent clauses are usually introduced by a subordinating conjunction (see 1g) or a relative pronoun (see 1b). Dependent clauses function as nouns, adjectives, or adverbs within a sentence. The exact relation in a sentence between the thoughts expressed in a dependent clause and the main clause is indicated by the subordinating conjunction or relative pronoun that joins them.

Adjective Clauses

An **adjective clause** modifies a noun or pronoun. It often begins with a relative pronoun (*who, whom, whose, that, which*) that refers to or is related to a noun or pronoun that preceded it. (See comma, 23c.)

> The trumpet player *who left the stage* fell asleep in the lounge. [Modifies the noun *player*]
>
> Anything *that stands on the seafront* will be leveled by the storm. [Modifies the pronoun *anything*]
>
> Karla is the spy *Smiley seeks.* [Modifies the noun *spy,* with the relative pronoun *that* or *whom* understood]

Adverb Clauses

An **adverb clause** modifies a verb, an adjective, or an adverb. It begins with a subordinating conjunction, such as *when, although, whenever, since, after, while, because, where, if, that,* or *than.*

> *Whenever he is asked*, he plays the banjo. [Modifies the verb *plays*]
>
> I am happy *because it is Saturday.* [Modifies the adjective *happy*]
>
> She studies more effectively *than I do.* [Modifies the adverb *effectively*]

Noun Clauses

A **noun clause** is a dependent clause that functions as a noun. It may serve as subject, predicate nominative, direct object, indirect object, or object of a preposition. The dependent clause is likely to begin with a relative pronoun. (See complements, 2g–2j.)

> *That life is difficult for some* means little to insensitive bureaucrats. [Subject]
>
> He described *what he wanted.* [Direct object]

Exercise 7

Combine each group of sentences by using dependent clauses as indicated in the instructions in brackets. You may need to change some words to avoid needless repetition. For example:

> Few people have heard of hydrocephalus. Hydrocephalus affects at least a million families. [Use *although* to form an adverb clause.]
>
> Although few people have heard of the disease, hydrocephalus affects at least a million families.

1. Hydrocephalus is caused by a buildup of fluid in the brain cavity.

   Hydrocephalus is often called "water on the brain." [Use *which* to

   form an adjective clause.]

2. As many as eight thousand babies are born with the defect every

   year. This number does not relieve the mark of shame attached

   to the disease. [Use *that* to form a noun clause.]

3. Some doctors have attempted to educate the public about the

   defect. These doctors are prominent in the medical profession.

Many people still believe that any child suffering from it will develop a head perhaps twice the normal size. [Use *although* to form an adverb clause and use *who* to form an adjective clause.]

4. Enlarged heads can be avoided. Doctors have developed an operation for hydrocephalics. The operation drains the fluid to avoid retardation in the patient. [Use *because* to form an adverb clause and use *that* to form an adjective clause.]

5. The surgical procedure has brought new hope to the parents of children suffering from the disease. They still worry about the future of their children. [Use *although* to form an adverb clause.]

5   Kinds of Sentences

Sentences can be classified according to their structure (simple, compound, complex, or compound-complex) and their purpose (declarative, imperative, interrogative, or exclamatory).

Sentence Structures

5a   **Simple sentences have only one main clause and no dependent clauses, although they may have several phrases.**

Years ago the family of a bride would supply the groom with a dowry. [One main clause]

The bride and the groom were not consulted about the choice of a mate and sometimes met each other for the first time on the day of their wedding. [One main clause with a compound subject and a compound predicate]

5b Compound sentences have two or more main clauses but no dependent clauses.

Chauvinism has fueled many political skirmishes, but jingoism has ignited wars. [Two main clauses joined by a comma and the coordinating conjunction *but*]

Some people are flattered into virtue; other people are bullied out of vice. [Two main clauses joined by a semicolon]

5c Complex sentences have one main clause and at least one dependent clause.

Although he was a cunning investor, Bennett went bankrupt. [One main clause and one dependent clause beginning with the subordinating conjunction *although*]

5d Compound-complex sentences have at least two main clauses and at least one dependent clause.

If they wish to live fully, most people need amusement to relax, and many people need intellectual challenges to develop their minds. [Two main clauses joined by a comma and the coordinating conjunction *and* and one dependent clause beginning with the subordinating conjunction *if*]

Sentence Purposes

5e A declarative sentence makes a statement.

Spelunking requires the skill of a mountain climber and the courage of a coal miner.

5f   An imperative sentence gives a command or makes a request.

Don't walk on the grass.
Please stay off the grass.

(See note, implied subject, 2a.)

5g   An interrogative sentence asks a question.

Which point of view is most valid?

5h   An exclamatory sentence expresses strong feeling.

The mountains are glorious!

Exercise 8

Write sentences according to the following directions.

1. Write a simple, declarative sentence that states a fact about your campus.
2. Using the coordinating conjunction *or,* write a compound sentence about a friend.
3. Write an interrogative sentence directed to a politician.
4. Write a declarative compound-complex sentence directed to a parent.
5. Write an imperative sentence that gently directs a child.
6. Write a complex sentence that deals with a foreign country.
7. Using a semicolon, write a compound sentence that deals with a sports event.
8. Using *who,* write a compound-complex sentence describing a friend.
9. Write a series of three simple sentences followed by a complex sentence that deals with a subject you read about in a newspaper.
10. Using a variety of sentence structures, describe a place that is important to you. Identify each sentence as simple, compound, complex, or compound-complex.

Sentence Errors

In some situations a noise or gesture will communicate. For instance, if you hear a shriek and glance out the window to see your neighbor holding a hammer in one hand while waving the other hand as if it were aflame, you would probably conclude that he had smashed a finger. Individual words also can communicate effectively. When you hear someone shout "Stop," "Run," or "Fire," you react, for not to react might be foolhardy. But in more complex situations, only sentences can effectively communicate. Like all languages, English has developed sentence conventions that help writers and speakers convey meaning clearly and accurately. While you will never be evaluated on how well you express the pain of a smashed finger or shout a warning, you will be evaluated as a college student, and later as a college graduate, on how clearly, correctly, and accurately you shape sentences. This section concentrates on common sentence errors and on ways to avoid those errors so that you can use sentences effectively.

6 Sentence Fragments *frag*

To stand as a main clause, a complete sentence must have a subject and a predicate and must not be introduced by a subordinating conjunction or a relative pronoun. (See chapter 2, Parts of sentences.)

A **sentence fragment** is a portion of a sentence that is punctuated as though it were a complete sentence. Sentence fragments are usually serious errors in writing. Except for a few situations, which are noted below, sentence fragments indicate that the writer lacks an understanding of the basic principles of sentence structure and is not fully in control of his or her writing. You can learn to avoid most sentence fragments by heeding the following guidelines.

6a Do not punctuate a dependent clause as a main clause.

A group of words introduced by a subordinating conjunction (such as *when, while, although, because, if, until*) or by a relative pronoun (such as *who, which, that*) functions as a dependent clause. Although dependent clauses have subjects and verbs, they can not stand alone as main clauses. You can correct such fragments by attaching the dependent clause to a main clause, by rewriting the dependent clause as a complete sentence, or by rewording the clause to eliminate the subordinating conjunction or relative pronoun. (See subordinating conjunctions, 1g; relative pronouns, 1b.)

> Dragon stories abound in the myths and legends of people everywhere. *As a study of early civilization will reveal.* [Fragment]

> Dragon stories abound in the myths and legends of people everywhere, *as a study of early civilization will reveal.* [Corrected as one sentence with a main clause and a dependent clause]

> One type of dragon popular in art is a huge beast with an armorlike skin and several heads capable of breathing fire. *Which makes it difficult to subdue.* [Fragment]

> One type of dragon popular in art is a huge beast with an armorlike skin and several heads capable of breathing fire. Such features make it difficult to subdue. [Corrected as two complete sentences]

> Drawings from widely separated cultures show dragons that are grotesque combinations of several animals. *That are familiar to the people living in that area.* [Fragment]

> Drawings from widely separated cultures show dragons that are grotesque combinations of several animals familiar to the people living in that area. [Corrected by eliminating the relative pronoun, thus changing the fragment to a phrase]

Words That Introduce Dependent Clauses

COMMON SUBORDINATING CONJUNCTIONS

after	as long as	because	in that
although	as much as	before	no matter how
as	as soon as	even though	since
as if	as though	if	so that
than	unless	when	wherever
though	until	whenever	while

RELATIVE PRONOUNS

that	which	whoever	whose
what	whichever	whom	
whatever	who	whomever	

Exercise 1

Correct the following sentence fragments by (1) attaching the dependent clause to a main clause, (2) rewriting the dependent clause as a main clause, or (3) rewording the clause to eliminate the subordinating conjunction or relative pronoun.

1. Any attempt to understand the popularity of dragon stories will have to begin with their origins. Which coincide with the origins of human civilization.

2. Then, as now, people searched for explanations for the mysterious forces of nature. Because knowledge is the first step toward control.

3. As though dragons were humans' most powerful enemy. Their behavior was used to explain earthquakes, fires, storms at sea, and sudden death.

4. Chinese dragons have had a better image, controlling rivers and bringing life giving rain. Though they could cause considerable trouble if angered.

5. Chinese dragons have also responded charitably to individual humans. Who were given wisdom and the ability to foretell the future. Because they treated the dragons with kindness.

6b Do not punctuate a phrase as a main clause.

A **phrase** is a word group used as a noun, verb, adjective, or adverb. Since such word groups lack a subject, a predicate verb, or both, they cannot stand alone. (See phrases, chapter 3.)

Phrase fragments can be corrected by joining them to main clauses or by rewriting them as complete sentences.

Some scholars have spent years studying ancient texts from civilizations around the globe. *Searching for a common origin of all later dragon lore.* [Participial phrase fragment]

Some scholars have spent years studying ancient texts from civilizations around the globe, searching for a common origin of all later dragon lore. [Corrected by attaching the participial phrase to the preceding main clause]

One candidate for the honor is Zu, a water monster of Sumerian myth, who was slain by Ninurta. *A warrior god who took for himself the names and characteristics of all the creatures he killed.* [Appositive phrase fragment]

One candidate for the honor is Zu, a water monster of Sumerian myth, who was slain by Ninurta. This warrior god took for himself the names and characteristics of all the creatures he killed. [Corrected by rewriting as two sentences]

In Babylonian stories about battles between dragons and gods. The defeated dragons were forced to live under the sea. [Prepositional phrase fragment]

In Babylonian stories about battles between dragons and gods, the defeated dragons were forced to live under the sea. [Corrected by attaching the prepositional phrase to the following main clause]

These dragons struggled constantly. *To free themselves and destroy the world.* [Infinitive phrase fragment]

These dragons struggled constantly to free themselves and destroy the world. [Corrected by attaching the infinitive phrase to the preceding main clause]

Exercise 2

Correct the following phrase fragments by joining them to the accompanying main clauses or by rewriting them as complete sentences.

1. Dragons appear in a variety of roles, symbolizing evil cultures, wisdom to others, and power to still others.

2. Sumerians thought of dragons as embodiments of evil. A concept later attached to the devil.

3. The Gnostics, early religious cults of Europe and Asia, used a figure of a dragon biting its own tail. To symbolize the cyclic nature of time and the continuity of life.

4. To convince the people that their leaders had the dragonlike qualities of strength and goodness. Early Chinese emperors adopted the dragon as a symbol of imperial power.

5. Although you may not believe they ever existed, the image of dragons survives in art, fiction, religious stories, and dreams. In every corner of the world.

6c Do not punctuate a part of a compound predicate as a main clause.

(See compound predicate, 2f; unnecessary commas, 24e.)

> According to one Greek tradition, dragons paradoxically sleep with their eyes open. *And see with them shut.* [Part of a compound predicate fragment]
>
> According to one Greek tradition, dragons paradoxically sleep with their eyes open, *and see with them shut.* [Still incorrect: compound predicate punctuated as two main clauses]
>
> According to one Greek tradition, dragons paradoxically sleep with their eyes open and see with them shut. [Correct]

6d Fragments are sometimes acceptable in special situations.

Use fragments such as the following sparingly and only when your purpose is clear.

ADVERTISING	Improved mileage!
HEADLINES	Two on Trial for Robbery
QUESTIONS AND ANSWERS	What next? Another term paper.
EXCLAMATIONS	Radical!
IN DIALOGUE	"Of course." "Wonderful."
FOR EMPHASIS	I've been patient, understanding, attentive, and gentle. Now it's over. No more Mr. Nice Guy!
AS TRANSITIONS	My final point.

Exercise 3

Correct each of the following fragments either by attaching it to a main clause or by rewriting the fragment as a complete sentence. Mark correct items with a *C*.

1. What explains the popularity of belief in dragons? In the absence of any scientific evidence that they ever existed.

2. Some scholars suggest that dragon stories originated from dim memories of prehistoric animals. And were passed on to later generations. Who embellished them to explain the history of their people.

3. The problem with this theory is that dinosaurs, pterodactyls, and similar animals that could have been the ancestors of dragon stories ceased to exist millions of years ago. Before human beings arrived on earth.

4. Others theorize that dragon stories represent a human psychological need. To imagine ourselves triumphant over enemies and evil forces.

5. The hero battles the many-headed monster threatening the beautiful young woman. Restores order to the world, and allows us to feel that we can control our lives, too.

6. Whatever the reason, dragons show a remarkable ability to survive. No matter how many have been killed, they are still with us.

7. Those of us who have not had the good fortune to see a live one can read about them. Or see them in our neighborhood theaters.

8. If books and films do not satisfy your urge to go dragon hunting. Find a damp, grassy, but rocky hillside remote from human habitation.

9. There, you may spot a particularly beautiful stone. That is really a dragon egg.

10. If you are patient, you may be witness to a dragon's hatching.

Take a lunch. Sometimes it takes a thousand years.

7   Comma Splices and Fused Sentences   *cs/fs*

Like unintentional sentence fragments, comma splices and fused or run-on sentences are serious errors in writing because they show that the writer is either careless or unaware of sentence structure. In speaking, you quite naturally run clauses together, linking or separating them with breaths and pauses. In writing, you must use coordinating conjunctions and punctuation marks to link or separate clauses. The key to avoiding comma splices and fused or run-on sentences is to recognize main clauses, dependent clauses, coordinating conjunctions, subordinating conjunctions, and conjunctive adverbs.

A **comma splice** occurs when main clauses are joined only by a comma. (See main clauses, 4a.)

> Some composers put notes down as rapidly as their hands can move across the paper, others write and rewrite slowly. [Comma splice]

A **fused** or **run-on sentence** occurs when main clauses are joined without a coordinating conjunction or any punctuation mark.

> In earlier centuries most composers were employed by churches or noblemen now they are usually employed by universities. [Fused sentence]

Comma splices and fused sentences can be corrected in four ways.
1. Use a period to make two separate sentences.

> Some composers put notes down as rapidly as their hands can move across the paper. Others write and rewrite slowly.

In earlier centuries most composers were employed by churches or noblemen. Now they are usually employed by universities.

2. Use a semicolon to show a close relation between the main clauses.

Some composers put notes down as rapidly as their hands can move across the table; others write and rewrite slowly.

In earlier centuries most composers were employed by churches or noblemen; now they are usually employed by universities.

NOTE: When two main clauses are joined by a conjunctive adverb (such as *nevertheless, consequently, however,* or *therefore*), a semicolon must come before the clause containing the conjunctive adverb. (See note on conjunctive adverbs, 1g.)

In earlier centuries most composers were employed by churches or noblemen; *however,* now they are usually employed by universities.

3. Use a comma and a coordinating conjunction to show the appropriate relation between the main clauses. (See coordinating conjunctions, 1g.)

Some composers put notes down as rapidly as their hands can move across the paper, *and* others write and rewrite slowly.

In earlier centuries most composers were employed by churches or noblemen, *but* now they are usually employed by universities.

4. Use a subordinating conjunction to introduce the less important clause. (See subordinating conjunctions, 1g.)

Although some composers put notes down as rapidly as their hands can move across the paper, others write and rewrite slowly.

In earlier centuries most composers were employed by churches or noblemen, *while now they are usually employed by universities.*

Exercise 4

Label each sentence as correct (C), fused (FS), or containing a comma splice (CS). Correct the fused sentences and comma splices in any of the four ways listed in the text.

1. Although she has studied for only two years, Laurie has already earned a black belt in aikido.

2. The meeting place for aikido practice is called a *dojo* the teacher is called *sensei.*

3. The students at Laurie's *dojo* work hard, many practice two or three hours every day.

4. Some of the movements are difficult to master however, everyone improves with practice.

5. Each movement is demonstrated by the *sensei,* he repeats the demonstration in slow motion.

6. Aikido is a fairly new martial art, it was developed in this century by Ueshiba Morihei of Japan.

7. The aikido form of self-defense involves neutralizing an attacker's power and causing him to become the victim of his own momentum.

8. Aikido students learn they do not need strength to repel an attack, they use the attacker's strength against him.

9. Each training session begins with warm-up and stretching exercises, then the students practice a movement until they can perform it in a smooth, seemingly effortless, motion.

10. By applying the physical and philosophical aspects of aikido to their daily lives, students learn self-defense and self-control.

Exercise 5

Correct the ten comma splices or fused sentences in the following paragraph, using all four methods of correction. The first sentence has been done as an example.

    Jazz is an American form of music that is difficult to define,/ because there are many kinds of jazz. Almost any popular music can be played as a jazz piece such an interpretation gives it a special swing or jump. Jazz musicians take the basic idea of a piece they are playing and change it to fit a personal style, this personal touch is known as improvisation, consequently jazz musicians can speak directly to their audience. Jazz rhythms are syncopated they have a bounce to them, stressing weak beats is at the heart of this rhythm. When jazz first started, it was always improvised. With the popularity of large dance bands that developed later, jazz arrangements were written down, at least for portions of the selection, nevertheless individual performers improvised solos between the arranged sections. Arranging jazz is difficult it is almost impossible to write everything down on paper, individual performers must rely on their feelings at the moment to supply the rest. Each band has its own style, therefore a new performer must fit his or her personal style to the group.

8 Subject and Verb Agreement *agr*

The subject of any sentence will determine whether the verb is singular or plural. If you wish to describe how a boy dresses, your subject is *boy* and you might write *The boy dresses sloppily.* If your subject is *boys,* your sentence might read *The boys dress sloppily.* In either case the verb must agree in number with the subject.

8a A verb must agree with its subject even when words come between them.

Many agreement problems arise because words often come between a subject and a verb, thus obscuring their relation.

> The *intricacy* of the overlapping, brightly colored patterns *makes* a viewer slightly dizzy at first.

In this sentence the singular noun *intricacy* is the subject, and the singular verb *makes* agrees with it. The plural noun *patterns* is the object of the preposition *of,* not the subject of the sentence. Some writers, however, might mistakenly believe *patterns* to be the subject and commit an agreement error by writing *The intricacy of the overlapping, brightly colored patterns make a viewer slightly dizzy at first.*

To determine which form of a verb agrees with the subject in sentences like this one, read the sentence, omitting all prepositional phrases.

The *intricacy* ~~of the overlapping, brightly colored patterns~~ *makes* a viewer slightly dizzy at first.

NOTE: Expressions such as *together with, as well as, in addition to,* and *along with* function as prepositions, not coordinating conjunctions. They do not, therefore, change the number of the subject.

The *candidate* as well as her relatives *was* pleased with the results. [The singular subject, *candidate,* takes a singular verb, *was.*]

The *neighbors* together with the inspector *were* concerned about the hazard. [The plural subject, *neighbors,* takes a plural verb, *were.*]

8b Two or more subjects joined by *and* usually take a plural verb.

The *chairman and* the *president battle* over the budget together. *Tom, Bill, and Beth are* correct.

NOTE: When the parts of a compound subject function as a single idea or refer to a single person or thing, they take a singular verb.

Apple pie and ice cream is my favorite dessert.
The *star and host* of the show *is* backstage.

When a compound subject is preceded by *each* or *every,* the verb is usually singular. Although these words refer to more than one, they imply consideration of one at a time.

Under the border guard's keen eye, *every pedestrian, cyclist,* and *motorist suffers* a close scrutiny.

When a compound subject is followed by *each,* the verb is singular.

Speaking and writing *each requires* a mastery of words. [The writer is referring to speaking and writing separately.]

8c Singular subjects joined by *or* or *nor* take singular verbs, and plural subjects joined by *or* or *nor* take plural verbs.

An early morning *swim or* tennis *game is* my waker-upper. [Singular subjects.]

Neither *players nor coaches* ever *arrive* on time. [Plural subjects.]

8d When a singular subject and a plural subject are joined by *or* or *nor,* the verb agrees with the subject nearer to it.

Neither *motorists nor rain discourages* a dedicated jogger.
Neither *rain nor motorists discourage* a dedicated jogger.

Since following this convention often leads to writing that sounds awkward, try to avoid the awkwardness problem by reworking such sentences.

AWKWARD   Neither *they nor I am* happy with the results.

REVISED   They are not happy with the results, and neither am I.

8e Generally, use singular verbs with indefinite pronouns.

Most indefinite pronouns (such as *anybody, anyone, anything, each, either, everybody, everyone, everything, neither, nobody, none, no one, one, some, somebody, someone,* and *something*) are singular and refer to a single unspecified person or thing; consequently, they take singular verbs.

Everyone on the team *was* excited about the game.
Neither of the twins *was* well disciplined.

A few indefinite pronouns (such as *all, any, none,* and *some*) may be singular or plural. Whether you use a singular or a plural verb depends on the noun or pronoun that the indefinite pronoun refers to.

The chairperson announced that *all* of the members *were* present. [*All* refers to *members,* so the verb is plural.]

The committee found that *all* of the report *was* helpful. [*All* refers to *report,* so the verb is singular.]

8f Collective nouns take singular or plural verbs depending on how they are used.

Collective nouns (such as *army, audience, class, committee, faculty, group, herd, public,* and *team*) are singular in form, but they name groups of individuals. When referring to a group as a single unit, a collective noun takes a singular verb.

Given time, the *public* always *sees* through political deception.

Some cynics claim that the American *family is* no longer functioning.

When referring to a group's members as individuals, a collective noun takes a plural verb. (See agreement of collective nouns and pronouns, 9d.)

The *faculty argue* among themselves about the value of general education courses.

The Rogers *family have been parking* their cars on our lawn.

8g Most nouns that are plural in form but singular in meaning take singular verbs.

Nouns such as *athletics, civics, economics, mathematics, measles, mumps, news, physics, politics, species,* and *statistics* are singular and take singular verbs.

Mumps is no longer a threat to Americans.
The *news* about the economy *is* bleak.

Words such as *trousers* and *scissors* are regarded as plural and take plural verbs, except when used after *pair*.

> These *shorts are* ripped.
> This *pair of shorts is* ripped.

8h The verb must agree with the subject even when the subject follows the verb and when the sentence begins with *there* or *here*.

> Where *is* the *truth?*
>
> Out of the pages of that best-selling novel *appear* eerie *characters,* mysterious *situations,* and philosophical *riddles.*

Don't mistake the expletives *there* and *here* for subjects. They merely signal that the subject follows the verb.

> There *are* several *answers* to the problem. [The actual subject is *answers.*]
>
> Here *is* a *bit* of advice. [The actual subject is *bit.*]

When a compound subject follows the verb in a sentence beginning with *there* or *here,* a singular verb is sometimes used, especially if the first item of the compound subject is singular. Such sentences are best rewritten.

> There *is* [*are*] a *can* of fruit and six *jars* of peanut butter in the cupboard.
>
> A can of fruit and six jars of peanut butter are in the cupboard. [Rewritten]

8i A linking verb must agree with its subject, not with the predicate nominative or predicate adjective.

> The *strength* of this pitching staff *is* the three rookie left-handers.

In this sentence *strength* is the subject. *Left-handers* is a predicate nominative following the linking verb *is*. The sentence could be rearranged to make *left-handers* the subject.

> The three rookie *left-handers are* the strength of this pitching staff.

Strength is now the predicate nominative.

> The best *hope* for the future *is* our children.
> Our *children are* the best hope for the future.

8j After the relative pronouns *who, which,* and *that,* use a singular verb when the antecedent is singular and a plural verb when the antecedent is plural.

The antecedent is the word that the pronoun refers to. (See antecedent, 1b; chapter 9.)

> Our elected officials obviously listen to *people* who *give* them campaign contributions. [*Who* refers to *people,* so the verb is plural.]

> The boss likes a *worker* who always *arrives* on time. [*Who* refers to *worker,* so the verb is singular.]

NOTE: Agreement errors involving relative pronouns often occur in sentences that include a phrase beginning with *one of the.* Look carefully at the sense of such sentences to determine whether the verb should be singular or plural.

> He is one of the *members* who *are* quarrelsome. [The antecedent of *who* is *members* because the sentence says that some members are quarrelsome. Therefore, the verb is plural.]

> She is *the only one* of the members who *has paid* the dues. [This sentence says that only one member paid the dues. The antecedent of *who* is *one,* so the verb is singular.]

She is only one of the *members* who *have paid* the dues. [This
sentence says that more than one member paid the dues, so the
antecedent of *who* is *members*, and the verb is plural.]

8k Use a singular verb when *every* or *many a* precedes a subject,
even a compound subject.

Although these words refer to more than one, they imply consideration of one at a time.

> *Every cave, gorge,* and *grove was* searched for the missing
> campers.

> *Many a motorist breathes* a sigh of relief when exiting from the
> freeway.

8l Expressions of time, money, measurement, weight, volume, and
fractions are singular when the amount is considered as a single
unit.

> By the time she arrived, *four-fifths* of the crowd *was* gone.
> *Three dollars is* a high price for a hot dog.
> *One hundred ninety pounds is* the average for this team.

When the amount is considered as separate units, use a plural verb.

> *One hundred ninety pounds* of muscle *were* pressing on my
> chest.

8m Titles and words named as words take singular verbs.

> Carl Jung's *Memories, Dreams, Reflections is* a fine work of
> autobiography.

> *Chitlins is* a variation of *chitterlings,* which refers to the part of
> the small intestines of pigs used for food.

Exercise 6

In the following sentences correct any errors in subject and verb agreement. If you find a correct sentence, mark it with a *C*.

1. A sum of over $400 million were spent to turn the Meadowlands marsh in New Jersey into a sports and entertainment complex.

2. Every domestic car and every imported car are required to pass the same safety inspection.

3. The committee are expected to announce the decision today.

4. Please bring me the pair of blue shorts that is hanging in the bathroom.

5. If you look at the map you will see there is three different routes the mail carrier have to cover each day.

6. Our children is the only hope we have for the future.

7. The students or the teacher order the theater tickets every month.

8. All of the seventeen-page information booklet are required reading.

9. The senator commented that politics are the art of the possible.

10. Where is the pants I bought last weekend?

11. The only chance we have to win rest with the defensive linemen.

12. Managers respect the advice of employees who work hard.

13. Every one of the journalism students want to attend the conference.

14. Ham and eggs are a popular American breakfast.

15. Here are a list of all the printing shops in our area.

16. *California Classics* by Lawrence Clark Powell are interesting reading.

17. The police officer as well as the onlookers were applauding the little girl's performance.

18. All the performers are from Brazil, and all the musical selections have a Latin beat.

19. The group argue about the fund-raising activities hour after hour.

20. Jerry Hopkins and his neighbors enjoys the peaceful summer evenings at the lake.

Exercise 7

In the following paragraph, correct the errors in subject and verb agreement.

Computerized psychological testing services around the country is gaining widespread use. A report published in recent months indicate that almost everybody taking the tests are pleased by the method. The automated testing proceeds in the following fashion: Sitting before a TV-like screen, a patient answers a group of questions that demands true/false responses or offers multiple-choice answers. Either a psychiatrist or a clinician who has been trained in psychiatry sit in another room and score the data and analyze the results. Immediately following the test, doctor and patient meets to discuss the outcome and plans an initial treatment. Some critics of computerized testing claim the testing dehumanizes the doctor-patient relationship, but neither doctors using the method nor patients undergoing the process seem to agree with the critics.

9 Pronoun and Antecedent Agreement *pron agr*

A pronoun must agree in person and number with its **antecedent,** the word to which the pronoun refers, and the reference must be clear. Singular pronouns refer to singular antecedents, and plural pronouns refer to plural antecedents. (See pronouns, 1b.)

> *Carla* drove *her* van to Mexico.
>
> The *travelers* piled *their* luggage on top of the van.
>
> Since *Carla* owned the van, *she* asked the other *passengers* to pay *their* share of the gasoline costs.

9a Use a plural pronoun to refer to a compound antecedent joined by *and.*

The coordinating conjunction *and* joins items together, creating a compound subject, so a plural pronoun is required.

> *Hugh and Aaron* practiced jujitsu until *they* collapsed on the mats.

9b Use a singular pronoun to refer to two or more singular antecedents joined by *or* or *nor*. Use a plural pronoun to refer to two or more plural antecedents joined by *or* or *nor*.

The coordinating conjunctions *or* and *nor* keep items separate for individual consideration. If the antecedents are singular and considered separately, a singular pronoun is required.

> *Erika or Pam* will give *her* flute rendition of Pachelbel's Canon in D.

Of course, if the separately considered antecedents are plural, a plural pronoun is required.

> Neither the *students nor* the *teachers* are presenting *their* position at the meeting.

NOTE: Confusion can arise when the pronoun refers to only one of the antecedents.

> Neither *Ann nor Silvina* could find *her* notebook. [Whose notebook?]

The meaning can be made clear simply by substituting the correct noun for the pronoun.

> Neither *Ann nor Silvina* could find *Ann's* notebook.

(See 18c.)

9c When a singular antecedent and a plural antecedent are joined by *or* or *nor*, use a pronoun that agrees with the nearer antecedent.

> The council *members* or the *mayor* will lose *her* supporters over this disagreement.

Since sentences that follow this convention, such as the preceding example, often sound awkward, writers usually rework them.

The *mayor* or the council *members* will lose supporters over this disagreement.

9d Generally use a singular pronoun to refer to a collective noun.

Words such as *army, audience, class, committee, group, herd, public,* and *team* are singular in form, but they name groups of individuals. When a collective noun refers to a group as a single unit, use a singular pronoun.

This *group* of students knows *its* way around Mexico.

When a collective noun refers to a group's members as individuals, use a plural pronoun. (See agreement of collective nouns and verbs, 8f.)

The *group* offered to pay *their* share of all expenses.

NOTE: Take special care to avoid mistakenly treating a collective noun as both singular and plural in the same sentence.

The hiring *committee arrives* at a decision only after *they have discussed* all the applicants. [Singular verb, plural pronoun, plural verb]

The hiring *committee arrives* at a decision only after *it has discussed* all the applicants. [Corrected]

9e Use singular pronouns to refer to indefinite pronouns used as antecedents.

Most indefinite pronouns—such as *anybody, anyone, each, everybody, everyone, nobody, one, none, somebody, someone,* and *something*—are singular and refer to a single unspecified person or thing; consequently, they call for singular pronouns.

Each of the women had *her* book published.
Everyone on the men's cross-country team ran *his* best race.
Something ominous made *its* presence felt in the woods.

In the preceding examples the gender of the antecedents is clear from the context, but often the gender of the antecedent of an indefinite pronoun is unknown or mixed. Traditionally in such cases, a masculine pronoun has been used to refer to the indefinite pronoun.

> *Everyone* living in the apartment building did *his* best to clean the halls.

Although men and women are probably living in the apartment building, grammatical convention calls for the masculine pronoun *his* to refer to the indefinite pronoun *everyone*. This practice, however, is changing because using *he* or *his* to refer to indefinite pronouns in the sentence ignores the presence of women. You can recast such a sentence by making the antecedent plural; by using *he or she, his or her;* or by avoiding pronouns that refer to indefinite pronouns.

> *People* living in the apartment did *their* best to clean the halls. [Making the antecedent plural]
>
> *Everyone* living in the apartment building did *his or her* best to clean the halls. [Using *his or her*]
>
> Everyone living in the apartment building kept the halls as clean as possible. [Avoiding pronouns referring to the indefinite pronoun]

NOTE: Avoid overusing *he or she, his or her.* Repeating those constructions excessively will make your writing unwieldy and monotonous. (See sexist language, 41g.) Never use a slash (/) as in his/her.

9f Use the relative pronouns *who, whom, which,* and *that* with the appropriate antecedents.

Who refers to persons and sometimes to animals that have names.

> Sandy is the one *who* enjoyed the trip most.
> Her canary, Sunshine, was the only pet *who* went on the trip.

Which refers to animals and things.

Their cat, *which* is pure-bred Siamese, cost a week's wages.

Andorra, *which* is located in the Pyrenees between Spain and France, is also called Andorra la Vella.

That refers to animals, things, and sometimes to persons when they are collective or anonymous. (See nonrestrictive and restrictive elements, 23c.)

The creek *that* flowed into the pasture has gone dry.
Do you believe the old saying "Dogs *that* bark will never bite"?
Acapulco is heaven for tourists *that* love tropical beaches.

NOTE: *Whose,* the possessive form of *who,* is often used to refer to animals and things to avoid awkward constructions that use *of which.*

This is a riddle the answer *of which* no longer interests me.
This is a riddle *whose* answer no longer interests me.

Exercise 8

Rewrite the following sentences according to the directions in brackets. Be sure to make all the changes necessary to keep the agreement of pronouns and antecedents correct.

1. The catalog and the schedule of classes contain the registration information you are seeking. [Change *and* to *or.*]

2. The counselors agree that English composition should be taken in the first year of college. [Change *The counselors* to *Each counselor.*]

3. Each year the dean or the president has her portrait painted by an outstanding art student. [Change *or* to *and.*]

4. The board of trustees submitted its proposals yesterday. [Change *The board of trustees* to *Some members of the board of trustees*.]

5. Someone attending the mother-and-daughter banquet forgot her coat. [Change *mother-and-daughter* to *father-and-son*.]

6. Either the crew or the rugby team uses the weight room on Monday afternoons. [Change *Either . . . or* to *and*.]

7. The class, which usually meets on Wednesday, forgot that it had agreed to meet on Saturday. [Change *The class* to *Some class members*.]

8. By using attractive visual displays, the business manager or the budget committee chairman can communicate his plans for spending tax money wisely. [Change *budget committee chairman* to *members of the budget committee*.]

9. The bear mascot, which is paraded at all home games, was donated to the university by the game wardens' association. [Change *The bear mascot* to *Bruno, the bear mascot*.]

10. Students who study every evening will perform well on examinations. [Change *Students* to *Anyone*.]

10 Case *case*

The **case** of nouns and pronouns indicates how the words function in a sentence. Nouns and most pronouns have only two case forms (that is, the spelling the word has when it is used in a particular case): the plain form (*day, someone*) and the possessive form (*day's, someone's*).

The pronouns *I, we, he, she, they,* and *who* have three different case forms: the subjective form, the objective form, and the possessive form. The pronouns *you* and *it* have one form for both the subjective and the objective case and a different form for the possessive case. (See possessive pronouns, 1b.)

Case

	SUBJECTIVE	OBJECTIVE	POSSESSIVE
Personal Pronouns			
Singular			
First person	I	me	my, mine
Second person	you	you	your, yours
Third person	he, she, it	him, her, it	his, her, hers, its
Plural			
First person	we	us	our, ours
Second person	you	you	your, yours
Third person	they	them	their, theirs
Relative or Interrogative Pronouns			
Singular	who	whom	whose
Plural	who	whom	whose

10a Use the subjective case of pronouns for subjects and for predicate nominatives.

Alicia and *I* went shopping. [Subject]

Since Marcus and *he* returned to Detroit, *she* has been lonely. [Subjects]

The scouts who had the most badges were Salvador and *he*. [Predicate nominative]

NOTE: When the subject is compound, as in *Alicia and I* and *Marcus and he,* beginning writers sometimes become confused about the selection of a pronoun. They would not write *Me went shopping,* but they might write *Alicia and me went shopping.* To avoid this error with compound subjects that include pronouns, try reading each subject separately with the verb.

In speech it is common practice to use the objective forms of personal pronouns as predicate nominatives in expressions beginning with *it is* or *it's: It's me, It is him, It's us, It's them.* Such use of the objective form is unacceptable in writing. Instead use *It is I, It is he, It is we,* and *It is they.*

10b Use the objective case when pronouns are direct objects, indirect objects, and objects of a preposition.

Bernie met Naomi and *me* at the museum. [Direct object]

The doorman gave *us* a map of the exhibits. [Indirect object]

A man dressed in a caveman costume sat by *me* on the bench. [Object of a preposition]

Exercise 9

For each of the following sentences, select the correct pronoun in the pair in parentheses. Identify each selected pronoun as a subject (S), a predicate nominative (PN), a direct object (DO), an indirect object (IO), or an object of a preposition (OP).

1. The lecture on Etruscan pottery interested Nguyen and (*I, me*).

2. The ones who laughed the most were Monica and (*she, her*).

3. I know I blushed when Sonia and (*she, her*) sat near (*we, us*).

4. That group's achievement is impressive, but the faculty expected (*they, them*) to excel.

5. Jorge wanted to use the car, so I gave (*he, him*) the keys.

10c Use the appropriate case when the pronoun *we* or *us* comes before a noun.

If the pronoun functions as a subject, use *we*.

We linguists meet once a year at a major university. [We meet.]

If the pronoun functions as an object, use *us*.

A number of *us* mycologists regularly collect mushrooms in the foothills. [A number of us collect.]

10d When a pronoun is used as an appositive, its case depends on the function of the word it refers to.

(See appositives, 3b.)

Two chemistry majors, Margarita and *he,* won science foundation awards. [The pronoun refers to *majors,* the subject of the sentence, so it is in the subjective case.]

Science foundation awards received by two chemistry majors, Margarita and *him,* highlighted the program. [*Majors* is now the object of the preposition *by,* so the pronoun is in the objective case.]

Exercise 10

Select the correct pronoun for each of the following sentences.

1. The artists, (*she, her*) and Shawn, will be at the festival booth all day.

2. (*We, Us*) customers are waiting for the festival to begin.

3. Many of (*we, us*) have been here since seven this morning.

4. The stormy weather ruined the day for the artists, Shawn and (*she, her*).

5. Nevertheless, (*we, us*) early birds enjoyed the chance to see the exhibits.

10e In elliptical, or incomplete, comparisons following *than* or *as,* the case of the pronoun depends on the meaning of the sentence.

In comparisons, *than* and *as* often introduce incomplete comparisons. The case of the pronoun in such constructions depends on how the incomplete clause would be completed.

Use the subjective case if the pronoun functions as the subject of the omitted clause.

I have been studying Spanish longer than *they* [have been studying Spanish].

She works as hard on projects as *he* [works on projects].

Use the objective case if the pronoun functions as the object in the omitted clause.

> For information, I rely on him more than [I rely on] *her.*
> I see Ngoc as much as [I see] *him.*

10f Use the objective case for pronouns that are subjects or objects of infinitives.

> The attorney considered *him* to be a prime suspect. [Subject of infinitive]
> He tried to trap *him* with tough questions. [Object of infinitive]

10g Usually use the possessive case of a pronoun or noun preceding a gerund.

A gerund is the present participle of a verb used as a noun. (See gerunds and gerund phrases, 3e.)

> What was the reason for *his* appearing tonight? [*His* modifies the gerund *appearing.*]
> *Dr. Rodriguez's* running for office pleased us all. [*Dr. Rodriguez's* modifies the gerund *running.*]

The possessive is not used when the present participle serves as an adjective. (See present participles, 3d.)

> The crowd watched *him* tottering on the tightrope. [*Tottering* is a present participle used as an adjective modifying *him.*]
> I often hear *Tom* talking in his sleep. [*Talking* is a present participle used as an adjective modifying *Tom.*]

Avoid using the possessive with a gerund when doing so creates an awkward construction.

AWKWARD	I am pleased about Nadeem's cooking dinner.
REVISED	I am pleased about Nadeem cooking dinner.
BETTER	I am pleased that Nadeem is cooking dinner.

Exercise 11

Select the correct pronoun for each of the following sentences.

1. The president ordered (*he, him, his*) to be ready at dawn.

2. Do you know the reason for (*he, him, his*) erratic driving?

3. Bok Hee has been more generous than (*they, them, their*).

4. The whole group watched (*he, him, his*) cooking the quesadillas.

5. We wanted to prove (*he, him, his*) wrong.

10h The case of the pronoun *who* is determined by its function in its own clause.

You can usually determine which case to use in interrogative sentences by answering the question the sentence poses.

> *Who* led England to victory? [*The prime minister* led England to victory: subject.]
>
> *Whom* shall we hold responsible? [We shall hold *her* responsible: direct object.]
>
> *Whom* is the letter addressed to? [The letter is addressed to *her:* object of the preposition *to.*]

In dependent clauses use *who* or *whoever* for all subjects; use *whom* or *whomever* for all objects. The case of the pronoun depends only on its function within the clause, not on the function of the clause in the sentence.

The Sisters of Mercy give help to *whoever* requests it. [*Whoever* is the subject of the clause *whoever requests it.* The entire clause is the object of the preposition *to.*]

I do not remember *whom* I met at the party. [*Whom* is the direct object of *met.* The entire clause *whom I met at the party* is the direct object of the verb *do remember.*]

To determine whether to use *who, whom, whoever,* or *whomever,* substitute a personal pronoun for the relative pronoun. The case of the personal pronoun is the correct case for the relative pronoun. If necessary, change the word order of the clause.

I do not recall (*who, whom*) I lent the book to.
I lent the book to *him* (or *her*). [Objective case]

Therefore, *whom* is the correct relative pronoun.

I do not recall *whom* I lent the book to.

Sometimes a dependent clause includes an expression such as *I think* or *he said.*

She is the woman (*who, whom*) he said called last night.

To decide between *who* and *whom* in such a construction, repeat the sentence without the intervening expression.

She is the woman *who* called last night.

Exercise 12

Select the correct pronoun in each of the following sentences.

1. The one-hundred-dollar prize will be given to (*whoever,*

   whomever) creates the most beautiful kite.

2. (*Who, Whom*) shall I file my report with?

3. (*Who, Whom*) will clean the chalkboards?

4. The honor goes to (*whoever, whomever*) I select.

5. The master is loved most by those (*who, whom*) share his beliefs.

11 Verb Forms and Verb Tense *verb*

Every verb has three principal forms: the infinitive (the plain form of the verb), the past, and the past participle.

Verb Forms

INFINITIVE	PAST	PAST PARTICIPLE
dance	danced	danced

The **infinitive** form of the verb usually appears in combination with *to* to form a verbal that functions as a noun, an adjective, or an adverb. (See 3c.) A **participle** is a verbal that functions as an adjective, an adverb, or a part of a verb phrase. (See 3d.)

All verbs form the **present participle** by the addition of *-ing* to the infinitive form. Neither a present participle nor a past participle can function as the verb in a sentence unless it is combined with one or more helping verbs.

Any verb may be combined with helping (or auxiliary) verbs to express time relations and other meanings. *Shall* and *will; have, has,* and *had; do, does,* and *did;* and forms of the verb be (*am, are, is, was, were, been, being*) are helping verbs used to indicate time and voice. (See tense, chapter 11; voice, chapter 13.) *Can, could, may, might, must, ought, shall, should, will,* and *would* are helping verbs used to indicate necessity, obligation, permission, or possibility.

> You *could* learn to ski.
> You *must* attend.
> She *should* know better.

Verbs have either regular or irregular forms. A **regular verb** forms its past and past participle by adding -*d* or -*ed* to the infinitive.

INFINITIVE	PAST	PAST PARTICIPLE
live	lived	lived
jump	jumped	jumped

An **irregular verb** forms its past and past participle in a different way from regular verbs. This difference may be a change in spelling or no change at all from the infinitive form. Spelling changes usually involve a change in vowels or the addition of an -*n* or -*en* ending.

INFINITIVE	PAST	PAST PARTICIPLE
swim	swam	swum
throw	threw	thrown
hit	hit	hit

The major difficulty you will confront in the use of irregular verbs is in selecting the correct past or past participle form. When in doubt, consult a dictionary. If a verb is regular, the dictionary does not include the past and past participle. If the verb is irregular, the dictionary includes the irregular forms.

Irregular Verbs

INFINITIVE	PAST	PAST PARTICIPLE
begin	began	begun
bite	bit	bitten
blow	blew	blown
break	broke	broken
bring	brought	brought
catch	caught	caught
choose	chose	chosen
come	came	come
creep	crept	crept
dig	dug	dug

Irregular Verbs

INFINITIVE	PAST	PAST PARTICIPLE
dive	dived or dove	dived
do	did	done
draw	drew	drawn
dream	dreamed or dreamt	dreamed or dreamt
drink	drank	drunk
drive	drove	driven
eat	ate	eaten
fall	fell	fallen
feel	felt	felt
find	found	found
fit	fit or fitted	fit or fitted
fling	flung	flung
fly	flew	flown
fly (baseball)	flied	flied
forbid	forbade or forbad	forbidden
forget	forgot	forgotten or forgot
get	got	got or gotten
go	went	gone
hurt	hurt	hurt
know	knew	known
lay (place or put)	laid	laid
lead	led	led
lend	lent	lent
lie (recline)	lay	lain
light	lighted or lit	lighted or lit
lose	lost	lost
pay	paid	paid
ride	rode	ridden
rise	rose	risen
run	ran	run
say	said	said
see	saw	seen
set (place or put)	set	set

Irregular Verbs

INFINITIVE	PAST	PAST PARTICIPLE
shine	shone or shined	shone or shined
shoot	shot	shot
sing	sang or sung	sung
sink	sank or sunk	sunk
sit (take a seat)	sat	sat
sleep	slept	slept
steal	stole	stolen
sting	stung	stung
swim	swam	swum
tear	tore	torn
throw	threw	thrown
wear	wore	worn
win	won	won
write	wrote	written

Exercise 13

With another student, test yourself on the principal forms of the irregular verbs in the list.

Exercise 14

Use a dictionary to determine the correct form of the irregular verb necessary to complete each sentence.

1. We knew the bananas _____ a great deal, but we had

    _____ to love them. (*cost, grow*)

2. By the time we _____ for the airport, he had

    _____ less nervous. (*leave, become*)

3. The carpenters had _____ a slide and _____ it to the children. (*build, give*)

4. We had _____ our views, but they had not _____ them. (*speak, hear*)

5. I had just _____ the window when the sky _____ up. (*shut, light*)

Verb Tense

Verb forms change to show the time of the action they express. The change in time (past, present, or future) is called **tense.**

11a **The present tense expresses action about something occurring now, at the present time.**

> I *believe* you.
> The light from below *creates* huge shadows on the wall.

The present tense also serves some special functions in writing:
Use the present tense to state a general truth or fact.

> Automobiles *require* fuel.
> A yard *equals* thirty-six inches.

Use the present tense to state what a writer does in his or her written work or to describe a character's activities in a written work.

> In her essay Tonya *argues* for mandatory installation of air bags.

Before the book ends the hero *discovers* the truth about the Lost Canyon Mine.

Use the present tense to describe elements in artistic works.

In the movie *Mishima*, Eiko Ishioka's designs *startle* and *intrigue* the audience.

The nonsensical conversation in Philip's stories *makes* readers uncomfortable.

Use the present tense to state habitual action.

She *studies* in the library every day.
Jeff always *keeps* his VW sparkling clean.

Use the infinitive form with *do* to create **emphasis.**

I *do get up* early!

NOTE: In all tenses you can show continuing action by using the **progressive tense,** which is the present participle of the verb together with a form of the helping verb *be.*

Li-Ching *is attending* Kettler College.

11b The past tense expresses action that occurred in the past but did not continue into the present.

I *slipped* on the icy street several times.
I *was slipping* on the ice when he grabbed my arm.

Use the infinitive form with *did* to create an emphatic form.

I *did slip* on the ice.

NOTE: Past action may be shown in other ways.

I *used to slip* on the icy streets.

verb

11c **The future tense expresses action about something happening in the future.**

The visitors from Oxford *will debate* four of our pre-law students next week.

The visitors from Oxford *will be debating* four of our pre-law students next week.

NOTE: Future action may be shown in other ways.

The visitors from Oxford *are going to debate* four of our pre-law students next week.

The visitors from Oxford and four of our pre-law students *are about to debate*.

11d **The present perfect tense expresses action occurring at no definite time in the past or action occurring in the past and continuing into the present.**

Environmentalists *have enlisted* the help of sensitive business people. [The action has not occurred at a specific time in the past.]

Environmentalists *have been enlisting* the help of sensitive business people. [The progressive form indicates that the past action continues into the present.]

11e **The past perfect tense expresses action completed in the past before another past action occurred.**

I *had flown* in a glider before I flew in a single-engine Cessna. [Flying in the glider preceded flying in the Cessna.]

After I *had been flying* for three months, I gave it up. [Flying for three months preceded giving it up.]

11f The future perfect tense expresses action that will be completed in the future before another action occurs.

By the end of the year 2000, the Galaxy Probe *will have traveled* through space for ten years.

By the end of the year 2000, the Galaxy Probe *will have been traveling* through space for ten years.

11g Use an appropriate sequence of verb tenses.

Sequence of verb tenses refers to the time relation expressed by verbs in main clauses and verbs in dependent clauses, infinitives, or participles. In the sentence *The crowd cheered when he served an ace,* the past tense of the verb *cheer (cheered)* is in sequence with the past tense of the verb *serve (served).* (See dependent clauses, 4b; verbals and verbal phrases, 3c–3d.)

Dependent Clauses

When the verb in the main clause of a complex sentence is in any tense other than the past or past perfect, make the verb tense in the dependent clause consistent with the meaning of the sentence.

Our political leaders *hope* that the federal budget *will be balanced* by the year 2002. [The sequence moves from the present tense, *hope,* in the main clause to the future tense, *will be balanced,* in the dependent clause.]

The president of the company *will visit* our department after she *has met* with the board. [The sequence moves from the future tense, *will visit,* in the main clause to the present perfect tense, *has met,* in the dependent clause.]

Kayla *will change* her major because she *thinks* that the computer field *will* soon *be* too crowded. [The sequence moves from the future tense, *will change,* in the main clause to the present tense, *thinks,* and the future tense, *will be,* in the dependent clauses.]

When the verb in the main clause is in the past or past perfect tense, use the past or past perfect tense in the dependent clause, except when the dependent clause is a general truth.

The pianist *blushed* as the audience *cheered.* [Past tense in both the main clause and the dependent clause]

The scout troop *had sold* a hundred coupons before the Christmas trees even *arrived.* [Past perfect tense in the main clause and past tense in the dependent clause]

The visitors from Taiwan soon *learned* that Americans *love* Chinese food. [Although the verb in the main clause is in the past tense, the verb in the dependent clause is in the present tense because *Americans love Chinese food* is a general truth not related to a specific time.]

Infinitives

Use the **present infinitive,** which is composed of the plain form of the verb preceded by *to* (as in *to dance, to sing, to grow*) to express action that takes place at the same time as or later than that of the verb in the main clause. Use the **present perfect infinitive,** which is composed of *to have* followed by a past participle (as in *to have danced, to have sung, to have grown*), to express action that takes place before that of the verb in the main clause. (See infinitives, 3c.)

Last July I wanted *to attend* summer school. [Present infinitive: Action takes place at the same time as that of the main verb, *wanted.*]

They hoped *to go.* They hope *to go.* [Present infinitive: Action takes place at a time later than the main verbs, *hoped* and *hope.*]

Maurice would like *to have entered* last week's race. [Present perfect infinitive: Action takes place before that of the main verb, *would like.* Note that *to enter,* the present infinitive, is not the correct form.]

Maurice would have liked *to enter* last week's race. [Present infinitive: Action takes place at the same time as that of the main verb, *would have liked.*]

Participles

Use the **present participle** to express action that takes place at the same time as that of the main verb. Use the **past participle** or the **present perfect participle** to express action that takes place earlier than that of the main verb. (See present participle, 3d.)

Running in the woods, he felt free of worries. [Present participle: The running occurs at the same time as the feeling.]

Encouraged by friends, Pat decided to attend college. [Past participle: The encouragement took place before the decision.]

Having danced all night, Maria slept past noon. [Present perfect participle: The dancing took place before the sleeping.]

Exercise 15

Select the verb form that is in sequence with the other verb or verbs in each of the following sentences.

1. The sudden ringing of the alarm clock reminded me that I (*have,*

    had) an appointment with the dentist in a few hours.

2. I am confident that I (*can, could*) pass the next history test.

3. I know that she will call me if she (*is, will be*) visiting the campus on her next trip.

4. Turning the corner to Rose Street, the mail carrier remembered that she (*had been, was*) bitten by a dog on this street.

5. (*Finishing, Having finished*) his shopping, Larry went to the Red Lion Inn for lunch.

6. The chief engineer will conduct further tests himself because he (*doubts, doubted*) that the first report (*is, was*) accurate.

7. Harold wrote his library report on Alice Walker because he (*knows, knew*) she (*wrote, writes*) with compassion and insight.

8. Rosa told Felipe that she (*will be, would be*) studying in the library last Friday.

9. His experiments proved that water (*boiled, boils*) at 212°F.

10. When I saw the movie I thought that I (*will be, would be*) more frightened than I (*had been, was*).

Exercise 16

Rewrite the following passage as if you were living in the twenty-first century and the events happened in the past. Change verb tenses wherever necessary. Your opening sentence will read as follows:

> Years ago throughout Orange County, visitors *seemed* unable to tell where fantasy *ended* and real life *began*.

Throughout Orange County, visitors seem unable to tell where fantasy ends and real life begins. One reason is theme architecture, which accounts for perhaps as much as 60 percent of the county's buildings. Within the county you can find triplex homes that look like English Tudor mansions, restaurants that look like a French chateau or a Mississippi riverboat, and a motel that resembles a Persian mosque. Theme architecture adds a dash of Disneyland to most neighborhoods. Visitors can travel from one exotic land to another within a few blocks. The variety bewilders visitors, but local residents take it in stride. The themes divide into several categories. Some homeowners prefer a Spanish mission style. Others choose the Mediterranean look. Still others want Tudor, Cape Cod, or plantation designs. One aspect of all this diversity is tragically real: as developers hack down the orange groves, they replace the trees with glittering fantasy structures.

Exercise 17

Rewrite the following passage as if the events were going to take place at some time in the future. Change verb tenses wherever necessary. Your opening sentence will read as follows:

> Tomorrow's female writer will face . . .

Today's female writer faces a peculiar confusion because she is susceptible to the images of women in literature. She goes to poetry or fiction looking for her role in the world, but she is disappointed. She is looking for guides, models, possibilities. But what she finds are many images of women in works by men. She discovers a terror and a dream. She encounters a *Belle Dame sans Merci* and a Daisy Buchanan. She does not find an image of herself, the struggling female writer.

12 Subjunctive Mood *mood*

The three **moods** of a verb indicate a writer's intent. The **indicative mood,** the one most frequently used, states a fact or an opinion or asks a question. The **imperative mood** gives a command or direction (usually with the subject *you* implied: *Be here at ten sharp*). The **subjunctive mood** expresses doubt or uncertainty, a condition contrary to fact, or a wish.

You will rarely have a problem with mood. In fact, the subjunctive mood, which can be problematic, is rarely used in current English. Nevertheless, you should master the remaining forms and the three uses of the subjunctive mood.

Forms of the Subjunctive

In the present tense the subjunctive mood consists of only the infinitive form of the verb no matter what the subject is. (See infinitive, 3c.)

> The choreographer urged that Boris *consider* a ballet career.
> [Present subjunctive]
>
> The guidelines demand that procedures *be* in effect tomorrow.
> [Present subjunctive]

In the past tense the only commonly used subjunctive verb form is *were.*

> If I *were* retired, I would live a carefree life. [Past subjunctive]

Uses of the Subjunctive

12a Use the subjunctive form *were* in sentences expressing a wish and in contrary-to-fact clauses beginning with *if.*

> I wish she *were* my teacher. [But she is not my teacher: expresses a wish.]
> I would be able to finish all my work if the day *were* thirty hours long. [But the day is twenty-four hours long: contrary-to-fact clause.]

12b Use the subjunctive form in *that* clauses following verbs that demand, request, or recommend.

> Jano's aunt urged that Brian *save* the money.
> The attorney asked that the witness *be* ready to testify.

NOTE: Often writers find substitute constructions for the subjunctive in sentences such as those above.

> Jano's aunt urged Brian to save the money.

12c Use the subjunctive form in some standard phrases and idioms.

> Peace *be* with you.
> Heaven *forbid!*
> *Come* rain or *come* shine.
> So *be* it!

Exercise 18

Revise the following sentences by using appropriate subjunctive verb forms.

1. If I was in charge, I would change our budget rules.

2. Since supply prices have soared, I wish the maximum petty cash disbursement was more than twenty-five dollars.

3. The present budget requires that a department head submits too many separate forms for a single purchase.

4. People laugh when I suggest changes, as if I was a comedian.

5. Heaven helps us.

13 Active and Passive Voice *pass*

Voice is the quality in verbs that shows whether a subject is the actor or is acted upon.

> The Tanaka Construction Company built the Statler Bridge. [The subject *Tanaka Construction Company* is the actor.]
>
> The Statler Bridge was built by the Tanaka Construction Company. [The subject *Statler Bridge* is being acted upon.]

Effective writing is vigorous and direct. In nearly all circumstances, the active voice achieves vigor and directness better than the passive voice. Consequently, use the active voice except when you do not know the doer of an action or when you want to emphasize the receiver of an action or the action itself.

Demonstrators from the New Earth Alliance *closed* the nuclear plant. [Active voice]

The nuclear plant *was closed* by demonstrators from the New Earth Alliance. [Passive voice]

These sentences contain the same information, but each emphasizes a different point. The active construction emphasizes the demonstrators because *demonstrators* is the subject. The passive construction emphasizes the nuclear plant because *nuclear plant* is the subject.

Transitive verbs have both active and passive voice. When a verb is in the **active voice,** the subject performs the action and the object receives the action. When a verb is in the **passive voice,** the subject receives the action. (See transitive verb, 1c.)

To form a passive construction, move the direct object of the sentence ahead of the verb; it thus becomes the subject. Use a form of *be* as a helping verb; the actual subject may be contained in a prepositional phrase. (See direct object, 2g.)

William Faulkner *won* a Pulitzer Prize in 1963. [Active voice]

A Pulitzer Prize *was won* by William Faulkner in 1963. [Passive voice: The direct object from the previous sentence, *Pulitzer Prize*, becomes the subject; *was* is added to the verb *won*; and the subject of the previous sentence, *William Faulkner*, becomes the object of the preposition *by*.]

Active sentences that have direct objects often have indirect objects also. When rewritten in a passive construction, either the direct object or the indirect object can become the subject, and the actual subject can be dropped. (See indirect object, 2h.)

The committee awarded Thuy a scholarship. [Active voice]

Thuy was awarded a scholarship. [Passive voice: Indirect object, *Thuy*, becomes the subject; the original subject, *committee*, is dropped.]

A scholarship was awarded to Thuy. [Passive voice: Direct object, *scholarship,* becomes the subject; the original subject, *committee,* is dropped.]

Although the meaning of each of the above sentences is the same, as the subject changes so does the emphasis: from *the committee* to *Thuy* to a *scholarship.* The choice depends on the writer's intention.

In most situations, use the active voice for several reasons:

The active voice is more concise.

An ancient soothsayer predicts the end of the world. [Active voice: nine words]

The end of the world is predicted by an ancient soothsayer. [Passive voice: eleven words)

The active voice emphasizes the actual subject and is, therefore, more direct.

The detectives who investigated the case earned the admiration of their fellow officers. [Active voice]

The admiration of their fellow officers was earned by the detectives who investigated the case. [Passive voice]

The active voice is more forceful.

Starks rifled a pass to Ewing under the basket. [Active voice]

A pass was rifled to Ewing under the basket by Starks. [Passive voice]

The passive voice is appropriate in several situations:

When you do not know the doer of the action.

The clubhouse was left a shambles, and the parking lot was littered with cans and garbage.

When you want to emphasize the receiver of the action.

Tomaso was wounded by falling bricks.

When you want to emphasize the action itself.

A curved incision was made behind the hairline so the scar would be concealed when the hair grew back.

Exercise 19

Rewrite the following passage, changing the passive constructions into active constructions.

A poison ivy rash is considered by some to be humorous. But it is not funny at all. A rash that has the intensity of a fresh mosquito bite and lasts for several days is caused by contact with the plant. The poison ivy reaction has been studied by scientists for centuries, but no preventive pill or inoculation has been found. The poisonous substance in the plant is called urushiol. After the skin has been touched by urushiol, the exposed area will soon be covered by blisters and weeping sores.

What can you do after coming into contact with poison ivy?

First, the urushiol should be washed off as soon as possible. Any available hand soap and plenty of scrubbing should be used. Then take a cold shower and soap yourself all over. The course of the reaction seems to be shortened by cold water. Finally, see a doctor.

14 Adjectives and Adverbs *adj/adv*

Adjectives and adverbs are frequently misused in writing. Errors involving adjectives and adverbs are easy to correct once you understand how the words function in a sentence.

Adjectives modify nouns and pronouns. Adverbs can modify verbs, adjectives, and other adverbs. You can form adverbs by adding *-ly* to adjectives (*rapid, rapidly; complete, completely; happy, happily; desperate, desperately*). But not all words ending in *-ly* are adverbs; some are adjectives (*womanly, lonely, saintly*). Some adverbs and adjectives have the same form (*well, late, early*), and some adverbs have two forms (*slow, slowly; quick, quickly; cheap, cheaply*).

14a Use adjectives to modify nouns and pronouns. Use adverbs to modify verbs, adjectives, and other adverbs.

An adjective modifies a noun or a pronoun.

> Jose is a *swift* runner.
> I prefer the *checkered* one.

An adverb, not an adjective, modifies a verb.

> Jose ran *swiftly.*

An adverb, not an adjective, modifies an adjective.

> Jose is *terribly* swift.

An adverb, not an adjective, modifies an adverb.

> Jose ran *very* swiftly.

14b Use an adjective after a linking verb to refer to the subject. Use an adverb to refer to the verb.

The most common linking verb is *be* and its forms—*am, are, is, was, were,* and *been.* Other common linking verbs include *seem, appear,*

become, grow, remain, prove, and *turn,* along with verbs of the senses
—*feel, look, smell, hear, taste.* When these verbs link the subject with a
modifier, use an adjective as the modifier. When the modifier
describes the verb, use an adverb.

> The climber felt *uneasy* about the darkening sky. [Adjective: *Uneasy* describes the climber.]

> The climber felt *uneasily* for a firm handhold. [Adverb: *Uneasily* describes how the climber used a hand to find a firm place to grip.]

14c After a direct object, use an adjective to modify the object. Use an adverb to modify the verb.

> The judges ranked the wine *excellent.* [Adjective: *Excellent* describes *wine.*]

> She revised her papers *thoroughly.* [Adverb: *Thoroughly* describes *revised.*]

14d Use the words *bad* and *badly* and *good* and *well* correctly.

Bad is an adjective; *badly* is an adverb. Since verbs of the senses—*feel, look, smell, hear, taste*—require adjectives to modify the subjects, use *bad,* not *badly,* after them.

> The diners felt *bad* after the third course.
> The rendering plant smells *bad* this evening.

Good is always an adjective, never an adverb.

INCORRECT	The team played *good* last night.
CORRECT	The team played *well* last night.
CORRECT	The team played a *good* game last night.

Well may be used as either an adjective or an adverb. As an adjective, *well* has three meanings.

To be in good health:

He seems *well* considering his ordeal.

To appear well dressed or groomed:

They look *well* in the new uniforms.

To be satisfactory:

All is *well*.

Exercise 20

Select the correct word to complete each sentence. Explain the function of each adjective or adverb you select.

1. The band marched (*brisk, briskly*) down the field.

2. Mario felt (*bad, badly*) about the argument.

3. Choosing what car to buy is becoming (*increasing, increasingly*) difficult.

4. The driver considered the route (*safe, safely*).

5. Mai takes a (*brisk, briskly*) walk every morning.

6. The pedestrian looked (*careless, carelessly*) at the traffic.

7. Carlos shook his head (*sympathetic, sympathetically*).

8. It was an (*extreme, extremely*) clever plan.

9. The quarterback executed the play (*well, good*).

10. The pedestrian looked (*careless, carelessly*) standing there.

14e Use the correct forms of adjectives and adverbs when making comparisons.

Adjectives and adverbs have three forms or degrees: the **positive,** or plain, form, which only describes; the **comparative,** which compares two things; and the **superlative,** which compares three or more things.

The comparative and superlative of most adjectives and adverbs are formed either by adding -*er* and -*est,* respectively, to the positive form or by placing *more* and *most* (or *less* and *least*), respectively, before the positive form.

Using *more* and *most* (or *less* and *least*) is the only way to form the comparative and superlative for most adverbs of two or more syllables and for adjectives of three or more syllables. Some adjectives of two syllables can add either -*er* and -*est* or *more* and *most.*

	POSITIVE	COMPARATIVE	SUPERLATIVE
ADJECTIVES	thick	thicker	thickest
	happy	happier	happiest
	beautiful	more beautiful	most beautiful
		less beautiful	least beautiful
ADVERBS	fast	faster	fastest
	often	more often	most often
	sadly	more sadly	most sadly

A few adjectives and adverbs change their spelling to form the comparative and superlative.

POSITIVE	COMPARATIVE	SUPERLATIVE
bad, badly	worse	worst
good, well	better	best
many, much	more	most
little	littler, less	littlest, least

Use the comparative form to compare two things.

> In August the sea seems *bluer* than the sky.
>
> Although the two tours cost the same, the one to Paris will be the *more exciting*.
>
> Her client was *less anxious* today than yesterday.

Use the superlative form to compare three or more things.

> Of the three agents, Bozarth has the *deadliest* charm.
>
> Apparently the *most* skilled of all the drivers, Randolph wins nearly every race.
>
> This novel is the *least* interesting in the series.

14f Do not use double comparatives or double superlatives.

INCORRECT	They are the *most happiest* couple I know.
CORRECT	They are the *happiest* couple I know.

14g Do not use comparative or superlative forms with words that cannot logically be compared.

Words such as *unique, perfect, dead, empty, infinite,* and *impossible* are absolute. That is, their positive form describes their only state. They cannot, therefore, be compared.

ILLOGICAL	Dr. Nastasi is the *most unique* surgeon.
CORRECT	Dr. Nastasi is a *unique* surgeon.

Exercise 21

Identify any errors in the use of adjective and adverb forms in the following sentences and correct the errors.

1. When the four horses turned into the stretch, My Game had the greater stamina.

2. Although he was the same height as Bridesmaid, his strides seemed the longest by a yard as Perez rose in the saddle and swung the crop to drive the thoroughbred toward the finish line.

3. My Game won in record time, proving to be the most fastest three-year-old to win the cup.

4. After the race, Perez said, "My Game is perhaps the most perfect horse I've ever ridden.

5. Whether Perez is right or wrong, today this marvelous animal was the better horse.

15 Reminders for ESL Writers

If English is not your native language, you may need to review the information in this section from time to time. It should be particularly useful when you are preparing a final draft of your paper. This section includes information about sentence completeness, correct verb forms and combinations, faulty repetitions, and the punctuation of coordinate elements—items that may still trouble you even though you have otherwise become quite fluent in English.

The reminders here supplement the fuller discussions presented in individual chapters. You should use this section in combination with the appropriate sections indicated by cross-references.

15a Check sentences for completeness.

(See also sentence fragments, chapter 6; sentence completeness, 20b.)

1. Some languages allow the omission of subjects or verbs when the meaning is clear. English allows the omission of a subject only in imperative sentences (*You* is the implied subject: *Brush your teeth.*), and a verb is nearly always required in every sentence or clause. (For an exception, see elliptical constructions, 20b.)

INCORRECT	Practice my saxophone every day. [No subject]
CORRECT	*I* practice my saxophone every day.
INCORRECT	Colorado a beautiful state. [No verb]
CORRECT	Colorado *is* a beautiful state.

An **expletive,** *there* or *it,* may be required in sentences in which the subject follows the verb.

INCORRECT	Are scary creatures in the park. [The subject *creatures* follows the verb *are.*]
CORRECT	*There* are scary creatures in the park. [Expletive required]
CORRECT	Scary creatures are in the park. [Usual subject-verb word order]
INCORRECT	Is difficult to master English. [The subject *English* follows the verb *is.*]
CORRECT	*It* is difficult to master English. [Expletive required]
CORRECT	English is difficult to master. [Usual subject-verb word order]

NOTE: *Is, are, was,* or *were* cannot begin a sentence unless the sentence is a question (Are you awake?) or an exclamation (Was I sick!).

Exercise 22

Read the following summary of an article about Hillary Clinton's early months in the White House. Find the missing subjects and verbs and add them to the text. There are five omission errors.

Hillary Rodham Clinton the wife of President Bill Clinton. Was appointed by her husband to lead a committee to study the issue of health care, which is one of the major problems in the United States. Is one of the problems Clinton promised to solve during his 1992 campaign. Are thousands of people living in the United States who do not receive proper health care. There are no easy solutions to this problem because is difficult to provide national health care at a reasonable cost.

2. In English, nouns are frequently preceded by **noun markers,** words that indicate that a noun is coming (though it might not be the next word). Common noun markers are articles, numbers, possessive nouns, possessive pronouns, and certain other pronouns.

Common Noun Markers

Articles: *a* or *the* refrigerator; *an* elephant
Numbers: *1500* aircraft; *seven* customers
Possessive nouns: *Natalie's* library; *Costa Rica's* forests
Possessive pronouns: *my, our, your, his, her, its, their*
Certain other pronouns: *all, every, any, each, either, neither, few, many, more, most, this, that, these, those, much, several, some, whose*

Modifiers may be placed between the noun marker and the noun.

> *an* or *the* old, trustworthy refrigerator
> *1500* high-performance aircraft
> *Natalie's* secret library
> *his, their, this, every* beat-up Chevy

You should have little trouble using numbers, pronouns, and possessive nouns as noun markers. The use of articles, though, is more complex. The following explanations should answer most of your questions about the use of articles in English.

Definite article

The definite article *the* is used before nouns that are specifically identified. (*The* comes from the root of an earlier English word meaning *that*.)

> Wear the sweater *that you bought yesterday.* [The italicized clause identifies which sweater.]

> As it turned out, Gina has the *funniest* comedy routine. [The superlative *funniest* identifies which routine. There can be only one funniest routine.]

> I'm cold. Please turn off the fan. [The situation makes identity clear.]

> The sun finally came out. [Since we have only one sun, the identity is clear.]

> A math problem kept me up all night. In class I had to admit the problem had me stumped. [The noun *problem* is unidentified at first and preceded by *a.* When mentioned again it is preceded by *the* because its identity is now clear—it is the problem that kept the writer up all night.]

NOTE: Because it is used only with nouns specifically identified, the definite article should not be used with plural or noncount nouns (see p. 92) when the meaning conveyed is "generally" or "all."

The cost of printing ~~the~~ newspapers is usually borne by advertising revenue.

Health magazines report studies about drinking ~~the~~ coffee.

Generally, do not use the definite article *the* with proper nouns. Proper nouns name people, places, and things: Anita Romano, France, Three Rivers Stadium. Although these nouns are specifically identified by their very nature, they ordinarily do not take *the.*

NOTE: There are exceptions to this rule in individual cases.

Some plural proper nouns: for example, the Pyrenees, the Sierra Nevadas, the Alps, the Great Lakes.

Some country names: Many countries have an official name that may take *the* and a shorter, more commonly used name that does not take *the.*

FORMAL NAME	COMMON NAME
the Italian Republic	Italy
the Commonwealth of Australia	Australia
the Hashemite Kingdom of Jordan	Jordan
the *Principality* of Liechtenstein	Liechtenstein
the United States of America	America*

In all these cases the article *the* is used for the descriptive portion of the name: republic, commonwealth, kingdom, principality, states.

Indefinite Articles

Use the indefinite articles *a* or *an* for singular count nouns not specifically identified. (*A* and *an* come from the root of an earlier English word meaning *one.*)

Most nouns in English refer to things that can be counted: one airplane, three candidates, seven assignments, twenty dollars. Some nouns in English are not countable: homework, sugar, information, rain.

---

*Commonly accepted as an alternative name for the United States of America, though strictly speaking, America refers to all of North and South America.

If a singular count noun is not specifically identified, use *a* or *an*, whichever is appropriate.

Computers started *a* revolution in data processing.
Clint works for *an* insurance company.

NOTE: The selection of *a* or *an* depends on the initial sound of the word immediately following the article, whether it is the noun or not. *A* is used before a consonant sound, *an* before a vowel sound.

a turtle	*an* ungainly turtle
an umbrella	*a* blue umbrella

A word beginning with the letter *h* may have either an initial consonant sound if it is aspirated (*hole*) or an initial vowel sound if it is not aspirated (*heiress*).

a hand	*an* hour

The indefinite articles *a* and *an* are not used with plural nouns.

Mariko borrowed money to cover ~~an~~ expenses.
The exhibit consisted of ~~a~~ hastily arranged groupings of native costumes.

Generally, the indefinite articles *a* and *an* are not used with noncount nouns. (See chart.)

Teresa wrote her paper on *pollution*.
While you are shopping, please get *coffee* and *soap*.
Love can overcome *poverty*.

A particular amount of a noncount noun can be indicated by placing a count noun first and using the noncount noun as the object of the preposition *of*.

a *sack* of rice	a *pile* of dirt
a *grain* of sand	a *piece* of jewelry

Some Common Noncount Nouns

ITEMS CONSIDERED AS A GROUP

baggage	furniture	luggage	traffic
clothing	homework	money	vocabulary
equipment	jewelry	success	work
food			

FLUIDS AND SOLIDS

blood	gold	silver	water
coffee	ice	soup	wood
gasoline	iron	tea	

FOOD

beef	cereal	cream	rice
bread	cheese	meat	salt
butter	flour	milk	sugar
candy	ice	pepper	

ABSTRACTIONS

advice	fun	knowledge	luck
beauty	happiness	laughter	truth
courage	intelligence	love	violence

NATURAL PHENOMENA

dew	fire	light	sunshine
darkness	fog	rain	wind
electricity	heat		

OTHER

dirt	grass	pollution	smoke
dust	hair	sand	smog

Exercise 23

Fill in the blanks with *a, an, the,* or *0* (no article) as appropriate. Be prepared to discuss the reasons for your choices.

Most college students drink a lot of _____ coffee to help them stay awake while they are studying. _____ most widely known ingredient in coffee is caffeine. Although caffeine is present in other beverages, _____ cup of coffee usually contains _____ highest concentration of this mild stimulant. That is why _____ college students are frequently seen carrying their insulated mugs of _____ hot coffee around campus. _____ morning class or _____ evening in the library would be unbearable without _____ help of some coffee.

15b Use correct verb combinations.

(See also verb forms, chapter 11.)

1. Main verbs and helping verbs

(See helping verbs, 1c.) English sentences often require combinations of helping verbs and main verbs. The discussion below will help you become familiar with the combinations that are acceptable.

HELPING VERBS

Three forms of do: *do, does, did*
Three forms of have: *have, has, had*
All forms of be: *be, is, was, were, are, am, been, being*
Modals: *can, could, may, might, must, shall, should, will, would*

In any combination of a helping verb and a main verb, the helping verb appears first.

After modals and forms of *do* (*do, does, did*), use the plain form of the verb.

may write	might go	should bring
do swim	does feel	did hurt

INCORRECT She might *goes* if you ask her.

CORRECT She might *go* if you ask her.

INCORRECT I do *wanting* you to go.

CORRECT I do *want* you to go.

INCORRECT Your answer does not *convinces* me.

CORRECT Your answer does not *convince* me.

INCORRECT Did you *finished* your paper?

CORRECT Did you *finish* your paper?

After forms of *have* (*have, has, had*), use the past participle to form one of the perfect tenses. (See tense, 11d–11f.)

have driven	has contributed	had slept

INCORRECT Those students must have *pass* the test.

CORRECT Those students must have *passed* the test.

INCORRECT Amina has *accomplish* a great deal today.

CORRECT Amina has *accomplished* a great deal today.

INCORRECT Luis had *finish* his sculpture just in time.

CORRECT Luis had *finished* his sculpture just in time.

After the helping verbs *is, was, were, are, am,* use a present participle to form one of the progressive tenses. (See *tense* in the glossary.)

is going	was swimming	were eating
are studying	am thinking	

INCORRECT Jason was *worked* on his car.

CORRECT Jason was *working* on his car.

Be and *been* must be preceded by other helping verbs and followed by a present participle to form one of the progressive tenses.

can or *could* be
may, might, or *must* be
shall or *should* be
will or *would* be
has, have, or *had* been
can or *could have* been
may, might, or *must have* been
shall or *should have* been
will or *would have* been

INCORRECT Nadia *be arriving* soon.

CORRECT Nadia *should be arriving* soon.

INCORRECT Minh *been sleeping* late.

CORRECT Minh *must have been sleeping* late.

After the helping verbs *is, was, were, are, am,* use a past participle to form the passive voice. (See passive voice, chapter 13.)

is repeated	was thrown	were submitted
are appreciated	am assisted	

INCORRECT The newsletter is *deliver* every Monday.

CORRECT The newsletter is *delivered* every Monday.

INCORRECT After the snow the branches were *bend*.

CORRECT After the snow the branches were *bent*.

Be, been, and *being* must be preceded by other helping verbs and followed by a past participle to form the passive voice.

is, was, were, are, or *am* being
can or *could* be
may, might, or *must* be
shall or *should* be
will or *would* be
can or *could have* been
may, might, or *must have* been
shall or *should have* been
will or *would have been*

INCORRECT	My life may have been *save* by the lifeguard.
CORRECT	My life may have been *saved* by the lifeguard.
INCORRECT	The photos were being *mount* in the albums.
CORRECT	The photos were being *mounted* in the albums.

NOTE: Intransitive verbs, those expressing action that has no object, cannot be used in the passive voice.

| INCORRECT | The stunt artist *was* grinned broadly. |
| CORRECT | The stunt artist grinned broadly. |

Exercise 24

Underline the correct verb form for each set of verbs in the following sentences. Be prepared to explain your answers.

1. Researchers (*have studied, have study*) the effects of television on children and teenagers for many years.

2. A report which (*was release, was released*) by the National Institute of Mental Health in 1982 indicates that violence on television (*is leading, is leads*) to aggressive behavior by children and teenagers who watch the programs.

3. Further research on television violence suggests that some young people (*be copying, may be copying*) the violent behavior they (*have saw, have seen*) on TV.

4. It appears that many television programs (*do not offer, do not offering*) a positive role model for children and young adults.

2. Phrasal Verbs

Sometimes a verb is combined with a preposition or an adverb. These combinations are called **phrasal verbs,** and the preposition or adverb is called a *particle*. English has many of these combinations. They are potentially confusing because many carry idiomatic meanings as well as, or in place of, the literal meaning you may expect. For example, "look up" may be used literally to mean "focus on something above you," but it is also used idiomatically to mean "search for information." Undoubtedly, you have run across other idiomatic two- or three-word verbs such as *pass out, get along with,* and *tear down.* Such verb + preposition or adverb combinations are everywhere in English, especially in informal writing, and they are becoming more acceptable in formal writing. Their meanings must usually be learned in context. All we can do here is list some of them for you and caution you about certain rules for their use.

Phrasal verbs are either *separable* or *nonseparable* depending upon whether an object can be inserted between the verb and the particle. *Clean up* is an example of a separable phrasal verb. Each of the following sentences is correct.

> This weekend I will *clean up* my room. [Object follows the particle]
>
> This weekend I will *clean* my room *up.* [Object placed before particle]
>
> This weekend I will *clean up.* [No object]

In the following chart nonseparable phrasal verbs have been marked [N].

Common Phrasal Verbs

ask out (*ask for a date*)
bring up (*mention; raise a child*)
call off (*cancel*)
call up (*call on telephone*)
come across [N] (*meet unexpectedly*)
drop in or drop by [N] (*visit unannounced*)
drop off (*leave someone or something at a place*)
fill out (*complete a form*)
get along [N] (*live satisfactorily*)
get along with [N] (*have a comfortable relationship with*)
get over [N] (*recover from something*)
give up (*stop trying*)
go over [N] (*review*)
hand in (*submit*)
hand out (*distribute*)
help out (*assist*)
keep on (*continue*)
leave out (*omit*)
make up (*become friendly again; do past work; invent*)
pass away [N] (*die*)
pass out (*lose consciousness; distribute items*)
point out (*call attention to*)
put away (*store someplace*)
put off (*postpone*)
run out of [N] (*have no more in stock*)
take off (*leave; remove something*)
take over (*control; take charge*)
turn down (*reject*)
wrap up (*complete*)

When the direct object is a pronoun, the particle *must* be separated from the verb.

My room is dirty, but I will *clean* it *up* this weekend.

It would be incorrect to say *clean up it*.

In nonseparable phrasal verbs the particle must follow the verb immediately.

> When the doors open I will *get on* the bus.
> Do you think Kevin Costner will *show up* at the premiere?

Exercise 25

Refer to the list of common phrasal verbs and fill in the blanks with a phrasal verb similar in meaning to the verb given under each blank. Be especially careful of the tense of each verb.

1. I was supposed to _____ my research paper last week.
   submit

2. However, I had _____ doing the paper for so long that I
   postponed

   _____ time and was unable to finish the assignment.
   had no more

3. My roommate suggested that I _____ my professor and
   telephone

   ask for an extension.

4. Fortunately, my professor said she would _____ me
   assist

   _____ and give me extra time to complete my paper.

5. She said I could _____ it _____ at her office next
   leave

   week.

3. Verbs followed by gerunds and infinitives

Some English verbs may be followed by gerunds but not infinitives, some may be followed by infinitives but not gerunds, and some may be followed by either gerunds or infinitives.

A gerund is a verbal ending in *-ing* that functions as a noun: *cooking, studying, painting.* (See gerund, 3e.) An infinitive is a verbal consisting of the plain form of a verb preceded (usually) by *to: to attend, to believe, to convince.* (See infinitives, 3c.)

> Did she mention *shopping* at the flea market? [Verb followed by a gerund]

> This gadget is guaranteed *to predict* every rainstorm. [Verb followed by an infinitive]

VERBS THAT MAY BE FOLLOWED BY A GERUND BUT NOT AN INFINITIVE

admit	discuss	mind	recall
appreciate	enjoy	miss	resent
avoid	escape	postpone	resist
consider	finish	practice	risk
delay	imagine	put off	suggest
deny	mention	quit	tolerate

> The city will not *tolerate skateboarding* on the boardwalk. [Do not write *tolerate to skateboard.*]

> Let's *discuss writing* the research paper. [Do not write *discuss to write.*]

VERBS THAT MAY BE FOLLOWED BY AN INFINITIVE BUT NOT A GERUND

afford	demand	hope	pretend
agree	deserve	learn	promise
appear	endeavor	manage	refuse
ask	expect	mean (intend)	seem
care	fail	need	threaten
claim	guarantee	offer	wait
choose	happen	plan	want
decide	hesitate	prepare	wish

NOTE: Some verbs followed by an infinitive must have a noun or pronoun between the verb and the infinitive: *advise, allow, cause, caution, challenge, condemn, convince, dare, direct, encourage, forbid, invite, permit, persuade, require, teach, tell, warn.*

> I *challenge you to do* your best.
> She *advised Shirley to avoid* bungee jumping.

Some verbs may be followed directly by an infinitive or have a noun or pronoun between the verb and the infinitive: *ask, expect, need, want.*

> I *want to go* to the museum.
> I *want you to go* to the museum.

VERBS THAT MAY BE FOLLOWED BY EITHER A GERUND OR AN INFINITIVE

bear	deserve	love	remember
begin	dread	neglect	start
can't stand	hate	prefer	stop
can't bear	intend	regret	try
continue	like		

> Tomorrow, I *start jogging.*
> Yesterday, I *started to jog.*
> Don't you *hate reading* these silly sentences?
> Don't you *hate to read* these silly sentences?

Exercise 26

Complete the following sentences with a gerund or an infinitive. Then write a brief dialogue between a friend and a police officer in which your friend reports a crime. Use five or six gerunds or infinitives in your dialogue.

1. Campus Security officers want students (*understand*)

   _____ how to protect themselves on campus.

2. They want students (*lock*) _____ the doors to their rooms at all times.

3. They also suggest (*walk*) _____ across campus with at least one other person, especially at night.

4. Moreover, campus police caution students (*avoid*) _____ (*walk*) _____ in dark areas.

5. The Security Office would appreciate (*know*) _____ about any strangers on campus or any unusual behavior.

6. Do not hesitate (*call*) _____ Security if you happen (*see*) _____ something that troubles you.

7. Security offices do not mind (*investigate*) _____ reports of potential crime. It is their job to ensure that students enjoy (*live*) _____ in a safe environment.

15c Avoid faulty repetitions.

1. The subject of a sentence should not be repeated.

> Running it is my favorite sport. [*It* refers to the subject *running*.]

This rule holds true even if a phrase or clause comes between the subject and the verb.

> The tall man with the red hair he is my neighbor.
> Professor Denton, who lectured on the Middle East, she used humor to make her points.

2. An adverb used to introduce an adjective clause should not be repeated. (See dependent clause, 11g.)

An adjective clause is a dependent clause that modifies a noun or pronoun.

The adverbs *when* and *where* in adjective clauses modify nouns indicating time and place.

> That was the year *when we graduated*. [The adjective clause refers to *year*.]
>
> That was the year when we graduated then. [*Then* also refers to *year*. It must not be included.]
>
> The reunion will be held in the park *where we held the Senior Picnic*. [The adjective clause refers to *park*.]
>
> The reunion will be held in the park where we held the Senior Picnic there. [*There* also refers to *park*. It must not be included.]

3. A relative pronoun used in an adjective clause as the object of a verb or the object of a preposition should not be repeated. (See relative pronouns, 1b and 15c.)

The relative pronouns *who, whom, that, which,* and *whose* introduce adjective clauses that modify a noun or pronoun. Each word in the adjective clause serves a grammatical function. Do not include another word that serves the same function.

> Carl's vacation was made enjoyable by the people *whom he was staying with*. [The relative pronoun *whom* is the object of the preposition *with*.]
>
> Carl's vacation was made enjoyable by the people whom he was staying with them. [*Them* is also the object of the preposition *with*. It must not be included.]

Exercise 27

Draw a line through the unnecessary repetition of subject, adverb, or relative pronoun in the following sentences. Which type of error in repetition do you think ESL students most frequently make?

1. The World Trade Center, which is located in New York City, it was severely damaged by a car bomb in February 1993.

2. The car bomb was placed in an underground garage where it could do the most damage there.

3. The massive explosion it blew a hole five stories deep and sent smoke to the top of the 110-story building.

4. The blast occurred in the middle of the day when thousands of people were at work then.

5. Six people they were killed, and more than 1000 they were injured.

6. Hundreds of businesses whose their offices were damaged had to relocate while the building was being repaired.

15d Avoid confusing present and past participles used as adjectives.

Present and past participles used as adjectives may precede the noun they modify or follow a linking verb. (See linking verbs, 1c.)

> We saw an *interesting* movie.
> The movie we saw was *interesting.*
> All *interested* people should attend the debate.
> Many people were *interested* in the debate.

As you can see from the examples above, the present participle describes the agent causing the feeling or reaction (*movie was interest-*

ing), and the past participle describes the person or thing having the feeling or reaction (*interested people*).

In your writing use the proper participle form for verbs such as these.

amazing, amazed   exciting, excited
amusing, amused   exhausting, exhausted
annoying, annoyed   fascinating, fascinated
boring, bored   frightening, frightened
confusing, confused   interesting, interested
depressing, depressed   shocking, shocked
disturbing, disturbed   surprising, surprised
embarrassing, embarrassed thrilling, thrilled

Exercise 28

Underline the correct participle for each sentence. Then write a paragraph describing your reaction to a movie you have seen recently, using present and past participles from the list in section 15d.

1. People across the country were (*shocking, shocked*) by the news of the earthquake in San Francisco in 1989.

2. The news on television showed how (*frightening, frightened*) and (*confusing, confused*) everyone was.

3. The death and destruction left the residents of the San Francisco area very (*depressing, depressed*).

4. However, the rescue of a man trapped for days was (*amazing, amazed*), and people were (*thrilling, thrilled*) to learn he had survived.

5. Cleaning up after the earthquake was (*exhausting, exhausted*) work, but the people of San Francisco were (*encouraging, encouraged*) by the kindness of their neighbors and friends who helped out.

6. It was (*fascinating, fascinated*) to see how quickly the city recovered from a major disaster.

15e Punctuate coordinate elements correctly.

Do not use a comma before a coordinating conjunction joining only two coordinate elements unless each element is an independent clause. (See comma, 23a.)

Coordinate elements are joined by a coordinating conjunction: *and, but, or, yet, for, nor,* and *so.*

Coordinate elements may be words, phrases, or clauses.

> *wood* or *iron* [Single words]
>
> *over the river* and *through the woods* [Phrases]
>
> Despair ruled the day *because we had lost our way* and *we had eaten all our food.* [Dependent clauses]

Each of the above examples contains no punctuation within the sentence. Use commas with coordinate words, phrases, and dependent clauses only when you have three or more items. (See comma, 23f.)

> *wind, sleet,* and *snow*
>
> *hiking in the hills, swimming in the lake,* and *relaxing by the fire*
>
> *Although the alarm failed to go off, my car had a flat tire,* and *the traffic was a mess,* I arrived at work on time.

If the coordinate elements are both independent clauses, then put a comma before the coordinating conjunction.

This morning my alarm failed to go off**,** and my car had a flat tire.

Exercise 29

Add commas where necessary to the sentences in the following paragraph. (*Hint:* Eleven commas are missing.)

Many Americans are taking overdoses of vitamins and minerals because they hope the supplements will stop colds prevent cancer relieve depression or boost energy. Doctors nurses and nutritionists are becoming concerned about people who take megadoses of these supplements. Vitamins are good for you but large doses of them can make you sick or even kill you. Excess amounts of vitamins are stored in tissues circulated in the blood or excreted. Taking too much of one vitamin caused a 62-year-old man to have a stroke and a 41-year-old woman to suffer high blood pressure. Too much vitamin B can lead to headaches nausea loss of sensation and an irregular heartbeat. Nutritionists recommend that people eat a healthy diet and check with their doctors for more advice on vitamins.

Sentence Clarity and Variety

In writing, you must hold a reader's attention. Shaping accurate sentences and maintaining the relation between words and ideas help to keep a reader moving from sentence to sentence but are not always enough in themselves. Too often, writing that may be correct is monotonous. You must, therefore, shape your thoughts in interesting ways. This section not only illustrates ways to write clear and accurate sentences but also illustrates ways to keep a reader interested in your paper's content.

16 Coordination and Subordination *coord/sub*

When a single sentence contains more than one clause, the clauses may be given equal or unequal emphasis. Clauses given equal emphasis in one sentence are **coordinate** and should be connected by a coordinating word or punctuation. Clauses given less emphasis in a sentence are **dependent,** or subordinate, and should be introduced by a subordinating word. (See clauses, chapter 4.)

> In recent years many Tibetans have moved to Switzerland, and now there is a famous Tibetan Institute of Rikon. [Two main clauses given equal emphasis and connected by the coordinating conjunction *and*]

> Because Switzerland is politically neutral, the country has become the headquarters for many international organizations. [Dependent clause introduced by the subordinating conjunction *because;* main clause begins with *the country*]

16a Use coordination to give main clauses equal emphasis.

To indicate the relation between coordinate ideas, select the proper coordinator.

COORDINATING CONJUNCTIONS						
and	but	for	nor	or	so	yet

CORRELATIVE CONJUNCTIONS

both . . . and   either . . . or   neither . . . nor
not only . . . but also   whether . . . or

CONJUNCTIVE ADVERBS

accordingly	finally	instead	nonetheless
also	furthermore	likewise	otherwise
anyhow	hence	meanwhile	still
anyway	however	moreover	then
besides	incidentally	nevertheless	therefore
consequently	indeed	next	thus

Different coordinators—coordinating conjunctions, correlative conjunctions, or conjunctive adverbs (see chart)—may be used to express different relations. The common kinds of relation between coordinate clauses are addition, contrast, choice, and result.

> I went to school in Colorado, *and* she went to school in Florida. [Addition]
>
> My school was often buried in snow, *but* her school was usually bathed in sunshine. [Contrast]
>
> Students *either* learn how to water-ski *or* they learn how to snow ski. [Choice]
>
> She wanted to learn how to snow ski; *therefore,* she visited me in Colorado. [Result]

(For correct punctuation marks to use with these coordinators see 25a–25c.)

16b Avoid faulty or excessive coordination.

Faulty coordination gives emphasis to unequal or unrelated clauses.

> Alice Adams has published four novels, and she lives in San Francisco.

The clause *she lives in San Francisco* has little or no connection to *Alice Adams has published four novels.* Therefore, the two clauses should not be coordinated. But the writer may want to include this information in the paragraph because it is interesting and perhaps important, even though it does not pertain directly to the main idea of the paragraph. Placing *she lives in San Francisco* in a separate sentence might detract from the paragraph's unity.

   Revise faulty coordination by putting part of the sentence in a dependent clause, modifying phrase, or appositive phrase.

> Alice Adams, *who lives in San Francisco,* has published four novels. [Dependent clause]
>
> Alice Adams, *from San Francisco,* has published four novels. [Modifying phrase]
>
> Alice Adams, *a San Francisco writer,* has published four novels. [Appositive phrase]

Excessive coordination—stringing main clauses together with coordinating conjunctions for no apparent purpose—can become monotonous for the reader. Excessive coordination also fails to show the relation between clauses.

> Alice Adams is a successful writer, and she lives in San Francisco, and she has received grants from the Guggenheim Foundation and the National Endowment for the Arts.

Revise excessive coordination by rewriting the sentence, using dependent clauses, modifying phrases, or appositive phrases.

> Alice Adams, a successful San Francisco writer, has received grants from the Guggenheim Foundation and the National Endowment for the Arts.

Exercise 1

Revise the following sentences to correct faulty or excessive coordination.

1. Eugene O'Neill was an American playwright, and he won a Nobel Prize for literature in 1936.

2. O'Neill had an unhappy childhood, and he told the story of his childhood in a play entitled *Long Day's Journey into Night,* and he said it was "written in tears and blood."

3. O'Neill's daughter Oona married Charlie Chaplin, but she married against her father's will.

4. One of O'Neill's plays, *The Iceman Cometh,* is full of symbols and hidden clues about its meaning, and it has probably been written about more than any other American play.

5. Louis Sheaffer wrote a biography of O'Neill, and he spent sixteen years researching and writing it, and his book won a Pulitzer Prize.

16c Use subordination to distinguish the main clause in a sentence from clauses of lesser importance.

Indicate the correct relation between main clauses and dependent clauses by the careful selection of subordinators—either a subordinating conjunction or a relative pronoun. (See chart that follows.)

COMMON SUBORDINATING CONJUNCTIONS

after	because	provided	until
although	before	since	when
as	how	so that	whenever
as if	if	than	where
as long as	in order that	that	wherever
as much as	inasmuch as	though	whether
as soon as	once	unless	while
as though			

RELATIVE PRONOUNS

that	which	whoever	whose
what	whichever	whom	
whatever	who	whomever	

Be sure to select the appropriate subordinator to show the relation between a dependent clause and a main clause. The choice of which clause to subordinate depends, of course, on your intention, but writers commonly select details of concession, identification, time, cause, condition, and purpose for subordination.

CONCESSION (*as if, though, although*)
Although Maria has difficulty concentrating, she plays chess well.

IDENTIFICATION (*that, when, who*)
My Uncle Luis, *who often plays chess,* could not believe her expertise.

TIME (*before, while, as soon as*)
As soon as my uncle sat down, Maria moved one of her pawns.

CAUSE (*since, because*)
Because he was too confident, Uncle Luis carelessly moved his knight to a vulnerable space.

CONDITION (*if, unless, provided, since*)

If Maria had wanted to take my uncle's knight with her pawn, she could have done it.

PURPOSE (*so that, in order that*)

She moved a bishop instead, *so that my uncle would be in check.*

Exercise 2

Combine each pair of sentences below into one sentence, subordinating one idea to another. For example:

> I need an English composition course to graduate. I am not planning to take one this year.
>
> Although I need an English composition course to graduate, I am not planning to take one this year.

1. My sister Carla loves to shop at airport duty-free stores. Her first overseas trip was to Paris. *because*

2. Carla gets to take several overseas trips every year. She works for an importing firm in Atlanta.

Although 3. Duty-free shops are not really duty-free to the consumer. She still saves money on perfumes, watches, scarves, and ties.

4. Carla arrives at the airport early and checks in. She heads for the duty-free shops.

5. She prefers the large selection of the airport duty-free shops. The on-plane duty-free shops are cheaper.

16d Avoid faulty or excessive subordination.

Faulty subordination occurs when the more important clause is placed in a subordinate position in the sentence or when the expected relation between clauses is reversed.

> Foreign-made goods are popular with American consumers although their import poses at least a short-term threat to the livelihood of some American workers. [In an article about the problems of the American worker, this sentence would take attention away from the worker and incorrectly emphasize *foreign-made goods.*]

> Although she easily won the Olympic trial, she had been training for only six months. [This sentence seems to say that she trained in spite of the fact that she easily won the trial.]

Correct faulty subordination by changing the position of the subordinating word or phrase.

> *Although foreign-made goods are popular with American consumers,* their import poses at least a short-term threat to the livelihood of some American workers.

> *Although she had been training for only six months,* she easily won the Olympic trial.

Excessive subordination occurs when a sentence contains a series of clauses, each subordinate to an earlier one.

> The lonesome trapper, who was a retired railroad worker who lived in a small cabin, enjoyed the rare occasions when a group of hikers wandered by his place, which was inaccessible for most of the year.

This sentence is confusing. The writer apparently just added information as it came to mind.

To correct excessive subordination, break the sentence into two or more sentences or change some of the dependent clauses to modifying phrases or appositives.

> The lonesome trapper, *a retired railroad worker,* lived in a small cabin. *Because his place was inaccessible for most of the year,* he enjoyed the rare occasions when a group of hikers wandered by.

One dependent clause, *who was a retired railroad worker,* has been changed to an appositive. A second dependent clause, *who lived in a small cabin,* is now the predicate of the first sentence. These changes make the sentence more direct. The subordinator of the third dependent clause has been changed from *which* (identification) to *because* (cause) to show clearly the connection between the inaccessibility of the cabin and the trapper's enjoyment of rare visits.

Exercise 3

Rewrite the following sentences, revising the faulty or excessive subordination in each. You may need to write more than one sentence for each item.

1. Eimi Yamada, who had been a teacher for more than twenty years, retired from Stanton University, which was founded in 1829 and which has an international reputation in the biological sciences, last year.

2. Professor Yamada, who is noted for her work on the chemistry of cells, has most of her research materials housed in her garage, which she has used as a library for a decade, ever since someone stole her Buick.

3. Her ancient Buick, which was a 1940 Century convertible that had been purchased for her by her mother when Professor Yamada graduated from high school, had been admired by every student who had ever seen her drive it through the streets of Stanton.

4. The man who stole Professor Yamada's Buick, which was beige and maroon, once failed the biology course that Professor Yamada taught.

5. Stanton University's student body, which numbers over two thousand, took up a collection and bought Professor Yamada a retirement present, which was another automobile to replace the one that was stolen many years ago

17 Placement of Modifiers *mm/dm*

A writer can confuse a reader by misplacing a modifier in a sentence. Be sure to place modifiers in your sentences so that a reader will be certain of the word or words they modify.

17a Place prepositional phrases and dependent clauses as close as possible to the words they modify.

CONFUSING   Our neighbor borrowed our lawn mower with a smile.

CLEAR   With a smile, our neighbor borrowed our lawn mower.

CONFUSING	The car has bad tires that I sold today.
CLEAR	The car that I sold today has bad tires.

Exercise 4

Revise the following sentences by rearranging the misplaced prepositional phrases and dependent clauses.

1. The woman cashed her check with a French accent.

2. His trial was postponed for three months for tax evasion.

3. The explorer described an earthquake during his lecture.

4. After the party the hostess gave balloons to all the children in the shape of fantastic animals.

5. The senator examined the rocks in his office taken from the moon.

17b Avoid writing squinting modifiers.

A **squinting modifier** can seem to modify the word either preceding or following it. The ambiguous result can confuse a reader.

SQUINTING	Mia told Antonio immediately to call the police. [Does *immediately* refer to *told* or to *to call?*]
REVISED	Immediately, Mia told Antonio to call the police.
REVISED	Mia told Antonio to call the police immediately.

Exercise 5

Revise the following sentences to clarify the confusion created by squinting modifiers.

1. Walking to work occasionally is an interesting experience.

2. News that the water had been shut off completely mystified me.

3. Reading his novel thoroughly delighted me.

4. Taking coffee breaks frequently disrupts production.

5. Young children given an allowance often waste the money.

17c Place limiting modifiers carefully.

Words such as *only, hardly, just, nearly, almost,* and *ever* can function in many positions in a sentence. They modify the expression immediately following them. Therefore, as these limiting modifiers change position in a sentence, the meaning of the sentence also changes.

> I will go *only* if he asks me. [Otherwise I will stay.]
> *Only* I will go if he asks me. [The others will not go.]
> I will go if *only* he asks me. [Please, ask me!]
> I will go if he asks *only* me. [If he asks others, I will stay.]

Exercise 6

Write another version of each sentence by moving the italicized modifier to a different position. Briefly describe the difference in meaning in the two sentences.

1. Henrietta lost *almost* one thousand dollars.

2. *Only* Clyde is ten years old.

3. Rachel *nearly* memorized a hundred Chinese verbs.

4. Andi *even* has a job.

5. Mr. Kobe *just* stared at Mike.

17d Avoid placing a lengthy modifier between the subject and the predicate of a sentence.

AWKWARD   The cost of attending college, because of inflation and reduced federal support, has risen sharply in recent years.

REVISED   The cost of attending college has risen sharply in recent years because of inflation and reduced federal support.

You may place short modifiers between a subject and a predicate.

The cost of attending college, *unfortunately,* has risen sharply in recent years.

17e Avoid placing a lengthy modifier between a verb and its complement.

AWKWARD   Anton seemed, to those who had visited him during the several weeks following his operation, discouraged.

REVISED   To those who had visited him during the several weeks following his operation, Anton seemed discouraged.

You may place single-word modifiers between a verb and its complement.

Anton seemed *mildly* discouraged.

17f Avoid placing a lengthy modifier within a verb phrase.

AWKWARD   Margo could have, if she had not joined the Army, been a police officer. [Interrupts the verb phrase *could have been*]

REVISED   If she had not joined the Army, Margo could have been a police officer.

You may use a single word modifier within a verb phrase.

He discovered he had been *cruelly* deserted.

17g Avoid splitting infinitives.

An infinitive consists of *to* plus the plain form of a verb: *to run, to complain, to speak.*

> **SPLIT INFINITIVE** When the locusts descended, the prairie residents prepared *to* hurriedly *depart.*
>
> **REVISED** When the locusts descended, the prairie residents hurriedly prepared *to depart.*

Occasionally a split infinitive will seem natural and appropriate. In fact, not splitting an infinitive can sometimes create an awkward or misleading sentence.

> His inability to clearly explain the issues cost him the election.

In the preceding sentence, the alternatives are more awkward than the split infinitive. *Clearly to explain* and *to explain clearly* sound excessively formal, and *to explain the issues clearly cost him the election* produces a squinting modifier.

Exercise 7

Change the position of the italicized modifier in each sentence to correct the awkward constructions.

1. Tenochtitlán, *until it was destroyed by Cortés's army in 1521,* served as the capital city of the Aztec empire.

2. Following the destruction of the capital, Cortés's men built, *with the forced labor of the Aztec survivors,* a magnificent new city.

3. Mexico City is, *by many visitors today*, considered one of the most beautiful cities in the world.

4. Some demographers expect the population of Mexico City to, *by the year 2000*, number over 30 million people.

5. A visitor today will, *if romantically inclined*, enjoy the numerous sidewalk cafés and strolling musicians.

17h Avoid writing dangling modifiers.

A dangling modifier is a phrase or clause that is not clearly attached to any word in the sentence. To correct a dangling modifier, change the subject of the main clause or rewrite the modifier as a complete clause.

DANGLING PARTICIPIAL PHRASE

Walking through the supermarket, the oranges looked tempting. [The oranges were walking?]

REVISED

Walking through the supermarket, *I noticed that* the oranges looked tempting. [Introductory participial phrase clearly modifies the new subject, *I.*]

As I was walking through the supermarket, the oranges looked tempting. [Introductory modifier is a complete clause.]

DANGLING INFINITIVE PHRASE

To understand world affairs, a daily newspaper should be read.

REVISED

To understand world affairs, *a person should read* a daily newspaper.

DANGLING PREPOSITIONAL PHRASE

After recovering from the treatments, my doctor told me to be more careful in the future.

REVISED

After I recovered from the treatments, my doctor told me to be more careful in the future.

DANGLING ELLIPTICAL CLAUSE

While a student at Rutgers, Shakespeare was my favorite author.

REVISED

While I was a student at Rutgers, Shakespeare was my favorite author.

Exercise 8

Revise the following sentences to eliminate dangling modifiers.

1. To learn about zombies, Haitian voodoo tradition was studied by E. Wade Davis.

2. After receiving a sample of "zombie powder," it was found by Davis to contain one critical ingredient: tetrodotoxin.

3. Being a powerful poison, Davis said tetrodotoxin is 160,000 times more potent than cocaine.

4. Produced by a species of puffer fish, a soldier passed out for twenty-four hours after he handled roasted fish entrails containing tetrodotoxin.

5. Under constant tetrodotoxin intoxication, researchers noted that

people acted like the zombies discussed in literature.

18 Pronoun Reference *ref*

Pronoun reference is the relation between a pronoun and its **antecedent.** (See antecedent, 1b; agreement of pronoun and antecedent, chapter 9.) If the pronoun reference is unclear, the sentence will confuse or misinform a reader.

18a Avoid using a pronoun to make a broad reference to an entire sentence or clause.

Sometimes inexperienced writers use *this, that,* or *it* to refer to an entire sentence or clause.

> Mystery is what I felt during my nightly walks through the streets of Paris. That is what I needed. [Does the pronoun *that* refer to *mystery* or to *nightly walks?*]

> Good managers know when to delegate responsibility. This allows them to concentrate on the broader aspects of a project. [This what?]

Confusing sentences such as the preceding examples can be made clear by rewriting the sentences or by using a summary noun after *this* or *that.*

> I needed the sense of mystery I felt during my nightly walks through the streets of Paris.

> Good managers know when to delegate responsibility. This knowledge (skill, ability) allows them to concentrate on the broader aspects of a project.

18b Avoid the indefinite use of it, they, and you.

In conversation *it* and *they* are often used to make vague reference to people and situations. In writing, more precise identification is usually needed.

VAGUE	*It* is said that gold prices are rising.
CLEAR	Today's newspaper predicted that gold prices will rise before next year.
VAGUE	*They* said it would rain tomorrow.
CLEAR	The weather forecaster on Channel 3 predicts rain for tomorrow.

You is also commonly used in conversation to refer vaguely to people in general. In writing, however, use the more formal *one* or less formal *a person* or *people*. *You* should be used as a personal pronoun.

VAGUE	When traveling in a foreign country, *you* should respect local customs.
CLEAR	When traveling in a foreign country, *a person* should respect local customs.

The use of *you* to refer to "you, the reader" is perfectly appropriate in all but the most formal writing.

> If you plan to become a history teacher, you should begin your education by reading Herodotus.

18c Make a pronoun refer clearly to one antecedent.

CONFUSING	After Yoshi studied with Kim for a week, she discovered that she still did not understand calculus. [The two *she*'s could refer to either Yoshi or Kim.]
CLEAR	After studying with Kim for a week, Yoshi discovered that Kim did not understand calculus.

CONFUSING	After Carlos bought the shingles and the boards, he discovered they were full of termites.
CLEAR	After Carlos bought the shingles and the boards, he discovered the shingles were full of termites.
CLEAR	After Carlos bought the shingles and the boards, he discovered the boards were full of termites.
CLEAR	After Carlos bought the shingles and the boards, he discovered that both were full of termites.

18d Use pronouns ending in *-self* or *-selves* only to refer to another word in the sentence.

Stacy returned the book to the library *herself.*

People who expect riches without effort are fooling *themselves.*

Avoid using pronouns ending in *-self* or *-selves* in place of a grammatically correct pronoun.

| INCORRECT | Between you and *myself,* I think our team will win. |
| CORRECT | Between you and *me,* I think our team will win. |

Exercise 9

Correct the faulty pronoun references in the following sentences. You may need to change words or rewrite entire sentences. For example:

Mary decided to live with Liz because her roommate had moved out.

Mary decided to live with Liz, whose roommate had moved out.

After losing her roommate, Mary decided to live with Liz.

1. Jason gave the notes to Raul that he had taken during the lecture.

2. After hours of lessons, he learned to water-ski, but this didn't impress his girlfriend.

3. I heard they're planning to widen the expressway to eight lanes.

4. Among Jose, you, and myself, the secret will be safe, but if we tell Alberto, we will hurt ourselves.

5. Joe Louis and Rocky Marciano were two great heavyweight boxing champions; however, after Marciano beat him in 1950, he never fought as well again.

6. I sometimes buy clothes at discount stores because they are good values.

7. As the tiny robot approached the cat it started hissing loudly.

8. The enchiladas are for ourselves and the fajitas are for them.

9. Tonya survived the three-car accident, which is evidence of her luck.

10. John changed his major and then had to drop all his classes. That's typical.

19 Consistency *shift*

The use of person, number, mood, subject, and voice should remain consistent within sentences. Faulty shifts in any of these elements indicate that the writer's thinking is not clear, and the meaning of the sentences will be obscured. Always review your sentences for consistency.

19a Write sentences that are consistent in person and number.

Most faulty shifts in person take place between second person and third person.

FAULTY SHIFT	If a beginning *driver* studies the vehicle code thoroughly, *you* should be able to pass the written test for a driving license. [Faulty shift from third to second person]
REVISED	If a beginning *driver* studies the vehicle code thoroughly, *he* or *she* should be able to pass the written test for a driving license. [Consistent third person]
REVISED	If *you* study the vehicle code thoroughly, *you* should be able to pass the written test for a driving license. [Consistent second person]

Number refers to the singular or plural form of nouns and pronouns. Most faulty shifts in number result from the use of a plural pronoun to refer to a singular noun. (See agreement of pronoun and antecedent, chapter 9; indefinite pronouns, 1b.)

FAULTY SHIFT	When a *mud flat* dries up, *they* do so in regular patterns of cracks. [Shift from singular to plural]
REVISED	When a *mud flat* dries up, *it* does so in regular patterns of cracks. [Consistently singular]
FAULTY SHIFT	When a *chemist* experiments with toxins, *they* exercise great caution. [Shift from singular to plural]
REVISED	When a *chemist* experiments with toxins, *he* or *she* exercises great caution. [Consistently singular]
REVISED	When *chemists* experiment with toxins, *they* exercise great caution. [Consistently plural]

19b Write sentences that are consistent in tense.

Tense refers to the time of an action indicated by the verbs in a sentence. Shifts in verb tense are often required to report time sequences accurately, but faulty shifts can confuse a reader. (See tense, 11g.)

FAULTY SHIFT	The suspected bicycle thief *ran* around the corner and *falls* into the arms of the police officer.
REVISED	The suspected bicycle thief *ran* around the corner and *fell* into the arms of the police officer.
FAULTY SHIFT	The escaping driver *speeds* around the corner and *veered* directly into the path of a motorcyclist.
REVISED	The escaping driver *sped* around the corner and *veered* directly into the path of a motorcyclist.

19c Write sentences that are consistent in mood.

The *mood* of a verb can be indicative, imperative, or subjunctive. Statements and questions are in the indicative mood; commands are in the imperative mood; and wishes and statements contrary to fact are in the subjunctive mood. Most faulty shifts in mood occur when a writer fails to follow through with the initial use of the imperative mood.

FAULTY SHIFT	*Save* coffee grounds, and you *should sprinkle* them around your rosebushes.
REVISED	*Save* coffee grounds and *sprinkle* them around your rosebushes.

19d Write sentences that are consistent in subject and voice.

A shift in subject or a shift from active to passive voice is awkward and possibly confusing.

| FAULTY SHIFT | In the game of curling, a *player slides* a heavy stone over the ice toward a target, and the *ice* in front of the stone *is swept* to influence its path. |

Because the subject shifts from *player* in the first clause to *ice* in the second clause, and the voice shifts from active (*slides*) to passive (*is swept*), a reader may be confused about who is doing the sweeping.

| REVISED | In the game of curling, a player slides a heavy stone over the ice toward a target, and *the player's teammates sweep* the ice in front of the stone to influence its path. |

A shift in subject and voice sometimes results in a dangling modifier.

| FAULTY SHIFT | *Shaking with fear,* the *sound* of an intruder *could be heard* in the kitchen. [The sound is shaking?] |

The subject of the main clause is *sound.* The introductory phrase *shaking with fear* is a dangling modifier because it does not sensibly relate to *sound.*

| REVISED | Shaking with fear, *we heard* the sound of an intruder in the kitchen. |

Now the subject is *we,* which clearly connects to *shaking with fear.*

19e Avoid unnecessary shifts between direct and indirect discourse.

Direct discourse reports the exact words of a speaker. **Indirect discourse** reports the gist of what a speaker said but not the speaker's exact words.

| DIRECT DISCOURSE | Father said, "I will be home at noon." |
| INDIRECT DISCOURSE | Father said that he would be home at noon. |

FAULTY SHIFT	"I'll be home at noon," Father said, and I should not eat the cookies.
REVISED	"I'll be home at noon," Father said. "Don't eat the cookies." [Direct discourse]
REVISED	Father told me that he would be home at noon and that I should not eat the cookies. [Indirect discourse]

Exercise 10

In these sentences, label each faulty shift in person, number, tense, mood, subject, voice, or discourse and revise each sentence to be consistent. If any sentences are already correct, mark them with a C.

1. Until yesterday, Ilse Denschlag had not heard from her brother for months, but last night he telephones her, and then they were meeting together in a dingy, underfurnished room on the eleventh floor of the Beckford Hotel.

2. He seemed perfectly calm, and he was obviously enjoying himself.

3. Carefully, he packed the tobacco deeper in the bowl of his pipe and a match was struck.

4. He held the match in his right hand, not bringing it to the bowl, and stares at her.

5. Then he shook the match out and asked her if she was surprised to see him and asked "Don't you wonder where I've been?"

6. "I can guess where you've been," Ilse replied with a laugh, "but I am surprised to see you."

7. "Well, sometimes a man has to come home or you forget where it is," he said, and his lips form a faint smile.

8. She remembered that little smile he had; they always preceded his sharing a special secret.

9. I know why he's home, she thought, but you better not spoil his fun.

10. "Don't tell me now," she said. "Tell me at dinner, and I think you should call Mom and Dad first."

19f Avoid shifting grammatical plans in a sentence.

> In Faulkner's often anthologized story "Barn Burning" poignantly reveals the conflicting loyalties in a young boy's life.

"*Barn Burning*" is used in this sentence as the object of the preposition *in,* but it is also used as the subject of the verb *reveals.* A word or group of words cannot function as both the object of the preposition and the subject of the main clause.

If the sentence begins with a prepositional phrase, the main clause has to have a subject of its own.

> In the often anthologized story "Barn Burning," Faulkner poignantly reveals the conflicting loyalties in a young boy's life.

If "*Barn Burning*" is to serve as the subject of *reveals,* the prepositional phrase must be eliminated.

> Faulkner's often anthologized story "Barn Burning" poignantly reveals the conflicting loyalties in a young boy's life.

19g Avoid faulty predication.

Faulty predication occurs when the subject and predicate of a sentence do not fit together in meaning.

FAULTY PREDICATION	The issue of gun control is an easy solution to a complicated problem. [The issue is not the solution.]
REVISED	The issue of gun control is complicated.
REVISED	Gun control is an easy solution to a complicated problem.
FAULTY PREDICATION	Nepotism is when [or where] officials appoint their relatives to desirable positions. [Nepotism is neither a time nor a place.]
REVISED	Nepotism is the appointing of relatives to desirable positions.
FAULTY PREDICATION	The reason he failed the examination is because he had a toothache.
REVISED	The reason he failed the examination is that he had a toothache.
REVISED	He failed the examination because he had a toothache.

Exercise 11
Revise the following sentences to avoid shifts in grammatical plan and faulty predication.

1. Banking is an idea that has always interested me.

2. While I was eating at the Turkish restaurant, is where the music excited me so much that I felt like dancing.

3. All over the campus seemed to be alive with flowers.

4. Pearls are when gems are formed inside oysters.

5. In *Light in August* by William Faulkner is difficult to understand.

20 Sentence Completeness *inc*

Most incomplete sentences are sentence fragments, but some sentences that are not fragments may still be incomplete because they lack certain words necessary for understanding.

20a Make all comparisons complete, clear, and logical.

INCOMPLETE	I think the Ace Construction Company treats its employees better. [Better than who?]
COMPLETE	I think the Ace Construction Company treats its employees better *than other contracting firms do.*
UNCLEAR	Susan is closer to me than Serena.
CLEAR	Susan is closer to me than Serena *is.*
CLEAR	Susan is closer to me than *she is* to Serena.
ILLOGICAL	To her, the silence of the desert at night was more terrifying than a coyote.
LOGICAL	To her, the silence of the desert at night was more terrifying than *the howl of a coyote.*

20b Do not omit words from the second part of a compound construction unless the omitted words are consistent in grammar or idiom with the earlier parallel words.

In elliptical constructions, writers omit words that are understood.

There are only two lasting bequests we can give our children: one is roots; the other, wings.

At eighteen I knew everything; at forty-five, nothing.

In the first example, the verb *is* is omitted before *wings* with no confusion in meaning. In fact, the omission serves to emphasize *wings*. In the second sentence, *I knew* is omitted before *nothing*. The comma in each sentence notes the omission of words. (See comma, 23l.) Both sentences are strengthened by the omissions. But if omitted words are not consistent in grammar or idiom, a **faulty ellipsis** occurs.

FAULTY	At eighteen I knew everything; now, nothing.
REVISED	At eighteen I knew everything; now *I know* nothing.
FAULTY	Humans have a strong belief and desire for love.
REVISED	Humans have a strong belief *in* and desire *for* love.

Exercise 12

Rewrite the following sentences to make all comparisons complete, clear, and logical and to correct faulty ellipses.

1. Many people believe that horses are more intelligent.

2. Jorge's wife, Sarah, always had confidence and admiration for Jorge's old horse.

3. His favorite plow horse used to plow three acres a day; now none.

4. Personally, I believe that Sarah wants a horse more than Jorge.

5. To me, the smooth ride of a car is better than a horse.

21 Parallelism //

Parallelism exists when two or more ideas are given equal weight and are expressed in the same grammatical form in a sentence. Clarity in written English requires that coordinate ideas, compared and contrasted ideas, and correlative constructions be expressed in parallel form—that is, a noun must be matched with a noun, a verb with a verb, a phrase with a phrase, and a clause with a clause. Parallelism can add clarity, interest, and impact to your writing.

21a Use parallelism for coordinate elements.

To earn a living, he worked *as a busboy at the faculty club* and *as a bellhop at the Bayshore Inn.* [Parallel prepositional phrases]

Clearing tables and *lugging suitcases* often left him *tired, disgusted,* and *discouraged* by Sunday night. [Parallel gerund phrases and parallel predicate adjectives]

If coordinate elements are not expressed in parallel grammatical form, sentences can be awkward and hard to understand.

FAULTY	Her greatest pleasures during the summer were *the dances at Hotspur's* and *sleeping until noon.* [A noun and a gerund phrase as predicate nominatives]
REVISED	Her greatest pleasures during the summer were *dancing at Hotspur's* and *sleeping until noon.* [Parallel gerund phrases]

Words such as the prepositions *by* and *in,* the *to* of the infinitive, the articles *a* or *an* and *the,* and the subordinate conjunction *that* should usually be repeated when they apply to both elements in a parallel construction.

| FAULTY | *By reading extensively* and *voting wisely,* Americans contribute to the democratic process. |
| REVISED | *By reading extensively* and *by voting wisely,* Americans contribute to the democratic process. |

Clauses beginning with *and who* or *and which* can be coordinated only with *who* or *which* clauses that precede them.

| FAULTY | May Lin a student *and who* has been a sales-clerk, won election to the school board. |
| REVISED | May Lin *who* is a student *and who* has been a salesclerk, won election to the school board. |

21b Use parallelism to compare and contrast ideas.

| FAULTY | Tisha said she would rather *put up with the hectic pace of life in the big city* than *to waste time in a little backwater town.* |
| REVISED | Tisha said she would rather *put up* with the hectic pace of life in the big city than *waste* time in a little backwater town. |

21c Use parallelism for correlative constructions.

Either . . . or, not only . . . but also, both . . . and, and similar correlative constructions should connect parallel sentence elements.

The same type of construction that follows the first half of the correlative should follow the second half.

| FAULTY | De Campo sent copies of his speech not only *to senators and representatives* but also *his friends and relatives.* |
| REVISED | De Campo sent copies of his speech not only *to* senators and representatives but also *to* his friends and relatives. |

FAULTY	Even at night, she can usually be found in her office either *listening to student problems* or she *works on her research.*
REVISED	Even at night, she can usually be found in her office either *listening* to student problems or *working* on her research.

Exercise 13

Correct faulty parallelism in the following sentences.

1. Endurance training helps not only the lungs but also is good for the heart.

2. Some of the best exercises are running, swimming, and walks.

3. Gymnasts may work out using parallel bars, rowing machines, and lifting weights.

4. All spectators enjoy watching athletes performing well and who win gracefully.

5. The outcome of many football games next season will depend on whether the kicker is successful, whether the quarterback will make the right calls, and if the team is healthy.

22 Sentence Variety *var*

A good writer avoids writing monotonous paragraphs and essays by varying the length and structure of sentences. The following paragraph has interesting content but too little variety in sentence length and structure. The monotonous result could put the reader to sleep.

var

The first settlers came to Sauk Centre, Minnesota, in 1857.
The seven settlers were from New England. They called themselves the Sauk Centre Townsite Company. They built the first
residence on a bluff above the reedy swamplands and the sand
flats of the river's swell. This first residence was only an excavation lined with poles. They organized the Sauk Valley Claim
Association in July of 1857. They built a log house on the river
bank and started to build a dam. They didn't complete the dam
because winter became too harsh. The partially constructed
dam was broken by melting ice in the spring. The residents
didn't give up. They established a post office in 1858. They
built a frame house in the next year. They finished the dam in
1860. They also built a sawmill and a blacksmith shop in 1860.
Joseph Casper, one of the residents, built a general store. Nellie
Pendergast was the first white child born there. She was born
in 1861. These people built a city where there had been only
sand and trails and a few Indians.

Every sentence in the paragraph begins with the subject and follows a similar pattern. Many of the sentences are between five and
eight words long, a pattern that gives the paragraph a repetitive drea-
riness. Most important, each sentence stands as an isolated fact;
therefore, the relations between ideas are not made clear.

Now read the way Mark Schorer actually wrote this material.

Thirty years before, there was nothing here but native earth,
rolling prairie, roving Indians, a crossing of stagecoach trails.
Then, in 1857, at the point where the Sauk River widens into
the nine or ten miles of Big Sauk Lake, the first settlers came—
seven New Englanders who called themselves the Sauk Centre
Townsite Company. On a bluff rising above the reedy swamplands and the sand flats of the river's swell, they established the
first residence in this place, an excavation lined with poles. In
July of 1857 a first general meeting of settlers organized the
Sauk Valley Claim Association, and before the rigor of Minnesota winter locked them in, they had begun the construction
of a dam and had built a log house on the river bank. When

the ice broke up in the spring of 1858, it swept away the partially constructed dam, but a post office was established in that year, the first frame residence went up in the next, and in 1860 a new dam was finished, a small sawmill was put into operation, and the first blacksmith shop. In 1861 one Joseph Casper built the first general store, and Nellie Pendergast, the first white child, was born.
—from *Sinclair Lewis: An American Life*

Of course, the first paragraph was written poorly to illustrate by contrast the value of varying sentence length and word order. Schorer's paragraph differs from the first paragraph in other ways, too, but the point should be clear: Vary the sentence beginnings, vary the sentence structure and length, and change the word order to create a piece that is lively, interesting, emphatic, and rhythmic.

22a Vary sentence beginnings.

Begin with the subject:

> *Americans* chew millions of pounds of chewing gum each year.

Begin with an adverb:

> *Surprisingly,* well over half of this gum is used in armed forces combat rations.

Begin with a prepositional phrase:

> *Before the importation of chicle from Mexico in the mid–1880s,* Americans chewed paraffin wax.

Begin with a participal phrase:

> *Seeking greater chewing pleasure,* Americans soon switched to chicle.

Begin with an infinitive phrase:

> *To advertise his gum,* William Wrigley, Jr., in 1915, mailed free sticks of gum to every telephone subscriber in the United States.

Begin with a coordinating conjunction when appropriate:

> I don't like candy. I don't like cookies. I don't like cakes or pies. *But* I can't live without my chewing gum!

Begin with a transitional expression when appropriate:

> Doctors used to believe that chewing gum was a health hazard. *However,* most doctors now agree that chewing gum contributes to a sense of well-being.

Exercise 14

For each of the following model sentences, write another sentence that imitates its structure. Identify how each sentence begins.

1. Near the state border, the two escaped convicts surrendered.

2. Running without track shoes, Mary Jo won the hundred-meter dash in record time.

3. Reluctantly, Clyde told the salesclerk that his credit card had expired.

4. Many brick buildings would topple during an earthquake.

5. To encourage the team, the coach gave a pep talk.

22b Vary sentence structures.

In a piece of writing you can achieve variety by alternating the structures of sentences.

A **simple sentence** has only one main clause.

Nobody owns a cat.

A **compound sentence** has two or more main clauses but no dependent clause.

Nobody owns cats, but many people feed them.

A **complex sentence** has one main clause and at least one dependent clause.

If a cat likes you, it will live with you.

A **compound-complex sentence** has at least two main clauses and at least one dependent clause.

If a cat dislikes you, it may leave your home, and it may never return.

Exercise 15

Identify the sentence structure of each sentence.

1. Tiny bones in a fish's ear tell the life story of the fish.

2. The bones are called otoliths, and they grow in rings.

3. Because otoliths are affected by known weather conditions, scientists can tell the age of the fish, and they can tell when the fish migrated.

4. In addition, if the fish has had a behavior change, the ear bones have recorded it.

5. Because the otoliths absorb heavy metal, scientists can examine them for signs of water pollution.

22c Vary sentence forms.

A **loose sentence** has its subject and predicate first, followed by modifiers and other amplification.

> Arteries carry blood, which is rich in oxygen, to the extremities of all warm-blooded animals, including birds.

A **periodic sentence** has most of its modification and amplification before the subject and predicate.

> Even with a temperature below ten degrees Fahrenheit, pheasants have warm bodies.

A **balanced sentence** is a compound or compound-complex sentence in which the clauses are parallel.

> Arteries transmit warm blood, and veins return the cooler blood. [Compound sentence]
>
> While they were studying zoology together, Bebe kept humming, and Ching kept mumbling. [Compound-complex sentence]

Exercise 16

Identify the form of each of the following sentences.

1. The Senate passed the tariff bill after a long debate.

2. Senator Milburn spoke for an hour, and Senator Reynaldo asked for some changes in the bill.

3. In the closing hours of the session, the Senate passed the tariff bill.

4. The president wanted a tariff bill, and Congress wanted one, too.

5. While the senators were debating, most of the reporters were interviewing the people in the balcony.

Exercise 17

Write sentences that conform to the following descriptions, using the model sentence as a guide.

1. Write a *simple, loose* sentence.

   Ether burns brightly.

2. Write a *simple, periodic* sentence.

   An organic compound, ether has industrial uses.

3. Write a *complex, periodic* sentence.

   While Donna Lee was experimenting in her laboratory, some ether caught fire.

4. Begin a *simple sentence* with a *prepositional phrase.*

   Before noon, her laboratory was destroyed.

5. Begin a *complex sentence* with a *dependent clause.*

   When the firefighters arrived, they saw only embers.

6. Write a *loose, complex* sentence.

   The firefighters returned to their station while Donna Lee remained at the scene.

7. Begin a *simple sentence* with a *participial phrase.*

   Reading her insurance policy, the young scientist looked sad.

8. Write a *periodic sentence* containing two *clauses.*

   After talking to her insurance agent, she called her father, and then she started to eat dinner.

9. End a *complex sentence* with a *prepositional phrase.*

   While she was eating, her brother walked into the kitchen.

10. Begin a *compound-complex sentence* with a *dependent clause.*

    After Donna Lee told her brother about her accident, he helped her with the dishes, and he later helped her rebuild her laboratory.

Punctuation

The following section illustrates the correct uses of punctuation. By punctuating your writing correctly, you will be supplying your readers with the cues they need to understand your written thought.

23 The Comma ,

The **comma** serves within sentences mainly to group words that belong together and to separate words that do not. The comma also has several conventional uses, such as in dates and addresses. Since the comma is the most frequently used, and misused, punctuation mark, you will be well on your way to controlling punctuation errors by mastering its use.

23a Use a comma before a coordinating conjunction (*and, but, or, nor, yet, so,* and *for*) linking two main clauses.

> The aging process is relentless, but most of us fight growing old.
>
> Professional athletes begin their careers out of love for sports, and a few keep that love.
>
> The road was littered with household goods, for the refugees could not carry the extra weight.

NOTE: Keep in mind that not every coordinating conjunction in a sentence joins main clauses. Often coordinating conjunctions create compound subjects or compound predicates.

> Every Saturday the lawyer walked seven miles to the widow's cabin *and* chopped a week's supply of firewood for her. [The coordinating conjunction *and* joins two verbs, *walked* and *chopped.* It is incorrect to separate two parts of a compound predicate with a comma.]
>
> We enjoy bagels *and* cream cheese for breakfast. [The coordinating conjunction *and* joins two nouns, *bagels* and *cream cheese;* do not use a comma.]

Exercise 1

Insert a comma before each coordinating conjunction linking main clauses. If a sentence is correct, mark it with a *C*.

1. The British used the name *America* to refer to the British colonies and the colonists used the term *American* to refer to natives.

2. The emerging country needed to establish a name or it would always be seen as an extension of Europe.

3. In 1697 Cotton Mather popularized the word *American* to mean an English colonist in America and by 1780 our language was called *American*.

4. By 1782 a citizen of the United States was called *American* but the term *Americanism* was not used until 1797.

5. Citizens of the United States call themselves *American* but seldom remember that citizens from other western hemisphere countries are also American.

23b Use a comma to set off introductory phrases and clauses from main clauses.

INTRODUCTORY PREPOSITIONAL PHRASE

By the end of next month, life in this house will change.
On the north shore of Kauai, two sharks attacked surfers.

INTRODUCTORY VERBAL PHRASE

To sail solo around the world, you must have courage.
Beaten by relentless winds, the caravan returned to the oasis.
Diving into the field, the hawk pursued its prey.

INTRODUCTORY CLAUSE

If the Alaska king crab population plummets, crab fishers will be bankrupted.

Whenever heavy rains hit southern California, hillside homes begin to slide.

Be careful to distinguish verbal modifiers from verbals that function as subjects. Verbal modifiers are usually separated from the main clause by a comma; verbals functioning as subjects never take a comma. (See gerunds and gerund phrases, 3e.)

Parachuting from an airplane, Darryl realized the joy of floating on the wind. [Verbal as modifier]

Parachuting from an airplane is Darryl's favorite pastime. [Verbal as subject]

You may omit a comma after a very short introductory clause or phrase if the omission does not cause a misreading.

CONFUSING	On each weekday morning exercise class begins at six.
CLEAR	On each weekday, morning exercise class begins at six.
CLEAR	In science we need to know when to persevere and when to quit.

Usually no comma is needed to separate adverb clauses placed at the end of a sentence. (See unnecessary commas, p. 167.)

Presidential news conferences offer more entertainment than information because reporters do not ask pointed questions.

Exercise 2

Insert commas where needed after introductory phrases and clauses in the following sentences. If a sentence is correct, mark it with a *C*.

1. In spite of an apparently inexhaustible supply the numbers of wild creatures are being depleted because of greed.

2. If you are tempted to spend $25,000 for a leopard-skin coat remember that each coat requires the pelts of seven animals.

3. Specializing in killing and stuffing a taxidermist in California illegally offered bighorn sheep to wealthy customers.

4. After exposure he confessed and paid a fine.

5. Handicapped by low budgets authorities seem to be losing the battle against poachers.

23c Use a comma to set off nonrestrictive elements. Do not use a comma to set off restrictive elements.

A **restrictive element** defines or identifies—that is, it restricts—the meaning of the noun it modifies and is essential to the meaning of the sentence. A **nonrestrictive element** may add important information to a sentence but is not essential to the meaning of the sentence.

> RESTRICTIVE   A student *who sets academic goals* will graduate in four years.

In the preceding sentence, the clause beginning with *who* is essential to the meaning of the sentence. Without the clause, the sentence will mean something else: *A student will graduate in four years.*

NONRESTRICTIVE   Robin Crisp, *who studies five hours daily,* will graduate in three years.

In the preceding sentence, the clause beginning with *who* adds factual information but is not essential. The basic meaning of the sentence is clear without it: *Robin Crisp will graduate in three years.*

1. Restrictive clauses and phrases are *not* set off by commas.

> Citizens *who are interested in politics* should run for public office. [The *who* clause defines which citizens should run for public office.]

> The mechanic *working on the Volkswagen* lost his temper. [The participial phrase identifies which mechanic lost his temper.]

NOTE: Clauses beginning with the relative pronoun *that* are almost always restrictive.

> The belief *that human beings are driven by subconscious drives* is common among psychoanalysts.

> Medical treatments *that are not approved by the American Medical Association* may be dangerous.

In a restrictive adjective clause, the relative pronoun introducing the clause may be dropped when it does not function as the subject of the relative clause.

> A tax increase is the only way [*that*] *our government can continue to function.*

> Pauncy could not find a politician [*whom or that*] *she respected.*

NOTE: Clauses and phrases modifying indefinite pronouns are almost always restrictive.

> Walt Disney is a genius to those *who make animated cartoons.* [The *who* clause restricts *those* to animated-cartoon makers.]

> I gave the report to someone *who was sitting at the desk.* [The *who* clause restricts *someone* to the person sitting behind the desk.]

Anyone *sleeping in the park* was awakened. [The participial phrase identifies the indefinite pronoun *anyone.*]

2. Nonrestrictive clauses and phrases should be set off by commas.

Venice, *which is noted for its Piazza San Marco,* was a favorite haunt for American writers. [The clause adds information but does not restrict the meaning of *Venice.*]

The right to free speech, *like breathing itself,* is essential to life. [The prepositional phrase does not restrict *right to free speech.*]

NOTE: Clauses and phrases that modify proper nouns are always nonrestrictive. (See proper nouns, 1a.)

Ernest Hemingway, *who had an interest in art,* claims to have learned to write fine descriptions by studying Impressionist paintings.

Sometimes a clause or phrase may be either restrictive or nonrestrictive. The writer must indicate how it is to be interpreted by using or omitting commas.

RESTRICTIVE	The engineers *who were trained as pilots* provided the technical advice. [The *who* clause restricts or defines *engineers.* The sentence means that not all engineers provided technical advice; only the ones trained as pilots did.]
NONRESTRICTIVE	The engineers, *who were trained as pilots,* provided the technical advice. [This sentence means that all the engineers were trained as pilots, and they gave the technical advice. The *who* clause is not essential to the meaning of the sentence.]

3. Nonrestrictive appositives should be set off by commas; restrictive appositives should not.

A restrictive appositive defines the noun it refers to in such a way that its absence from the sentence would leave the meaning unclear.

NONRESTRICTIVE	Ralph Williams, *a frequent personality on late-night television,* made millions selling used cars.
NONRESTRICTIVE	Baby gray whales, *huge creatures at birth,* consume up to fifty gallons of milk daily.
NONRESTRICTIVE	"Mending Wall," *one of Robert Frost's narrative poems,* deals with two differing world views.
RESTRICTIVE	The actor Whoopi Goldberg is known for both her comedic and her dramatic roles.
RESTRICTIVE	The Greek hero *Perseus* slew the dragon and freed Andromeda.
RESTRICTIVE	James Dickey's poem "*Looking for the Buckhead Boys*" portrays a middle-aged man's attempt to reconnect with his youth.

Exercise 3

In the following sentences, insert commas to set off nonrestrictive clauses, phrases, and appositives. If a sentence is correct as written, underline the restrictive or nonrestrictive element and mark the sentence with a *C*.

1. Edgar Allan Poe a nineteenth-century American writer wrote the first murder mystery.

2. "The Murders in the Rue Morgue" published in 1841 presents C. Auguste Dupin the world's first modern detective.

3. In Dupin, Poe created a detective who solved murders through observation and reason often drawing a solution that appears miraculous.

4. Poe also created the "locked room" story a mystery in which a murdered victim is found in a room locked from inside.

5. James Fenimore Cooper another American writer created the first espionage novel.

6. Cooper's *The Spy* which was based on historical notes from the American Revolution appeared even before Poe's work.

7. Cooper who is known for his romantic Indian tales created a formula that future espionage writers would use.

8. Mark Twain who is not considered to be a mystery writer contributed to detective fiction by being the first author to use fingerprints to help solve a crime.

9. Mystery writers today must use new methods of detection since crime technology has become so sophisticated.

10. Anyone who reads or writes mysteries must wonder if science will put an end to the fine art of fictional murder.

Exercise 4

Combine the following sentences according to the directions given in brackets. After you have combined the sentences, be sure to punctuate them correctly. For example:

> The tradition of detective stories with murder in the family is an old one. Human beings have always had murder in their hearts. [Use *since* to form an adverbial clause.]
>
> COMBINED: *Since human beings have always had murder in their hearts,* the tradition of detective stories with murder in the family is an old one.

1. Cain killed his brother Abel in an Old Testament story of the first murder. Cain was jealous of Abel. [Use *who* to form an adjective clause.]

2. Some serious mystery readers claim that *Oedipus Rex* is the first detective story. *Oedipus Rex* is an early Greek play. [Use an appositive phrase.]

3. Oedipus seeks his true identity. He has inadvertently killed his father and married his mother. [Use *who* to form an adjective clause.]

4. Clearly, *Oedipus Rex* is a murder mystery. The play ends ironically when the detective discovers he is the killer. [Use *that* to form an adjective clause.]

5. Shakespeare's *Hamlet* can also be viewed as a mystery. *Hamlet* is an Elizabethan tragedy. It deals with a brother murdering his brother and ascending to the throne of Denmark. [Use an appositive phrase and an adjective phrase beginning with *that*.]

6. Hamlet must first prove that his uncle murdered his father. Hamlet was the son of the slain king. [Use an appositive phrase.]

7. Both *Oedipus Rex* and *Hamlet* concentrate on solving a family murder. They thrill many audiences today. [Use a present participial phrase.]

8. Modern detective writer Ross Macdonald also weaves his mysteries around family crimes. They often use murder or a disappearance to motivate the investigation. [Use *which* to form an adjective clause.]

9. *The Galton Case* begins with a mother who wishes to be reconciled with her son. *The Galton Case* is an early Macdonald mystery. The son has disappeared without a trace. [Use an appositive phrase and an adjective clause beginning with *who*.]

10. By the novel's end, Macdonald's detective has revealed a murder and unraveled the family's snarled history. The detective's name is Lew Archer. [Use an appositive.]

23d Use commas to set off parenthetical expressions that function as transitions, express afterthoughts, or offer supplemental information.

Parenthetical expressions interrupt the flow of a sentence. Transitional phrases such as *for example, on the other hand,* and *in fact* are parenthetical and usually are set off by commas.

> Driving on freeways and turnpikes, *for example,* is four times more dangerous than flying.

Commas are usually needed to set off conjunctive adverbs, such as *accordingly, besides, consequently, furthermore, hence, however, indeed, instead, likewise, meanwhile, moreover, nevertheless, otherwise, therefore,* and *thus.* (See semicolon, 25b.)

> Several bystanders who witnessed the crime identified the thief; *nevertheless,* he was released from custody because of a technicality. [Before a clause]
>
> Several bystanders who witnessed the crime identified the thief; he was released from custody, *however,* because of a technicality. [Within a clause]

Always use commas to set off *however* when it is used as a conjunctive adverb; do not use commas to set off *however* when it is an adverb meaning "no matter how."

> Sixteen engineers gave similar testimony; *however,* the Senate committee was swayed by the attorney general's dissenting view. [Conjunctive adverb]
>
> *However* reasonable the expert testimony, the committee still votes according to party attitudes. [Adverb]

Afterthoughts and supplemental information should be set off with commas.

> Mystery writers, *some critics maintain,* try to make sense of murder.

23e Use a comma to set off mild interjections, words of direct address, and *yes* and *no*.

Oh, I didn't mean to buy so many groceries!
Stop playing those video games, *Ji.*
No, I cannot be there early.

Exercise 5

Insert commas as necessary to set off parenthetical expressions and words of direct address in the following sentences. If a sentence is correct, mark it with a *C*.

1. However much Americans love their Big Macs and chocolate shakes, many are sacrificing their affair with junk food for a new commitment.

2. Bulging biceps, rippled stomachs, and yes even sinewy necks are the new shapes people yearn for.

3. Regardless of the pain and endless hours spent pumping iron men and women are dedicating themselves to furious body-building.

4. Will chiseled muscles lead to healthier lives? No not if weightlifting is merely an escape from time's relentless craftsmanship.

5. Moreover many bodybuilders express their desire to become a new-age Rambo.

23f Use commas between words, phrases, and clauses in a series consisting of three or more items of equal importance.

Three well-known Japanese novelists are *Junichirō Tanizaki*, *Yasunari Kawabata*, and *Yukio Mishima*. [Nouns]

To plan successfully, you must *clarify* the goal, *define* the objectives, *establish* a deadline, and *charge* ahead. [Predicates]

Driving luxury sedans, *eating gourmet food*, and *drinking fine wine* are Camelita's fantasies. [Participial phrases]

When Aaron awoke, he did not know *who he was*, *where he had been*, or *what would happen next*. [Dependent clauses]

Although the final comma in a series is optional, including it can prevent misreading.

I took the following courses: digital computers, software manufacturing, word processing, and data retrieval. [The final comma makes it clear that word processing and data retrieval are separate courses.]

NOTE: No comma is necessary between items in a series all joined by *and* or *or*.

Whole grains and nuts and yogurt are the staples in Quintana's diet.

23g Use a comma between coordinate adjectives not joined by *and*. Do not use a comma between cumulative adjectives.

Coordinate adjectives are two or more adjectives that modify the same noun or pronoun.

Informative, *imaginative*, *appealing* advertising should be more common. [*Informative, imaginative,* and *appealing* modify advertising.]

Advertising is often no more than a *deceptive, dull* appeal to one's insecurity. [*Deceptive* and *dull* modify *appeal.*]

NOTE: A comma is never used between the last adjective in a series and the noun it modifies.

Cumulative adjectives modify the adjectives that follow them as well as a noun or pronoun.

His life was dedicated to achieving a *single personal* goal. [*Single* modifies *personal* and *goal.*]

The exhibition of *ancient Tunisian* mosaics will close next week. [*Ancient* modifies *Tunisian* and *mosaics.*]

Two simple tests can help you tell the difference between coordinate and cumulative adjectives. If you can change the order of the adjectives or place the word *and* between them, the series is coordinate and requires commas.

Intelligent, sensitive, witty films are seldom produced in Hollywood.

Sensitive, witty, intelligent films are seldom produced in Hollywood.

Intelligent *and* sensitive *and* witty films are seldom produced in Hollywood.

The preceding adjective series meets both tests; therefore, it is a coordinate series and should be separated by commas.

International peace organizations supported antinuclear demonstrations in the world's capitals.

Peace international organizations supported antinuclear demonstrations in the world's capitals.

International and peace organizations supported antinuclear demonstrations in the world's capitals.

The adjective series *international peace* does not meet either test; therefore, it is a cumulative series and should not be separated by commas.

Exercise 6

Insert commas as necessary within a series or between coordinate adjectives in the following sentences. Include the last comma in a series. If a sentence is correct, mark it with a *C*.

1. Early colonists brought such words as *bandit robber highwayman* and *outlaw* with them from England.

2. Freezing weather personal dignity or increasing population demanded that the first privy be built.

3. The history of the circus goes back to the days of the Roman Empire when chariot races gladiator fights and animal shows were featured activities.

4. Hungry for adventure seeking land to farm and willing to risk life and limb, thousands of Mississippi settlers caught the Oregon fever.

5. Tall and lean brooding and gentle Abraham Lincoln was the imposing figure who led a divided confused country during the Civil War.

23h Use the comma to set off absolute phrases.

An **absolute phrase** modifies an entire sentence rather than a word or phrase, but it is not grammatically related to the rest of the sentence. Absolute phrases are always nonrestrictive—that is, they always supply important but nonessential information to a sentence.

The Doberman leaped at Rashid's *throat, teeth snapping, eyes flashing anger.*

Their feet aching from the journey, the four campers climbed into their sleeping bags.

Anuka, *her fingers gripping the wheel,* accelerated into the curve.

23i Use the comma to set off contrasting expressions and interrogative elements.

Love, not hate, is the essence of renewal. [Contrasting expression]

Each person has the responsibility for his or her behavior, *right?* [Interrogative element]

23j Use the comma to set off expressions such as *she said* or *he wrote* from direct quotations.

The *Tao Te Ching* says, "Not collecting treasures prevents stealing."

"I cannot and will not cut my conscience to fit this year's fashions," wrote Lillian Hellman.

"One writes out of one thing only," says James Baldwin, "one's own experience."

If the expression comes between two or more sentences of quotation, use a period after the expression to indicate the end of the first sentence.

"The apartment house is nearly finished," she said. "I never thought I would see the day."

(See quotation marks, 28d; colon, 26e.)

Omit the comma if a quotation ends with an exclamation point or question mark.

"Why all this indecision?" she asked.

NOTE: When a comma follows a quotation, always place it within the quotation marks, not after or under them.

"Of course," she replied.

Exercise 7

Insert commas as necessary in the following sentences to set off absolute phrases, contrasting expressions, interrogative elements, and explanatory words used with a direct quotation.

1. Many food faddists like to eat natural meat not just the domesticated meat displayed in most supermarkets.

2. Natural meat is game not the kind you play on ball fields and includes a variety of wildlife found in America's forests and mountain ranges.

3. Free for the taking some game is coveted more than others. Venison for instance is the most popular game served at American tables.

4. One chef praises muskrat chili certainly not as common as Texas chili right?

5. Some food faddists see game as a preferred dish in specialty restaurants. "Seldom is the taste so aroused as when a platter of sputtering moose steaks or a brace of mallards is placed on a table" one critic writes. "It's like experiencing the American wilderness in the heart of Manhattan" he claims.

23k Use a comma according to established conventions in numbers, addresses, place names, dates, and friendly letters.

1. Separate long numbers into groups of three beginning from the right.

> 12,345   222,498   231,547,211

In four-digit numbers the comma is optional.

> 5,676 or 5676

2. Separate each item in an address when the address is run together in a line. Do not use the comma to set off the zip code.

> 600 Wisconsin Avenue, South Milwaukee, Wisconsin 53172
> 600 Wisconsin Avenue
> South Milwaukee, Wisconsin 53172

3. Separate each item in a place name.

> I forwarded the package to Harvard University, Cambridge, Massachusetts, where she now teaches.

4. Separate the month and day from the year in a date.

> The reception will be held at the Hilton on September 21, 1999, in the Twilight Room.

If the day precedes the month, do not use commas.

> 21 September 1999

5. Set off the salutation and close of a friendly letter.

> Dear Uncle Joe Bob,   Yours truly,

Exercise 8

Insert commas as necessary in the following letter, including optional commas.

March 16 1990

Dear Dat

I have just accepted a sales position with a firm in Newport
Beach California about forty-five miles south of Los Angeles.
The base salary is $25000 a year but with commissions I could
make another $5000 to $10000.

The company will have a training position opening next month.
Are you interested? Let me know. My new address is 2701 Fairview
Road Costa Mesa CA 92626.

Your friend

Hoa Thi

23I   Use a comma to prevent misunderstanding and to show the omission of an understood word.

1. To prevent a misunderstanding:

CONFUSING	On Monday morning schedules will be revised.
CLEAR	On Monday, morning schedules will be revised.
CLEAR	On Monday morning, schedules will be revised.

2. To show an omission:

The French drink wine; the Germans, beer.

For Dr. Sanchez to give one *A* is rare; for him to give two,
unprecedented.

24 Unnecessary Commas *no ,*

Excessive use of the comma may confuse a reader by separating sentence elements that belong together. The following rules specify when a comma is not necessary.

24a Do not use a comma between a subject and its verb unless a sentence element that comes between them requires a comma.

INCORRECT	Fully grown killer whales, are as long as thirty feet and as heavy as ten tons.
CORRECT	Fully grown killer whales are as long as thirty feet and as heavy as ten tons.
CORRECT	Fully grown killer whales, which travel in pods of ten to twenty, are as long as thirty feet and as heavy as ten tons.

24b Do not use a comma between a verb and its object or its complement.

INCORRECT	A killer whale will eat, anything it can catch.
CORRECT	A killer whale will eat anything it can catch.

24c Do not use a comma between a preposition and its object.

INCORRECT	Killer whales live in, practically all the tropical oceans of the world.
CORRECT	Killer whales live in practically all the tropical oceans of the world.

24d Do not use a comma between an adverb and the word it modifies or between an adjective and the word it modifies.

INCORRECT   The killer whale has been described as the most socially, intelligent, animal in the world. [*Socially* modifies *intelligent; intelligent* modifies *animal.*]

CORRECT   The killer whale has been described as the most socially intelligent animal in the world.

(See coordinate adjectives and cumulative adjectives, 23g.)

24e Do not use a comma between compound words, phrases, or dependent clauses joined by a coordinating conjunction.

INCORRECT   The engine, and the grill are the most famous features of the Rolls-Royce. [Compound subject joined by conjunction *and*]

CORRECT   The engine and the grill are the most famous features of the Rolls-Royce.

INCORRECT   A Rolls-Royce has eighty thousand parts, and takes three months to build. [Compound predicate joined by conjunction *and*]

CORRECT   A Rolls-Royce has eighty thousand parts and takes three months to build.

INCORRECT   The Rolls-Royce is proof that fine work is still being done, and that people will pay any price for quality. [Two dependent clauses beginning with *that* and joined by conjunction *and*]

CORRECT   The Rolls-Royce is proof that fine work is still being done and that people will pay any price for quality.

(See compound subject and compound predicate, 2c–2f.)

24f Do not use commas to separate restrictive elements from the rest of the sentence.

INCORRECT   The first car, created by Henry Royce and Charles Rolls, was built in 1904. [The sentence falsely suggests that Royce and Rolls built the first automobile.]

CORRECT   The first car created by Henry Royce and Charles Rolls was built in 1904.

INCORRECT   Fritz Wirth's article, "An Empire on Four Wheels," appeared in January. [This sentence would be correctly punctuated only if Wirth wrote one article.]

CORRECT   Fritz Wirth's article "An Empire on Four Wheels" appeared in January.

(See restrictive elements, 23c.)

24g Do not use a comma after *such as* and *like.*

INCORRECT   Some writers, such as, Gabriel García Márquez and Mario Vargas Llosa, influenced contemporary American writers.

CORRECT   Some writers, such as Gabriel García Márquez and Mario Vargas Llosa, influenced contemporary American writers.

24h Do not use a comma before the first or after the last item in a series unless a rule requires it.

INCORRECT   Reading, writing, and arithmetic, should be the spine of education.

CORRECT   Reading, writing, and arithmetic should be the spine of education.

INCORRECT	Popular college subjects today are, psychology, business, and engineering.
CORRECT	Popular college subjects today are psychology, business, and engineering.
CORRECT	Popular college subjects today are, among others, psychology, business, and engineering. [A rule requires that the phrase *among others* be set off.]

24i Do not use a comma to introduce indirect discourse.

INCORRECT	The Tao teaches that, muddy waters left alone will become clear.
CORRECT	The Tao teaches that muddy waters left alone will become clear.

24j Do not use a comma before *than* in a comparison.

INCORRECT	Hang gliding is more exciting, than skydiving.
CORRECT	Hang gliding is more exciting than skydiving.

24k Do not use a comma with a period, a question mark, an exclamation point, or a dash, all of which stand by themselves.

INCORRECT	"Return the money at once!", he pleaded.
CORRECT	"Return the money at once!" he pleaded.

Exercise 9: Review

Correct the following sentences by inserting commas where they are needed and by deleting them where they are not needed. Include all optional commas. If any sentence is correct, mark it with a *C*.

1. The life of the Chinese heroine Meng Chiang Nu, the Pumpkin Girl, is an example of loyalty dedication and self-sacrifice.

2. The story begins with two families the Meng and the Chiang.

3. During the planting season one year each family planted pumpkins at the foot of a wall that marked the boundary of their properties.

4. Growing rapidly, pumpkin vines soon began to climb the wall and at the top they joined and produced a pumpkin larger than anyone had ever seen before.

5. According to the story the families agreed to divide the pumpkin but when they cut it open they found a tiny baby girl inside.

6. To show she belonged to both the Meng family and the Chiang family they called her Meng Chiang.

7. At about the same time, the Emperor Shih Huang Ti started to build the Great Wall of China.

8. Each time the emperor's men put up a section of the wall however it collapsed before another section could be built.

9. The emperor who felt discouraged sent for the wisest men in the empire to advise him.

10. One wise man told him the only way to stop the collapse, would be to bury a living person in the wall every mile.

11. Since the wall was to extend ten thousand miles the plan would call for the sacrifice of ten thousand people!

12. Another wise man whispered to the emperor "Your Eminence living nearby is a poor man. Since his name Wan means ten thousand bury him in the wall and your great enterprise will be strong along its entire length."

13. Yes, Wan was poor, but he was not stupid.

14. When he heard of the plan he ran, and ran, and ran, until at nightfall he found himself high, in the branches of a tree in a peaceful isolated garden.

15. Beneath him he saw a beautiful girl bathing naked in a pool.

16. Of course it was Meng Chiang grown to womanhood.

17. She sang softly of love, and said aloud "If any man should see me now I would happily be his wife forever."

18. Wan forgot his own safety for a moment and climbed down from the tree and claimed his bride.

19. Unfortunately the emperor's men arrived just after the wedding seized the bridegroom and carried him off to be buried alive in the Great Wall.

20. Having heard of Wan's fate years later Meng Chiang made the hazardous journey to the wall to search for her husband's body.

21. Out of sympathy for her plight, a section of the wall collapsed, and her husband's bones fell out.

22. She was taken to the emperor who was stunned by her great beauty and vowed to marry her.

23. Seeing that the emperor was determined to marry her Meng Chiang asked only that a high altar be built in memory of her husband.

24. On their wedding day Meng Chiang climbed to the top of the altar cursed the emperor for his cruelty and threw herself to her death.

25. The emperor commanded his men to cut her body into little pieces but each piece of her flesh turned into a beautiful silver fish and her soul lives in these fish as a tribute to faithfulness.

25 The Semicolon ;

A **semicolon** is used, in a limited number of situations, as a substitute for a period to indicate a close relation between main clauses and as a substitute for a comma to improve clarity

;

25a Use a semicolon between main clauses that are closely related in meaning and are not joined by a coordinating conjunction.

In Irish folklore the Sidhe (pronounced "she") spirits sometimes appear as men and women; other times they appear as birds and beasts. The Sidhe travel as clouds of dust; they rest as blades of grass.

There must be some basis for deciding whether to use two main clauses with a semicolon between them or two sentences with a period. Generally, the division into separate sentences is better. A semicolon should be used only when the ideas in the two main clauses are so closely related that a period would make too strong a break between them. (See coordinating conjunctions, 1g; comma splices and fused sentences, chapter 7.)

Stylistically, the semicolon may be used to create a balance between closely related clauses.

Mystics trust spirits; realists trust only facts.
Mystics trust spirits; realists, only facts.

(See sentence completeness, 20b.)

25b Use a semicolon to separate main clauses joined by conjunctive adverbs.

In folklore the Sidhe live under Ireland's rocky soil or beneath the mutinous seas; consequently, some Irish claim the Sidhe are never far from them.

(See note, conjunctive adverbs, 1g.)

NOTE: When a conjunctive adverb immediately follows a semicolon (as in the preceding example), always put a comma after the conjunctive adverb. When a conjunctive adverb does not immediately follow the semicolon, put commas before and after the conjunctive adverb.

The Sidhe live on cold potatoes and milk left on hearths and at thresholds of Irish homes; when feasting, however, they resort to theft and rob Irish cellars of good wines.

25c Use a semicolon to separate main clauses joined by coordinating conjunctions when the main clauses are long and complex or have internal punctuation.

The Sidhe sing in glens, dance on boulders, and play hurling in the fields; but they also curse, bicker, and fight each other.

25d Use semicolons to separate phrases or clauses in a series if they are long or contain commas.

Partial to humans, Sidhe spirits will help them in their work; aid them in the search for hidden money, lost jewels, and buried gold; and treat their sick pets, ailing livestock, and ill children.

25e Avoid misusing the semicolon.

Do not use a semicolon to join dependent clauses or phrases and main clauses.

INCORRECT	According to some enthusiasts; only ten thousand Sidhe exist.
CORRECT	According to some enthusiasts, only ten thousand Sidhe exist.
INCORRECT	Some believe the Sidhe are headed toward extinction; because fewer and fewer people believe in them.
CORRECT	Some believe the Sidhe are headed toward extinction because fewer and fewer people believe in them.

Do not use a semicolon to introduce a list.

INCORRECT	Perhaps the Sidhe will join the ranks of other imaginary creatures; such as unicorns, leprechauns, and magical dwarfs.
CORRECT	Perhaps the Sidhe will join the ranks of other imaginary creatures, such as unicorns, leprechauns, and magical dwarfs.
CORRECT	Perhaps the Sidhe will join the ranks of other imaginary creatures: unicorns, leprechauns, and magical dwarfs.

(See colon, 26a; dash, 27b.)

Exercise 10

Delete the unnecessary or incorrect commas and semicolons and insert the correct punctuation in the following sentences. If any sentence is correct, mark it with a *C*.

1. Whereas imaginary creatures may fall from memory, the real mysteries of the world will always arouse our curiosity.

2. One mystery involves strange carvings, many the size of three-story buildings, found on Easter Island; another involves cave drawings at Lascaux, France, painted fifteen to twenty thousand years ago.

3. Easter Island is tiny, volcanic, barren, and isolated; nevertheless, plenty of insects and hordes of rats live there.

4. Mysterious statues dominate the island, their threatening expressions presiding over the landscape.

5. Their faces all share similar features, such as long ears, large eyes, and jutting chins.

6. Some of the statues are toppled over, most, however, still stand, all still have topknots made from red stone.

7. The paintings in the Lascaux caves, are equally mysterious, however, the mystery surrounds their purpose, not their origin.

8. Some historians claim the paintings represent hunting magic, others see in them a great symbolic idea that is beyond our understanding, still others view them as simply the result of creative impulses.

9. Whatever their motivations; the Lascaux cave painters created groups of pictures in sixty-six caves. This achievement required many skills; including the ability to extract minerals from the ground, pound them to powder, and mix them with grease.

10. As children we huddle together in the darkness and scare each other with tales of mysterious monsters, as adults we curl up under a reading lamp with a good book and wonder about the mysterious creations of humankind.

:

26 The Colon :

A **colon** introduces sentence elements that explain, illustrate, or amplify portions of a sentence. A colon also introduces formal quotations and separates subtitles and titles, subdivisions of time, parts of biblical citations, and city and publisher in bibliographic entries.

26a Use a colon to introduce a series following a complete sentence.

Maya Angelou is best known for four volumes of autobiography: *I Know Why the Caged Bird Sings, Gather Together in My Name, Singin' and Swingin' and Gettin' Merry Like Christmas,* and *The Heart of a Woman.*

They stood on a hilltop and watched the crowd pour across the bridge: families pulling carts piled high with furniture, soldiers in torn uniforms and dragging their rifles by the strap, and children, crying, lost, helpless.

26b Use a colon after *the following* or *as follows* to introduce a statement or series.

In the upper-right-hand corner on your paper write the following: name, course number, assignment number, and date.

The secret to understanding history is as follows: whatever goes around will come around.

26c Use a colon to announce a second main clause that explains the first.

She has no doubts about her future: she will first attend medical school and then train as a psychiatrist.

NOTE: Capitalizing the first word of a main clause that follows a colon depends on the style you are following. (See capitals, 34a.)

26d Use a colon to introduce a final appositive.

August 6, 1945, is a day we should never forget: the day humanity ignited the earth.

26e Use a colon to introduce a long or formal quotation.

In 1962 Rachel Carson's *Silent Spring* sounded the warning:

The most alarming of all man's assaults upon the environment is the contamination of air, earth, rivers, and sea with dangerous and even lethal materials. This pollution is for the most part irrecoverable; the chain of evil it initiates not only in the world that must support life but in living tissues is for the most part irreversible. In this now universal contamination of the environment, chemicals are the sinister and little-recognized partners of radiation in changing the very nature of the world—the very nature of life itself.

26f Use a colon to separate subtitles and titles, subdivisions of time, parts of biblical citations, and city and publisher in bibliographic entries.

The Origins of the English Language: A Social and Linguistic History
1:13 A.M.   12:34 P.M.   Matthew 4:6–10
New York: HarperCollins, 1996

NOTE: The MLA and some other styles use a period for biblical citations: Matthew 4. 6–10.

:

26g Use a colon at the end of a formal salutation.

Dear Mr. and Mrs. Fritz:
To Whom It May Concern:

26h Do not misuse the colon by placing it after a linking verb (separating the verb from its direct object) or a preposition or by placing it in a sentence that lacks a formal introduction for what follows.

INCORRECT	You will need: toothbrush, toothpaste, razor, shaving cream, and change of clothes.
CORRECT	You will need toothbrush, toothpaste, razor, shaving cream, and change of clothes.
INCORRECT	Finchamp, a well-traveled man, has lived in: Paris, London, Rome, Dublin, and Berlin.
CORRECT	Finchamp, a well-traveled man, has lived in Paris, London, Rome, Dublin, and Berlin.
INCORRECT	Bluegrass music makes use of several stringed instruments, such as: banjo, guitar, mandolin, and fiddle.
CORRECT	Bluegrass music makes use of several stringed instruments, such as banjo, guitar, mandolin, and fiddle.

Exercise 11

Use a colon to combine each group of sentences into a single sentence. You will have to revise wording and exclude some words to make the combined sentences read correctly.

1. He drove twelve hours nonstop for one reason. ~~That reason was~~ to arrive before the opening kickoff.

2. The philosopher Sören Kierkegaard contemplated the future with a simply stated attitude. ~~He defined it~~ as fear and trembling.

3. *Yahoos* were introduced in Jonathan Swift's *Gulliver's Travels.* ~~They are a race of~~ brutish, degraded creatures who have the form and all the vices of human beings.

4. Our forests, our hills, our prairies all have one thing in common. They will soon succumb to land development.

5. Propaganda devices have been given catchy names. Some of the names are "glittering generalities," "bandwagon," "testimonial," "plain folks," and "poisoning the well."

27 The Dash —

The most common uses of the **dash** are to emphasize a sentence element and to indicate a break in tone or thought. Do not use a dash habitually in place of a comma, a semicolon, parentheses, or a period. Reserve dashes for situations calling for special emphasis or for the infrequent situations when only a dash will make your meaning clear.

In a typed paper make a dash by joining two hyphens (--) without spaces before or after them.

27a Use dashes to emphasize appositives and parenthetical expressions.

Judge Sarah Riley sentenced O'Neil—the treasurer of Local 1026 and once the friend of local politicians—to five years. [Appositive]

The craft of surgery—though some would call it an art—demands the steady hand of a miniaturist to work the scalpel through a web of arteries and veins. [Parenthetical expression]

27b Use a dash to separate a series that comes at the beginning of a sentence.

Aching feet and ankles, throbbing shins, clicking knees, and crumbling hip joints—these physical ailments result from running on asphalt or cement.

27c Use a dash for special emphasis or clarity.

Gary March decided to outrage his associates by wearing gray slacks, a brown sport coat, and a pink shirt—but no one noticed. [Emphasis]

The meeting was attended by two consultants—a historian and a psychologist. [Clarity]

In the last example a dash must be used rather than a comma to make it clear that the meeting was attended by two consultants, not by four people—two consultants, a historian, and a psychologist.

27d Use dashes to show a break in tone or thought.

"I don't—well—I just can't."
"Can't what?"
"Can't seem— OK—I will if you help."

27e Use a dash to precede an author's name after a formal quotation that stands separately from the text, such as an epigraph.

Fasten your seat belts. We're going to have a bumpy night.
——Bette Davis

28 Quotation marks " "

The main use of **quotation marks** is to assist a reader by indicating the beginning and the end of a direct quotation from speech or writing.

28a Use double quotation marks (" ") to enclose direct quotations from speakers or writers.

In a recent lecture on contemporary art, Professor Alvarez said, "Until the general acceptance of Georgia O'Keeffe's work, artists were divided into two groups—artists and female painters. Now we have just one group—artists."

Art historian Sam Hunter sees Georgia O'Keeffe's work as emerging from and going beyond biomorphic abstraction: "O'Keeffe seemed able to invest abstract painting with fresh content and significant new forms."

When quoting a passage that takes up more than four lines in a typewritten paper, do not use quotation marks (unless they appear in the original); instead, set off the quotation from the rest of the paper by putting it in block form. That is, indent the entire passage ten spaces (or one inch) and double-space the lines. The first line of the passage should be indented an additional three spaces (or one-fourth inch) if it marks the beginning of a paragraph.

All of us are familiar with the superstitious belief that the number 13 is unlucky. But we are not, of course, the only culture that worries about numbers. The famous linguist Charles Berlitz notes,

> In both Chinese and Japanese, the word "four," shi, sounds like the word "death." The Japanese often substitute another word for "four"-yotsu, taken from an alternative system of counting. License numbers using 4 in certain combinations are shunned by Chinese car owners in Hong Kong, Taiwan, and Singapore. They especially avoid the number 1414, which in speech resembles the words "definite death, definite death."

The indention of the quoted paragraph indicates that it is all a quotation. Note, too, that the words *four, death,* and *definite death* are placed within quotation marks because those marks appeared in the original.

When directly quoting poetry, work a quotation of one line or less into the text and enclose it within quotation marks.

> Shelley tellingly countered Ozymandias's proclamation of omnipotence with the short, ironic comment, "Nothing beside remains."

A quotation of two lines of poetry may be worked into the text of your paper or set off from it. To work the lines into the text, separate them with a slash (with one space before and after the slash) and enclose the entire quotation in quotation marks.

In T. S. Eliot's poem "The Love Song of J. Alfred Prufrock," Prufrock's isolation is echoed in the lines "I have heard the mermaids singing, each to each. / I do not think that they will sing to me."

To set off the lines of poetry from the text, begin each line on a new line, indent it ten spaces (or one inch) unless the poet used varying indentation, and double-space the lines. Omit the quotation marks.

In T. S. Eliot's poem "The Love Song of J. Alfred Prufrock," Prufrock's isolation is echoed in the lines

> I have heard the mermaids singing, each to each.
>
> I do not think that they will sing to me.

A poetry quotation of three or more lines should be set off from the text in block form and presented just as it is printed in the original. Do not use quotation marks and slashes.

When quoting conversation or writing fictional dialogue, put quotation marks around the exact words spoken. Do not enclose descriptive phrases or attributions in quotation marks. Begin a new paragraph for each speaker.

"Where is he?" Mae asked, coming around the corner of the house with a mop and bucket in her hands. "Is he gone?"

"I dunno, Mom," Stacy replied. "He was here a minute ago." She yawned and scratched the back of her head vigorously. "Probably gone huntin' again."

If one speaker or writer is quoted without interruption for more than one paragraph, put quotation marks at the beginning of each paragraph but at the end of only the last paragraph.

NOTE: Do not use quotation marks to enclose indirect quotations—written or spoken information that you have rewritten or summarized in your words.

> His purpose, he said, was to break with the traditions of the past and bring new life to the film industry.

28b Use quotation marks to enclose the titles of articles, essays, short stories, short poems, songs, chapter titles and other subdivisions of books or periodicals, and episodes of radio and television programs.

(See italics, 37a.)

> Shirley Jackson's "The Lottery" exposes a small community's blind obedience to tradition. [Short story]
>
> "The Microbe Hunters" is this week's episode of *Nova.* [Television episode]
>
> Chapter 2, "Entering the Aerobics Program," tells how to take the first step toward improving the cardiovascular system. [Chapter title]

NOTE: Do not use quotation marks to enclose the titles or section titles of your own papers.

28c Occasionally quotation marks serve to enclose a word used in a special sense.

> I had to take the job. I needed the "bread."

NOTE: Do not use quotation marks to create an ironic tone, change the meaning of a word, or justify the use of nonstandard English.

> INAPPROPRIATE   Just being late to class was "traumatic" enough, but when the instructor peered over his glasses and "growled," "Again," I just "totally flipped."

APPROPRIATE   Just being late to class was bad enough, but when the instructor peered over his glasses and growled, "Again," I was really embarrassed.

28d Follow standard practice when using other marks of punctuation with quotation marks.

1. Always place commas and periods that follow a quotation *inside* quotation marks.

> Although Tom Bender said, "Writers who endure will always write about what they know," he spent years describing the journeys of characters who became lost in exotic lands he never visited.

> Scanning the crowd for her son, she said, "It's like looking for a needle in a haystack."

2. Always place colons and semicolons *outside* quotation marks.

> Some of Aunt Maude's favorite expressions are "He runs around like a chicken with its head cut off"; "Where there's smoke there's fire"; "Don't count your chickens until they've hatched": expressions from the common pot of American clichés.

3. Enclose dashes, question marks, and exclamation points in quotation marks only if they belong to the quotation.

> "That's terrible! How can they expect—" she screamed in disbelief.

> I am sure you resent him for always asking, "But what does it all mean?"

> Long after she had turned the corner, she could still hear him calling, "Eva! Eva!"

When a dash, question mark, or exclamation point is not part of a direct quotation, do not enclose it within quotation marks.

"Something is rotten in the state of Denmark"—and I intend to find out what it is!

Have you ever wanted to tell him, "I don't want to work here anymore"**?**

Please! Stop saying, "Something is rotten in the state of Denmark"**!**

28e Use single quotation marks (' ') to enclose a direct quotation within a quotation.

"Let me remind you," the professor said, "of the words of Edward R. Murrow, 'We cannot defend freedom abroad by deserting it at home.'"

Exercise 12

Supply quotation marks where they are needed and place punctuation marks correctly in the following sentences. If a quotation should be set off in block form, place a *B* to indicate at which point the block would begin and an *E* to indicate where it would end. Make any other changes that would be necessary to handle a block quotation correctly. If no quotation marks are needed in a sentence, mark it with a *C*.

1. Of all Flannery O'Connor's short stories, A Good Man Is Hard to

   Find best embodies the full range of her style.

2. O'Connor, Michael Finnegan wrote, mastered the use of carica-

   ture in character development.

3. The dictionary defines *caricature* as follows: The exaggeration of certain human characteristics in order to create a satiric effect.

4. The portrait of Mrs. Freeman in the short story Good Country People is an example of caricature: Besides the neutral expression that she wore when she was alone, Mrs. Freeman had two others, forward and reverse, that she used in all her human dealings. Her forward expression was steady and driving like the advance of a heavy truck. She seldom used the other expression because it was not often necessary for her to retract a statement. O'Connor even uses the name *Freeman* ironically because Mrs. Freeman is no more free than the speeding truck she is compared to.

5. To reveal the limited natures of her characters, O'Connor often fills their speech with stock phrases, such as Nothing is perfect; That is life; and You're the wheel behind the wheel.

6. Sometimes her characters seem too strange to be real, but like all writers who will endure, she draws her material from life, thus following Alexander Pope's dictate: Know then thyself, presume not God to scan; / The proper study of Mankind is Man.

7. She studied people, and the absurdity of much of the world delighted her. Sally Fitzgerald writes about O'Connor's letters,

She regaled us with Hadacol advertisements; birth announcements of infants with names that had to be read to be believed; such news items as the attendance of Roy Rogers' horse at a church service in California.

8. Could her intense interest in the absurd behavior of people continue one critic asked and still remain fresh?

9. I've reached the point where I can't do again what I can do well she wrote in a letter and the larger things I need to do now, I doubt my capacity for doing.

10. Many prefer distant landscapes such as the magical kingdom in Coleridge's short poem Kubla Khan, which begins In Xanadu did Kubla Khan / A stately pleasure-dome decree: / Where Alph, the sacred river ran / Through caverns measureless to man / Down to a sunless sea.

29 The Ellipsis Mark . . .

An **ellipsis mark** (**. . .**) indicates that one or more words within a quotation have been intentionally omitted, either to avoid including unnecessary or irrelevant portions of a quoted passage or to mark an unfinished statement in dialogue.

29a Use an ellipsis mark to indicate an omission in a quotation that you have edited to fit the purposes of a paper.

ORIGINAL PASSAGE

All his books in the Yoknapatawpha cycle are part of the same living pattern. It is the pattern, not the printed volumes in which part of it is recorded, that is Faulkner's real achievement. Its existence helps to explain one feature of his work: that each novel, each long or short story, seems to reveal more than it states explicitly and to have a subject bigger than itself. All the separate works are like blocks of marble from the same quarry: they show the veins and faults of the mother rock. Or else—to use a rather strained figure—they are like wooden planks that were cut, not from a log, but from a still-living tree. The planks are planed and chiseled into their final shapes, but the tree itself heals over the wound and continues to grow.

—Malcolm Cowley

EDITED WITHIN A PAPER

Malcolm Cowley praises the interconnectedness of Faulkner's work:

> All his books in the Yoknapatawpha cycle are part of the same living pattern. It is the pattern . . . that is Faulkner's real achievement . . . . Each novel, each long or short story, seems to reveal more than it states explicitly and to have a subject bigger than itself.

Note that when a complete sentence comes before an omission, as in the sentence that ends with *achievement,* you should place a period at the end of the sentence before the ellipsis mark. Note also that a complete sentence, even if it is only part of the original sentence, is capitalized (see 34a). Finally, note that although the quotation is part of a larger paragraph, an ellipsis mark is not used at the end of the quotation.

29b Use a row of evenly spaced periods to indicate that one or more paragraphs of prose or one or more lines of poetry have been omitted from a quotation.

And for all this, nature is never spent;

There lives the dearest freshness deep down things;

. . . .

Because the Holy Ghost over the bent

World broods with warm breast and with ah! bright wings.

–Gerard Manley Hopkins, "God's Grandeur"

29c Use an ellipsis mark to indicate an unfinished statement in speech or dialogue.

Barry's nervousness got him off to a bad start: "I'm not sure how to begin. It seems as if • • • I don't know how to tell • • • I don't want to appear • • • Miss Jones • • • can I call you Mildred?"

30 Parentheses ( )

Parentheses separate incidental information from the rest of the sentence. They serve approximately the same function as commas and dashes in some situations, though each mark gives a different emphasis to the inserted information.

( )

Bernard Slye, the famous movie actor, was this year's grand marshal. [Commas imply that the inserted information is equal in importance to *Bernard Slye.*

Bernard Slye—the famous movie actor—was this year's grand marshal. [Dashes give the inserted information more emphasis.]

Bernard Slye (the famous movie actor) was this year's grand marshal. [Parentheses imply that the inserted information is incidental.]

All three of the preceding sentences are punctuated correctly. Usually, however, commas, dashes, and parentheses are not used interchangeably but are used with different kinds of inserted information. (See comma, 23b–23d; dash, 27a–27d.)

Billie Jean Stanford, one of our town's leading citizens, donated one thousand dollars to the earthquake relief fund. [Commas used for inserted information that departs from the thought of the rest of the sentence.]

Billie Jean Stanford—bless her kind heart—donated one thousand dollars to the earthquake relief fund. [Dashes used for a strong break in sentence continuity.]

Billie Jean Stanford (Bob's mother) donated one thousand dollars to the earthquake relief fund. [Parentheses used for inserted information of only incidental interest.]

30a Use parentheses to enclose parenthetical descriptions or explanations.

Zablonsky Hall (its brick exterior almost entirely covered with ivy) stands at the top of the hill. [Description]

The lecture on phototaxis (the movement of an organism in response to the stimulus of light) gave Nadia the idea for her animated film. [Explanation]

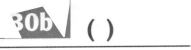

If a parenthetical sentence comes between two sentences, it should begin with a capital letter and end with a period, question mark, or exclamation point.

> My uncle was born in 1928. **(**What a year that was!**)** Bread was nine cents a loaf and a new Ford cost about five hundred dollars.

NOTE: Nonessential elements take no special punctuation other than the parentheses. At times punctuation marks may follow the parentheses if those marks are part of the main sentence.

> When I feel my stomach churning from fear **(**usually on the morning of a midterm or final**)**, I do deep-breathing exercises.

30b Use parentheses to enclose letters or figures that label items in a series.

> To begin playing tennis well, you must remember these three fundamental points: **(1)** tennis is a sideways game, **(2)** the backhanded stroke makes a loop, and **(3)** the follow-through should end high.

NOTE: When lists are set off from text, the letters and figures labeling them are usually not enclosed in parentheses.

31 Brackets *[ ]*

Always use **brackets** to enclose your own comments that explain, clarify, or correct the words of a writer you quote.

> Flora spoke in a soft voice to the other campers: "In all my years **[**she had been a ranger at Pig Pines for seven summers**]**, I've never seen a more beautiful sunrise." [Words added for explanation]

> Ibrahim, the unenthusiastic protagonist, "surveyed the wreckage **[**of the airplane**]** and smiled." [Words added for clarity]

The tall, dark-haired man finally spoke: "[I] try to mind my own business. [Why don't] you do the same?" [Words added for sentence completeness.]

The word *sic,* a Latin term meaning "thus it is," placed in brackets indicates an error that you have let stand in a quotation and that you did not make when you copied the quotation.

Roberts set the scene: "And then nite [*sic*] seemed to crush the castle under a heavy blanket of gloom."

Use *sic* only for errors, not for disagreements you may have with a writer you are quoting.

32 The Slash /

The **slash,** or virgule, separates lines of poetry worked into the text of a paper.

Faustus is astounded at the beauty of Helen, whom Mephistopheles has summoned to his room: "Was this the face that launch'd a thousand ships, **/** And burnt the topless towers of Ilium? **/** Sweet Helen, make me immortal with a kiss."

(See direct quotations, 28a.)

The slash is also used to indicate two options.

Students may now take eight units of credit**/**no-credit courses.

NOTE: Do not join pronouns with a slash when referring to non–gender-specific antecedents. Instead, use *or.*

INCORRECT	CORRECT
he/she	he or she
him/her	him or her
his/her(s)	his or her(s)

33 End Punctuation

The Period .

33a Use a period to end sentences that are statements, mild commands, or indirect questions.

The theater department presents a Shakespearean play every year. [Statement]

Be sure to buy your tickets early. [Mild command]

My uncle asked me which play would be performed this year. [Indirect question]

33b Use periods with most abbreviations.

Ms.	Dr.	Ave.	i.e.
Mr.	Ph.D.	Blvd.	e.g.

NOTE: Although the title *Ms.,* used before a name in place of *Miss* or *Mrs.,* is not an abbreviation, it is still followed by a period: *Ms. Hansen.*

Generally, BC and AD do not take periods. No periods are needed in certain common abbreviations or in abbreviations of the names of well-known companies, agencies, or organizations.

NBA	CNN	CBS	IBM
TV	USA(or U.S.A.)	NCAA	VW

Do not use periods after U.S. Postal Service (zip code) abbreviations for states.

CA	MA	VT	WY
NY	OK	NC	AL

Do not use two periods at the end of a sentence.

LaToya received her R.N.

The Question Mark ?

33c Use a question mark after a direct question.

What changes led to this increase in production**?**

33d Use a question mark within parentheses to indicate doubt about the accuracy of a date or number.

The Peloponnesian War ended in 404 BC (**?**) with a victory for Sparta.

Do not use a question mark within parentheses in an attempt to indicate sarcasm.

  INCORRECT I never saw such a hardworking (?) engineer.

Instead, shape your words to convey your intention.

  CORRECT Jon is seldom accused of being hardworking.

The Exclamation Point !

33e Use an exclamation point after interjections, strong commands, and emphatic statements.

Man**!** Look at that little S-car go. [Interjection]
"Go away**!**" she shouted. "Get out of here**!**" [Strong command]
I will never give up**!** [Emphatic statement]

!

Do not use an exclamation point within parentheses to indicate sarcasm or amazement.

INCORRECT   Gail's winning essay (!) was printed in the *Clarion*.

Instead, shape your words to convey your meaning.

CORRECT   I couldn't believe Gail won the contest and had her essay printed in the *Clarion*.

NOTE: Only one mark of end punctuation is used. Do not combine marks of end punctuation.

INCORRECT   How can you do this to me?!
CORRECT   How can you do this to me?

NOTE: A period is not used as end punctuation for the title of a work. A question mark or an exclamation point is used when appropriate.

Their Eyes Were Watching God
Shopping for a New Car?
Do It Now!

Mechanics

Handing in a paper with errors in mechanics is much like giving an after-dinner speech without knowing you have lettuce in your teeth. No matter how brilliant your phrasing, no matter how appropriate your gestures or witty your anecdotes, the audience will be distracted by the green bits between your incisors. You already know the importance of avoiding spelling errors—no other errors are so quickly noticed and condemned—but you should also know the importance of avoiding errors in capitalization, in the uses of apostrophes, abbreviations, italics, hyphens, and numbers. This part covers the conventions of mechanics. By following these conventions, you will avoid distracting a reader's attention from the ideas in your paper.

34 Capitals *caps/lc*

34a Capitalize the first word of every sentence.

The fog drifted across the field.
Who is responsible for the engine failure?
Do not touch the kettle.

NOTE: Capitalizing the first word of question fragments in a series is optional. Both of the following examples are correct.

What is the best way to become successful? by hard work? through education? by luck?

What is the best way to become successful? By hard work? Through education? By luck?

Capitalizing the first word of a sentence following a colon depends upon the style you are following. The Modern Language Association (MLA) lowercases the first word if the sentence is other than a rule or principle. The American Psychological Association (APA) always capitalizes the first word. (See the MLA and APA styles, 50a–50b.)

The eye does more than scan the physical world: it reveals the soul.

The eye does more than scan the physical world: It reveals the soul.

34b Always capitalize the interjection *O* and the personal pronoun *I* as well as contractions made with *I,* such as *I've* and *I'm.*

I beseech Thee, O Father, to help me in my troubles.

Before I write an essay, I outline the main points of my argument.

Although I've been reading French for three years, I'm still uncomfortable speaking it.

34c Capitalize the first and last words and every important word in the titles of your papers and of books, plays, short stories, poems, essays, songs, films, and works of art. Do not capitalize coordinating conjunctions, articles, the *to* of infinitives, and prepositions unless they begin or end a title.

Guinness Book of World Records [Book]
Fatal Attraction [Movie]
"Traveling through the Dark" [Poem]

NOTE 1: Capitalize the word immediately following a colon in a title.

The Uses of Enchantment: The Meaning and Importance of Fairy Tales

NOTE 2: Capitalize the first word in a hyphenated compound within a title. Capitalize the other parts of the hyphenated compound if they are nouns or adjectives or are as important as the first word.

"A Clean, Well-Lighted Place"
"Mysteries of Hide-and-Seek"
The Do-It-Yourself Environmental Handbook

NOTE 3: The APA capitalizes prepositions of four letters or more.

One Flew Over the Cuckoo's Nest

34d Capitalize the first word in directly quoted sentences or dialogue.

In *Love and Will*, psychologist Rollo May writes, "The striking thing about love and will in our day is that, whereas in the past they were always held up to us as the *answer* to life's predicaments, they have now become the *problem*."

"This is illegal," the detective whispered, taking the crisp twenties. "We're in it together, I guess."

NOTE: Do not capitalize the first word after an interruption between parts of a quoted sentence.

"Politicians must be courageous," the senator said, "for if they are not, they will never make unpopular decisions."

34e Capitalize the first word in every line of poetry.

To see a world in a grain of sand
And a heaven in a wild flower,
Hold infinity in the palm of your hand
And eternity in an hour.

—William Blake, "Auguries of Innocence"

If the poet does not follow this convention, use the poet's style.

anyone lived in a pretty how town
(with up so floating many bells down)
spring summer autumn winter
he sang his didn't he danced his did.

—e. e. cummings, "anyone lived in a pretty how town"

34f Capitalize proper nouns, proper adjectives, and words used to form essential parts of proper names.

PROPER NOUNS	PROPER ADJECTIVES	COMMON NOUNS
Freud	Freudian	psychoanalyst
Texas	Texan	state
France	French	country

The following is a representative list of words that typically are capitalized. Do not capitalize an article that precedes a proper noun unless it is part of the noun.

SPECIFIC PERSONS, PLACES, THINGS

Pat Kubis	the Tower of London
the Atlantic Ocean	*The Old Curiosity Shop*
the Washington Monument	the Grand Canyon
Europe	the *Los Angeles Times*

HISTORIC EVENTS, PERIODS, MOVEMENTS, DOCUMENTS

Desert Storm	the Enlightenment
the Boston Tea Party	the Roaring Twenties
the Middle Ages	the Bill of Rights

NOTE: Do not capitalize centuries, as in eighteenth century, nineteenth century, and so on.

DAYS OF THE WEEK, MONTHS, HOLIDAYS

Friday	September	Fourth of July

ASSOCIATIONS, ORGANIZATIONS, GOVERNMENT DEPARTMENTS, POLITICAL PARTIES

American Bar Association	Postal Service
League of Women Voters	House of Representatives
Boston Symphony Orchestra	Republican Party
Metropolitan Museum of Art	Democrats

NAMES OF EDUCATIONAL INSTITUTIONS, DEPARTMENTS, COURSES, DEGREES

Westbrook College	History 150
Department of English	Bachelor of Arts

RELIGIONS, RELIGIOUS FOLLOWERS, RELIGIOUS TERMS

Christianity, Christians	Judgment Day
Judaism, Jews	Allah
Buddhism, Buddhists	Holy Ghost
Hinduism, Hindus	the Virgin
God	

NOTE: Capitalizing pronouns referring to God is optional in general writing but required in most religious writing. Do not capitalize *who, whom,* or *whose* when referring to God.

RACES, TRIBES, NATIONALITIES, AND THEIR LANGUAGES

Native American	European
Iroquois	Gaelic
African American	Asian
Irish	Yugoslav
Latino	

NOTE: Capitalizing *black* and *white* when referring to people is optional. Both of the following examples are correct.

In American cities, Blacks and Whites are struggling to revitalize neglected neighborhoods.

In American cities, blacks and whites are struggling to revitalize neglected neighborhoods.

NAMES OF CELESTIAL BODIES

Mars	the North Star	the Big Dipper	the Milky Way

TRADE NAMES

Nintendo	Ford	Frisbee	Coke	Xerox

34g Capitalize titles when they come before proper names, and capitalize abbreviations for academic degrees when they come after proper names.

Chancellor Carmen Herrera　Carmen Herrera M.D.
President Cecelia Perdomo　Cecelia Perdomo Ph.D.

NOTE: Generally, do not capitalize titles that follow a name.

Harold Thomas, treasurer
Adelina Tapparo, professor of history

34h Capitalize abbreviations that indicate time, divisions of government, national and international organizations, businesses, and call letters of radio and television stations.

AD	P.M. (or p.m.)	NATO
BC	YMCA	IBM
A.M. (or a.m.)	FDIC	WQXR

34i Avoid common mistakes in capitalization.

Do not capitalize common nouns used in place of proper nouns.

INCORRECT	I plan to enroll in College next Fall.
CORRECT	I plan to enroll in college next fall.
CORRECT	I plan to enroll in Bradley College next September.

Do not capitalize the seasons or academic years or terms.

spring　　　fall　　　senior year　　　winter quarter

Do not capitalize words denoting family relations unless they are part of or a substitute for proper nouns.

cap/lc

INCORRECT	My Mother met my Father on an ocean voyage.
CORRECT	My mother met my father on an ocean voyage.
CORRECT	Mother met Father on an ocean voyage.

Do not capitalize general directions unless they refer to specific geographical areas.

south	the South
east	the East
western	East Manhattan

Exercise 1

In the following paragraph, capitalize words as necessary. Consult a dictionary if you are in doubt.

in american literature, satire has helped us examine human experience and smile. humorist kurt vonnegut, author of satiric novels such as *cat's cradle, slaughterhouse five, breakfast of champions,* and *galapagos,* believes humankind is in trouble. "our brains," vonnegut says, "are too large." according to vonnegut, nature goofed: *homo sapiens's* highly developed cerebral lobes are responsible for the world's troubles. "our brains are terribly oversized," he says, "and must keep creating things to do." he charges that big brains are responsible for the near destruction of native american culture. humankind's big brains caused the civil war and world war I. big brains created the third reich in germany that led to world war II and created death camps like dachau and belsen. humankind's oversized brain made the nuclear weapons that were dropped on hiroshima and nagasaki. vonnegut believes our big brains can be used to solve all our problems, but will it happen? he does not know. after all, human beings now think they are the intellectual center of the universe, when in reality they are nothing more than a speck of dust in the milky way.

35 The Apostrophe ,

The **apostrophe** indicates possession, the omission of letters in words, and the plurals of letters and words used as words.

35a Use an apostrophe to form the possessive case for nouns and indefinite pronouns.

To form the possessive of singular nouns, plural nouns not ending in -s, and indefinite pronouns (such as *no one, someone,* and *everybody*), add -'s. (See indefinite pronouns, 1b.)

> Akemi's novel is about an ex-governor's climb to the presidency.
> History exists because of humankind's outstanding achievement: the creation of written language.
> If only he could be someone's friend, anyone's—but he felt doomed to be everyone's curse.

To form the possessive of singular nouns ending in -s, add 's.

> He rushed into the boss's office.
> Little is known about Cheryl Moses's life in Paris during the Depression.
> James's reptile collection gives me an eerie feeling.

In the following examples, only the apostrophe is added because adding 's would make pronunciation difficult.

> James' snake collection gives me an eerie feeling.
> The court listened to Socrates' speech.

To form the possessive of plural words ending in -s, add only an apostrophe.

> The girls' basketball team won.
> The victory was the Mustangs' first.

To form the possessive of compound words, add 's or an apostrophe (following the rules for forming possessives) to the last word only.

> My son-in-law's job is threatened by military cutbacks.

When two or more nouns show joint possession, add 's to the last noun in the group.

> Raoul, Gus, and Meera's business is facing stiff competition.
> [Raoul, Gus, and Meera own the business together.]

When two or more nouns show individual possession, add 's to each noun in the group.

> Raoul's, Gus's, and Meera's businesses are facing stiff competition.
>
> [Raoul, Gus, and Meera each have a business separate from the others.]

Exercise 2

Insert apostrophes as needed in the following sentences.

1. *Sophies Choice* advanced William Styrons reputation as Americas leading novelist.

2. A kangaroos hop can span forty-two yards.

3. Groves and Flaggs fates are intertwined.

4. The Childrens Book Shoppe on 15th Street holds Kids

   Time, an hour of storytelling, three times each week.

5. Fathers Day and Mothers Day are celebrated yearly, but no spe-

   cial day has been designated for fathers- and mothers-in-law.

35b Do not use an apostrophe with possessive pronouns, such as
his, hers, its, ours, yours, theirs, and *whose.*

> The manuscript is *theirs;* the income is *ours.*
> If you want the truth, it is *yours.*

NOTE: Be careful not to confuse the possessive pronouns *its, whose, your,* and *their* with the contractions *it's* (it is), *who's* (who is), *you're* (you are), and *they're* (they are).

35c Use the apostrophe to mark omissions in contractions.

> it's (it is)
> we're (we are)
> don't (do not)
> o'clock (of the clock)
> class of '57 (class of 1957)

35d Use *'s* to form the plurals of letters and words used as words.

> When speaking publicly do not use *well*'s, *huh*'s, and *you know*'s.
> I got two *A*'s and three *B*'s.
> Dot your *i*'s and cross your *t*'s.

NOTE: Letters and words used as words are italicized, but the 's is not italicized as part of the word. (In handwritten and typed papers, italics are indicated by underlining. See italics, chapter 37.)

Exercise 3

Delete or insert apostrophes in the following sentences. Correct any mistakes in possessive pronouns. If any sentence is correct, mark it with a C.

1. Mississippi is spelled with four *s*s and four *i*s.

2. Who's 57 Ford is this? Hers or his?

3. Its the house on the corner.

4. She became rich in the state's lottery.

5. His *what ifs* make the world sound gloomy.

6. It was our mistake, not hers.

7. Who's responsibility is it?

8. The summer of 1992 was as hot as an angry dragons breath.

9. *Whys* and *how comes* seem to breed on the tongue of every four-year-old.

10. Many writers confuse *their* or *there* with *they're* and *your* with *youre*.

36 Abbreviations *ab*

In most writing, avoid using abbreviations unless they are commonly accepted.

36a Abbreviate titles before a proper name, if you wish.

Mr. Douglas Miner	Ms. Florence Nesbitt
Mrs. Catherine Rojas	Dr. Hanh Tran
Prof. Wilma Stewart	Rev. Marion Sylvester
Gen. Doyle Fujimoto	Msgr. Ramon Alvarez

NOTE: Do not abbreviate a title if it is not used with a proper name.

INCORRECT	The Maj. deployed the volunteers in an awkward formation.
CORRECT	The major deployed the volunteers in an awkward formation.
CORRECT	Maj. Olson deployed the volunteers in an awkward formation.

36b Abbreviate titles immediately following proper names.

Yung Kee, M.D.	Donald Sporakowski, Ph.D.
Sumi Inoue, LL.D.	Maude Cook, Ed.D.
Marion Feldman, Jr.	Marion Feldman, Sr.

NOTE: You may use abbreviations for academic degrees without proper names.

She has one goal—to earn an LL.D. by 1998.

36c Use familiar abbreviations for names of corporations, organizations, and countries.

NBC	FBI
AOL	USA (or U.S.A.)
AFL-CIO	IRS

NOTE: If a name that you plan to use repeatedly is not well known and can be abbreviated, you may write the full name followed by the abbreviation in parentheses the first time you use it. You may then use the abbreviation throughout the paper.

> Parents, teachers, and students formed the Committee for Educational Excellence of Orange County (CEEOC) to improve classroom teaching. CEEOC raises money to support experimental programs that might go unfunded because of limited state resources.

36d Use the commonly accepted abbreviations *a.m., p.m., bc, ad, no.,* and the symbol *$* with specific dates and numbers only.

12:01 a.m. (or A.M.)	1:00 p.m. (or P.M.)
21 BC	AD 1061
no. 12	$5,501

NOTE: BC always follows a date; AD always precedes a date.

36e Use common English and Latin abbreviations in tables, footnotes, reference lists, and comments placed inside parentheses.

Hobson, Sydney, et al. *A Hiker's Guide to South America.* 4th ed. 3 vols. New York: Wainwright, 1989.

The four defendants (i.e., Humphreys, Kettler, Rodda, and Gandy) had to be restrained.

36f In most writing, do not abbreviate personal names, calendar terms, courses of study, divisions of written works, units of measurement, and geographical names.

PERSONAL NAMES

Edward [not Edw.] Walden wrote three unpublished books.

NAMES OF DAYS, MONTHS, AND HOLIDAYS

The Monday [not Mon.] before Christmas [not Xmas] is the earliest I begin to shop.

Virgos are born during the second half of August [not Aug.] and the first half of September [not Sept.].

NOTE 1: MLA style abbreviates the name of the month in the list of works cited; APA style, however, spells out the name of the month in the reference list. (See 50a–50b.)

EDUCATIONAL COURSES

You must take literature [not lit.] and biology [not bio.] to finish the general education requirements.

DIVISIONS OF WRITTEN WORKS

Study section [not sec.] 4, chapter [not ch.] 3.

UNITS OF MEASUREMENT

The car skidded 106 feet [not ft.] and 7 inches [not in.].

NOTE 2: Long, familiar phrases, such as *miles per hour,* are usually abbreviated (mph).

The Porsche nosed into the turn at 120 mph, fishtailed, and then screeched down the highway.

GEOGRAPHICAL NAMES

The outstanding characteristic of Los Angeles [not L.A.], California [not Calif.], is that it seems to be able to stretch itself from the Mexican [not Mex.] border to San Francisco.

He grew up in Huntington Park [not Pk.] on Randolph Street [not St.] near Miles Avenue [not Ave.].

NOTE 3: Certain familiar abbreviations for countries are acceptable: USA (or U.S.A.).

37 Italics *ital*

Use underlining to represent italic (or *slanted*) type when distinguishing certain titles, words, and phrases in typed and handwritten papers.

37a Underline the titles of books, periodicals, newspapers, pamphlets, plays and films, long poems and long musical compositions, television and radio shows, and works of visual art.

(See quotation marks, 28b.)

When underlining a title, be precise. Do not underline an initial article (*a, an, the*) unless it is part of the title.

BOOKS
<u>The Color Purple</u>
<u>The Adventures of Huckleberry Finn</u>

PERIODICALS
<u>Harper's</u>
<u>Time</u>

NEWSPAPERS
the <u>Manchester Guardian</u>
<u>The New York Times</u>

PAMPHLETS
<u>How to Say No</u>
<u>The Dangers of Sugar</u>

PLAYS AND FILMS
<u>The Rocky Horror Picture Show</u>
Miller's <u>Death of a Salesman</u>

LONG POEMS AND MUSICAL COMPOSITIONS
Eliot's <u>The Waste Land</u>
<u>The Nutcracker Suite</u>

TELEVISION AND RADIO SHOWS
Seinfeld
Speaking of Sports

WORKS OF VISUAL ART
da Vinci's Mona Lisa
Michelangelo's David

NOTE: Names of legal documents, the Bible, and parts of the Bible are not underlined.

INCORRECT	The Bill of Rights contains the first ten amendments to the Constitution.
CORRECT	The Bill of Rights contains the first ten amendments to the Constitution.
INCORRECT	The Bible is composed of the Old Testament and the New Testament.
CORRECT	The Bible is composed of the Old Testament and the New Testament.

37b Underline the names of spacecraft, aircraft, ships, and trains.

Discovery   The Spirit of St. Louis
the Titanic   the Orient Express

37c Underline non-English words and phrases that have not become common expressions.

Harrods, Europe's largest department store, tries to live up to its motto–Omnia, omnibus, ubique–everyone, everything, everywhere.

Foreign words that have been absorbed into English do not need to be underlined. For example, the words *cliché* and *genre,* both French, are commonly used in English and, therefore, are not underlined.

When in doubt, consult a dictionary to see if a foreign word or phrase should be underlined.

NOTE: Most commonly used foreign abbreviations—i.e., etc., ibid, op. cit., and sic—are not italicized.

37d Underline words, letters, numbers, phrases, and symbols when they are referred to as such.

When writing a paper, you should not use & for and.

Someone had painted an X on the oak.

The voters are tired of maybe and perhaps.

"Mind your p's and q's" was my grandmother's favorite expression.

NOTE: You can use quotation marks instead of underlining to set off a word you are defining. Both of the following styles are correct, but use one style consistently throughout a paper.

Bumbershoot, which is slang for umbrella, is the result of merging umbr from umbrella and shoot from parachute.

"Bumbershoot," which is slang for "umbrella," is the result of merging "umbr" from "umbrella" and "shoot" from "parachute."

37e Underlining may be used to show emphasis.

I wrote that I wanted the entire amount.

Excessive underlining, however, will only distract the reader and diminish the emphasis.

I wrote that I wanted the entire amount.

37f Do not underline the titles of your own papers.

Propaganda: Five Ways to Trick a Consumer

Do underline the title of another work included in your title.

The Message of The Autobiography of Malcolm X

38 The Hyphen *hyph*

Use the **hyphen** to divide words, form compounds, and add some prefixes, suffixes, and letters to words.

38a Use a hyphen to indicate that a word is broken at the end of a typed or handwritten line.

Emergency volunteers, medical workers, and avia-
tion experts began sifting through the wreckage.

NOTE: Be sure to divide words between syllables. Whenever you are unsure of the syllabication of a word, check a dictionary. Do not break a one-syllable word.

38b Use a hyphen to form certain compound words.

cross-reference	clear-cut
mother-in-law	half-moon
deep-fry	bull's-eye
jack-o-lantern	great-grandfather

NOTE: Since most compound words are not hyphenated, check a dictionary whenever you are uncertain about whether to hyphenate a compound word.

38c Use a hyphen to join two or more words that serve as a single descriptive word before a noun.

The one-eyed, one-armed cowboy could hold his own in any two-bit joint he stumbled into.

In Pentagon jargon, two-syllable names indicate jets, and one-syllable names indicate piston-driven aircraft.

Since taking a course in crafts, Beth has produced some well-designed furniture.

The twenty-year-old adventurer will lecture tomorrow.

NOTE: When the descriptive phrase comes after the noun, the words usually are not hyphenated.

> Beth's furniture is well designed.
> The adventurer, who is twenty years old, will lecture tomorrow.

But when such a phrase is used as a noun, it is hyphenated.

> The adventurer, a daring twenty-year-old, will lecture tomorrow.

38d Use a hyphen to spell out the compound numbers twenty-one to ninety-nine and fractions.

seventy-five	ninety-nine
one-half	three-fourths

38e Use a hyphen to join certain prefixes, suffixes, and letters to words.

Use a hyphen to join a prefix to a word beginning with a capital letter.

> Those who criticize foreign policy are sometimes accused of being anti-American.

Use a hyphen between words and the prefixes *self-*, *all-*, and *ex-* (meaning formerly) as well as the suffix *-elect*.

self-control	all-encompassing
ex-student	president-elect

Use a hyphen to join single letters to words.

Z-transfer	U-turn
T-shirt	F-sharp

38f Use suspended hyphens for hyphenated words in a series.

> My mother-, father-, and brother-in-law graduated from Lochlin High School.

38g Use a hyphen to avoid confusion.

In creating compound words, use a hyphen rather than doubling vowels and tripling consonants.

> The current college administration has an anti-intellectual [not antiintellectual] attitude.
>
> When the wind blows, the chimes make bell-like [not *belllike*] music.
>
> The concept of a college without walls is like a wall-less [not *wallless*] room—full of wind.

Use a hyphen to avoid ambiguity.

> re-creation (something created anew)
> recreation (a diverting activity)
>
> re-sign (to sign again)
> resign (to give up a position)

39 Numbers *num*

Follow established customs when using numbers in written work.

39a Spell out any number consisting of one or two words.

> *Eighty-five* cyclists started, but only *twenty-one finished.*
>
> The race covered *four hundred* miles of tough Mexican desert over a period of *three* days.

39b Use figures for any number that requires more than two words to spell out.

> In Kobe, Japan, 5,300 people lost their lives in an earthquake that left over 200,000 homeless.

NOTE: Be consistent. If there are several numbers, some of which are one or two words and others of which are more than two words, use numerals for all of them. Also, if numbers are used frequently in a discussion, use numerals for all of them.

39c Use a combination of figures and words for numbers when such a combination will keep your writing clear.

The president invited fifty 10-year-olds to the Easter celebration.

39d Use figures for dates; time; addresses; scores and other numerical results; percentages, decimals, and fractions; pages and divisions of written works; and exact amounts of money.

DAYS AND YEARS

November 11, 1996   13 BC   AD 1492   the 1990s

The forms *1st, 2nd,* and so on, as well as *fourth, fifth,* and so on, are sometimes used in dates but only when the year is omitted: *December 5th, December fifth.*

TIME OF DAY

12:15 p.m.   1300 hours   5:43 a.m.

If you are not using a.m. or p.m., write the time in words.

We will meet at twelve-thirty, and we will leave at one o'clock.

ADDRESSES

4345 Sandburg Way   4 Upper Newport Plaza

SCORES, STATISTICS, RESULTS OF SURVEYS

The Hawks beat the Hornets 133 to 102.
You must score over 600 to qualify.

Out of the 500 surveyed, 498 recognized the name *Tyrone Power,* but only 56 knew he had been an actor, and 16 said they had never seen one but had heard they were great to drive.

PERCENTAGES, DECIMALS, FRACTIONS

23 percent (or 23%)   98.6   12⅓

PAGES AND DIVISIONS OF WRITTEN WORKS

page 3, pages 110–12   chapter 2   volume 5
act 4   scene 1   lines 5–22

EXACT AMOUNTS OF MONEY

$100,871 $19.76 $123 million

39e Spell out any number that begins a sentence.

Two hundred and thirteen [not 213] voted for the amendment; no one voted against it.

Revising the sentence may be more effective than spelling out the number.

The amendment passed 213 to 0.

Exercise 4

Correct the faulty use of numbers in the following sentences. If any sentence is correct, mark it with a *C*.

1. In Super Bowl V at Miami's Orange Bowl, Dallas and Baltimore were tied thirteen to thirteen with 5 seconds left when the Colts' Jim O'Brien kicked a field goal.

2. 42.5 million people live in Zaire, which has a growth rate of three point three percent.

3. Massive mud slides have been known to reach speeds of sixty mph.

4. On October 18th, 1864, 15 Confederate raiders robbed 3 banks in

St. Albans, Vermont, and buried $114,522 in gold and currency,

82½ percent of the town's total capital.

5. Nearly 1000 fans were turned away from the auditorium gates

even though they had paid as much as $34.50 for seats.

40 Spelling *sp*

Difficulty with spelling is a highly individual problem. Most of us have compiled a personal list of spelling demons, words such as *occasion, separate, rhythm, negotiator,* and *strategy.* When we use a word from our demon list, we remind ourselves to double-check its spelling. We double-check because we know readers consider misspellings among the most distracting and careless errors a writer can commit.

Nobody improves poor spelling without working at it. To get started, use a dictionary to check the spelling of words you are uncertain about. Keep a list of words you look up and practice spelling them by using one or more of the following techniques. (See chapter 41, "Appropriate Language.")

40a Visualize the correct spelling of a troublesome word.

Write the troublesome word correctly and concentrate on how it looks on the page. Then look away and visualize the word. Do this over and over until you can actually imagine how the word, with the troublesome letters emphasized, appears on the page.

Some people help themselves visualize a word by capitalizing the part of the word that is the most difficult to spell.

      sTRATegy   accoMModate
      proCEDure   govERNment

40b Practice writing a troublesome word several times.

Repeatedly writing a troublesome word will help you break an old habit and replace it with a new one. Write the word slowly at first and then rapidly until the correct spelling comes naturally.

40c Pronounce the syllables of a troublesome word carefully and accurately.

Mispronunciation often leads to misspelling. If you repeatedly pronounce a troublesome word as it appears in a dictionary, you can begin correcting some of your misspellings.

ac ci den tal ly	ath lete
(not accident*ly*)	(not ath*e*lete)
light ning	nu cle ar
(not light*e*ning)	(not nuc*ular*)

40d Proofread your written work for misspellings.

After you have proofread a paper for errors in grammar, punctuation, and mechanics, proofread it one more time for spelling errors. The best way to proofread is to read the paper backward—that is, read the last word first, then read the word just before that, and so on, until you reach the first word. This procedure will help you examine the words themselves without being distracted by the ideas in the paper.

If you are writing on a word processor that has a spelling function, make sure to use the spelling checker after you complete each draft. Beware, however, that you will still need to proofread your paper carefully, for the spelling checker cannot distinguish between misused homophones (whole, hole) and typographical errors that create actual words (form, from; the, she).

40e Distinguish between *ie* and *ei*.

The vowel combinations in the second syllables of *relief* and *perceive* sound alike, but the syllables are spelled differently. Confused? Apply the familiar jingle to help clear up the confusion: Place an *i* before *e* except after *c* or when pronounced like *a* as in *neighbor* and *weigh*.

> *i* before *e* : chief, grief, belief
> *e* before *i* following *c:* ceiling, conceit
> *e* before *i* when the sound is *a* : eight, sleigh

Exceptions include either, neither, foreign, forfeit, height, leisure, weird, seize, sheik.

Exercise 5

Complete the following words, filling in the blanks with *ie* or *ei*, whichever is appropriate.

1. l___sure		6. th___f	
2. c___ling		7. n___ce	
3. ach___ve		8. perc___ve	
4. for___gn		9. p___ce	
5. rec___pt		10. w___rd	

40f Usually drop a silent final *-e* before a suffix that begins with a vowel.

> come + ing = coming   fame + ous = famous
> force + ible = forcible   love + able = lovable

EXCEPTIONS: (1) Keep a final *-e* to prevent confusion with other words: *dyeing* to distinguish it from *dying; singeing* to distinguish it from *singing*. (2) Keep a final *-e* to prevent mispronunciation:

mileage, not *milage.* (3) Keep a final *-e* after *c* or *g* to preserve the soft sound of the consonant: *notice* + *able* = *noticeable; courage* + *ous* = *courageous.*

40g Usually keep a silent final *-e* before a suffix beginning with a consonant.

arrange + ment = arrangement   care + ful = careful

Exceptions include *awful, ninth.* The final *-e* is sometimes dropped before a suffix beginning with a consonant when *-e* is preceded by a vowel.

true + ly = truly   argue + ment = argument

40h When a final *-y* is preceded by a consonant, change the *y* to *i* before a suffix except when the suffix begins with *i.*

-y preceded by a consonant:

try + ed = tried   messy + er = messier

-y preceded by a vowel:

obey + ed = obeyed   sway + s = sways

Suffix beginning with *i:*

apply + ing = applying   try + ing = trying

40i Double the final consonant before a suffix beginning with a vowel if (1) the word has only one syllable or is stressed on the last syllable and (2) the word ends in a single consonant preceded by a single vowel.

One-syllable word; final consonant preceded by a single vowel:

drop + ing = dropping   stop + ing = stopping

Stress on the last syllable; final consonant preceded by a single vowel:

forget + ing = forgetting   submit + ed = submitted

Last syllable unstressed:

benefit + ed = benefited   prefer + able = preferable

Exercise 6

Add the final suffix to the words below by writing the words in the right-hand column. Be able to explain the rule that applies to each word. Check doubtful spellings in a dictionary.

1. unwrap + ed _____

2. stubborn + ness _____

3. plant + ing _____

4. ski + ing _____

5. commit + ed _____

6. casual + ly _____

7. move + ing _____

8. merry + ly _____

9. argue + ment _____

10. write + ing _____

40j Observe the conventions for forming plurals of nouns.

Most nouns form the plural by adding -s.

book, books; chair, chairs; pen, pens

Nouns ending in *-s, -sh, -ch,* or *-x* form the plural by adding *-es.*

dress, dresses; bush, bushes; church, churches; fox, foxes

The plural of nouns ending in *-y* preceded by a consonant is formed by changing the *y* to *i* and adding *-es.*

enemy, enemies; fly, flies; sky, skies

EXCEPTION: Family names ending in *-y* such as *McCherry, McCherrys; Haessly, Haesslys.*

The plural of most nouns ending in *-f* or *-fe* is formed by adding *-s.* The plural of some nouns ending in *-f* or *-fe* is formed by changing the *f* to *v* and adding *-s* or *-es.*

Add *-s:*

chief, chiefs; dwarf, dwarfs; roof, roofs

Change *f* to *v* and add *-s* or *-es:*

calf, calves; knife, knives; hoof, hooves; leaf, leaves

The plural of nouns ending in *-o* preceded by a vowel is formed by adding *-s.* The plural of nouns ending in *-o* preceded by a consonant is formed by adding either *-s* or *-es.*

-o preceded by a vowel:

radio, radios; studio, studios

-o preceded by a consonant:

mosquito, mosquitoes; potato, potatoes

EXCEPTION: Musical terms ending in *-o* form the plural by adding *-s.*

piano, pianos; solo, solos

The plural of a few nouns is formed by irregular methods.

child, children; goose, geese; mouse, mice; ox, oxen; tooth, teeth; woman, women

Some nouns borrowed from French, Greek, and Latin retain the plural form of the original language.

> alumnus, alumni; analysis, analyses; basis, bases; datum, data; medium, media; phenomenon, phenomena

Some nouns are the same in plural and singular forms.

> deer   Chinese   species   trout

The plural of compound nouns written as one word is formed by adding -s or -es. The plural of compound nouns consisting of a noun and a modifier is formed by making the noun plural.

> leftover, leftovers; strongbox, strongboxes; mother-in-law, mothers-in-law; passer-by, passers-by

Exercise 7

Write the plural forms of each of the following words. Be able to explain your spelling according to the rules for forming plurals. Refer to a dictionary when in doubt.

1. father-in-law
2. cameo
3. roof
4. loss
5. box
6. crisis
7. loaf
8. alumnus
9. Kelly
10. approach

40k Learn the meaning and correct spelling of commonly confused words.

accept:	to receive
except:	to exclude
advice:	counsel (noun)
advise:	to give advice (verb)

affect:	to influence (verb)
effect:	a result (noun); to accomplish (verb)
all ready:	prepared
already:	previously
brake:	to stop
break:	to smash
buy:	to purchase
by:	near
capital:	accumulated wealth; uppercase letter; city serving as seat of government (lowercase for state, uppercase for federal)
capitol:	building in which legislative body meets (lowercase for state, uppercase for federal)
choose:	to select
chose:	past tense of *choose*
cite:	to quote
sight:	ability to see
site:	a place
complement:	something that completes
compliment:	flattering remark
conscience:	moral sense (noun)
conscious:	aware (adj.)
coarse:	rough (adj.)
course:	path, procedure, process (noun)
decent:	moral (adj.)
descent:	a way down (noun)
dissent:	disagree (verb); difference of opinion (noun)
desert:	barren land
desert:	to abandon
dessert:	last course of a meal
formally:	in a formal manner
formerly:	previously
forth:	forward
fourth:	after third

hear:	to perceive by ear (verb)
here:	in this place (adv.)
heard:	past tense of *hear*
herd:	group of animals
instance:	an example
instants:	moments
its:	possessive of *it*
it's:	contraction of *it is*
lead:	to show the way (verb); a metal (noun)
led:	past tense of *to lead*
lessen:	to make less
lesson:	something learned
loose:	to free from restraint (verb); not fastened (adj.)
lose:	to misplace; to be deprived of (verb)
passed:	past tense of *pass*
past:	no longer current (adj.); an earlier time (noun); beyond in time or place (prep.)
peace:	absence of strife
piece:	a part of something
plain:	clear (adj.); level land (noun)
plane:	airplane; carpenter's tool
principal:	most important (adj.); leader (noun)
principle:	basic truth or law (noun)
right:	correct (adj.)
rite:	ceremony (noun)
write:	to record (verb)
road:	a driving surface
rode:	past tense of *ride*
stationary:	unmoving
stationery:	writing paper
their:	possessive of *they*
there:	in that place
they're:	contraction of *they are*

to:	toward
too:	also; excess amount
two:	the number following one
weak:	not strong
week:	Sunday through Saturday
weather:	condition of climate
whether:	if, either
who's:	contraction of *who is*
whose:	possessive of *who*
your:	possessive of *you*
you're:	contraction of *you are*

Exercise 8

For each of the following sentences, circle the correct word in parentheses.

1. The ancient temple was the (*cite, sight, site*) of mysterious rituals.

2. The coat does not (*complement, compliment*) the dress.

3. Her job is to (*advice, advise*) the board, not make its decisions.

4. You must contribute (*weather, whether*) you want to or not.

5. The boys were not (*conscience, conscious*) of the damage they did.

6. I think I know (*who's, whose*) thumbprint that is.

7. He stands as (*stationary, stationery*) as a statue.

8. There is a (*principal, principle*) cause for his joy—money!

9. Can you identify the (*affect, effect*) of the chemical?

10. (*Accept, Except*) for Roberta, no one was in the house last night.

401 Learn to spell frequently misspelled words.

The following is a list of one hundred commonly misspelled words.

absence	emphasize	occurrence	safety
academic	existence	optimistic	salary
accidentally	familiar	parallel	satellite
accommodate	fascinate	pastime	secretary
achieve	February	personnel	seize
across	foreign	precede	separate
all right	forty	prejudice	sergeant
already	friend	prevalent	similar
apparent	fulfill	privilege	sincerely
appearance	government	probably	sophomore
athletic	grammar	procedure	specimen
attendance	harass	proceed	strategy
believe	height	quantity	subtly
benefited	independent	quiet	succeed
Britain	intelligence	quite	succession
business	license	quizzes	surprise
calendar	luxury	receive	temperament
candidate	maneuver	reference	tendency
cemetery	marriage	referred	thorough
definite	mathematics	referring	tragedy
desperate	misspelled	reminisce	usually
develop	neither	repetition	vacuum
dilemma	ninth	rhythm	vengeance
dining	occasion	ridiculous	weird
embarrass	occur	sacrifice	writing

Exercise 9

Test yourself on the list of frequently misspelled words by asking someone to read the words aloud so that you can spell them..

Diction

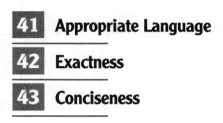

233

appr

Diction refers to the choice and use of words. Dictionaries of English are filled with words and their meanings, but so too is the mind of anyone who speaks the language. You know the meanings of such words as *child, dance, sincere, immediately, theirs, after,* and *yellow.* Your knowledge of these and thousands of other words enables you to understand them when they are used in combination with other words. Suppose a government official announced

A spy was stopped before discovering Project X15.

You might not know what "Project X15" is, but if you understand the word *spy,* you know the sentence is about a person who was prevented from finding out about a secret project while employed by another government or agency. This information is part of the definition of *spy.* But there is more: the mind's emotional connection with the word *spy.* Most likely you *feel* that a spy is treacherous and deceptive, someone you could never trust.

Now suppose the spy in the announcement was actually a reporter trying to collect information for a story about a project that a government agency wanted to keep secret. For an official to describe the reporter as a spy would not only be inaccurate; it would also color your view of the experience by tugging at your emotions. Indeed, the use of *spy* would have misled you.

Such is just one example of the power and danger in choosing and using words. As a writer, you should use appropriate language and be as accurate and concise as you can. You must control your diction and keep your thoughts logically consistent—skills discussed in this part.

41 Appropriate Language *appr*

The appropriateness and accuracy of your words are just as important as grammar, punctuation, and mechanics. To develop skill in diction, sharpen your knowledge of words and, after studying the guidelines in this part, trust in your own judgment. Using appropriate and accurate words often has more to do with your sensitivity to the English language than with your knowledge of its rules. Finally, when in doubt about a particular usage, consult a dependable dictionary, such as one of these:

> *The American Heritage Dictionary of the English Language*
> *Merriam-Webster's Collegiate Dictionary*
> *Webster's New World Dictionary of the American Language*

41a Use standard American English.

Standard American English is used in literature and printed documents, is taught in schools, is written by political and business leaders, and is propagated by the mass media—television, radio, newspapers, and magazines. In most writing, standard English is appropriate.

Nonstandard English consists of variations of standard English (especially in certain pronoun cases and verb forms) not found in the speech or writing of those who have been trained in standard American English.

STANDARD	The guest *brought* homemade pie for dessert.
NONSTANDARD	The guest *brung* homemade pie for dessert.
STANDARD	Nina is the woman *who* broke the record.
NONSTANDARD	Nina is the woman *what* broke the record.
STANDARD	He sings to *himself.*
NONSTANDARD	He sings to *hisself.*

Standard American English can be **formal** or **informal.** Informal (sometimes called *colloquial*) writing is characterized by common expressions taken from spoken English.

INFORMAL	If the mayor would *get together with* the city manager, *they'd* solve the problem.
FORMAL	If the mayor would *meet with* the city manager, *they would* solve the problem.

INFORMAL	I *don't get* why the refund took *all these* weeks to *get here.*
FORMAL	I *do not understand* why the refund took *several* weeks *to arrive.*

Contractions, such as *they'd* and *don't,* are common in informal writing; in formal writing the words are usually written out—*they would, do not.*

Informal English is appropriate for casual essays, diaries, personal letters or reflections, and creative works whose authors attempt to capture the sounds and rhythms of everyday speech. But because most of the writing you do in college and in a profession—serious essays, theses, reports, and memos—will be formal, you should generally avoid words and expressions labeled "informal" or "colloquial" in a dictionary. Also, be especially careful to avoid mixing informal and formal writing in the same work.

MIXED	According to Philip Larsen's report, two thousand people willingly shell out twenty dollars a year to belong to the Marilyn Monroe Fan Club. For that amount they're considered dues-paying members and are entitled to receive the latest word on the club's publications, on the going price for Marilyn Monroe playing cards or jigsaw puzzles, and on the annual get-together at her graveside.
CONSISTENTLY FORMAL	According to Philip Larsen's report, two thousand members of the Marilyn Monroe Fan Club willingly *pay* twenty dollars a year *to learn* about the club's latest publications, the *cost* of a set of Marilyn Monroe playing cards or of a Marilyn Monroe jigsaw puzzle, and the annual *gathering* at her graveside.

41b Avoid using slang.

Slang comes from a specialized, often colorful vocabulary that grows out of the experience of a group of people with common interests, such as actors, astronauts, athletes, computer scientists, copywriters, musicians, street gangs, and truckers. Eventually, some slang passes into standard usage; *jazz* and *A-bomb* are two words that once were slang expressions but are now part of standard English. More often slang makes an appearance, increases in use, and then shifts its meaning or becomes dated. The writer of the following sentence uses current slang expressions.

> *Jean de Florette* is a *downer* to watch. The *flick* portrays a *smack* from Paris who lacks the *smarts* to survive on a farm.

Earlier slang might express the same thoughts with the words *tear jerker, pic, brain,* and *savvy.*

When you wish to use a slang term to create a dramatic effect, do so: "With so much money in campaign donations, Wiener is a *shoo-in.*" But generally, avoid using slang in your written work because it is imprecise and may be confusing or misleading to a reader.

IMPRECISE	The journalist was *bummed* after the judge *laid a heavy trip on him* for contempt of court.
PRECISE	The journalist was *stunned* after the judge *sentenced him to thirty days in county jail* for contempt of court.

41c Avoid using regional expressions.

Regional differences exist in the use of some words and phrases. Do you *carry* or *drive* your friends to the mall? Do you *draw water* or *run water* from a *faucet,* a *spigot,* or a *tap?* Words such as these will not confuse your reader, but in writing you should avoid expressions that are not generally used outside a particular region.

| REGIONAL | The committee had a *right nice* meeting. We wish *you all* could have *come.* |
| GENERAL | The committee had a *productive* meeting. We wish *all of you* could have *attended.* |

41d Avoid using obsolete or archaic words and neologisms.

In a dictionary, items labeled "obsolete" or "archaic" are words or meanings that have fallen from general use. **Obsolete** indicates that a word or a specific meaning is no longer used at all. *Coy* meaning "to caress" and *cote* meaning "to pass" are labeled "obsolete." **Archaic** indicates that a word or meaning appears only in special contexts. *Anon* meaning "at once" and *methinks* meaning "it seems" are labeled "archaic."

Neologisms are words or terms that have come into use so recently that they may still be unacceptable in general writing. Some former neologisms, such as *astronaut, bookmobile, fallout, supersonic,* and *smog,* have become acceptable. But most neologisms pass quickly from use, and you should avoid using them unless they become widely accepted.

41e Use technical terms, or jargon, with care.

When writing for a group of literature specialists, you may use the terms *persona, verisimilitude,* and *motif* with confidence that your readers will understand them. These are technical terms that literature specialists freely use. Most fields and activities have technical vocabularies, and a person who studies a field or pursues an activity soon learns the specialized vocabulary that characterizes it. A person who has studied finance will use the terms *put, call,* and *margin* with ease. A skier will feel equally at ease talking about *moguls, whiteouts,* and *schussing.* But without explanation, such terms are inappropriate for a general audience. When you are writing for a general audience, therefore, avoid using technical terms. If you must use them, be sure to define them.

Exercise 1

Revise the following paragraphs by changing words or phrases that may be informal, slang, regional, obsolete, or archaic expressions, neologisms, or technical terms. Feel free to consult a dependable dictionary that includes usage labels to determine the appropriateness of expressions and to find suitable substitutes. (See the dictionary list, p. 235.)

In 1945 Vice President Harry S. Truman unexpectedly became president when Franklin Roosevelt died in office. When Truman took the oath of office, he was so jittery that the words would not come to him and his voice petered out, so he took out a slip of paper with the oath written on it and held it on top of the Bible. Then his voice began to function, and he read the words in a real nice manner. The next day he laid his feelings on a group of reporters: "Boys, if you ever pray, pray for me now!" During his first months in office, Truman could not duck the decision to use the atomic bomb against Japan, a decision that not only brought World War II to an end but also demonstrated that human beings had created the power to waste the entire world.

After the war, Truman lost the heavy-duty political support Roosevelt had previously gathered; consequently, in the 1946 midterm elections Republicans gained control of both houses of Congress for the first time since 1930. Betwixt the attacks of the opposition party and the sniping of rebellious members of his own party, Truman appeared to be on the ropes politically, yet he continued his plans to run for re-election in 1948.

41f Avoid pretentious language.

Write in simple English. Beginning writers often make their writing excessively showy, perhaps from a misconceived desire to sound impressive or even poetic. Unfortunately, the result is often pretentious.

> **PRETENTIOUS** At day's end the evening solitude descended on the sea-swept coast.
>
> **REVISED** At sunset the beach grew quiet.
>
> **PRETENTIOUS** This college is predicated on the belief that diligent and sustained effort will be rewarded.
>
> **REVISED** This college rewards hard work.

To write in simple English, always choose the common word over the fancy one. If you want to say "Drinking will destroy the liver," do not write "Imbibing alcoholic beverages in vast quantities will lead to the degeneration of one of the body's most important organs."

Exercise 2

While keeping their basic meaning, revise the following sentences by using simple English.

1. The ability to orate before the multitude is accrued through repetitive effort.

2. Vinification is an ancient art that has been revitalized by modern technological innovations.

3. Dr. Chen's verbal meanderings amaze and mystify his students.

4. Among his peers he was the sole champion for those who wished to privatize the U.S. Postal Service.

5. We must face the dangers of an inexorable rise in population today or find an agreed-upon solution for thousands of starving infants and children in the near future.

41g Avoid sexist language.

In your writing, avoid usages that may disregard or insult your readers or that rely on stereotypes. English traditionally contains an implicit sexual bias, such as in the use of the masculine pronouns *he, him,* and *his* to refer to individual members of a given occupation or of a group composed of both men and women.

BIASED	A *doctor* must pass the state medical examination before *he* can be licensed to practice.
BIASED	A mystery *novelist* concentrates on *his* plot, whereas a suspense *novelist* concentrates on *his* action.
BIASED	*Man* must assume responsibility for the preservation of the natural world.
BIASED	*Freshmen congressmen* must serve several years before they gain enough seniority to become committee *chairmen.*

These usages ignore the fact that women also occupy these positions or participate in these groups, thus implicitly diminishing their roles.

You can avoid sexual bias in your writing by applying several techniques.

1. Replace masculine pronouns with an article (*a, an, the*).

   REVISED   A mystery novelist concentrates on *the* plot,
                    whereas a suspense novelist concentrates on
                    the action.

2. Change the nouns and pronouns from singular to plural.

   REVISED   *Doctors* must pass the state medical examina-
                    tion before *they* can be licensed to practice.

3. Revise the sentence to eliminate the need for a pronoun.

   REVISED   Before practicing, a doctor must pass the
                    state medical examination.

   REVISED   To practice medicine, a doctor must first
                    pass the state medical examination.

   REVISED   A mystery novelist concentrates on plot,
                    whereas a suspense novelist concentrates on
                    action.

4. Use compounds, such as *he or she* and *him or her*.

   REVISED   A doctor must pass the state medical exami-
                    nation before *he or she* can begin to practice.

Stylistically, however, these compounds can sound awkward
when frequently repeated, so use them sparingly.

   AWKWARD   A mystery novelist concentrates on *his or her*
                    plot, whereas a suspense novelist concen-
                    trates on *his or her* action. The mystery nov-
                    elist must construct *his or her* plot in great
                    detail so both *his or her* characters and *his or
                    her* readers will not be able to solve the crime
                    too soon in *his or her* story.

REVISED	A mystery novelist concentrates on *the* plot, whereas the suspense novelist concentrates on *the* action. The mystery novelist must construct *his or her* plot in great detail so both *the* characters and *the* readers will not be able to solve the crime too soon in *the* story.

5. Avoid the traditional masculine and feminine stereotypes by using gender-neutral language to refer to both men and women.

SEXIST	NONSEXIST
man, mankind	human, humanity, humankind, people
female doctor	doctor
male nurse	nurse
chairman	chairwoman (if a woman), chairperson, or chair
councilman	councilmember
fireman	fire fighter
policeman	police officer
businessman, businesswoman	executive
businessmen	business people
poetess	poet
coed	student
waiter, waitress	server
stewardess, steward	flight attendant
gal Friday	assistant

6. Use parallel constructions for men and women.

SEXIST	Both *Dr.* John Bernstein and *Mrs.* Selma Rosa, who is also a doctor, attended the meeting.
NONSEXIST	Both *Dr.* John Bernstein and *Dr.* Selma Rosa attended the meeting.

Exercise 3

Revise the following passage to eliminate sexually biased language.

A writer's primary task is to fulfill the purpose of his book. He must first develop a sense of his reader and a strategy for addressing him: Whom is the essay directed to? How much does his reader know about the subject? How much time is he likely to spend reading the book? Will he want a straightforward treatment of the subject? Will he want extensive background information? These are questions every writer must ask himself. If he doesn't, he will not develop a feel for his reader, that is, for the person who sits behind his desk or in his easy chair, book in hand, under his reading lamp.

Exercise 4

Find nonsexist terms to replace the sexist ones.

1. cleaning lady
2. stewardess
3. actress
4. Father Christmas
5. Mother Nature
6. sportsmanship
7. ladylike
8. newsboy
9. anchorwoman
10. airman

42 Exactness *exact*

To be exact in writing, you must find the words that best fit the meaning you wish to convey. Exactness requires not only that you concentrate on the meanings of words you use but also that you develop keen sensitivity to the differences in tone of some words. If you are inexact, you risk misleading or confusing your reader.

42a Distinguish between a word's denotation and connotation.

Denotation refers to a word's concrete meaning as found in the dictionary. **Connotation** refers to what a word implies or suggests. According to one dictionary, the word *snake* denotes "any of a wide variety of limbless reptiles with an elongated, scaly body, lidless eyes, and a tapering tail." For some people the word **snake** may connote treachery or evil, and for others, wisdom or healing. Pay close attention to both the denotation and the connotation of the words you use. Otherwise your words might clash, as in the following sentence.

> The speaker manipulated the audience by presenting the evidence to refute their arguments.

Manipulated denotes deviousness on the part of the speaker, but *refute* has the connotation of reasonably proving something false. The two words do not fit well together. To correct the clash of meanings, the writer should use words with more compatible denotations and connotations.

> The speaker convinced the audience by presenting the evidence to refute their arguments.

> The speaker manipulated the audience by presenting only the evidence that would disprove their arguments.

You must also take special care when selecting a word from among **synonyms,** words that have nearly the same meaning. *Depart, retreat,* and *flee; emulate, copy,* and *mimic* are two groups of synonyms.

Although synonyms are close in denotation, they usually differ in connotation. It is much different to write "Harold's speech was funny" than to write "Harold's speech was laughable."

When the connotations of words arouse exceptionally strong feelings, we consider the words loaded. **Loaded words** appeal to emotion rather than to reason. A copywriter using loaded language might describe a company as carrying on the tradition of *free enterprise* while claiming that a competitor is *price gouging*. A politician might call himself or herself a *progressive* while calling an opponent a *do-gooder*. Loaded words are the tools of advertisers and other propagandists. If you use loaded words, your writing will seem not only inexact but also biased.

Exercise 5

Replace each italicized word with a word that has a similar denotation but a connotation better fitted to the sentence.

1. To be a successful high-fashion model, a woman or man must be

   emaciated and graceful.

2. Success also depends on an ability to improve from hearing a

   photographer's constant *ridicule* and to survive arduous hours in

   a studio.

3. Unlike actors, models are not hired because of their *quirky profiles*.

4. Instead, their facial features must be *bland*, and their bodies must

   seem to come from the same mold.

5. Successful high-fashion modeling has its *payoffs* but also its

   drawbacks—constant routine and *relentless* dieting.

Exercise 6

Revise the following paragraph to replace any loaded words and phrases with language that is less emotionally charged.

Secretly, the president's agents in Congress are threatening to smother hard working Americans with new taxes. These greedy politicians are plotting to impose a value-added tax to support social boondoggles that conservative legislators have always resisted. Patriotic taxpayers throughout the heart of the country are beginning to resist, too.

42b Do not rely exclusively on abstract and general words. Be as concrete and specific as you can.

Abstract words refer to qualities, ideas, and actions that we cannot experience through our senses: *culture, friendship, loyalty, democracy.* **Concrete words** refer to things we can experience through our senses: *orange, blood, scream, laugh, hug, tick, swamp.*

General words refer to large groups of people or things. The word *athlete* includes everyone who seriously pursues a sport. **Specific words** refer to one particular part of a general group. *Professional athlete* limits the group of athletes to those who are paid for their athletic performances. Other specific words for *athlete* include *professional tennis player; professional female tennis player; top ten female tennis players;* and *Steffi Graf, one of the top ten female tennis players.* Notice that *general* and *specific* are relative terms and that language becomes more specific as it moves from the general group to a unique example of the group—from *athlete* to *Steffi Graf* in this case.

Experienced writers know the value of concrete and specific words. Inexperienced writers tend to overuse abstract and general words, and consequently their work is often inexact and lifeless.

GENERAL	In English 170 we studied the world's leading contemporary writers.
SPECIFIC	In English 170 we studied the works of *Alice Walker, Ursula K. le Guin, Gabriel García Márquez, and Raymond Carver.*
GENERAL	After major trials, jurors are often interviewed for their opinions.
SPECIFIC	After major trials, jurors are often interviewed *by newspaper and television reporters who seek to find out the jurors' versions of the deliberations.*
GENERAL	The amount set by the government as the poverty level for a family of four is not much to live on.
SPECIFIC	The *$13,000* set by the government as the poverty level for a family of four *will not buy many $3.50 hamburgers, $5 six-packs, $50 tickets for Bruce Springsteen concerts, and $15 T-shirts, let alone bread, milk, vegetables, and meat for four hungry mouths.*

Exercise 7

Make these sentences more precise by revising the general words and phrases with concrete and specific language.

1. The film was *thrilling.*

2. The city was *quickly destroyed.*

3. The sea was *dangerous.*

4. The senator *lost her temper.*

5. My brother *irritates me.*

42c Use idioms correctly.

An **idiom** is a fixed phrase with a single meaning that cannot be determined from the definitions of the individual words in the phrase. If a person said, "The waiter *flew into a rage*," most native speakers of English would know that the waiter became angry. If, however, a non-native speaker were to translate the phrase *flew into a rage* word by word, the meaning would seem absurd. People learn the idiomatic expressions of their language naturally and have little difficulty understanding and using most of them. Occasionally, however, even experienced writers make errors in using an idiom that combines an adjective or verb and a preposition. "Independent *of* outside influence" is a meaningful idiom, whereas "independent *from* outside influence" is not a meaningful phrase. Whenever you are in doubt about which preposition to use with a word, look up the word in a dictionary. Here are common idioms and examples of their use.

abide *by*	We must abide by the rules.
according *to*	According to the evidence, he must be innocent.
agree *with* (a person)	I agree with Noah.
agree *to* (a proposal)	I cannot, however, agree to his proposal.
agree *on* (a course of action)	Moreover, we cannot agree on any plan.
angry *with*	The children are angry with the babysitter.
charge *for* (a purchase)	The charge for cocoa butter is excessive.
charge *with* (a crime)	The manager has been charged with fraud.
comply *with*	Everyone must comply with the regulations.
compare *to* (something in a different class)	Do not compare psychiatry to witchcraft.

compare *with* (something in the same class)	You can compare a Freudian with a Jungian.
concur *with* (a person)	Jones concurs with Fussel.
concur *in* (an opinion)	I concur in your wish to transfer.
confide *in* or *to*	Ching had no time to confide her secret to me. She confides in her roommate.
die *of* or *from*	He may die from grief.
differ *with* (disagree)	Nguyen differs with Yoshi over the presidential candidate.
differ *from* (be unlike)	Gibson's style differs from Redford's.
differ *about* or *over* (a question)	We differ about how food should be cooked.
different *from*	Living in a dormitory is different from living in an apartment.
identical *to* or *with*	One cannot be identical to the other.
ignorant *of*	Carmen is ignorant of basic table etiquette.
inferior *to*	Is a life of toil inferior to a life of ease?
occupied *by* (a person)	We found our cabin occupied by two stranded hikers.
occupied *in* (thought)	He was occupied in thought when the pain struck.
occupied *with* (a thing)	She has been occupied with the book for a year.
prior *to*	Prior to appearing in court, he wrote the accused a letter.
superior *to*	Some cat owners feel that their pets are superior to dogs in intelligence.

42d Use figurative language carefully.

Writers use figurative language to draw a comparison between two things that are essentially different but alike in some underlying and surprising way. By making comparisons, writers not only help their readers understand what is being said but also add vigor to their prose. The most common figures of speech are simile and metaphor.

In a **simile** a writer expresses a comparison directly by using *like* or *as*.

> Her forward expression was steady and driving like the advance of a heavy truck.
>
> —Flannery O'Connor
>
> The bowie knife is as American as the half-ton pickup truck.
> —Geoffrey Norman

Through **metaphor** a writer expresses a comparison indirectly, without using *like* or *as*.

> A sleeping child gives me the impression of a traveler in a very far country.
>
> —Ralph Waldo Emerson
>
> I refuse to accept the notion that nation after nation must spiral down a militaristic stairway into the hell of nuclear war.
> —Martin Luther King, Jr.

Personification and hyperbole are less common figures of speech. Writers use **personification** to give ideas, animals, and objects human qualities.

> When the wind swept through the forest, the trees moaned, and among their branches birds complained.

Through **hyperbole** a writer creates an exaggeration.

> Mike Finnegan's tennis game has hit bottom, unless he returns to the court another time.

To be exact, a figure of speech must always clarify a writer's thought by making it understandable in other terms. Sometimes, however, a figure of speech will miss the mark or fall flat because it is trite or overblown.

> Her smile is as warm as a crackling fire on a snowy evening.
> [Trite simile]

Another figure of speech gone wrong is the *mixed metaphor,* which combines two or more incompatible comparisons.

MIXED METAPHOR	Ideas that *blaze* in his mind often *crash* in his writing.
REVISED	Ideas that *blaze* in his mind often *smolder* in his writing.
REVISED	Ideas that *race* in his mind often *crash* in his writing.

Exercise 8

Revise the following mixed metaphors to make the comparisons consistent.

1. The scalpel cuts through the flesh, leaving a road of blood.

2. The speaker bathed her audience in a blanket of nonsense.

3. She stirs figurative language into her writing the way a cook adds vegetables to a stew—a dash of simile, a pinch of metaphor.

4. His arms flapping, the student flew to the lectern and barked for silence.

5. Reformers once imagined that prisons could be lapidary shops where the soul could be polished after the flaws had been surgically cut away.

42e Avoid trite expressions.

A **trite expression,** sometimes called a *cliché* or *stock phrase,* is an expression that was fresh and striking at one time but through overuse has become stale. Trite phrases include exhausted figures of speech (*hit the nail on the head*), wedded adjectives and nouns (*a well-rounded personality*), and overused phrases (*the finer things in life*). Trite phrases may come easily to mind when you feel rushed in your writing. But when you revise your work and come across one, strike it out and reword your thought in a fresh way. These are some common trite phrases to avoid.

a must	as a matter of fact
a thinking person	at this point in time
all in all	cold as ice
all walks of life	depths of despair
aroused our curiosity	face the music
flat as a pancake	none the worse for wear
in a very real sense	pure as newly fallen snow
in the final analysis	quick as a flash
in the world of today	sadder but wiser
last but not least	silent as the grave
method in his madness	smart as a whip
never a dull moment	strong as an ox

Exercise 9

Revise the following sentences, substituting fresh thoughts for trite expressions.

1. It is safe to say that Tom Pham looks like a timid tax attorney who would feel butterflies in his stomach if he ever heard a raised voice.

2. But looks are deceptive; Pham is a fierce negotiator who takes the bull by the horns and never gives an inch in collective bargaining sessions.

3. His endurance is such that he can go nose to nose with an opponent for twelve hours straight and leave the table none the worse for wear.

4. Although some see collective bargaining as child's play, Gus realizes that the incomes of two thousand union members hang in the balance.

5. He takes seriously his responsibility to get the best deal he can and never drops the ball—or a dime.

43 Conciseness *con*

Make your writing concise by deleting words and phrases that add nothing to your meaning. Scrutinize your sentences for empty phrases, needless repetition, jargon, and euphemism. When you find such oversights, cross them out and search your vocabulary for more direct and forceful ways to state your thoughts. Being concise does not necessarily mean your writing will be skimpy; it means your writing will be free of useless words.

43a Avoid empty phrases.

Empty phrases do little more than add useless words to your writing. Whenever they appear in your work, cut them out or revise them.

WORDY	In the world of today, eighteen-year-olds can find only minimum-wage jobs. [*In the world of today* is an empty phrase.]
REVISED	*Today* eighteen-year-olds can find only minimum-wage jobs.

Many empty phrases develop from such all-purpose words as *angle, area, aspect, case, character, fact, factor, field, kind, nature, process, situation,* and *type.* Watch for them and cut wherever you can.

Often one word will do the work of an entire empty phrase; substitute the single word for the phrase.

FOR	SUBSTITUTE
at all times	always
at this point in time	now
at that point in time	then
at any point in time	whenever
by means of	by
come into conflict	conflict (verb)
due to the fact that	because
for the purpose of	for
for the reason that	because
give consideration to	consider
give encouragement to	encourage
in order to	to
in the event that	if
in the final analysis	finally
make contact with	call
of the opinion that	think
regardless of the fact that	although
the fact that	that
until such time as	until

Exercise 10

Revise the following sentences by deleting empty words or phrases or by substituting single words for empty phrases.

1. At the present time sales indicate that biographies of film stars

   are the type of book more readers want.

2. It is usually the case that these tales give encouragement to the public's fantasies.

3. The 1966 story of Hedy Lamarr's life was so steamy that in order to keep an aspect of her public dignity, she claimed that the book revealed too much and denounced it as obscene.

4. But at this point in time stars seem pleased to reveal shocking details of their lives due to the fact that confession sells books.

5. With big money at stake, you can easily come to the realization why Marlon Brando announced that his 1994 as-told-to publication would be candid about his love life, and why not, since it's too late for him to change his makeup.

43b Avoid needless repetition.

At times you will repeat words for parallel structure or for emphasis. But careless repetition leads to awkward, wordy sentences.

REPETITIOUS	The grizzly bear is probably the world's most ferocious bear.
REVISED	The grizzly is probably the world's most ferocious bear.
REPETITIOUS	Economists say that the recession will continue, and I continue to believe them.
REVISED	Economists say that the recession will continue, and I *still* believe them.

43c Avoid redundant phrases.

A **redundant phrase** says the same thing twice: *visible to the eye, large in size.*

REDUNDANT	The central character in this novel is a mysterious figure beyond understanding.
REVISED	The central character in this novel is a mysterious figure.

The following list includes some common redundancies. Be aware of them and watch for them and others that appear in your own writing. Whenever you find a redundancy, strike it. The italicized words below are redundant.

advance *forward*	disappear *from view*
autobiography *of her life*	*end* result
basic fundamentals	*factual* truth
circle *around*	*important* essential
close proximity	refer or revert *back*
combine *together*	repeat *again*
consensus of *opinion*	round *in shape*
continue *to go on*	

Exercise 11

Improve these sentences by revising them for ineffective repetition and redundancy.

1. From my point of view, I believe parents do not allow their children enough time to discover their creative interests.

2. Twice a day millions of people listen to public radio while continuing on their daily schedules.

3. In the United States, American citizens often make heroes out of the country's severest critics.

4. The book puts forth an extraordinary and exceptional deception aimed at convincing readers that philosophy is superior to and better than any other intellectual pursuit.

5. Nearly square in shape and reddish-brown with yellow stripes in color, the puffer fish is covered with spines that make it look more like a spiny medieval weapon than a fish.

43d Avoid excessive use of euphemism.

A **euphemism** is a word or phrase substituted for other words that are considered harsh or blunt. The funeral industry, for instance, substitutes *loved one* for *corpse, vault* for *coffin,* and *final resting place* for *grave.* Common euphemisms generally refer to experiences in our daily lives—birth, bodily functions, sex, aging, death—and they are often necessary for tactfulness. No doubt most of us prefer to ask a waiter for directions to the restroom rather than to the toilet.

Indeed, common euphemisms such as *restroom* are harmless, but other euphemisms, especially those created by private and public institutions, often are designed to distract us from the realities of poverty, unemployment, and war. We've become accustomed to the euphemisms of *low-income, inner city,* and *correctional facility* as substitutes for *poor, slum,* and *prison.* Plumbers may be referred to as *sanitation engineers,* teachers as *learning directors,* and salespeople as *account executives,* yet they still fix pipes, correct papers, and sell products. In war the act of burning villages and herding people into detention camps has been called *pacification,* and the lies of public officials have been euphemistically named *inoperative statements.*

Because euphemism is pervasive in our society, you must guard against its slipping into your finished work. If you identify euphemisms when rereading a passage you have written, rephrase them in more accurate, concrete language.

EUPHEMISTIC	The whole area was underdeveloped and crowded with the disadvantaged, who seemed to be living on a marginal diet. Several families often lived together in a small dwelling, sometimes with no more than a single water source to serve them and several other homes together.
REVISED	The whole area was a slum and crowded with starving people who seemed to have no more to eat than rice and water. Sometimes several families crammed themselves into two-room hovels made of cardboard and sticks. The only water they had came from a single tap shared by fifteen or twenty such shacks.

Use euphemism when tact calls for you to do so, but avoid using it when your work requires a direct rendering of the material. Do not use it to deceive.

Exercise 12

Make these sentences concise by eliminating jargon and euphemism and recasting the sentences in plain, straightforward English.

1. The chairman and the director must resolve the intense feelings that arose during their recent negative encounter.

2. When I was a young girl living in a deteriorating residential section of town, I vowed to develop the capital necessary to buy a ranch.

3. Beware—pre-owned car dealers embellish information regarding the quality of their products to enhance their monthly revenue.

4. On the basis of information from visual surveillance, the air force chief of staff ordered the squadron to carry out a surgical bombing action over the enemy's capital.

5. My Uncle Ramsey passed away while staying overnight in a near-by motor lodge in the company of a female companion the family had never met.

Paragraphs, Essays, and Research Papers

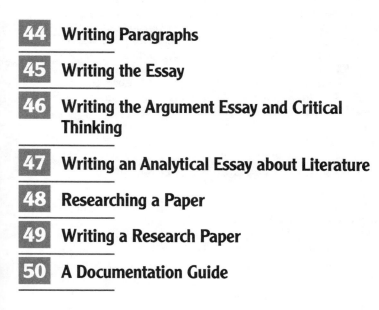

261

Each piece of writing has its own audience, its own purpose, and its own content. Moreover, no two writers hold exactly the same views or express themselves in exactly the same ways. Yet despite the unique characteristics of written works and writers, beneath all clear, effective writing is some underlying structure that directs the reader's attention from point to point. When reading, you are probably unaware of a structure because you seek information to fill the gaps in your knowledge. But when writing, you must create an underlying structure for your work and use it to arrange your ideas as carefully as a mapmaker charts a wilderness for an uninitiated traveler. Paragraphs, essays, and research papers—the subjects of this part—all have underlying structures that you can master with practice. But remember: if your written work lacks a clear design structure, your reader may stumble into a verbal thicket and stray from the main path of your thought.

44 Writing Paragraphs *par,* ¶

A paragraph consists of several related sentences that develop one unit of content. A paragraph may stand alone as a brief work, but usually it functions as part of a longer piece of writing. The division of prose into paragraphs guides a reader through a paper by presenting content in individually organized, easily digested portions of thought.

A well-constructed paragraph is unified (all of its sentences are focused on the same idea), coherent (the thought proceeds logically from sentence to sentence), and fully developed (it contains enough information to convey the idea in a reasonably thorough manner). The end of a paragraph signals completion of the thought and prepares the reader to shift attention, at least slightly, to the beginning of the next paragraph.

In a sense, an essay is created by bringing together a series of related paragraphs, each one a brief composition itself. As you read the selections used as examples throughout this chapter, be aware that they are one-paragraph excerpts taken from longer essays. As you complete the paragraph-length exercises at the end of this chapter, you will be writing the kind of building blocks that you will use for longer papers.

How long should a paragraph be? Paragraph length depends on many factors: the complexity of the idea; the method of development; the length of adjacent paragraphs; and the age, knowledge, interest, and educational background of the intended audience. In college writing, thoughtful paragraphs usually range from 125 to 200 words because of their complexity. The best approach is not to worry much about paragraph length. Instead, concentrate on the unity and on the development of the paragraph.

The following is an undeveloped paragraph from an early draft of student writer Dan Leonard's essay on facts and myths related to dinosaurs.

> In early Hollywood adventure films, dinosaurs roamed the earth with humans. If this had been true, of course, we humans would also be extinct. Scientists now hypothesize that dinosaurs met their end because of a worldwide catastrophe. Over 65 million years ago, the hypothesis goes, a huge meteorite crashed into the earth. The impact is thought to have kicked up enough dust to block sunlight for a long time, which would lower temperatures. A worldwide fire could have added other dangers. If humans had been living then, they would never have survived.

When revising his essay, and more particularly this paragraph, Dan added specific details and developed more fully the supporting information.

> In the film classic *One Million B.C.,* dinosaurs roamed the earth with humans. In fact, *Tyrannosaurus rex* seemed especially fond of human flesh. Of course, this is just "Hollywood history," a form of mythmaking that pays little attention to geological or anthropological facts. Actually, if we humans had

once shared the earth with dinosaurs, we too would be extinct. Scientists now hypothesize that dinosaurs met their end because of a worldwide catastrophe that threatened all living creatures. Over 65 million years ago, the hypothesis goes, a huge meteorite crashed into the earth. The impact is thought to have kicked up enough dust to block sunlight for a long time, triggering extinctions by lowering temperatures and killing vegetation. A worldwide fire could have added other dangers. Apart from burning or choking in the smoke, living creatures could have perished from newly formed toxic compounds or from an eventual warming of temperatures triggered by carbon monoxide that the fire poured into the atmosphere. If humans had been living as the makers of *One Million B.C.* portray us, we would never have survived to watch our ancestors in hand-to-claw combat on the silver screen.

44a State the single idea of a paragraph in a topic sentence.

A **topic sentence** identifies the main idea of a paragraph. For the reader, the topic sentence gives the idea of the paragraph in a convenient capsule form so that he or she knows what the more specific sentences of the paragraph add up to. For the writer, the topic sentence serves as a guide, reminding the writer of the paragraph's boundaries and, therefore, helping to assure a well-unified paragraph.

The following paragraph, taken from business major Maria Dallos's essay on the advantages of earning a college degree, begins with a brief topic sentence that effectively announces to readers that the rest of the paragraph will consist of information showing that earning a college degree has some economic advantages.

TOPIC SENTENCE	From an economic perspective, earning a college degree is a sound investment. College tuition can cost anywhere from $1,490 a year
SUPPORTING ANALYSIS	at a state-supported university to as high as $30,000 a year at an expensive private

university, such as Harvard, Stanford, the University of Southern California, or Yale. When you add to tuition costs another $8,000 a year for books and living expenses, the final spread is $9,490 to $38,000 a year or $37,950 to $152,000 for an entire four years. No matter where you fall within the range, this price tag is hefty, especially if you figure you could be earning money on a job instead of attending college. But the payoff from earning a degree is substantial also. The difference between having a college degree and a high school diploma these days is $600,000 in income over a working lifetime. Calculating forty years on the job, that amounts to $15,000-a-year differential for college graduates. Clearly, college is a sound investment, but as my grandmother used to say, "It takes money to make money."

CLOSE

Topic Sentence Characteristics

An effective topic sentence has three characteristics:

1. Includes a subject and controlling idea
2. Is limited
3. Can be developed

Subject and Controlling Idea

The subject identifies the topic of the paragraph, and the controlling idea identifies what aspects of the topic will be discussed.

Hong Kong has a fascinating mixture of European and Asiatic traditions.

¶

This sentence placed at the beginning of a paragraph tells a reader that Hong Kong is the topic and that the writer plans to discuss the European and Asiatic traditions of the city, not its economy, population, or style of government.

Limitability

The subject and controlling idea of a topic sentence must be limited enough to be discussed fully within a single paragraph.

GENERAL	The works of James Agee often include information from several academic disciplines.
LIMITED	James Agee's *Let Us Now Praise Famous Men* includes content drawn from history, sociology, and philosophy.
GENERAL	Sometimes concerts can be dangerous.
LIMITED	Concert promoters could reduce the number and severity of spectator injuries by following a few simple rules of crowd control.
GENERAL	Bolivia is an interesting country.
LIMITED	Bolivia has some spectacular mountains.

Development

A topic sentence must lend itself to development. The controlling idea has to be one that can be amplified or illustrated. If the controlling idea is strictly factual, it allows no development.

FACTUAL	Northwestern is a university in Illinois.
REVISED	Northwestern, a university in Illinois, is noted for its outstanding drama faculty.

Placement

Although placing a topic sentence at the beginning of a paragraph is sound practice, writers sometimes place it in another part of the paragraph or, if the controlling idea can be clearly understood from the discussion within the paragraph, leave it out entirely.

When a writer places a topic sentence at the end of a paragraph, it often serves as a climax to the details that come before it. Biology major Saul Castro, in a paragraph from a report focusing on the benefits of genetic engineering, places the topic sentence last.

INFORMATION RELATED TO THE TOPIC SENTENCE
Recently scientists used a bacterium called *Agrobacterium tumefaciens* to transfer a special insect- and disease-resistant gene into the cells of walnut tree plants. Test proved that the insect- and disease-resistant characteristics of the special gene had been successfully incorporated into the walnut plant's genetic material. Clearly, this genetic feat has major implications for growers who produce America's $300-million-a-year walnut crop; moreover, it also has important implications for health-minded consumers.

TOPIC SENTENCE
When researchers are able to transfer insect- and disease-resistant genes to all food-bearing plants, genetic engineering can be used to protect us all from the poisonous insecticides and pesticides that growers use on their crops.

Implied Topic Sentence

When a writer leaves out a topic sentence, the discussion must be so clear that the controlling idea of the paragraph is strongly implied. In the following paragraph, Jody Farjami, a social ecology major, leaves out the topic sentence, but it might be stated as "Development is destroying the environment beyond the city."

After spending August working as a camp counselor at a YMCA camp in the mountains, I headed home. Since the thought of a trip through the city always depresses me, calling up visions of housing tracts pasted together and of jammed freeways that lead to the city's concrete heart where gray towers spear into the afternoon pall, I decided to take the longer but more scenic route north of the city. I was in for a surprise. When I crossed the last ridge just before the sun went down and began the descent to the coastal plain, I saw that the fields of crops and citrus I remembered having been there had vanished. In their place were housing projects, shopping centers, gas stations, trailer parks, and schoolyards. The whole scene reminded me of a huge bowl heaped with junk and covered over with a layer of haze thick as gauze. I felt I was entering a nightmare. Certainly all this growth couldn't have happened in a single month, but then I remembered I had not traveled this particular route for almost ten years. I wanted to escape the numbing scene, so I stepped on the gas pedal and pointed my VW toward home.

Closure

Often when a writer begins a paragraph with a topic sentence, he or she will close the paragraph with a *clincher,* a sentence that restates the controlling idea in different words, summarizes the discussion, or gives the writer's response to the material, which may be ironic or humorous. The next example closes with a clincher.

TOPIC SENTENCE

REASONS

As sources of ideas, professors simply cannot compete with books. Books can be found to fit almost every need, temper, or interest. Books can be read when you are in the mood; they do not have to be taken in periodic doses. Books are both more personal and more impersonal than professors. Books have an inner confidence which individuals seldom show; they rarely have to be on the defensive. Books can afford to be bold and courageous and exploratory; they do not have to be so careful of boards of trustees, colleagues, and community opinion. Books are infinitely diverse; they run the gamut of human activity. Books can be found to express every point of view; if you want a different point of view, you can read a different book. (Incidentally, this is the closest approximation to objectivity you are likely ever to get in humanistic and social studies.)

CLINCHER *Even your professor is at his best when he writes books and articles; the teaching performance rarely equals the written effort.*

—William G. Carleton,
"Take Your College in Stride"

Exercise 1

These topic sentences are either too general or too factual. Revise each to make it an effective topic sentence.

1. Some states require motorists to wear seat belts.

2. Vandalism is a problem in urban areas.

3. Many Americans try different diets from time to time.

4. Going to college is expensive.

5. Grading policies are different for different classes.

6. Everyone believes that travel is educational.

7. Large stores usually have consumer complaint departments.

8. In spite of all the evidence, my sister believes that spinach alone will give a person tremendous strength.

9. I like people who assume responsibility for their actions.

10. Hollywood films have both good and bad features.

Exercise 2

Using one of the topic sentences you wrote in Exercise 1, develop a complete paragraph.

44b Maintain unity throughout a paragraph.

To achieve **unity** in a paragraph, you must not only have a clear controlling idea but must also stick to that idea. The writer of the following paragraph digresses from the controlling idea stated in the first sentence.

TOPIC SENTENCE   Attending this college can be unexpectedly dangerous. Last week in the parking lot my friend Bill accidentally bumped the side of a pickup truck. Just as he was finishing a note to leave on the windshield, the owner came up, scowled at the grapefruit-size dent, and punched Bill in the nose. He then drove off without looking back or taking Bill's
DIGRESSION   name and address. At least Bill didn't have to pay for the damage. Three days ago a bicyclist wearing portable radio earphones plowed into a psychology instructor, and both went sprawling over the walkway. Yesterday in the zoology lab, a four-foot snake slipped from its cage. No one noticed until it struck at one student, sending him and four
DIGRESSION   others into shock. The lab technician came

in, snatched up the snake, and stuffed it back into the cage. No one plans to sue the college, but those students have a good case if any of them would press it.

Because of digressions from the controlling idea, the paragraph is flawed. To correct it, the writer deleted some of the unnecessary comments and subordinated others.

DIGRESSION ELIMINATED

Attending this college can be unexpectedly dangerous. Last week in the parking lot my friend Bill accidentally bumped the side of a pickup truck. Just as he was finishing a note to leave on the windshield, the owner came up, scowled at the grapefruit-size dent, and punched Bill in the nose. Three days ago a bicyclist wearing portable radio earphones plowed into a psychology instructor, and both went sprawling over the walkway. Yesterday in the zoology lab, a four-foot snake slipped from its cage. No one noticed until it struck at one student, sending him and four others into shock before a lab technician came in, snatched up the snake, and stuffed it back into the cage.

DIGRESSION ELIMINATED

Exercise 3

The following sentences are taken from Robert I. Tilling's "A Volcanologist's Perspective." Several sentences are from one paragraph. Others are from different parts of the article. Determine which sentences should be included in a unified paragraph with the following topic sentence.

Volcanic eruptions have had a profound influence on mankind.

1. Civilizations have flourished in regions blessed with fertile soils derived from the breakdown of nutrient-rich volcanic materials.

2. The volcanoes in the Ring of Fire zone are what scientists call composite volcanoes.

3. The violent, destructive unleashings of volcanic fury that accompanied the catastrophic blast of Mount St. Helens have imprinted their marks on mind and landscape.

4. Some of the world's most majestic and inspirational mountain and seashore scenery, including the entire state of Hawaii, has been created by volcanic action and subsequent erosion.

5. Most of the world's approximately five hundred active volcanoes are located along or near such boundaries between shifting plates.

6. The Pacific Basin provides excellent examples of these two types of volcanoes.

7. The earth's surface is broken into lithospheric slabs, or plates.

8. As one volcano dies, however, a new volcano begins to form behind it over the hot spot.

9. More fundamentally, life on earth as we know it would not have evolved at all were it not for volcanic exhalations that occurred

over hundreds of millions of years and formed the primitive but

life-giving atmosphere and oceans.

10. Composite volcanoes predominantly erupt highly viscous

(sticky) magma.

44C Achieve coherence by putting details in proper order.

One way to keep a paragraph coherent is to arrange the sentences in a pattern that will generate an orderly, natural flow of ideas. Five possible methods are illustrated on the next few pages. You will find these methods useful in some situations, but the most suitable arrangement for any given paper will depend on your particular purpose and content.

Time Order

Narrative paragraphs—those that tell a story or series of incidents—usually arrange themselves naturally in the order in which the events occurred. Often a narrative structure is an effective way of giving a reader information, as Vince Cagney does in his essay on unique occupations.

TOPIC SENTENCE	Bill Meek, a marine biologist and entrepreneur, manages an unusual enterprise. Using a hoe, a suction hose, and lots of elbow grease, Meek rakes and vacuums up mussels that cling to the long legs of oil platforms located off the coast. He sells the mussels to restaurants that pay top prices for them. His day begins at sunrise on a dock where he checks his equipment and meets his small crew for the three-mile trip to the oil platform. Once at the platform the sun is well up and he peers into the aquamarine depths to take an informal inventory. The
EVENT 1	
EVENT 2	

EVENT 3

EVENT 4

EVENT 5

CLOSE

mussels grow rapidly on the platform legs to a depth of forty feet, but below forty feet there isn't enough light to nourish plankton on which mussels feed. By 8:00 the harvesting work begins. Two divers in wet suits jump into the sea. They are equipped with air hoses and mouthpieces for breathing, a hoe, and a corrugated plastic tube to suck up the mussels. One man will loosen the mussels while the other vacuums. Once the work is under way, a compressor generates the pressure that sucks the mussels through the tube to the surface where they are collected into a tumbling wire-mesh container. The container turns throughout the collecting process, allowing barnacles, seaweed, and salt water to cascade back into the ocean while retaining the larger mussels. By early afternoon the harvest is done and the crew heads for shore. Within hours, the mussels will be steaming on the stoves of local restaurants.

Spatial Order

Descriptive paragraphs lend themselves quite easily to a spatial arrangement—from left to right, from right to left, from near to far, from the center outward, and so on. In the following paragraph from a gallery report, Alice Lee describes a painting from the top down.

Topic sentence sets the purpose and direction. Notice the use of guiding phrases, such as "At the top," "in the upper middle ground," and "in the lower foreground."

At the top of Dunlap's "Picnic," clouds are gathering as if ready to erupt with rain. Between the sky and shore, in the upper middle ground, the sea is edged with whitecaps and a line of sailboats lean into the wind, heading for safe harbor. On shore, in the lower foreground, two children stand facing the sea and a third stares back at a man and woman sitting on the sand, a fearful expression on the child's face. The couple she stares at are the focus of the canvas, taking up a third of the space. Dunlap only represents the back of the man's head and just a slice of his profile. He seems to be staring beyond the children at the impending squall. The woman is staring at him, a neutral expression on her face, but she appears to have the faint trace of a bruise on her cheek. Behind her, in the lower left corner, is a watermelon with a butcher knife leaning against it, the knife tip in the sand.

Order of Climax

Some paragraphs lend themselves to an arrangement of details or examples according to increasing importance. In the following paragraph, economics major Phyllis Baysinger places a dramatic anecdote last.

MAIN IDEA INTRODUCED	Modern technology is transforming the workplace. Teleconferencing now allows meetings to be held by telecast so that business people can "meet" without traveling to
THREE BRIEF ASSERTIONS	other cities. Current photocopy technology facilitates decision making by printing and sending material around the globe in seconds. The desktop computer allows people not only to work at home but even to work
FOURTH ASSERTION	on airplanes. But no technological break through seems to have revolutionized the office more than the simple car phone. Business can now be carried on even in traffic jams. In fact, the car phone has made

CLIMAX   business people so mobile that they sometimes fail to report to the office. For example, an entertainment executive was calling
his attorney at a red light when he noticed
his partner pull up alongside his Mercedes.
When his attorney picked up the phone, she
immediately began to complain about how
hard the partner was to reach. The executive
rolled down his window, leaned across the
seat with the phone in hand, and said, "It's
for you!"

General-to-Specific, Specific-to-General Order

Most paragraphs begin with a general comment—usually contained
in a topic sentence—and follow with specific details, reasons, or
examples that support the generalization. Some paragraphs, however,
reverse this order by beginning with specific details, reasons, or examples and ending with a general observation that summarizes the paragraph's meaning.

A paragraph from fiction writer Jackie Carlton's essay "Getting
Started" begins from the generalization that writers pursue storytelling in different ways. She then moves from the general—how others discover their stories—to the specific—her method of story creation.

GENERALIZATION   In discussing writing habits with members of my fiction-writers workshop, I found
that they pursue stories in a couple of ways.

GENERAL
EXAMPLE 1   Many begin with a plot in mind. They start
by outlining its dramatic points and soon
characters and a setting begin to fill in the

GENERAL
EXAMPLE 2   empty spaces. Others begin with a character,
someone they've seen on campus, in a
restaurant, strolling through a mall or riding
a bus—anyone that seems to hold their

SPECIFIC
EXAMPLE

attention. They begin with questions: Where does she live? Who are her friends? What kind of trouble is she in? And so on. Soon a portrait emerges and a story follows. I begin with an image, a mental picture that might even come to me in a dream. This image does not have to be dramatic, just arresting, something that nudges me into exploring its significance. I then find myself visualizing the image, allowing it to create a feeling in me. Finally, after the image has matured in my imagination, I sit at my desk, usually very early in the morning with a single desk light on, and begin to "sketch" the image in words, writing in large sweeps that make me think of action painters. Eventually the sketch includes characters, a dramatic situation, and a plot. Soon, although I never rush the process, I will have a rough draft. Once I

CLOSE

reach the rough draft stage, I know the fun is over and revising and editing begin.

This paragraph moves from the specific to the general—from physical details of Rainy Mountain and the surrounding plain to the generalization that one can imagine creation having begun in such a spot.

SPECIFIC
DETAILS

A single knoll rises out of the plain in Oklahoma, north and west of the Wichita Range. For my people, the Kiowas, it is an old landmark, and they gave it the name Rainy Mountain. The hardest weather in the world is there. Winter brings blizzards, hot tornadic winds arise in the spring, and in summer the prairie is an anvil's edge. The grass turns brittle and brown, and it cracks beneath your feet. There are green belts

along the rivers and creeks, linear groves of
hickory and pecan, willow and witch hazel.
At a distance in July or August the steaming
foliage seems almost to writhe in fire. Great
green and yellow grasshoppers are everywhere in the tall grass, popping up like corn
to sting the flesh, and tortoises crawl about
on the red earth, going nowhere in the plenty of time. Loneliness is an aspect of the
land. All things in the plain are isolate; there
is no confusion of objects in the eye, but *one*

GENERALIZATION hill or *one* tree or *one* man. To look upon
that landscape in the early morning, with the
sun at your back, is to lose the sense of pro-
portion. Your imagination comes to life, and
this, you think, is where Creation was begun.

—N. Scott Momaday,
The Way to Rainy Mountain

Exercise 4

The following paragraphs were coherent as originally written, but
now the sentence order has been changed. By following a specific
order (time, space, climax, generalization), rearrange the sentences so
that the paragraphs are coherent once again.

1. (1) Before I started grammar school, I knew all the neighbor-
    hood's marvelous places: the avocado tree where my friends
    and I used to climb to an ancient tree house that had been
    built by children before us, the park where old-timers would sit
    on the benches and laugh at our wild games, the abandoned
    garage where we used to spy at the neighborhood through
    knotholes. (2) My earliest memories center on playing in that
    house: pushing trucks over the hardwood floors, my pajama
    knees mopping up the morning dust; rummaging through my
    mother's pan drawers and banging pans on the linoleum; and

hiding behind the overstuffed couch whenever I was called for lunch. (3) Driven out by a severe drought, my parents came from the cornfields of Nebraska to the house where they lived for thirty-five years. (4) I was born in the back bedroom because, as my mother said, "There just wasn't enough time to get to a hospital." (5) When I first began to walk, the backyard seemed to stretch the length of a football field, and there I would chase my older brothers and sisters until I would fall down, breathless and sweating.

2.   (1) The other was thin and reminded me of a deer loping through a meadow. (2) Yesterday, I sat alone in the bleachers and watched the day come to a close. (3) The horizon was turning deep orange while the sun sank behind the ridge of a hill. (4) I felt alone and glanced back at the track to see the joggers like two ghosts fade with the light. (5) They circled the track—four, five, six laps. (6) One was heavy and scuffled along like a tired buffalo, his head bobbing from side to side. (7) On the track below the bleachers two men jogged. (8) The horizon turned indigo, and the sky began to fill with stars scattered like chips of glass tossed on a dark highway. (9) Not far in the distance the university was silhouetted against the orange background, a few lights speckling its dark outline. (10) Soon the light was almost gone.

44d Achieve coherence by using transitional words and phrases.

When a paragraph is coherent, the writer's thought flows from the first sentence to the last. One way to maintain coherence is by using words and phrases that indicate the relation of one sentence to the preceding one. The coordinating conjunctions *and, but, for, or, so, nor,* and *yet* serve this purpose, but English provides a variety of other words that function as transitions. Use them to create clarity in your work.

To Show Similarity

likewise, similarly, moreover

To Show Differences or Contrast

but, however, still, yet, nevertheless, on the one hand/on the other hand, on the contrary, in contrast

To Show Addition

moreover, and, in addition, equally important, next, first, second, third, again, also, too, besides, furthermore

To Show Time and Process

soon, in the meantime, afterward, later, meanwhile, while, earlier, finally, simultaneously, next, the next step

To Show Direction

here, there, over there, beyond, nearby, opposite, under, above, to the left, to the right, in the distance

To Announce an End

in conclusion, to summarize, finally, on the whole

To Announce a Restatement

in short, in other words, in brief, to put it differently

To Indicate a Result

therefore, then, as a result, consequently, accordingly, thus, thereupon

The following narrative paragraph becomes cohesive through the use of transitional words and phrases (shown in italics) that support the time order of the events.

> At first glance Tod seems to be a typical four-year-old: scruffy, sun-bleached hair, a few freckles, worn cords, short-sleeved shirt, and tattered tennis shoes. But behind his boyish

appearance he seems to be a loner. *During the first class,* he was the only child who did not raise his hand to answer a question or share an experience. He was attentive *at first* but soon lost interest. *Once* he reached out a finger to poke a boy in front of him, and then stopped, perhaps thinking better of it. *Finally,* his thumb went into his mouth. *As soon as* the class broke up, he headed for the monkey bars, where he climbed to the highest rung and sat, his eyes staring toward a distant hill. No one tried to approach him, however. The other children, most of whom chased around the play yard, seemed to respect his wish for privacy. *Later,* when the class regrouped for story time, Tod didn't show as much interest as he had during the sharing session. He seemed more interested in using a fingernail to trace the cracks in the wall than in listening to *Winnie-the-Pooh.*

44e Achieve coherence by repeating key words and phrases.

A writer maintains coherence by repeating key words and phrases to stress the major points and to smooth the flow of the sentences. Pronouns referring to clearly established antecedents function in the same way. In the following paragraph the repeated words are in italics.

> Public speaking differs from acting in that the *speaker* rarely, if ever, reveals any character or personality traits other than his own. A central problem of the *actor* is to create a character for his audience. There are other differences. The *public speaker* usually works alone. The *actor,* unless he is performing a monodrama, usually works with a group. A *public speaker* does not ordinarily use scenery, costume, or make-up to help him express and communicate as the *actor* does. He may on some occasions employ special lighting effects and platform decorations to reinforce his message. Further, the *public speaker* deals only with his own composition while the *actor,* like the oral reader, has all the problems of interpreting the words of

another. He serves as a sort of middleman for the playwright and reveals the intentions of a director. Thus, the purposes of the *actor* are at once like and unlike those of the *public speaker*. The *actor* may seek to elicit primarily utilitarian responses or to gain aesthetic responses depending upon the nature of the material with which he works.

> —John F. Wilson and Carroll E. Arnold,
> *Public Speaking as a Liberal Art*

44f Achieve coherence by using parallel structure.

By repeating a particular structure in successive sentences, a writer can create a parallel form that will guide a reader smoothly from the first sentence to the last. The repeated structure emphasizes the relation of the sentences to the paragraph's controlling idea. Parallel structures are italicized in the following paragraph from Mark Reuter's impressionistic essay on California.

> Historically, California has been a place as much in the imagination as a place on any map. *In the minds of the '49ers, California offered* gold nuggets, shallow streams, and meadows. *In the minds of farmers wiped out in the Depression, California offered* rich soil and abundant potential. *In the minds of impressionable teenagers, California offered* champagne, silver slippers, and fame at the corner of Sunset and Vine. But too often *adventurous Easterners sold* everything to pursue the dream of gold and ended up losing it all to swindlers. *Depression victims were* sometimes greeted by hostile ranchers who carried rifles and drove them away from the fertile valleys. And many *young actors ended up* living on the streets, the stars in their eyes faded.

Exercise 5

Choose a subject and write a paragraph containing parallel structure.

44g Develop the paragraph according to your subject and purpose.

The topic sentence of a paragraph should be adequately supported with convincing, specific material. Some methods of arranging that supporting material are illustrated on the following pages. They are guides only, not rigid requirements to which your paragraphs must conform. The nature of your content, your paper's purpose, and the way a paragraph fits with others in a larger piece of writing will help you determine the most effective way to develop it.

Examples and Details

One common way to develop a paragraph is by using examples and details. Examples and details supply relevant information as well as the specifics a reader needs to understand a writer's point. They are so important that many other methods of development depend on them. The following paragraph illustrates with details the effects of DDT spraying.

> Soon after the spraying had ended there were unmistakable signs that all was not well. Within two days dead and dying fish, including many young salmon, were found along the banks of the stream. Brook trout also appeared among the dead fish, and along the roads and in the woods birds were dying. All the life of the stream was stilled. Before the spraying there had been a rich assortment of the water life that forms the food of salmon and trout—caddis fly larvae, living in loosely fitting protective cases of leaves, stems or gravel cemented together with saliva, stonefly nymphs clinging to rocks in the swirling currents, and the wormlike larvae of blackflies edging the stones under riffles or where the stream spills over steeply slanting rocks. But now the stream insects were dead, killed by the DDT, and there was nothing for a young salmon to eat.
>
> —Rachel Carson,
> *Silent Spring*

This next paragraph uses three factual examples.

> The popular image of the frontier as a place of violence is only partly due to the fact the place often was violent. Most of it is due to hype, particularly Hollywood hype. The truth is many more people have died in Hollywood westerns than ever died on the real frontier (Indian wars considered apart). In the real Dodge City, for instance, there were just five killings in 1878, the most homicidal year in the little town's frontier history—scarcely enough to sustain a typical two-hour movie. In the most violent year in Deadwood, South Dakota, only four people were killed. In the worst year in Tombstone, home of the shoot-out at the OK Corral, only five people were killed. The only reason the OK Corral shoot-out even became famous was that town boosters deliberately overplayed the drama to attract new settlers. "They eventually cashed in on the tourist boom," historian W. Eugene Hollon says, "by inventing a myth about a town too tough to die."
>
> —Richard Shenkman,
> *Legends, Lies, and Cherished Myths*

Comparison and Contrast

A paragraph developed by comparison and contrast discusses the similarities and differences between two subjects. Each may also be used separately. Sometimes the content of such a paragraph is presented in blocks—all the details about one side of the comparison or contrast are presented first, followed by all the details about the other side. Tom Henry's paragraph below compares and contrasts the prehistoric mastodon with the elephant.

> When I first saw the reproduction of the prehistoric mastodon, I thought of elephants I had seen in circuses and zoos. Like the modern elephant, the mastodon is large, with legs that remind me of sturdy tree trunks. The ancient beast had large, floppy ears and a long trunk that he could use as a tool for gathering food. But after a closer look, I saw some

major differences between the modern elephant and the prehistoric mastodon. The mastodon's tusks grew longer and curved upward at a sharper angle. Unlike the elephant with its thick, almost hairless hide, the mastodon was matted with long, thick hair. And although the mastodon was large, it was not as tremendous in size as its modern descendant.

Another way to organize the details of a comparison or contrast paragraph, particularly when you have many points to make about the subject, is to move back and forth between them, point by point. In the following paragraph, Jim Cartozian begins an essay on modern American writers by contrasting Ernest Hemingway and William Faulkner.

No modern American writers have gained as much worldwide critical recognition as Ernest Hemingway and William Faulkner, and no two could be more different. Both did win the coveted Nobel Prize for literature, but when the mild-mannered Faulkner won first, Hemingway is said to have lost his temper and then sulked. Both were publishing at a young age, but Hemingway attracted popular attention early in his career while Faulkner worked in near obscurity. Hemingway became America's first modern literary media star. Magazines featured spreads of his war exploits, his African safaris, and his bullfighting adventures. Faulkner, in contrast, was never a media celebrity. Instead, he seemed to embody the lifestyle of small-town Southern gentry, spending most of his quiet life in Oxford, Mississippi. Hemingway's novels and stories were often set in exotic locales like France, Spain, and Cuba; Faulkner set his works in the South, primarily in the mythical Yoknopatawpha County. Each dealt with very different visions: Hemingway's work displays psychologically wounded characters struggling to establish a personal code of values in an absurd world. Faulkner's work displays characters who are victims of history, suffering because of the sins of their ancestors, the men who wrenched the land from Native Americans and enslaved Native Africans. In 1961 Hemingway died violently by his own hand; in 1962 Faulkner died peacefully.

Analogy

Analogy is a figurative comparison that helps explain a complicated or abstract idea by comparing it to a simpler idea or more concrete image. In an analogy, the items compared are from different classes. A writer might compare the life of a human being to a river, for example. In most ways the two are not alike, but in suggestive ways they *are* alike—both flow smoothly at times, turbulently at other times; both change as they follow their paths; both find destinations that change their very nature. Analogies can help you show things to your reader in different ways, but you must take care not to press an analogy too far, or it can become foolish.

The following paragraph compares the earth's atmosphere to a window. The writer succeeds because he uses our familiarity with windows to enlighten us about the functions of the atmosphere.

> The atmosphere of Earth acts like any window in serving two very important functions. It lets light in and it permits us to look out. It also serves as a shield to keep out dangerous or uncomfortable things. A normal glazed window lets us keep our houses warm by keeping out cold air, and it prevents rain, dirt, and unwelcome insects and animals from coming in. As we have already seen, Earth's atmospheric window also helps to keep our planet at a comfortable temperature by holding back radiated heat and protecting us from dangerous levels of ultraviolet light.
>
> —Lester del Rey,
> *The Mysterious Sky*

When analogies are not used effectively to explain a complicated or abstract idea, they can become unintentionally comic. In the following whimsical paragraph, Russ Williams recounts his high school football coach's comparison of football to war.

> When I recall my high school football days, I remember how my coach's thinking seemed to be dominated by a single analogy—the football field is a battlefield. He treated his players like war heroes. When one of us made an outstanding tack-

le, ran for a touchdown, or intercepted a pass, he would say "Great, you deserve a Medal of Honor." If one were hurt during the game, he would say, "That deserves the Purple Heart." My coach, who once played for Ohio State's Woody Hayes, the "Rommel" of the gridiron, claimed the best defense was the siege. He claimed a successful offense must attack on all fronts. After each play, new battlelines are drawn and the purpose of the game is to penetrate the enemy's line or to strike around it, like a tank division going into action. He spoke of "blitzes," "traps," "zones," and "bombs." Often he and his assistants would "strategize" in the "war room," like Pentagon generals. I was once impressed by my coach's comparison of football to war, but no longer. In fact, when I recall the realistic details of my football experience—that is, a broken nose, two chipped teeth, cracked ribs, and shattered kneecaps—I do not think of battlefield heroes and Purple Hearts, I think of victims who have been mugged.

Classification

Classification is a method of organizing information into general categories. The purpose of such grouping is to clarify the nature of each category. In this sense, classification is a kind of indirect or implied comparison or contrast because the qualities that place an item in one class also distinguish it from items belonging to other classes. In the following example, Elena Peralta offers an informal classification of comic book collectors. She introduces her categories in the opening of the paragraph. She then sketches some broad characteristics each group possesses and cites specific comic book titles appropriate for each category.

> One fascinating off-beat hobbyist is the comic book collector. Usually pale, wearing glasses, bushy-haired and disheveled, collectors can be found rummaging through pile after pile of unsorted secondhand comics in magazine marts across the

country. Comic book collectors, the serious ones, seem to fall into four major groups: Antiquarians, Mercenaries, Idolators, and Compulsive Completers. The Antiquarian cares only for age value; subject matter is of no concern. He is looking for a 1933 *Funnies on Parade* from the days when men were men and comics were comics. To the Mercenary, value is all-important. Certain numbers and titles ring a bell in his cash-register brain and start him furtively checking through a half dozen price sheets. A pristine first edition of *Action Comics* (value: $4000) would suit him just fine. The Idolator couldn't care less about age or value. He's looking for favorites: a *Sheena*, a *Flash Gordon*, or another *Incredible Hulk*. Hiding in a corner, reading those he can't afford to buy, the Idolator will be the last one out of the mart at night and the first one back in the morning. The most frustrated collector is the Compulsive Completer. He'll examine and reject thousands of comics in his search for a badly needed *Felix the Cat* to complete a year's set or the one *Howdy Doody* missing from his collection. But no matter what the reason for collecting, these hobbyists share a common trait: They love the thrill of the hunt.

Cause and Effect

Cause-and-effect paragraphs explore why something happened or explain what happened as a result of something else. Sometimes such a paragraph deals only with causes because the effects are already clear. A paragraph might explore the reasons for a movie star's popularity without needing to demonstrate that the person really was a star, for example. Or a cause-and-effect paragraph could concentrate on effects because a given cause clearly exists, and the only question remaining is "What happened as a result?" Such a paragraph might explain the effects of unemployment or of an increase in taxes. Sometimes it is appropriate to discuss both causes and effects in a paragraph. The following paragraph concentrates on the cause-and-effect relationship between television violence and real-life violence.

Much of the research that has led to the conclusion that TV and movie violence could cause aggressive behavior in some children has stemmed from the work in the area of imitative learning or modeling which, reduced to its simplest expression, might be termed "monkey see, monkey do."

CAUSE

Research by Stanford psychologist Albert Bandura has shown that even brief exposure

EFFECT

to novel aggressive behavior *on a one-time basis* can be repeated in free play by as high as 88 percent of the young children seeing it

CAUSE

on TV. Dr. Bandura also demonstrated that even a single viewing of a novel aggressive

EFFECT

act could be recalled and produced by children six months later, without any intervening exposure. Earlier studies have estimated that the average child between the ages of 5

DETAILS RELATED TO CAUSE

and 15 will witness, during this 10-year period, the violent destruction of more than 13,400 fellow humans. This means that through several hours of TV watching, a child may see more violence than the average adult experiences in a lifetime. Killing is as common as taking a walk, a gun more natur-

OVERALL EFFECT

al than an umbrella. Children are thus taught to take pride in force and violence and to feel ashamed of ordinary sympathy.

—Victor B. Cline,
"How TV Violence Damages Your Children"

Definition

One kind of definition is the dictionary definition, which provides a synonym (*slice* = to cut) or shows how a word fits into a general class (*astronomy* = the science that studies the universe). Using a paragraph to define a term allows for a thorough discussion. Such a paragraph might begin, as does a dictionary definition, by identifying a term as belonging to a general class and differentiating it from other members of the class; it might also include synonyms. Or it might illustrate the term with examples, discuss the word's origins, compare it to similar words, or tell what it is not.

The following paragraphs go beyond a dictionary definition to show the rich background of urban legends.

GENERAL CLASS	Urban legends are realistic stories that are said to have happened recently. Like old legends of lost mines, buried treasure, and ghosts, they usually have an ironic or
DIFFERENTIATION	supernatural twist. They belong to a subclass of folk narratives that (unlike fairy tales) . . . are set in the recent past, involving ordinary human beings rather than extraordinary gods and demigods. Unlike
DIFFERENTIATION	rumors, which are generally fragmentary or vague reports, legends have a specific narrative quality and tend to attach themselves to different local settings. Although they may explain or incorporate current rumors, legends tend to have a longer life and wider acceptance; rumors flourish and then die out rather quickly. Urban legends
CHARACTERISTICS	circulate, by word of mouth, among the "folk" of modern society, but the mass media frequently help to disseminate and validate them. While they vary in particular details from one telling to another, they preserve a central core of traditional themes. In some instances these seemingly fresh stories are merely updatings of classic folklore plots, while other urban leg-

EXAMPLES

ends spring directly from recent conditions and then develop their own traditional patterns in repeated retellings. For example, "The Vanishing Hitchhiker," which describes the disappearance of a rider picked up on a highway, has evolved from a 19th-century horse-and-buggy legend into modern variants incorporating freeway travel. A story called "Alligators in the Sewers," on the other hand, goes back no further than the 1930s and seems to be a New York City invention. Often, it begins with people who bring pet baby alligators back from Florida and eventually flush them down the drains.

—Jan Harold Brunvand,
Alligators in Sewers

Process

A process paragraph explains how to do something or how something works. Process paragraphs are usually developed step by step in a chronological or logical sequence. This process paragraph explains how stripes are put into striped toothpaste, following a step-by-step chronology—the construction of the tube, the filling of the tube, and the mechanics of use by consumers.

Although it's intriguing to imagine the peppermint stripes neatly wound inside the tube, actually stripes don't go into the paste until it's on its way out. A small hollow tube, with slots running lengthwise, extends from the neck of the toothpaste tube back into the interior a short distance. When the toothpaste tube is filled, red paste—the striping material—is inserted first, thus filling the conical area around the hollow tube at the front. (It must not, however, reach beyond the point to which the hollow tube extends into the toothpaste tube.) The remainder of the dispenser is filled with the familiar white stuff. When you squeeze the toothpaste tube, pressure is applied to the white paste, which in turn presses on the red paste at the head of the tube. The red then passes through the slots and onto the white, which is moving through the inserted tube—and which emerges with five red stripes.

—Caroline Sutton,
How Do They Do That?

Exercise 6

Write one paragraph for each of the following methods of development. Select your own topic or use a topic from the list. Once you have selected a topic, phrase a topic sentence with a clear controlling idea that seems appropriate for the method of development.

1. **Examples and details**
   body language
   superstitions
   good teaching
   sports rivalries
2. **Comparison and contrast**
   dress styles
   artists
   religious beliefs
   political beliefs
3. **Classification**
   college majors
   rock groups
   lifestyles
   comedians
4. **Analogy**
   Compare something and a musical instrument.
   Compare education and something.
   Compare something and freeway traffic.
   Compare something and a garbage disposal.

5. **Cause and effect**
   weather and human behavior
   computers and people
   packaging and retail sales
   noise and health
6. **Definition**
   respectability
   wisdom
   cowardice
   bigotry
7. **Process**
   training for physical competition
   cooking for one hundred people
   teaching someone to ski
   making an item of jewelry

45 Writing the Essay *essay*

Most papers you write in college are essays. **Essays** are nonfiction compositions in which you analyze or interpret a limited subject. Whereas a journalism article reports the facts of an event and a lab report precisely details the facts of an experiment, an essay expresses your understanding and opinion of a topic. Your interpretation is based on your research, knowledge, observations, experience, insight, and values.

45a Understand the writer-reader relationship.

When composing an essay, imagine that you are participating in a relationship. This relationship is between you and your readers. Every relationship has its obligations. In the writer-reader relationship, your obligation is to meet your readers' expectation that you will use common essay principles to guide them through the reading process.

Readers Expect an Essay to Have a Clear Purpose.

One principle readers expect to find in an effective essay is a clear purpose—a specific goal that you wish to accomplish. The purposes of essays can be divided into four categories.

> ### *Purposes of Essays*
>
> 1. To narrate
> 2. To describe
> 3. To explain
> 4. To argue

A **narrative essay** tells a story by relating a sequence of events. An essay on the criminal justice system, written as a narrative, might trace the chronology of a typical day in the life of a district attorney.

A **descriptive essay** uses details and images to depict a scene, an event, a person, an object, or a setting. You might write a descriptive essay that re-creates a courtroom scene for its emotional impact.

An **expository essay** explains, informs, analyzes, or interprets. You might explain the causes of a particular crime, inform your readers about several approaches to ending street crime, analyze the effects of crime on a community, or interpret what crime suggests about a community.

An **argumentative essay** attempts to persuade readers to take some action or to convince them to accept your position on a debatable issue. You might try to persuade your readers to join a crime alert program or argue against police harassment of teenagers.

These purposes are not rigid. You might, for example, use descriptive or narrative techniques in an argumentative essay. You might supply useful and interesting information in a narrative essay. Try thinking of your essay as having a dominant purpose, one your readers will sense even though you use several techniques.

Readers Expect an Essay to Follow a Pattern.

Readers expect essays to be organized in clear patterns. In a general sense, the principles of paragraph writing also apply to essay writing. Just as a paragraph has a topic sentence that expresses the main idea, an essay has a **thesis statement** that states and limits the writer's main point. An essay, like a paragraph, should be *unified,* with every part clearly related to the idea expressed in the thesis statement. An essay, like a paragraph, should be *coherent,* with the thoughts expressed in sentences connected by the same techniques used in paragraphs: repetition of key words and phrases, rephrasing of key ideas, and use of transitional words and phrases. Finally, to fulfill a purpose, both paragraphs and essays require thorough supporting explanation and detail.

An essay is composed of several paragraphs. College essays, typically 500 to 1500 words in length, usually follow a general pattern composed of three main parts: an introduction, a discussion, and a conclusion.

1. The *introduction,* usually composed of one or two paragraphs, presents the thesis statement and any background information that readers might need to understand the discussion. An effective introduction arouses reader interest and limits the discussion that follows.

2. The *discussion* usually contains several paragraphs, each organized by a topic sentence that relates to the thesis statement. The discussion paragraphs develop the ideas expressed in the thesis statement in a detailed, thorough manner.

3. The *conclusion,* usually no more than a single paragraph, gives a sense of completion to the essay. Often, though not always, the conclusion restates the thesis statement and touches on the essay's subpoints.

An Essay Structure

Introduction—one or two paragraphs that contain the thesis statement.

Background information prepares the reader for the thesis.

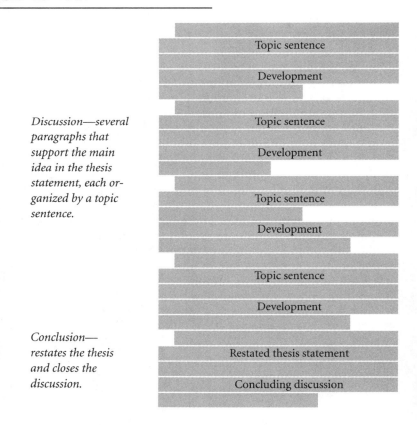

Discussion—several paragraphs that support the main idea in the thesis statement, each organized by a topic sentence.

Topic sentence

Development

Topic sentence

Development

Topic sentence

Development

Topic sentence

Development

Conclusion— restates the thesis and closes the discussion.

Restated thesis statement

Concluding discussion

Readers Expect Essay Paragraphs to Reflect Effective Strategies.

Just as readers expect essays to follow a clear pattern, they expect the paragraphs in essays to be developed in an orderly fashion. Since an essay is composed of several paragraphs, it might contain a variety of paragraph strategies (see paragraph development, 44g).

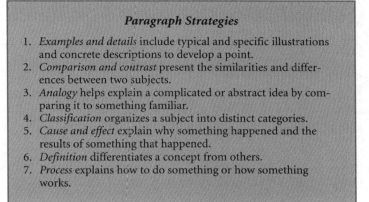

Paragraph Strategies

1. *Examples and details* include typical and specific illustrations and concrete descriptions to develop a point.
2. *Comparison and contrast* present the similarities and differences between two subjects.
3. *Analogy* helps explain a complicated or abstract idea by comparing it to something familiar.
4. *Classification* organizes a subject into distinct categories.
5. *Cause and effect* explain why something happened and the results of something that happened.
6. *Definition* differentiates a concept from others.
7. *Process* explains how to do something or how something works.

Think of these paragraph development strategies as a repertoire to draw from. The sooner you master them, the sooner you will gain control of essay writing.

45b Study a student essay.

Now examine the final draft of an essay written in response to an assignment directing students to discuss "social influences that operate in daily life." Following the essay is a complete discussion of the composing process that student author John Halliwell used to complete his final draft. First read what Halliwell says about the essay.

> Reading the final draft of my essay you might think it was easy to compose. It wasn't. I developed it by applying composing techniques. This essay was especially difficult. It took at least three drafts before I finished it.

I developed the content from my own ideas, class notes, some reading, and advertisements. I had too much information to fit into a simple essay. This made me work hard at organization. Establishing my dominant purpose helped me sort all the parts out. Basically, I wanted to explain how we, meaning most everyone, are influenced by calculated persuasive techniques.

Now examine Halliwell's final draft before reading the discussion of the composing process that follows.

John Halliwell
Professor Dees
English 1
9 September 1996

Title prepares readers for the essay's main subject.

Two-paragraph introduction begins with an anecdote.

Subtle Persuasion

Recently, a student stood outside the cafeteria entrance. He handed out samples of toiletries, a colorful bag containing shaving cream, cologne, a plastic razor, toothpaste, and toothbrush. He smiled and said, "If you use these free samples, you will know they are the best."

Second introductory paragraph analyzes the opening anecdote and defines reciprocity.

Was this merely a corporation's kind gesture? Perhaps, but on closer examination it could be a subtle form of persuasion. Generally, many of us have been trained to believe that repaying a favor with a favor is important, even if the first favor was not requested. Some of us will often return an unrequested favor rather than feel the pain of being indebted. This behavior pattern has not been lost on those who wish

Thesis statement is integrated into the text.

to influence others. For example, politicians have learned that favors are returned with votes. Charities mail unrequested personal address labels to potential contributors. Companies offer free samples. All are using a persuasive technique based on reciprocity. A politician, charity, or company seems to be saying, "I have done you a favor. I expect you to do me a favor." Reciprocity is only one of several subtle strategies used to influence our decisions.

Discussion section begins.

Topic sentence prepares readers for discussion of social validation.

Another of these strategies takes the form of social validation. At certain times everyone is uncertain about how to behave. Perhaps in a restaurant someone will be uncertain about what fork to use for the salad. At a wedding another person might be uncertain about how to greet the bride. At a religious gathering yet another person might be uncertain about how to participate in an unfamiliar ceremony. In typical situations such as these, we tend to decide correct behavior based on what other people do or think. This behavior is a form of social validation, one person turning to another to avoid making a mistake in public. Uncertainty and social validation are powerful tools when used to influence people. For example, in a simple way social validation is at work when a jar marked "tips" is placed by a cash register in a self-service coffee bar. Simply, the jar suggests that it is socially correct to tip even though no

Defines social validation with examples from common experience.

service has been given. In a more complex way, social validation is at work in advertisements where ordinary people offer testimonials for products ranging from soap to pickup trucks. Do such advertisements work? The desire for social validation indicates that we all look to others as guides when in doubt. When we view those others as similar to ourselves, we are likely to be influenced by them.

Topic sentence prepares readers for discussion of mindless consistency.

Most of us have been trained to be consistent. Unfortunately, we sometimes remain consistent when to do so makes no sense. The exploitation of "mindless consistency" is another strategy that works to influence our behavior. The strategy usually involves someone getting another person to agree to a small commitment, often called the "foot in the door" tactic. Once a small commitment is made, making a second larger commitment is easier. The

An extended hypothetical example showing mindless consistency at work.

strategy is most successful when a chain of commitments follows. Salespersons of auto dealers have perfected this method of influencing customers. For example, the first commitment actually takes place when a potential customer steps into a showroom and walks up to a car. "It's a beauty, isn't it?" the smiling salesperson might ask. "Yes," the customer replies, mainly being courteous, but, of course, the salesperson knows a second commitment, one consistent with the first, has been made. A series of small steps follow: "Feel that leather interior. Feels rich, doesn't it? Sit behind the wheel; comfortable, right? Let's test drive it, okay?" Soon the unwary customer might be sitting on the other side of a desk, signing a sales contract–all because of the powerful influence of mindless consistency.

As children, many of us were conditioned to defer not only to parents, but also to such authority figures as teachers, police personnel, and adults in general. Indeed, deferring to authority in many situations is beneficial, but authority when used as a strategy to influence us can be exploitive. For example, actor Robert Young played a character named Dr. Marcus Welby, Jr., in a classic 1970s television series. For years after the series ended, he represented products in commercials by projecting the authority of the Dr. Welby image. We all view doctors as authority figures, and Robert Young seemed to personify everyone's ideal medical practitioner, even though he had only acted the role.

In many contemporary advertisements, the use of authority seems to be even more powerful. Authorities add prestige to a product in ways that influence sales. Consider, for example, Nike athletic shoes. Obviously, consumers are not influenced by being told how well an athletic shoe is stitched; they are influenced by

Topic sentence prepares readers for discussion of authority as used to exploit the unwary.

A common example from vintage television.

This paragraph continues to develop the topic of authority, using a current ad campaign as an example.

the authority figures associated with the shoes. Why else would Nike pay millions to feature basketball star Michael Jordan making slam dunks or tennis champion André Agassi making powerful serves? The prestige these world-class athletes bring to Nike products is part of a strategy to use authority to influence consumer decisions.

Conclusion begins.

Rephrases the thesis and reminds readers of the key points.

These subtle persuasive strategies are all established in common human behavior. Indeed, most people feel obligated to return favors, even those they have not requested. We all have looked to others for guidance and approval. We are trained to pursue consistent behavior. No one can avoid the impact of authority on his or her life. Though we as individuals may not be influenced by these strategies all of the time, it is hard to escape their influence some of the time.

Halliwell has met his responsibility to his readers. His essay has a clear purpose and a clear thesis statement. It follows a clear pattern with an introduction that presents the thesis statement, a discussion that develops the subpoints of the thesis statement, and a conclusion that effectively closes the discussion. Finally, the discussion paragraphs reflect sound paragraph strategies—all of which fulfills a reader's expectation.

The Composing Process

Few writers can take up a pen or sit at a keyboard and compose an effective essay from beginning to end. Writing is a recursive process—that is, writers usually work and rework a piece, moving ahead in creative spurts and then faltering before once again picking up speed and moving toward completion. Usually the composing process leads to two, three, or even four working drafts before a final manuscript is ready to submit.

If possible, compose your work on a word processor; it will allow you to concentrate on the composition itself—on your ideas and how to present them—rather than on the retyping or rewriting that each draft would require. Word processors facilitate the composing process by enabling you to easily insert, delete, and move passages and then to print out the entire piece with little effort.

Although we present the stages of the composing process in chronological order, you will find that you might need to circle back to the beginning of the process to generate more ideas or alter your plan. If you use common composing techniques, are persistent and thoughtful, and use time wisely, however, you can create a product that you will be proud of.

45c Assess the writing situation.

Many writing decisions depend on the elements of each individual writing situation.

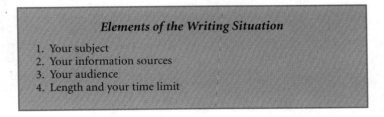

Elements of the Writing Situation

1. Your subject
2. Your information sources
3. Your audience
4. Length and your time limit

Subject

The subjects of most college writing assignments are given to you. In political science you might analyze a political cartoon or explain local campaign fund-raising restrictions. In business you might identify the reasons for the fluctuating value of the dollar. In literature you might interpret a short story or poem. Other times, however, you can choose your own subject. In this situation, select a subject you know something about or one you can quickly research.

Information Sources

Personal experience allows you to explore your life—often the best source of information—for subjects. You might write about how your neighborhood has changed over the years or how an event changed your vision of the world—all based on your individual experience.

Direct observation sends you into the world as an observer. You might observe and then write about the behavior of strangers gathered in confined places, such as elevators, lunch counters, and crowded public transportation. You might observe and analyze a television program, a film, or a series of advertisements.

Reading is the basis of your college education. Many of the writing situations you face will be based on the careful reading of a text—that is, a book, essay, short story, or poem. In these situations, be sure not to let your paper become an extended summary; instead, concentrate on interpretating the work and support your interpretation with details and examples from the text.

Questionnaires and interviews can also serve as rich information sources for essays. A psychology instructor might ask you to use questionnaire information as the source for an essay on student attitudes toward such subjects as work, family values, child rearing, or marriage. For a law course you might be asked to interview several legal authorities, such as a judge, a defense attorney, a prosecuting attorney, and a police officer, and then use the interview information in an essay.

Audience

Write your essays with a particular audience—that is, readership—in mind. In college writing, your audience is usually your instructor. Your task is to convince him or her that you have fulfilled the assignment, your information is valid, and your conclusions are reasonable. Other audiences may include fellow students, professionals from a particular field, and community members. Often, your audience will be too diverse to be categorized. This is the universal audience. When writing for a universal audience, you might have to seek common elements that involve everyone in the audience. A common audience might be consumers, males, females, students, teenagers, or senior citizens. Once you have a sense of your universal audience, you can shape your material for them: "All consumers are targets . . . ," "No matter how many semesters you have completed at this campus . . . ," or "For those of you over fifty-five . . . ."

Questions for Audience Analysis

1. Is my audience a group or an individual?
2. What is my relationship to my audience?
3. How much does my audience know about the subject?
4. Should I consider my audience's age, gender, education, political bias, or social values?
5. Is reading ability a consideration? Can my audience follow a complex discussion? Do I need to simplify the discussion?

Length and Time Limit

In college assignments, your instructor will assign an approximate length to the paper and a due date. The length of an essay and the time you have to write it have a direct bearing on the writing situation. For example, you need to restrict your subject more for a 500-word essay than for a 1500-word essay. If you have two weeks to write an essay, you will not have much time to research the subject, and if you are writing an in-class essay, you will not have much time to plan the essay. In any case, you must accurately assess the length of a paper and the time you have to write it and then adjust your writing behavior appropriately.

Exercise 7

First identify what information sources could be used to develop the following subjects. Then identify who the audience might be.

1. Whether campus security guards overstep their authority

2. The influence of psychiatrist Carl Jung's theory of the unconscious on painter Jackson Pollock

3. The effects of political polling on voters

4. How photographs reveal family relationships

5. Unexpected sources of noise pollution

45d Find a subject.

If you have the freedom to select your own subject for an essay, the most effective procedure is to select a subject quickly rather than to wait too long for inspiration. Beware, though, because not all subjects are suitable for college essays. For example, do not write an essay based on your summer vacation, a trite subject that has plagued English teachers for generations.

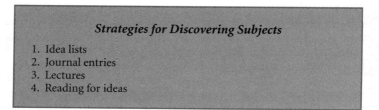

Strategies for Discovering Subjects

1. Idea lists
2. Journal entries
3. Lectures
4. Reading for ideas

Pick a subject that reflects the content and spirit of the course. Plunge into serious issues and explore significant concepts. Your subject should force you to use specific examples and concrete details. Remember, the quality of a subject can show that you are an engaged writer who is willing to encounter your world.

If a suitable subject does not come to mind immediately, actively pursue one through one of several strategies.

1. Make a *list* of possibilities. Give yourself thirty minutes of uninterrupted time and jot down subjects that come to mind. Items on your list do not need to be extensive entries. Merely sketch an item in a phrase or a sentence.

2. If you keep a *journal,* browse through it, searching for an engaging entry. If an entry engages you, it will engage your readers.

3. Recall a recent classroom *lecture.* Perhaps a professor stimulated your curiosity or reminded you of a strong opinion you hold, either of which might inspire an essay.

4. *Skim* a newsmagazine or newspaper until a subject catches your attention. Jot down your thoughts; use them as a starting point.

Being assigned a topic does not necessarily make writing easier. An assignment might be harder to complete than a subject you generate yourself, because you might skip the exploration process and plunge directly into a first draft. To avoid this mistake, keep the following principle in mind.

> If an assignment does not provide a workable subject, you must create a subject.

To do so, you can use the strategies listed above. For example, consider the Halliwell essay that you have already examined. Halliwell's essay was based on an assignment that followed a critical thinking unit in freshman composition.

"Social influences" offers a general area for exploration, but the topic is much too broad to be discussed successfully in a single essay. Halliwell, therefore, developed an idea list with the term *social influences* as the starting point.

> ### *Halliwell's Assignment*
>
> In four to five typed pages, discuss social influences that operate in daily life. You may use lecture notes, personal experience, and first-hand observations as information sources.

Social Influences

1. Parents, relatives influence children—role models, authority, love, anger.
2. Teachers, police officers, other authority figures influence our behavior.
3. Political campaigns and politicians influence voters—image, favors, promises.
4. Religious figures influence their followers—guilt, love, kindness.
5. Television influences viewers—entertainment programs, news, commercials.
6. Charities try to influence donors.
7. Celebrities, such as music stars, film actors, television personalities, influence fans.
8. Influence tactics—guilt, trust, hope.
9. Trained behavior patterns are used to influence people.
10. Government lying—is this influence? No. It's deception.
11. Photography is a powerful influence in films like *J.F.K.* and *Born on the Fourth of July.*

Developing an idea list helped Halliwell find a topic for further exploration. No particular entry gave him a clear subject, Halliwell says, but the list externalized his thinking and began a more analytical process.

> When I first reviewed my idea list, I felt lost. Nothing on the list would work as an essay. Then I began to examine the items differently.

My thought went something like this: many items suggested authority figures who serve as role models. We emulate role models, and they give us advice. From them we also gain a sense of self-worth. These two ideas began to connect in my imagination.

Then my attention fell on two brief entries, influence tactics and trained behavior. People are trained to listen to authorities and to trust authorities. Authority gives us self-worth, advice. How do authorities abuse their roles? They use trust, guilt, hope. I felt I had found a direction.

I knew my essay would examine ways that common behavior is used to influence decisions.

Halliwell's experience with this early stage in the composing process is not unusual. A subject or a direction presents itself only after a writer becomes deeply involved. Writers must re-examine their material, redevelop it, combine ideas, and seek patterns among existing ideas.

45e Narrow the subject so that it can be covered in a single essay.

The first thoughts you have about possible essay subjects will more than likely be too broad. If you select a subject such as the anti–nuclear energy movement, the history of television, or child development, you will end up with an uninteresting essay consisting of general statements because only general statements will allow you to cover the broad territory you have mapped. Avoid this trap. In fact, by narrowing your subject to manageable size, you are taking charge of the assignment.

Suppose you are assigned the subject of analyzing gender roles on television. After composing an idea list of possible subjects, you decide to explore one item from your list—the role of women in situation comedy. This subject, of course, is too large for a single essay. You would have to examine representative programs of all situation comedies that feature women—an impossible task.

You begin the narrowing process. You might concentrate on specific comedies: a current comedy, such as *Murphy Brown, Roseanne,* or *The Simpsons;* or a vintage comedy, such as *Ozzie and Harriet, The Honeymooners,* or *I Love Lucy.* Perhaps you have a special interest in *I Love Lucy* and enjoy watching reruns of this show. Your subject is now narrowed to *I Love Lucy,* which would lead you to review several representative shows to identify the female roles the show portrays. In the end, you might concentrate on Lucy herself and examine her role in one show, thus narrowing the subject even more.

John Halliwell, the author of "Subtle Persuasion," narrowed his subject even further once he formulated it from his idea list. He began with the general observation that our behavior is used to influence our decisions but soon realized that "behavior" is a very broad concept. He limited his subject to "methods used to influence our decisions." He decided to identify and explain some common tactics that affected him most, the kind that most people probably experience.

Later, as he was brainstorming his subject, the idea of behavior came back. Writers often change the scope or phrasing of a subject as they move through the composing process. Keep in mind that writing is a process of trial and revision. Do not hesitate to change your subject if you see new possibilities as you proceed.

Exercise 8

Narrow the following subjects by writing three progressively more limited topics. For example:

   Music
      Country and western music
         Male and female relations in country and western ballads
            Attitudes toward marriage in current country and western ballads

1. novels
2. style
3. advertising
4. survival
5. manners
6. shopping malls
7. film
8. health
9. greed
10. conformity

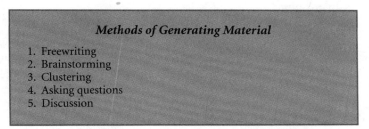

45f Use associational thinking to generate material.

Once you have narrowed a subject to a specific topic, you are ready to discover what you know about it and to explore ways to develop it. There are several methods you can use to generate material for future drafts. They are sometimes called *prewriting strategies* or *invention techniques*.

> ### *Methods of Generating Material*
> 1. Freewriting
> 2. Brainstorming
> 3. Clustering
> 4. Asking questions
> 5. Discussion

These invention techniques activate associational thinking and restrict analytical thinking. The association process is characteristic of the early stages of writing, and the analytical process is characteristic of the later stages. By using *associational thinking*, writers generate ideas, events, examples, and metaphors—the raw material of fresh, interesting writing. By using *analytical thinking*, writers judge content, shape structure, and examine logic—the critical evaluation that results in accurate, coherent writing. Through associational thinking, writers *invent* their material; through analytical thinking, writers evaluate and organize the material for their readers.

Once you begin to explore a subject, allow your mind to follow its thought patterns, associating one thought with another without worrying whether the connections are logical. When you use associational thinking, resist the urge to analyze your thoughts. Instead, encourage the random exploration of your imagination.

Freewriting

Freewriting means writing down everything that comes to mind without judging its value. Your goal is to create an associative flow of ideas without being distracted by concerns for grammar, punctuation, spelling, or logic. Once you have a narrowed subject, no matter how tentative, you can place your freewriting in focus by jotting down the subject at the top of the page. Then set a time or page limit goal for yourself and begin the freewriting session.

Brainstorming

Brainstorming is similar to freewriting, but you arrange the material in an extended list. The list entries are quickly jotted down in phrases or short sentences. The entries should include just enough detail to remind you of their significance when you review the list. Your goal in brainstorming is not to be comprehensive but to capture thought fragments on the fly. Later you can add more detail to the entries that are appropriate to your essay.

Clustering

Clustering offers a way to generate ideas and show the relationships among them. To develop material through clustering, write your topic in the center of a piece of paper; then, as you think of ideas connected with your subject, arrange them around the edges of the page or in clusters of similar items. For example, a student who was composing an essay on rude behavior developed the following cluster diagram.

Asking Questions

Another method of generating material is to frame questions about the subject, sometimes referred to as *journalist questions:* Who? What? When? Where? Why? How? Of course, not every question will be appropriate for your subject, but using the ones that are can begin an associational chain that will generate material for your essay and help you view your subject from different perspectives.

Cluster Diagram for Rude Behavior

For example, the subject of rude behavior could be approached through the following questions.

> What is rude behavior?
> Who is rude?
> Who is affected by rudeness?
> Who can change rude behavior?
> What causes rudeness?
> What is my attitude toward rudeness?
> What are other attitudes about rudeness?
> When did I first become interested in rudeness?
> Where does rude behavior take place?
> Why are people rude?
> Where have I seen rude behavior?
> How can rude behavior be changed?

When you allow your mind to explore your subject freely by asking such questions as these, you can generate material quickly.

Discussion

Writers often describe the writing process as lonely. Indeed, in many ways it is, for at some point, a writer must sit down by him- or herself to complete the essay. But in the meantime, writers find that discussing or brainstorming their projects with other people helps them generate ideas and material. For example, you may become part of a writing group that discusses class assignments. When you discuss your project, be sure to take notes that will add to your composing process. You may also consult a writing buddy—another student or a friend who is more experienced with writing than you are. Finally, you can engage your instructor in a discussion of your project to test your ideas against another point of view.

Discussions of this sort will help you generate ideas and perhaps refine them, but you must also commit them to paper. Ultimately, this responsibility is yours.

John Halliwell's Process at Work

To generate material that led to "Subtle Persuasion," John Halliwell used several invention techniques, as he points out.

> Once I narrowed the subject—ways common behavior is used to influence decisions—I took it to my writing group. We generated a long list of questions, several of which I found helpful.
>
> What common behavior traits do most people share?
> What behavior traits are used to influence people?
> Who uses them?
> Why do they use them?
> How are they used?
>
> Then we spent the rest of my group time brainstorming a response to the first question. For example, here are several of the items on the brainstorming list.
>
> People are selfish.
> People are self-sacrificing.
> People feel guilt.
> People trust authority.
> People are insecure.
> People need to be accepted.
> People need to be valued.
> People feel indebted to others.
>
> The next day I began to respond to the remaining questions. I used both brainstorming and freewriting to generate responses. When I finished I had several pages to work through.

Using several invention techniques to generate material is not unusual. Once you begin to use associational thinking, you might find yourself, like Halliwell, first making lists, then writing questions, then freewriting to explore the questions. No single invention technique is appropriate for all writing situations. Use one or a combination of several to explore your subject.

Exercise 9

To start a 500- to 750-word essay, select three of the following subjects, or choose three other subjects that interest you, and narrow
their focus. For one subject, brainstorm until you have developed a
list of at least fifteen items related to the topic, or freewrite about the
topic for thirty minutes. Write without concern for phrasing, organization, grammar, punctuation, or spelling. For the second subject,
create a list of appropriate questions based on Who? What? When?
Why? and How? Follow each question with an answer, if possible. For
the third subject, create a cluster of at least fifteen items. Include secondary clusters when appropriate.

improving health	damaging health
gun control	making money
escaping the rat race	becoming involved
messages in dreams	space travel
effective teaching	lost causes
capital punishment	fashion trends
angry students	competitive sports
American memories	lost opportunities
living in poverty	obtaining knowledge
being manipulated	shocking films

45g Use analytical thinking to evaluate your prewritten material.

Evaluating the material generated by invention techniques can be difficult. You will discover quickly that much of your material will not
help you develop an effective essay. You must strike out useless observations, odd digressions, clichéd thinking, stalled musings, and dead-
end ideas. You must search for a fresh perspective, interesting ideas,
and observations that can be developed as examples.

This phase of the composing process will also reveal what you do
not know about a subject. This knowledge can direct your search to
reading, a review of class notes, or discussions with relatives, friends,
or instructors.

The fourth paragraph of John Halliwell's "Subtle Persuasion" grew out of the following freewriting. Notice that the freewritten material is unstructured, reflecting his associational thinking process. Halliwell has evaluated it, crossing out what he identifies as unhelpful.

Insecurity–most people I know need people to tell them they're okay. They feel insecure about different things. ~~I know I do. I feel insecure in English, that's for sure. Too many smacks. They already know how to write.~~ I like people to like me, this is important. I also turn to others for advice when I am uncertain about how to behave. I remember going to a Buddhist ceremony and didn't know what to do when I heard a gong. I asked my friend. She said just do what I do. I watched her so I wouldn't embarrass myself. I remember when I didn't know which fork to use at a formal dinner. Other things:

We see others used in ads as ordinary people.

Example

Do you tip at coffee shops? The jar says so. I'm uneasy at weddings, never knowing which side to sit on or how to talk to the bride. People in commercials give us advice all the time. When we buy certain products, do we do it because we need them or because others will see us in a certain way?

Key point

Why do advertisers use "ordinary people"? The psychologists call it social validation–see psychology notes ...

Two ideas from this prewritten material that find their way into Halliwell's final draft of his essay are social validation and the use of ordinary people in advertisements. In this freewriting fragment, he also uncovers some typical examples from his own experience that he reworks for paragraph three of the final draft.

Exercise 10

Select one of the three subjects you used to practice prewriting strategies for Exercise 9, p. 316, and evaluate your prewritten material. (If you need more material to develop a 500- to 750-word essay, continue the prewriting process.) Strike out useless observations, odd digressions, and clichéd thinking. Identify the material you can use in an essay and note aspects of the subject that you might need more information about.

45h Clarify your dominant purpose.

Until this point, you will have used a topic to guide the composing process. Now, as you analyze your material, you should clarify your purpose by writing a purpose statement. The purpose statement should identify your subject and how you propose to develop it. Later in the process, the purpose statement will become the basis for a more formal thesis statement.

An effective purpose statement can usually be stated in a single sentence.

> I plan to analyze the role of Lucy as a gender stereotype in the situation comedy *I Love Lucy.*

This writer's subject is quite clear: the character Lucille Ball plays as a gender stereotype. The writer will develop the subject by exposition, thus writing an expository essay.

Now consider another statement of purpose.

I propose to argue that public rudeness damages campus life.

This writer's subject is also clear: the effects of public rudeness on campus life. The subject will be developed in an argumentative essay.

After analyzing his prewriting material, John Halliwell wrote a purpose statement for his essay.

I want to explain how self-interested groups use several ways to influence the public.

Halliwell's subject is clear: the effect of persuasive techniques. He will develop his subject in an expository essay.

Your purpose might change as you continue through the composing process, but in the meantime it will help you develop a tentative plan.

Exercise 11

Clarify a dominant purpose for the subject you evaluated in Exercise 10, p. 318. Write it in a complete sentence.

45i Sketch an informal plan.

Use your purpose statement to sketch an informal plan for your essay. Think of this stage of the composing process as sorting and grouping your prewritten material. More than likely, the sorting and grouping process began when you first evaluated your prewriting notes. By sketching an informal plan, you will be organizing your material in a clear pattern to fulfill your purpose. Besides getting a general sense of how your essay will be structured, by identifying major points and examples you will also discover what other information you need to gather.

An informal plan might take the shape of your purpose statement and a phrase list of major points. Halliwell's informal plan took this shape.

Self-interested people have subtle ways to influence the public.

—Reciprocity: expecting an unrequested favor to be returned.
  Examples: student at cafeteria, charities, politicians

—Social validation: people turn to others.
  Examples: religious ceremonies, formal dining, tip jar, advertisements that feature ordinary people

—Consistency: parents, teachers, teach children to be consistent.
  How does consistency work? Sales (develop an example, foot-in-the-door technique)

—Authority: parents, teachers, police officers, celebrities.
  Examples: Celebrities in ad campaigns—Nike sports shoes. Find another example.

Clustering techniques that are used to generate material during the invention process can also serve as informal outlines. Halliwell's informal sketch in cluster form might resemble the one that follows.

Exercise 12

Examine the material you have developed for your 500- to 750-word essay, that is, the prewritten material and the purpose statement. Make an informal plan for your essay by selecting and organizing the ideas and information from the prewriting.

45j Write a clear, limited thesis statement.

If there is one moment in the composing process when an essay's final direction and shape become clear, it is when you write a thesis statement. A thesis statement serves as an essay's intellectual center for both writers and readers.

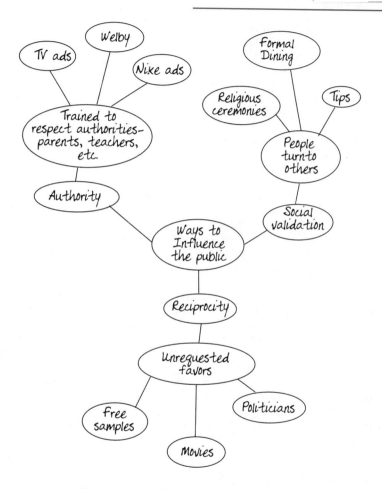

Cluster Diagram for Halliwell's Informal Plan

For writers, a **thesis statement** identifies and limits the subject, establishes the dominant purpose, and unifies the discussion. Once you have a clear thesis statement, you will find it easier to make decisions about what to include in and exclude from the discussion paragraphs and how to conclude an essay. If you have trouble developing your thesis statement, then you know you must seek more information (either by returning to earlier drafts or by generating additional material) to fill out the content.

For readers, a thesis statement tells what the essay will cover and helps put discussion paragraphs in perspective. Imagine the confusion that a reader would experience if you develop several paragraphs but fail to provide the necessary focal point to understand their purpose. A thesis statement provides that perspective.

An effective thesis statement, usually expressed in a single sentence, goes beyond a purpose statement by specifically identifying the content of the essay and limiting the discussion.

If you were writing about violence, for example, you might begin with the following thesis statement.

> Violence is destroying the safety of U.S. cities.

When writing your first draft, however, you would discover that this thesis statement is much too broad for a three- or four-page essay. At best you could develop only a few very general observations, all unsupported by specific details. As a consequence, you would have to limit the thesis statement.

Writers limit their thesis statements in two ways. First, they limit the subject part of the statement. As it stands, the subject of the above thesis statement is violence. But violence covers a large territory— murder, muggings, police brutality, and so on. Concentrating on one aspect of violence would limit the subject.

> *Street violence* is destroying the safety of U.S. cities.
> *Gang violence* is destroying the safety of U.S. cities.
> *Random violence* is destroying the safety of U.S. cities.

Street violence, gang violence, and random violence are more limited than the general subject of violence. However, the statements are still too broad for a brief essay.

Second, writers narrow the predicate part of the statement—in this example, the part that reads "is destroying the safety of U.S. cities." "U.S. cities" covers all the territory from Bangor, Maine, to Honolulu. You could narrow the predicate part of the thesis statement to a particular city, town, or neighborhood.

> Street violence *is destroying the safety of Newport Heights.*
> Gang violence *is destroying the safety of my apartment complex.*
> Random violence *is destroying the safety of our campus.*

These thesis statements are now manageable. You could develop them from personal observation, interviews, surveys, police reports, and newspaper articles—all readily available information sources.

An effective thesis statement is always stated precisely. Vague language and overly general assertions may misguide your reader. Use precise language, not fuzzy words, to phrase your thesis statement.

VAGUE	The examination of fairy tales is fascinating.
PRECISE	"Cinderella" reveals common stereotypes of women.

The second example, phrased precisely in specific language, leaves no room for confusion.

Finally, an effective thesis statement makes a promise to develop its subject—a promise which the writer must keep or risk writing an unsuccessful essay.

Consider, for example, these three thesis statements.

> Kevin Costner's *Dances with Wolves* and John Ford's *The Searchers* create conflicting images of Native Americans. [The promise: to explain through comparison and contrast the image of Native Americans in two blockbuster films.]

Although murder is humankind's most repugnant crime, the death penalty should be abolished. [The promise: to argue that capital punishment should be ended.]

Cigarette advertisements can be divided into four categories. [The promise: to classify cigarette advertisements.]

When writing your thesis statement, do not confuse it with a title, a factual statement, or a purpose statement. Titles orient readers, but they are not detailed enough to reveal much about an essay's limited focus and direction. Factual statements do not lend themselves to development; they are dead ends. Purpose statements are often similar to thesis statements, but they are usually less refined and become stylistically intrusive when inserted into essays. Compare the following.

TITLE	*Sesame Street:* The Hidden Message
FACTUAL STATEMENT	*Sesame Street* is a successful children's education program.
PURPOSE STATEMENT	I am going to argue that *Sesame Street* emphasizes entertainment over education.
THESIS STATEMENT	Although it is identified as television's finest children's education program, *Sesame Street* communicates the message that entertainment is more important than education.

John Halliwell's thesis evolved from the purpose statement he used to sketch his informal plan. After several attempts, Halliwell phrased his thesis as follows:

Self-interested people use several ways based on typical behavior to influence our decisions.

By analyzing the elements of his thesis, Halliwell could see that he would be promising the reader that he would identify several typical behaviors and explain how self-interested people use them to manipulate others. Who are these self-interested people? By returning to his prewritten material, Halliwell identified them as politicians, advertisers, salespeople, and even people who operate charities.

Exercise 13

The following thesis statements are ineffective. Identify their problems and rewrite them so that they are effective.

1. U.S. schools are not doing their job.

2. Film: A window to the world

3. I want to explain how magazine advertisements use fear to sell products.

4. The state has set aside 3800 acres of sand dunes for land preservation.

5. Help—the cry of the homeless

Exercise 14

Write a thesis statement for the essay you have been developing.

45k Make a formal plan with a reader in mind.

If you have not done so already, now is the time to determine the nature of your audience—that is, who, exactly, your reader is. Your reader will influence choices that you make about the essay's content. If you are writing an in-class essay for an instructor, you would want to show the full range of your understanding of the subject. If writing for fellow students, you would select examples that would relate to their experience. If writing for a universal audience, you would select examples that reflect broad experience.

For example, although John Halliwell was responding to a Freshman Composition assignment, he decided to direct his paper to a universal audience. He knew he would have to select common examples and explain his ideas in ways that many people would understand. This decision and the formulation of his thesis meant that he was ready to develop a more formal plan for his essay.

One method for planning your essay is to write a more formal outline, one that identifies the thesis and lists the supporting points. For short essays, an informal outline may be effective, but for longer essays a formal outline will provide a more detailed view of the final arrangement.

Formal outlines include the thesis statement, the subpoints, and various levels of detail depending on the subject's complexity. They can be written in topic or sentence form. The main items will be identified by roman numerals, the first sublevel of items by capital letters, the second sublevel by arabic numerals, the third sublevel by lowercase letters, the fourth sublevel by arabic numerals enclosed in parentheses, and the fifth sublevel by lowercase letters enclosed in parentheses. All letters and numbers at the same level are indented to fall directly under one another. You will rarely need all six levels, especially for college essays.

FORMAL OUTLINE STRUCTURE

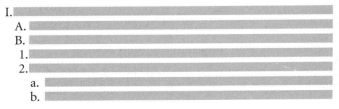

```
(1) ▓▓▓▓▓▓▓▓▓▓▓▓▓▓▓▓▓▓▓▓▓▓▓▓
(2) ▓▓▓▓▓▓▓▓▓▓▓▓▓▓▓▓▓▓▓▓▓▓▓▓
    (a) ▓▓▓▓▓▓▓▓▓▓▓▓▓▓▓▓▓▓▓▓
    (b) ▓▓▓▓▓▓▓▓▓▓▓▓▓▓▓▓▓▓▓▓
II. ▓▓▓▓▓▓▓▓▓▓▓▓▓▓▓▓▓▓▓▓▓▓▓▓▓
```

Notice that each level is a division of the level above it. There must be two items at every level because, logically, a topic cannot be divided into one item. There cannot be an *A* without a *B* or a *1* without a *2*, for example. Of course, there may be more than two items at any level.

All items at the same level must be expressed in parallel grammatical structure, and the first word of each item must be capitalized. The following example is a formal topic outline for "Subtle Persuasion."

Thesis: Self-interested people use several ways based on typical behavior to influence our decisions.

   I. Reciprocity suggests favors must be repaid.
      A. Companies give free samples.
      B. Politicians do favors.
      C. Charities give free address labels.
  II. Social validation plays on uncertainty.
      A. Unfamiliar social situations create uncertainty.
       1. Wedding etiquette creates unease.
       2. Religious ceremonies may be unfamiliar.
      B. Social validation is an influence.
       1. Tip jar at the coffee house creates pressure.
       2. Advertisements feature ordinary people.
 III. Mindless consistency plays on early training.
      A. "Foot-in-the-door" establishes causal chain.
      B. Auto dealers build mindless consistency.
 IV. Authority influences decisions.
      A. Dr. Welby commercials reflect authority.
      B. Nike commercials use stars.
       1. Michael Jordan shoots hoops.
       2. André Agassi serves aces.
  V. These persuasive strategies are hard to escape.

Developing a formal outline such as Halliwell's forces you to arrange your material for a reader. Throughout the process of constructing a formal outline, you will draw on the informal outline you constructed earlier, your prewriting material, and any other material you collected. About his outlining process, Halliwell says,

> To start, I laid my informal plan, prewriting, and class notes on my desk. I kept moving through the material and experimenting with the outline. Since I was writing for a universal audience, I knew I needed to include more examples, especially under point four where I planned to use Nike. I remembered Dr. Welby commercials, but I couldn't remember the actor. A couple of questions and a glance at *The Film Encyclopedia* gave me the information. He is Robert Young, a film actor and television star who played the lead in *Marcus Welby, M.D.,* in a very popular television series in the late 1960s and 1970s.

Too often, beginning writers want to skip formal planning, yet a formal plan can be an important part of the composing process, one that will help you determine your essay's final arrangement.

Exercise 15

If appropriate, develop a formal outline for your essay.

45l Choose a suitable tone for your essay.

After all the planning is completed, you will be ready to write the first draft of your essay. Before you begin writing, think about the attitude you wish to convey to your readers. Tone embodies your attitude—it is reflected in what you say and how you say it. In college writing, try to achieve a reasonable tone, one that shows you understand your subject and have respect for it and for your readers. Most college writing reflects standard American English, which can be formal or informal writing (see 41a). Although readers generally appreciate lively language, they can be repelled by sarcasm or slang inserted into a serious discussion.

Writing a Working Draft

When you begin a first draft—that is, a working draft—remember that you will probably write several more drafts before you complete the final manuscript. With the knowledge that several drafts lie ahead, you can more easily accept that a working draft will never be perfect. Instead of being concerned with perfection at this stage, merely try to keep your writing moving by concentrating on content and structure. Later you can refine and rephrase your sentences.

Also keep in mind that not all first drafts begin at the beginning and go to the end. You might begin with the introduction, or you might begin with a discussion paragraph and return to the introduction or conclusion later. In any case, your goal should be to keep your writing going. You can circle back and fill in information when necessary—but always keep writing with an eye toward completing the working draft.

45m Write an introduction that includes the thesis statement and captures a reader's interest.

An introduction presents the thesis, the discussion paragraphs develop the thesis, and the conclusion rounds out the discussion. Actually, an effective introduction does more than present the thesis; it showcases the thesis, displaying it in a way the reader cannot miss. Remember, your thesis statement is your promise to the reader. Do not let the reader miss your promise.

An introduction should also draw readers into an essay, arousing their interest and providing them with intriguing background material. Traditional introductions usually reflect common strategies.

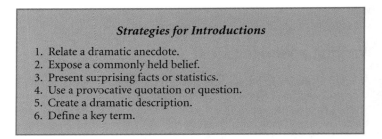

Strategies for Introductions

1. Relate a dramatic anecdote.
2. Expose a commonly held belief.
3. Present surprising facts or statistics.
4. Use a provocative quotation or question.
5. Create a dramatic description.
6. Define a key term.

For most essays, your introduction will be a paragraph or two, usually ending with the thesis statement. For example, student writer Joan Ackers places her thesis at the end of a series of brief descriptions.

> From a page in a high-fashion magazine, an attractive woman in boots, jeans, and bomber jacket stares at the reader. From the back of a newsmagazine, a cowboy in hat and sheepskin coat leans on a fence and stares at the distant mountains. On another page, a young couple sit in a tavern and stare lovingly into each other's eyes, and on yet another page a camel in tuxedo struts its stuff in a nightclub. These are all central images in cigarette advertisements, and each figure is smoking. Generally, *cigarette advertisers employ powerful imagery to sell their products.*

John Halliwell, in "Subtle Persuasion," devotes two paragraphs to his introduction and closes with his thesis statement. Whether composed of one or two paragraphs, an introduction should be no longer than one-fifth of the entire essay. Remember that an introduction should arouse your reader's interest and showcase your thesis.

45n Write the discussion paragraphs.

Discussion paragraphs develop the thesis statement. Discussion paragraphs present the subpoints and supporting details necessary to convince your reader that the thesis is reasonable. In other words, the discussion keeps the promise implied in the thesis.

To be effective, discussion paragraphs should follow three paragraph conventions (see 44a–44g).

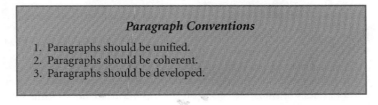

> ### *Paragraph Conventions*
>
> 1. Paragraphs should be unified.
> 2. Paragraphs should be coherent.
> 3. Paragraphs should be developed.

Unity. Discussion paragraphs are unified when the information they present clearly relates to the idea expressed in the topic sentence. Remember—the topic sentence advances the thesis statement's promise by identifying and developing one subpoint.

Coherence. Discussion paragraphs are coherent when readers move smoothly and logically from one sentence to another—that is, when the main idea advances from sentence to sentence in a well-constructed verbal web. When a paragraph lacks coherence, readers will lose interest.

> ### *Techniques to Achieve Coherence*
>
> 1. Put details in proper order (44c).
> 2. Use transitional words and phrases (44d).
> 3. Repeat key words and phrases (44e).
> 4. Use parallel structure (44f).
> 5. Follow traditional development strategies (44g).

Development. Beginning writers often ask, How long should a discussion paragraph be? Paragraph length depends on several considerations.

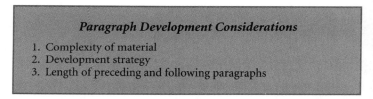

Paragraph Development Considerations
1. Complexity of material
2. Development strategy
3. Length of preceding and following paragraphs

Most important, a discussion paragraph should be developed enough to do justice to its main idea in the topic sentence.

Well-developed paragraphs might contain examples, definitions, comparisons, causes, effects, facts, and statistics—all presented in enough detail to make a paragraph several hundred words long. Or a paragraph might serve as a transition between subpoints of a thesis statement and be only a sentence or two. When a discussion paragraph becomes exceptionally long, writers will often separate the material into two or more paragraphs to ease the reading process, even though the information amplifies the main idea of a single topic sentence.

While composing an essay, you might discover that you need more information to develop an effective paragraph. There are several actions you can take. First, you can return to your prewriting for an idea. Second, you can provide greater detail to the idea that currently exists. Third, you can consult outside sources for more information. The process of inventing and acquiring material continues until the final draft is complete.

450 Write the conclusion.

Too often, beginning writers treat conclusions in a perfunctory manner—a couple of general statements about the subject and a rapid

"That's all, folks" to close. Experienced writers, in contrast, use a different strategy based on the simple principle that readers remember best what they read last. Experienced writers therefore treat writing a conclusion as a challenge, one that demands skill and concentration. Generally, they use one of the following four common strategies to conclude their essays.

Strategies for Conclusions

1. Review the subpoints and restate the essay's thesis statement.
2. Recommend a course of action.
3. Offer a prediction based on the discussion.
4. Present an appropriate quotation or anecdote that leads a reader to reflect about the subject.

Remember that a conclusion must flow logically from the essay. If it does not, it will seem merely tacked on.

Exercise 16

Write the first draft of your essay.

Revising the Working Draft

Once you have a well-structured and well-developed working draft in hand, you are ready to begin revising. Before you begin, however, set aside your draft for a while—overnight if possible—to gain a more objective perspective.

To begin revising, imagine that your reader is sitting by your shoulder as you make revision decisions. When you add content, improve organization, or sharpen your sentences, you are doing so for the reader, the person you want to understand your thesis and to follow its development.

Revising a draft, like composing it, takes place in stages. First, writers revise the major elements, such as content, organization, and point of view. Then, once the major elements are supportive, logical, and consistent, they revise the smaller elements, such as sentence clarity and word selection.

45p Revise for content, organization, and point of view.

Reread your working draft with an eye toward strengthening the content. You might have to add more information or delete some material. Moreover, you will probably need to compose another draft to accommodate the changes.

Adding Content

Some writers skimp on content in their working drafts. They choose to move quickly through the draft, hitting the high points while planning to add detail during the revision stage. To develop more content, they sometimes return to the beginning of the composing process to generate more material—that is, they will develop a list of details, create another cluster, or seek more information.

Deleting Content

Some writers purposefully overwrite their first drafts, knowing that they have generated excessive information. Other times, writers overemphasize a minor point or include too much detail to support it. In these cases the content must be trimmed.

The content of John Halliwell's "Subtle Persuasion" was heavily revised for the final draft. During the revision process, he decided he needed to strengthen the opening with an anecdote. When he added the anecdote, he was forced to delete other sentences. Below is Halliwell's handwritten anecdote and revised introduction.

Recently, I saw a student in a white coat standing outside the entrance to the cafeteria. He gave away samples of toiletries, a colorful bag containing shaving cream, cologne, a plastic razor, toothpaste and toothbrush. He smiled and said, "If you will use these free samples, you will know they are the best."

Was this merely a corporations' kind gesture? Perhaps, but on closer examination it could be a subtle form of persuasion.

~~In almost any department store or supermarket people offer free samples. In department stores they offer perfume and after-shave lotion, in supermarkets, cheeses and dips. These gifts seem to make the manufacturer seem generous. Although manufacturers might be generous, they are also using a subtle form of persuasion.~~ Most of us have been trained to believe that repaying a favor with a favor is important. This is true even if the first favor was not requested. Some of us will often return an unrequested favor rather than feel the pain of being indebted. This behavior has not been lost on those who wish to influence us. ~~They use this behavior to persuade us to their ends.~~ For example, politicians have learned that favors are returned with votes. Charities mail unrequested personal address labels to potential contributors. Companies offer free samples. These politicians, charities, and companies are using a persuasive technique based on reciprocity. A politician, charity, or company seems to be saying, "I have done you a favor. I expect you to do me a favor." Self-interested people use several other ways based on typical behavior to influence our decisions.

Reread your working draft with an eye toward organization. At the most general level, this draft should have a distinct introduction, discussion, and conclusion. But more specifically, each discussion paragraph should be organized by a topic sentence that connects directly to the thesis statement.

Begin by examining the thesis statement and the topic sentences. Your topic sentences should relate directly to the thesis. For example, during the revision of "Subtle Persuasion," John Halliwell revised his thesis statement by adding the key word *strategies.*

Halliwell's Working Thesis

Self-interested people use several ways based on typical behavior to influence our decisions.

Halliwell's Revised Thesis

Self-interested people use several strategies based on typical behavior to influence our decisions.

He then revised each topic sentence to include the key word *strategies,* thus creating a coherent web that connects the thesis statement with each discussion paragraph.

For the final draft, Halliwell integrated the thesis statement into his text more smoothly. He deleted *self-interested people* and *based on typical behavior* because both were obvious in his text.

> ### Halliwell's Final Thesis
> Reciprocity is only one of several subtle strategies used to influence our decisions.
>
> ### Halliwell's Topic Sentences
> Another of these strategies takes the form of social validation.
> The exploitation of "mindless consistency" is another strategy that works to influence our behavior.
> Authority when used as a strategy to influence behavior can be exploitive.

Once the topic sentences are revised so they clearly relate to the thesis statement, check each body paragraph to be sure the content relates directly to the topic sentence. Finally, examine the conclusion to see that it follows logically from the discussion. It is important to make sure your conclusion restates or at least echoes the thesis statement.

Reread your essay to be sure the point of view is consistent. In the broadest sense, writers present their material from a personal or impersonal point of view. A personal point of view places the writer in the experience, which is reflected by the use of personal pronouns (*I, me, my, we, us, our*). Sometimes writers address their readers directly, which is reflected in second-person pronouns (*you, your*). An impersonal point of view seldom directly addresses the reader or uses personal pronouns. Personal point of view usually presents personal experience and observation; impersonal point of view usually presents reports and research.

Your material will usually dictate which point of view to use. You would not write about your childhood experiences in an impersonal way, nor would you write from historical, social, or scientific research in a personal way. When revising for point of view, ask yourself where the material came from. From research? From reports by others? From personal experience? The point of view will follow from the answer.

John Halliwell, in "Subtle Persuasion," wrote from a personal point of view. The information comes from his experience and observations. But he chooses not to use the first person pronoun *I*, which characterizes a great deal of personal writing, because he selects material that a universal audience would recognize and share. During revision, he made the point of view consistent by deleting *I* and emphasizing *we* and *us* to show that everyone has encountered these manipulative techniques.

> Another of these strategies takes the form of social validation.
> *everyone is*
> At certain times, ~~I have been~~ uncertain about how to behave.
> *Perhaps*   *someone will be*
> ~~Once~~ in a restaurant ~~I was~~ uncertain about what fork to use
>   *ͻ*
> for the salad, ~~so I watch which fork my date picked up first.~~
>   *,*   *another person might be*
> ~~Another time~~ at a wedding ~~I was~~ uncertain about how to greet
>   *ͻ*
> the bride, ~~so I asked my friend.~~ At a religious gathering
> *yet another person*
> ~~you~~ might be uncertain about how to participate in an unfa-
>   *we*
> miliar ceremony. In typical situations such as these, ~~I, like~~
> ~~most people,~~ tend to decide correct behavior based on what
> other people do or think.

Exercise 17

Revise your first draft for content, organization, and point of view. Reread your essay. Note points that might need more development or support. Generate more content and work it into your paper. Reread for organization, making sure that the discussion paragraphs reflect the thesis statement. Reread for point of view, making the necessary revisions to keep the point of view consistent. Revise the draft once again, if necessary.

45q Revise and edit sentences.

Once you are satisfied that the paper's organization is logical, the content is well developed and balanced, and the point of view is consistent, then you are ready to focus on the individual sentences.

Revise your sentences with an eye for effectiveness—that is, for clarity, variety, conciseness, diction, and style. Begin with a new, clean draft. Reread the essay slowly, preferably out loud. The ear often detects problems that the eye misses. As you read, make improvements directly on the page.

Once the individual sentences say and mean precisely what you need them to, then edit them for correctness: check their grammar, spelling, mechanics, and punctuation. Also make these changes directly on the page. Print out a new, clean draft that includes all of these changes.

For ESL Writers

Before revising and editing your sentences, review chapter 15, "Reminders for ESL Writers," to review common mistakes that second-language students make.

1. Sentence Completeness
2. Verb Combinations
3. Faulty Repetitions
4. Participles Used as Adjectives
5. Coordinate Elements

After incorporating the changes he made in his introduction to "Subtle Persuasion," John Halliwell revised and edited his introductory paragraph in the following fashion.

Recently, a student in a white coat stood outside the entrance
~~to the~~ cafeteria. He ~~gave away~~ *handed out* samples of toiletries, a colorful

bag containing shaving cream, cologne, a plastic razor, tooth-

paste, and toothbrush. He smiled and said, "If you use these

free samples, you will know they are the best."

Generally, many of us
~~Most of us~~ have been trained to believe that repaying a

favor with a favor is important. ~~This is true~~ even if the first

favor was not requested. Some of us will often return an

unrequested favor rather than feel the pain of being indebted.

pattern
This behavior has not been lost on those who wish to influence
others
~~us.~~ For example, politicians have learned that favors are

returned with votes. Charities mail unrequested personal

address labels to potential contributors. Companies offer free

All
samples. ~~These politicians, charities, and companies~~ are using

a persuasive technique based on reciprocity. A politician,

charity, or company seems to be saying, "I have done you a

Reciprocity is only one of
favor. I expect you to do me a favor." ~~Self-interested people use~~

subtle *used*
several strategies ~~based on typical behavior~~ to influence our

decisions.

Exercise 18

Revise your essay for clarity, variety, and correctness.

45r Proofread the final draft and write a title.

Once you have thoroughly revised and edited your essay, you are ready to prepare the final manuscript (see manuscript form, 45s) and write a title.

Proofreading requires a special kind of attention. You are looking for such errors as misspellings, missing words, dropped endings of words, and typographical mistakes. Some writers proofread their manuscripts by reading them backward, one sentence at a time. Reading backward in this fashion will distract your mind from the essay's meaning so that you can concentrate on the essay's technical features. Keep in mind that you are now preparing the draft your reader will see. A carefully proofread essay will reflect the effort you have given the entire project.

Often the last step in the composing process is writing the title. A title is not an afterthought, a phrase hastily typed at the top of the page before you rush to class. A title actually begins the essay and should suggest the general subject while serving as an invitation to read the essay. A title should be brief but interesting and may be taken directly from the essay itself. Often, however, a title will echo a thought that runs through the essay.

John Halliwell offers the following comment about his title.

> "Subtle Persuasion" came to me while I was editing my final draft. I realized that it was a recurring phrase throughout the essay and captured the idea that people who use the techniques I identified were not bashing us over the head, but in a way seducing us in very subtle ways.

Exercise 19

As a final step, proofread and title your essay.

45s Use proper manuscript form.

Following standard manuscript form is a courtesy to the reader. These standard guidelines, as set by the Modern Language Association, make a paper easy to read.

Materials

For handwritten papers use 8½-by–11-inch lined white paper with neat edges, not pages torn from a spiral notebook. Use black or blue ink—not green or red—and write on one side only. Skip every other line to make reading and correcting easier.

For typewritten or computer-printed papers use 8½-by–11-inch white typing paper. Do not use onionskin because it is flimsy; do not use erasable bond because it smudges. You may use correction fluid ("white out") to cover any typing errors you have made. Double-space between lines and type on one side only. Be sure that you have a fresh ribbon in the typewriter and that the keys are clean.

Use a type style or font that is standard and easily readable—that is not italic, cursive, or outlined. For computer-printed manuscripts, use a letter-quality printer or a dot matrix printer in a letter-quality mode.

Unless otherwise directed, use a paper clip to hold the pages together. Many instructors do not like pages stapled together, and no instructor likes the upper-left-hand corner to have been dog-eared to hold the pages in place.

Margins

Leave margins of one inch on all sides of the paper to avoid a crowded appearance. On lined white paper, the vertical line indicates a proper left-hand margin. On most computers, justification of the right margin creates awkwardly spaced lines. Turn the right justification control off while formatting your paper on a computer.

Indentions

Indent the first line of every paragraph uniformly—one inch in a handwritten manuscript, five spaces in a typewritten one, one-half inch in a typeset one.

Paging

Place the page number, in arabic numerals (*2*, not *II*), without a period or parentheses, in the upper-right-hand corner, one-half inch from the top of each page. You may omit the number on the first page, but if you choose to include it, center it at the bottom.

Identification

Include your name, your instructor's name, the course title and number, the date, and any other information your instructor requests. Place that information on separate double-spaced lines, beginning in the upper-left-hand corner of the first page. Place the line that your name is on, one inch from the top of the page. Also put your last name in the upper-right-hand corner, with the page number: Halliwell 3. (See the sample research paper, 49e.)

Title

In handwritten papers on lined paper, place the title in the center of the first line and begin the first sentence two lines below it. In typed papers, double-space below the date and center your title on the page. Begin the first sentence two lines below it. Capitalize the first and last words, any word that follows a colon, and all other words except articles, conjunctions, and prepositions. Do not underline the title or place quotation marks around it. If, however, the title of another work or a quotation is part of your title, underline or use quotation marks as appropriate. (See quotation marks, 28b; italics, 37a; capitals, 34c.)

45t Follow guidelines for peer review sessions.

Writers sometimes have difficulty seeing problems in their essays because they have worked so closely with the material. What seems clear to them may be confusing to a reader who has intellectual and emotional distance from the essay. Sharing an early draft with classmates in peer review sessions during the revision process reveals confusing areas of a draft and often points the way to revision.

In many English composition courses, instructors set aside class time for students to respond to early drafts. For these peer review sessions, an instructor will usually provide a list of specific guidelines

based on the assignment's requirements. He or she will arrange the class in small groups, establish a review process, and then set the process in motion.

In courses other than composition, instructors seldom organize peer review sessions, yet informal peer review sessions can be a valuable asset in these courses. You may wish, therefore, to organize informal review sessions in which you and three or four of your classmates respond to early drafts.

Offer Specific Responses

The most effective responses are those that identify a draft's strengths and weaknesses. Vague and general observations do little to help a writer. For example, the following two reviewers responded to a fellow student's essay introduction. One response is ineffective, and the other is effective.

INEFFECTIVE RESPONSE

Overall the introduction is terrific. You set up the thesis well, and I know what the discussion will cover. The wording of the thesis is a little weak. You may want to revise it.

There is little in this response that identifies in specific terms what the writer is doing that makes the introduction "terrific," nor is there a suggestion that will help the writer improve the thesis statement.

EFFECTIVE RESPONSE

Your introduction is particularly effective. You use specific, dramatic examples, then you close with a thesis statement that leads smoothly into the following discussion. Unlike the examples, however, your thesis statement is weakly worded. I suggest you rewrite it and use a verb and a key phrase that you can repeat or reword throughout the rest of the paper to help you create unity. Your key verb is now "use." Try rewriting the thesis by using a word such as "trick," "fool," or "seduce." A more active verb will give your paper more energy.

344 *Writing the Essay*

The latter response clearly identifies the introduction's strength—that is, specific, dramatic examples—and then identifies and suggests a solution for a problem in the thesis sentence.

Writing Responses

When you respond to someone else's draft, do not be distracted by surface errors—that is, do not correct grammar, punctuation, and mechanics. Inform the writer that these errors exist, but it is the writer's job to proofread carefully and correct such errors. Instead, concentrate on the larger elements. Keep in mind, too, that it is better to write your responses on a separate sheet of paper than on the draft itself.

Questions for Peer Review Responses

1. What is the dominant purpose and thesis statement?
2. Does the overall structure develop logically?
3. Where is the writing confusing?
4. Should more information or examples be added? Why?
5. What is the essay's main strength? What are its weaknesses?

During peer review sessions, remember that your task is not to rewrite the draft but to respond as a reader and to offer suggestions for improvement.

Discussing Responses

Until writers have experience with peer review, they may be sensitive to what they perceive as criticism. When discussing a draft with a writer, it is usually best to offer objectively descriptive comments rather than subjectively evaluative comments.

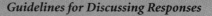

> ### Guidelines for Discussing Responses
>
> 1. A review session should be a dialogue between you and the writer, not a monologue.
> 2. Ask questions. Develop a clear understanding of the writer's goals.
> 3. Use your notes and begin by stating the draft's strengths.
> 4. Link suggestions for improvement to the writer's goals.
> 5. Close by summarizing ways the writer can improve the draft.

Integrating Peer Responses

You must evaluate the responses you receive during a peer review session. This evaluation is not always easy. Sometimes the responses will conflict, often reflecting one reader's blind spot or bias rather than identifying a particular problem in your draft. Other times the responses will agree, giving you a clear direction for revision. It is up to you to decide which responses are appropriate and which are inappropriate based on your goals for the draft. Remember, ultimately the responsibility for the final draft is yours, not your reviewers'.

46 Writing the Argument Essay and Critical Thinking *arg*

Thinking generally means any sort of mental activity, from idle daydreaming to rigid mathematical analysis. *Critical thinking* specifically refers to the thought processes that engage the mind in deliberate inquiry. *Analysis, synthesis,* and *evaluation* are three mental activities essential to critical thinking.

> ### *Critical Thinking Activities*
>
> 1. *Analysis* emphasizes breaking down a problem into parts to examine their relationship.
> 2. *Synthesis* emphasizes the process of combining separate ideas to create a new pattern that was not clearly apparent before.
> 3. *Evaluation* involves assessing the reasoning behind a position to judge its validity.

In writing, critical thinking finds its most direct expression in argumentation. By using argumentation, writers attempt to change or reinforce a reader's opinion or to move that reader to take action. Often an argument essay may be emotionally charged, appealing to a reader's feelings with emotional detail or biased language. This is called *persuasive argument.* Or an argument essay may be highly rational, appealing to a reader's intellect with logical discussion. This is called *logical argument.* Political writing relies heavily on persuasive argument, whereas academic writing relies heavily on logical argument. With the exception of highly scientific argument, however, an argument essay seldom appeals only to emotion or only to reason.

A general guideline to follow is that an argument essay should be primarily rational or it may fail to convince a critical reader. Successful writers of effective arguments usually present their opinions persuasively but develop ample and strong evidence. This practice impresses upon readers that the writer is *ethical*—that is, a well-informed, reasonable person committed to his or her position and, therefore, worthy of being believed.

46a Evaluate facts and opinions you might use in an essay.

When writing an argument essay, you will take a stand on a debatable issue, a stand that relies on reasoned opinion, not on clear-cut facts.

A **fact** in itself is not debatable. A factual statement reflects how something actually exists and can be objectively verified. These are factual statements: Republican presidents held the White House for twelve years, from 1980 to 1992. The moon is earth's only satellite. Hawaii became a state in 1959.

Statistics are collections of numerical facts. For example, the average American uses three gallons of paint a week. This amount adds up to more than a billion gallons every year, enough to fill a lake 20 feet deep, 4 miles long, and 1 mile wide. Statistics are often referred to as *alleged facts*. An alleged fact is one that needs verification before people will accept it. For example, the statement "The junk mail Americans receive in one day could produce enough energy to heat 250,000 homes" may be a fact, but it would not be accepted without further verification.

When analyzing an argument—your own or that of another writer—you must often separate fact from opinion. **Opinion** is what a person believes and is not necessarily true merely because someone believes it. Opinions can take several forms.

A **preference** expresses taste—that is, what someone likes or dislikes. Such statements as "Suspense movies are my favorite" or "Racquetball is a great workout" express a person's preference. Generally, preferences offer no grounds for argument. How can someone be wrong for liking a type of movie or a particular sport?

A **judgment** is an opinion with a basis for support. Preferences can often be restated as judgments. For example, the statement "Suspense movies, more than romances or westerns, reflect society's ills" can be discussed reasonably by concentrating on the social criticism embedded in romance, western, and suspense movies. The statement "Racquetball offers a more sustained aerobic workout than tennis does" creates the opportunity to compare the physical demands of racquetball and tennis. Both statements clearly reflect opinions that can be supported to convince readers of their validity.

An **inference** is a conclusion drawn from a fact or set of facts. An inference does not embody a judgment but rather forms an assumption from evidence. For example, in your hometown the elementary school is overcrowded, no new teachers will be hired because of budget cuts, the city council has just approved the building of a thousand homes, and an apartment complex is scheduled to open. From these facts you may reasonably infer that next year the elementary school will be even more crowded than it currently is.

As with all inferences, yours is subject to testing. You may or may not be correct. For example, the bulk of school overcrowding might be caused by students in their last year of elementary school, the state might increase school funding, the approved homes might not be built for three years, and the apartments might be slated for elderly housing—all of which could invalidate your inference.

An **interpretation** offers an opinion on the significance or meaning of something. An interpretation is speculative, an attempt to look beneath the surface at a deeper truth. Personal experience, literary works, cultural phenomena, and historical events are often used as the basis of interpretation.

In the political arena, suspicious facts often fuel conflicting interpretations. For example, the Japanese military's surprise bombing of Pearl Harbor on December 7, 1941, brought the United States into World War II. Later, some historians charged that President Roosevelt had advance knowledge of the attack but did not warn our military. Their accusation is based mainly on the interpretation of one suspicious fact: by the summer of 1940, the United States had cracked Japan's top-secret diplomatic code, which enabled intelligence agencies to monitor messages to and from Tokyo. Some historians interpret this to mean that President Roosevelt wanted to use the attack as a reason to involve the United States in World War II. To counter this interpretation, however, other historians have pointed out that code-breaking intelligence could not have prevented the attack on Pearl Harbor because Japan did not send any messages about the planned attack.

The validity of an interpretation is usually difficult to verify. Often only careful analysis will reveal whether a particular interpretation of an act or an event is accurate.

46b Identify a purpose and develop a strategy for an argument essay.

Identifying the purpose of an argument essay is similar to identifying the purpose of any other essay (see 45a, p. 294; 45h). A purpose statement should identify the subject and how you wish to develop it. Consider the following examples.

> I want to argue that the use of animals in scientific research is necessary to protect humankind.

The subject is quite clear. The writer will discuss animals used in scientific research. The method of development is also clear. The writer will argue that research using animals is necessary.

> I want to convince my readers that campus police should be armed.

The subject is arming campus police, and the writer will argue to do so.

> I will argue that films featuring characters who smoke cigarettes should carry the surgeon general's warning that smoking is hazardous to a smoker's health.

Here, too, the subject—films featuring characters who smoke—and the method of development—to argue that the public should be warned about the hazards of smoking—are clear.

Once you have a clear purpose statement, you are ready to create a strategy to use in the development of your paper. Developing a strategy for an argument essay is much like creating an informal plan for an expository essay, but with a major difference. In an argument essay, you must develop a list of arguments that support your position and a list of arguments that oppose your position.

List Supporting Arguments.

Begin by developing a list of arguments you might use to support your position. Suppose you want to argue that films featuring characters who smoke cigarettes should carry the surgeon general's warning. You might develop a list of supporting arguments similar to the following:

—Scientific evidence shows that smoking is hazardous to health.
  —Smoking causes lung cancer.
  —Smoking affects the fetuses of pregnant women.
  —Smoking causes emphysema.
—Because of the health hazards of smoking, advertisements for cigarettes have been banned from television and radio. Moreover, cigarette advertisements in magazines carry a warning of the health hazards of smoking.
—Many classic films feature romantic characters who smoke. A famous actor, Humphrey Bogart, died of lung cancer.
—Many current films perpetuate smoking by featuring romantic characters who smoke.
—Several cigarette companies realize the advertising value of having film characters smoke their brands and have paid film companies to feature their brands.

List Opposing Arguments.

Once you have listed supporting arguments, list opposing arguments. An effective tactic for developing a list of opposing arguments is to discuss the issue with someone who disagrees with your position. The discussion can provide you with valuable information you might have overlooked. Here is a list of opposing arguments against identifying movies that feature characters who smoke.

—There is no practical way to evaluate the impact on viewer behavior of characters who smoke in films.
—Much information already exists about the hazards of smoking, so film viewers must already be aware of the dangers.
—Films reflect reality. Many people smoke, so why should films be held accountable for reflecting that reality?
—Forcing film companies to label films is just one more government attempt to interfere with free expression in the arts.

Reconsider your Position.

After developing a list of supporting and opposing arguments, you might reconsider your position. Perhaps the supporting arguments are weak and the opposing arguments are strong. In this situation you would probably be unable to convince readers that you are right, even though you still believe in your original position. Perhaps your position is oversimplified, too extreme, or merely rooted in a preference. In these situations you might rethink your position, attempting to search beyond the obvious; modify your extreme thinking, or rephrase your preference so you can support it.

Consider your Audience.

An important part of creating a strategy for an argument essay is to consider your audience carefully (see 45c, p. 304). Are you writing for readers who might already agree with your position? Are you writing for hostile readers? Are you writing for readers who are uninformed? For senior citizens? For students?

By identifying your audience, you will be able to decide which arguments to emphasize. For example, to convince parents that movies featuring characters who smoke should display a health warning, you might emphasize that teenagers often model their behavior on entertainers. You might further emphasize that even though information about the dangers of smoking is broadly publicized, the teen market for cigarettes is expanding.

46c Develop and evaluate evidence to support your arguments.

Once your purpose and strategy are identified, you must compile evidence to support your position. Only accurate and effective evidence will persuade readers to accept your position and reject the opposing position.

If any of your evidence is based on research, you must acknowledge your sources (see 49c). There are several different types of evidence you can use in an argument essay, but some types are more convincing than others.

Using Facts and Statistics

Often the most convincing argument you can develop is based on facts and statistics. Facts and statistics, when used appropriately, are irrefutable but will not carry an argument in themselves. Instead, they serve as the basis for an inference. For example, research from the Industry Safety Council in Washington, DC, points out the following facts about automobile tires.

> —Americans wear nearly 50 million pounds of rubber off their tires every two weeks, enough to make 3.25 million new tires from scratch.
> —Some 240–260 million tires are discarded each year in the United States.
> —Billions of tires currently fill up landfill space.
> —It takes half a barrel of crude oil to produce the rubber in one truck tire.

In themselves these facts are merely surprising in their magnitude, but if used to argue a case for recycling tires, they could be compelling.

When using facts and statistics, you must be sure the inferences you draw are reasonable. No one, for example, can dispute the fact that four powerful advocates of African American rights—John F. Kennedy, Malcolm X, Martin Luther King, Jr., and Robert Kennedy—were assassinated in the 1960s. But the interpretation of this fact as proof of a powerful anti–civil rights conspiracy is highly debatable.

Using Informed Authorities

In daily life we rely on a variety of authorities. Dentists evaluate the condition of our teeth. Critics recommend films and books. Weather forecasters tell us to prepare for rain or sunshine. In an argument essay you can rely on authority to support your opinion, but you must be sure your authority is an expert in the field. To argue for special psychological treatment for children who are victims of natural catastrophes, rely on developmental psychologists, not law enforcement officers. To argue for government-supported child care, rely on educational experts, not political activists.

Avoid using recognized experts in one field as authorities in an unrelated field. For example, a Nobel Prize–winning biologist might have opinions about the economy but is probably not an authority on the economy.

Also avoid using biased authorities. For example, a film executive's opinion about the social effects of violence in popular movies probably will not be objective.

Avoid using *nameless* authorities. Although "doctors maintain," "three hundred scientists surveyed," and "nationally recognized educators" are often cited by advertisers, to do so in an argument essay would detract from its credibility.

Using Observations

You can rely on your own observations and the observations of others as evidence to support your opinion. In fact, often the most vivid and dramatic evidence results from personal observations. A traveler's report from a foreign country; a friend's exchange with law enforcement officers; your own encounter with the college bureaucracy; or a visit to a polluted river, beach, or industrial site—all can add color and significant information to an argument essay.

When using personal observations as evidence, do all you can to present accurate information. You know how accurate a description of your own experience is because you lived it, but when you present the experience of others, you are, in effect, vouching for its veracity. It is often wise, therefore, to include more than one account of the same event.

Personal observations become even more compelling when used in conjunction with other forms of evidence. For example, to develop an argument to convince officials to protect an ecologically sensitive salt marsh, you might visit the site and report your observations. If your observations can also be supported by authorities, facts, and statistics, then your observation and the argument's validity will be difficult to challenge.

Three Criteria to Evaluate Evidence

1. *Evidence should be relevant:* Evidence should support an argument directly. It should not digress from the point.
2. *Evidence should be representative:* Evidence should embody the full range of opinion. Expert opinion and personal observations should be typical, not exceptional.
3. *Evidence should be sufficient:* Evidence should be ample enough to support your point. The amount of evidence needed to be sufficient depends on the audience and the point.

46d Confront the opposition.

During the evidence-gathering process, keep in mind that you must confront the opposing arguments you identified when planning a strategy. If you neglect to confront the opposition, your essay will be ineffective because you will not have dissuaded the reader from those opposing arguments. By confronting objections to your position, you are actively convincing readers that your arguments are sound and that you are a reasonable person, thus making your case even stronger.

You can confront opposing arguments by showing that they are unreasonable, unfair, or even weak and emotional. If, however, the opposing position is so compelling that it is not easily dismissed, then concede its strength and go on to make an even stronger case for your position.

46e Write an argumentative thesis statement and sketch a plan.

An argumentative thesis statement, sometimes referred to as a *proposition,* serves as the center of your essay (see 45j). Take a stand in your thesis; that is, clearly state your position so readers will have no doubt about your sympathies.

> Television stations should not be allowed to broadcast children's programs that feature violent encounters.

> Class attendance should not be a factor in grading.

> The high-fashion fur industry should be stopped.

Sometimes you might identify the opposing position in your thesis statement.

> Although censoring magazines that feature nudity would violate freedom of expression, these magazines should not be sold in community vending machines.

> Even though some ranchers will lose livestock to wolf packs, for ecological reasons wolves should be reintroduced into the western national parks.

> Police maintain that they do not target college-age drivers, but the evidence shows that police consistently abuse their authority near the university.

Notice that in each of these statements the writer takes a clear stand on a debatable point, one with which reasonable people could disagree.

Once you have written a clear thesis statement, you are ready to plan the development of your essay in sentence form. The points you state in your development plan can serve as topic sentences for the finished essay. Your thesis statement and development plan, therefore, will give you a sketch or rough outline for your final paper. Consider the following example. The writer wanted to argue that movie violence should not be censored. Furthermore, he wanted to convince his readers that the skillful use of violence heightens audience interest.

THESIS	Despite charges that movie violence triggers social violence, the evidence shows that no causal relationship exists between imaginary violence and human behavior, and, moreover, violence used skillfully in movies heightens audience interest.
DEVELOPMENT	—Some movies use violence in irresponsible ways.
	—No study has shown a causal connection between movie violence and actual violent behavior.
	—Since violence pervades actual life, viewers demand that movies depict violence to reflect reality.
	—Although many movies feature gratuitous violence, others use skillfully crafted violence to engage viewers in positive ways.
	—Even such mild fare as *Bambi* and *The Wizard of Oz* use carefully crafted violence to heighten viewer awareness.
	—The careful crafting of violence to achieve dramatic purposes has its roots in classical literature.

The development pattern of this essay is clear. The author would first write an introduction that presents the thesis statement. He would then concede that many movies feature gratuitous violence, but he would also point out that even if gratuitous violence is a characteristic of many films, it still has no proven effect on audience behavior. Next the writer would develop the supporting arguments: violence is part of real life; skillfully crafted violence engages viewers in positive ways; even classic children's films use violence; and finally, violence plays a significant role in literature in general.

46f Compose your essay.

Argument essays are structured like most expository essays. They have three main parts: an introduction, a discussion, and a conclusion (see 45a, p. 295).

The Introduction

An argument may be won or lost in the introduction. To write an effective introduction, you must achieve two goals. First, an introduction should put you on common ground with readers who might not share your views. It is always a mistake to write a strident introduction that may offend readers whose support you are trying to gain. Instead, encourage readers to identify with your position. Show that you share their values. Present yourself as a thoughtful, reasonable person whose opinions should be considered seriously.

Second, end your introduction by clearly expressing in a thesis statement your position on an issue. If your thesis statement is not presented clearly and concisely, readers might decide that you are uncertain about your own views, and are perhaps using the essay to define your position rather than to argue for it.

Although there are many introductory strategies, three are commonly used.

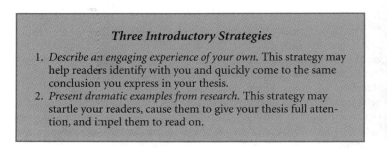

Three Introductory Strategies

1. *Describe an engaging experience of your own.* This strategy may help readers identify with you and quickly come to the same conclusion you express in your thesis.
2. *Present dramatic examples from research.* This strategy may startle your readers, cause them to give your thesis full attention, and impel them to read on.

> 3. *Quote a notable authority.* This strategy shows that you have thoughtfully considered your position and placed it in a philosophical context. When quoting a notable authority, do not let the quotation stand alone, unexplained. Instead, explain it as a significant reflection of your position.

The Discussion

As with an expository essay, an argument essay's discussion section is composed of several paragraphs. You should accomplish two goals in the discussion. First, present the evidence that supports your position. Arrange your support in paragraphs organized by topic sentences. Each paragraph should further your argument, sticking to the point and marshaling evidence in a logical sequence.

Second, confront and refute opposing arguments. Generally, writers use one of two strategies to refute opposing arguments. One strategy is to present the opposing arguments early, following the introduction and thesis statement. This is an especially effective strategy to use if the opposing arguments are brief and relatively weak. The tactic is to state the opposing arguments succinctly and then point out their deficiencies. Michael W. Hirschorn uses this tactic in "Facing Up to Sexism." Hirschorn argues that the Harvard College newspaper, *The Crimson,* should have refused to publish a recruitment advertisement for *Playboy.* Early in the discussion, he states two opposing arguments and refutes them.

> Some will argue that refusing to publish an advertisement infringes on freedom of speech. Not really, for advertising is not free speech, and, in any case, the *Playboy* ad is not an opinion. As one editor noted at Sunday's in-house discussion of the ad issue, one must be able to disagree with an opinion, and the counter argument to the *Playboy* solicitation is "No, a *Playboy* photographer will *not* be at the Somerville Holiday Inn this week."

After confronting these two opposing arguments, Hirschorn concentrates on his supporting arguments.

A second strategy that writers use to confront opposing arguments is to refute them from paragraph to paragraph throughout the discussion. This tactic is especially effective if the opposing arguments are lengthy and complex. Pediatrician Ron Karpati uses this tactic to argue that, contrary to the claims of animal rights activists, animals are necessary for medical research. The following example is one of his several discussion paragraphs that directly refute an opposing argument.

> Much is made of the pain inflicted on these animals in the name of medical science. The animal-rights activists contend that this is evidence of our malevolent and sadistic nature. A more reasonable argument, however, can be advanced in our defense. Life is often cruel, both to animals and human beings. Teenagers get thrown from the back of a pickup truck and suffer severe head injuries. Toddlers, barely able to walk, find themselves at the bottom of a swimming pool while a parent checks the mail. Physicians hoping to alleviate the pain and suffering these tragedies cause have three choices: create an animal model of the injury or disease and use that model to understand the process and test new therapies; experiment on human beings—some experiments will succeed, most will fail—or finally, leave medical knowledge static, hoping that accidental discoveries will lead us to the advances.
>
> —Ron Karpati,
> "A Scientist: 'I Am the Enemy'"

The Conclusion

The conclusion of an argument essay should effectively emphasize the writer's position. Writers tend to emphasize their positions directly by summarizing the thesis and main points or indirectly by using various techniques that appeal to the reader's reason or emotions.

> ### *Three Concluding Strategies*
>
> 1. *Relate a personal experience.* Just as a personal experience can serve as an effective opening, it can also dramatically conclude an argument essay. The experience should clearly reinforce your position.
> 2. *Make a direct appeal to readers.* Direct appeals often embody a call to action or a call to solve a specific problem.
> 3. *Describe the consequences.* If an essay argues for specific action, an effective conclusion can project the consequences of not taking action.

46g Evaluate inductive and deductive reasoning with care.

Inductive reasoning moves from specific evidence to a general conclusion. You have been using inductive reasoning throughout your life. For example, imagine that you were given the wrong date the first time you registered for college classes. Against all reason, you were not allowed to register even though you had waited in line for an hour. "Come back Friday," you were told. "That's the right day." The second semester, you discovered that the class numbers had been printed incorrectly, and you had to return to revise your schedule. The third semester, the procedure went well, but you discovered on the first day of classes that you were not on any class roster. "We just can't explain it," a clerk said. "I guess it was a computer glitch." By induction—that is, by interpreting the meaning of these experiences—you conclude that your college's registration procedures are frustrating.

Inductive arguments are built piece by piece. As the evidence mounts, your reader is persuaded to accept the conclusion you intend. For example, one student argued that her college had an

advanced gender awareness program. She began with the question regarding gender awareness at Riverbank College. She then planned to present the evidence inductively.

QUESTION
Is Riverbank College responsible in the area of gender bias?

EVIDENCE
—Riverbank College has gender awareness workshops for students, faculty, administrators, and support staff.
—The college has revised its course catalog, class schedule, and policy statements to embody gender-neutral language.
—The college has created a standing committee to review and arbitrate gender-related issues.
—The college has instituted new procedures to eliminate gender bias.

CONCLUSION
Evidence shows that Riverbank College has an advanced gender awareness program.

Conclusions drawn from inductive reasoning are usually referred to as *probable conclusions.* They are, in fact, inferences subject to close examination (see 46a). The reader's acceptance of a conclusion that follows from inductive reasoning is often referred to as the *inductive leap.* When constructing or evaluating an inductive argument, you must be sure that the probable conclusion is clearly connected to the evidence.

Deductive reasoning is the opposite of inductive reasoning. Deductive reasoning begins with general assumptions called *premises* and draws specific conclusions that follow logically from the premises. In formal logic, this pattern is called a *syllogism.* Syllogisms always include a *major premise, a minor premise,* and a *necessary conclusion,* which is the logical result of the two premises. The classic example of syllogistic form comes to us from the philosopher Aristotle.

MAJOR PREMISE	All humans are mortal.
MINOR PREMISE	Socrates is human.
CONCLUSION	Therefore, Socrates is mortal.

When you evaluate a syllogism, keep in mind that accuracy is the key to its validity. If the major and minor premises are accurate, then the conclusion will be accurate and logically sound. Syllogisms, however, can be illogical. For example, an inaccurate major premise may make a syllogism illogical.

MAJOR PREMISE	Computer programmers are shy and seldom socialize.
MINOR PREMISE	Joan Adams is our first female computer programmer.
CONCLUSION	Therefore, she will obviously be shy and seldom socialize with fellow employees.

Clearly, the major premise, which reflects a stereotypical image of computer programmers, is inaccurate. Ask yourself, Are all computer programmers shy and antisocial? At one time or another, aren't most people shy, and don't they sometimes avoid social contact? Because the major premise is inaccurate, the conclusion is inaccurate.

Sometimes the slippery use of language makes a syllogism inaccurate. Consider the use of *good student* and *accept* in this flawed syllogism.

MAJOR PREMISE	All good students accept that teachers have the responsibility for grading their class performance.
MINOR PREMISE	Harold Ward is disputing his history grade from last semester.
CONCLUSION	Therefore, Harold is not a good student.

Good student is a vague concept, too vague to identify a category of students accurately. What does *accept* mean in this context? Teachers make mistakes when grading. Is it unreasonable to ask for a grade change because of a mistake? Colleges have provisions to challenge grades that students believe are unfair. Does using this procedure mean a person is not a "good" student? Clearly, because the language is used deceptively in the premises, the conclusion is illogical.

Syllogisms may also be illogical because they are improperly constructed. First, evaluate a properly constructed syllogism.

MAJOR PREMISE   All economists must master statistics.

In a properly constructed syllogism, the subject of the major premise—in this example, economists—must be repeated in the minor premise.

MINOR PREMISE   Leslie is an economist.

The conclusion then follows necessarily from the major and minor premises.

CONCLUSION   Therefore, Leslie has mastered statistics.

The syllogism is properly constructed and, therefore, logical. Now evaluate the following invalid syllogism.

MAJOR PREMISE   All economists must master statistics.

MINOR PREMISE   Social psychologists must master statistics.

CONCLUSION   Therefore, social psychologists are also economists.

This syllogism is improperly constructed because the minor premise does not repeat the subject of the major premise. The conclusion, therefore, is illogical.

Like inductive reasoning, deductive reasoning can help organize an argument. Deductive arguments, however, are never presented quite as simply in writing as in the skeletal form of syllogisms used to illustrate them.

For example, many deductive arguments do not state one of the premises. The reader must infer this premise. Consider the following syllogistic argument with a major premise, a minor premise, and a conclusion.

> Migrating Canada geese are disappearing from the marshes where they forage each winter. People frighten Canada geese. We must, therefore, restrict the use of the marshes during migration.

Now examine the same argument without the minor premise

> Migrating Canada geese are disappearing from the marshes where they forage each winter, so we must restrict the use of the marshes during migration.

A deductive argument with an unstated premise needs to be evaluated with care, since the omitted premise may be inaccurate. In evaluating the preceding example, you might ask these questions: Do many people visit the marshes during winter months? Are fewer geese migrating south? Have the geese found better foraging sites? Of course, in a successfully developed argument essay, the writer would anticipate these questions and develop evidence to support the conclusion.

46h Avoid committing logical fallacies.

Logical fallacies are common mistakes in reasoning. The word *fallacy* means "deception" or "a fault in reasoning." An argument tainted by logical fallacies is ineffective. Study the nine common fallacies. Remember, you must scrutinize every argument to detect fallacious reasoning.

Hasty Generalization

Writers commit hasty generalization when they draw conclusions from insufficient or unrepresentative evidence.

> In recent years, almost every major college athletic program has been investigated by the NCAA for recruitment violations. Every year, at least one team is placed on probation as a result of these investigations. Clearly those in charge of college athletics must be immoral.

The writer is drawing a conclusion from insufficient evidence. Are all violations of complex regulations a matter of immorality? Perhaps some of the violations are inadvertent or technical. As for the investigations and penalties, they could be an indication of rigorous enforcement of the rules rather than of widespread immorality.

> During the last year, three of five award-winning films concentrated on family violence. An examination of family violence was just broadcast on national television. No doubt these events indicate that family violence is on the rise.

Three films and a television program do not represent a trend. The conclusion that family violence is rising could be substantiated with statistics and reports from such authorities as psychologists, sociologists, and law enforcement officials.

> Politicians, whether currently in office or not, should not be allowed to sit on the boards of nonprofit organizations, such as charities, foundations, and educational institutions. We all know that to win an election a person must always compromise common standards of ethics. Politicians are notorious for representing the individual interests of their supporters and then seeking their financial support in the next election. All of us should fight to keep nonprofit organizations free from this kind of corrupt behavior.

The above argument is based on a common hasty generalization called *stereotyping*. Stereotypes are conclusions—usually negative—drawn from limited information about a particular group of people. Stereotypes have power because many people accept them uncritically and they are often confirmed in the media. For example, if you already believe that politicians are corrupt, your stereotype will be reinforced by political scandals you read about in newspapers and see reported on television. Yet the reality is that only a few politicians of the thousands holding office in city, county, state, and federal governments are ever involved in corruption.

Oversimplification

Writers oversimplify when they ignore essential information from which a conclusion is drawn. Too often, writers are eager to offer a simple explanation for a complicated problem.

> Getting a good grade in a composition class may involve a lot of your time, but there is nothing difficult about it. All you have to do is meet the required word length and avoid errors in grammar and punctuation.

As you doubtless know by now, a good grade in a composition class also requires clear thinking, organizational skills, and a good deal of effort and practice at writing.

Faulty Either/Or Reasoning

Writers commit the either/or fallacy by assuming there are only two alternatives when, in fact, there are many. The slogan "America, love it or leave it," implies that love of country must be unqualified, which has the effect of excluding constructive criticism.

> Drug use is destroying the social order of American cities. The drug problem is so monumental that no one can afford to be neutral. Are we going to do nothing and let criminals rule our cities? Or are we going to give our police more power so that they can control drug traffickers, dealers, and users?

Of course, other actions are possible—initiate public education, fund rehabilitation for drug users, develop agreements with other countries to curtail drug traffic, and so on. The choices are not just between doing nothing and increasing police power.

Post Hoc Argument

When writers assume that one event causes a second event simply because the second follows the first in time, they are committing the *post hoc, ergo propter hoc* ("after this, therefore because of this") fallacy.

> Some people think that microwave ovens are a health threat. I disagree. Our family purchased a microwave oven two years ago. Since then, none of us has seen a doctor.

As stated, the only relation between the purchase of a microwave oven and the good health of this family is that one followed the other in time. Time sequence alone cannot prove the existence of a cause-and-effect relationship.

Non Sequitur

The Latin phrase *non sequitur* means "it does not follow." Writers commit this fallacy when their conclusions do not logically follow from their premises.

> Ryan Beach has the highest per capita income in the state, but it has the lowest-paid police force, city employees, and school-teachers. These facts are revealing. They show that those with money know how to keep government expenses under control.

Many factors contribute to per capita income. Perhaps in a small beach town a few wealthy landowners drive up the average income. Moreover, individuals do not directly pay for city government and schools. These are paid for by tax dollars that may come from state or local government. And, finally, elected city and school officials—none of whom in this specific case may be wealthy—determine employee salaries. Clearly, this writer's conclusion does not follow from the premises.

False Analogy

A writer using false analogy assumes that if two things are similar in one or more characteristics, then they are similar in other characteristics.

> Some people cannot be educated. You can't make a silk purse out of a sow's ear.

Applying the apparent wisdom of folk sayings to real-life situations usually results in false analogy. Education does not change valueless things into valuable things, as the folk saying suggests. It develops already existing intelligence further.

> The European experience in World War II is clear. The lessons should not be ignored. You cannot ignore the rise of a dictator, and you cannot successfully negotiate with one to avoid a war. The best solution is to attack an enemy before he attacks.

Conditions today are not the same as they were before World War II. To compare pre–World War II conditions to the world today is to fall into the trap of false analogy.

Ad Hominem Argument

The Latin phrase *ad hominem* means "to the man." Writers use the *ad hominem* argument when they attack the person who is connected with an issue rather than concentrating on the issue itself.

> The senator has made an interesting case for eliminating the inheritance tax. No wonder! When his father dies, he will inherit millions!

In this statement the writer ignores the senator's arguments for abolishing the inheritance tax and focuses on his personal situation.

> Do not believe film critics. They are all frustrated actors or directors who could not succeed in the film industry.

The statement attacks the film critics rather than discussing inaccuracies or bias in their reviews.

Begging the Question

A frequent error that writers make is reasoning in a circle or "begging the question," as circular reasoning is commonly referred to. In its most fundamental form, a circular argument ends up where it began—merely restructuring the original assumption without introducing actual information.

Welfare recipients are lazy because they don't like to work. Have you heard about someone on welfare who likes to work? That's because welfare recipients are lazy.

The argument travels in a circle, confirming the assumption it makes in the opening assertion.

Emotional Appeals

In critically examining your own and other writers' arguments for errors in reasoning, you should also be aware of several propaganda devices used to sway an audience. Propaganda devices are used to shape opinion by appealing to emotion rather than to reason. In argument essays written for college courses, you win support for your position through reasonable argument, not emotional appeals.

Five Emotional Appeals

1. **Glittering generalities** are virtue words that appeal to such emotions as love, generosity, motherhood, brotherhood, the American way, the natural world, and so on. Writers using glittering generalities frequently use such words as *truth, freedom, honor,* and *love* for the emotions they trigger.
2. **Name calling** is an obvious but surprisingly effective tactic. The tactic, which is often used in conjunction with *ad hominem* arguments, is designed to belittle or arouse contempt for a person or an idea.
3. **Testimonial** involves having loved or respected persons give statements of support (testimonials) for a particular cause, idea, or product. The persons giving the testimonials may not be experts; in fact, they may know nothing at all about the subject.
4. **Plain folks** is the opposite of testimonial. This device differs from testimonial in that the appeal comes from ordinary people with ordinary backgrounds as opposed to the rich and famous.
5. **Bandwagon** appeals to the strong desire to be one of the crowd, part of a peer group, and not to be excluded.

Exercise 20

Identify the logical fallacies in these brief arguments. Be prepared to discuss your choices.

1. I think Ms. Sawyer is the best history teacher at our school. She is a strong conservative.

2. We must reject gun-control laws or sacrifice a sacred right granted to us by the Constitution.

3. Glenview College always has a winning football team because its coach believes in team spirit.

4. The least promising students achieve the greatest success as adults. Winston Churchill's teacher predicted he would be a failure, and William Faulkner, who won the Nobel Prize for literature, never even earned a college degree.

5. Ancient religious leaders were responsible for the sun's rising because they went to high ground every morning and prayed for the sun god to return.

6. Jan is intelligent and hardworking. There is no doubt she will rise to the top of her field.

7. A brain absorbs information just as a sponge absorbs water. But eventually a sponge becomes saturated; it cannot hold any more water. Students, too, reach a saturation point, and then it is foolish to expect them to soak up more information.

8. If I had not gone out of my way to pick up Mia this morning, the car would not have broken down.

9. I do not see how young people can enjoy his music; he has been arrested several times, and his wife left him because he was cruel.

10. Lola Allure, the star of stage, screen, and television, starts every day with Skinny Wafers. Don't you think you should too?

Exercise 21

Write an argument essay in which you express one of your own deeply felt opinions. If the subject you select has undergone extensive public discussion, assume that your reader is familiar with the general elements of the debate and develop specific evidence based on your own observations, reading, and experience. Use the following list to spark your thinking, but do not feel bound by the subjects. Remember, the suggestions are merely broad subjects; any one of them must be narrowed and focused (see 45e, 45h, 45j).

1. Euthanasia
2. Censorship
3. Television violence
4. Film ratings
5. Legalized drugs
6. Animal rights
7. Student codes of conduct
8. Disruptive behavior in public places
9. Subliminal messages in music
10. People on public assistance should work
11. Sex education in public schools
12. Hiring quotas
13. Smoking in public places
14. Alternative ways to combat drug use
15. The power of the beauty myth

47 Writing an Analytical Essay about Literature *lit*

The process of writing analytical essays about literature involves breaking up a work of fiction, poetry, or drama into its component parts and concentrating on a single element of the work.

47a Select an appropriate subject for analysis.

When selecting a single element as the subject of your analysis, be sure that the element is central to the work's meaning. If the author of a short story made little use of symbols, then you would be mistaken to analyze the use of symbols in that story. If the psychological development of a character, however, were central to the story, then writing a character analysis would be appropriate.

Traditionally, analytical essays have concentrated on several subjects, many of which are discussed in the following paragraphs.

Characterization refers to the way in which an author presents the characters within a work. Two types of characters appear in fiction and drama—flat and round. A *flat character* usually has a single outstanding trait and stays the same throughout a work. A *round character* may have several traits, usually learns from his or her experiences, and changes in the course of the work. An analysis of character might begin with the following questions: How is this character developed? What is he or she like? In what ways does he or she learn or change?

Plot usually refers to the meaningful arrangement of events in a narrative. Authors arrange events in patterns and establish causal relations among them. For the most part, plot is generated by conflict. At a simple level, conflict arises when a character wants to achieve something but must overcome barriers to reach his or her goal. Conflict may be external or internal. *Internal conflict* takes place within the mind of a character, whereas *external conflict* takes place between characters or between a character and the forces of nature. To write about the plot of a narrative work, begin your analysis with these questions: What conflicts does the work embody? How are the conflicts related? Which conflicts are external and which are internal? How does conflict affect the characters?

Point of view refers to the means by which a work is narrated. At the simplest level, a narrative can be told through the first person (a character in the work) or the third person (the author is implied as the narrator). When using first person, an author must sustain the work's psychological reality by using the language and reflecting the attitudes and opinions of the character who is telling the story. Because of its complexity, a first-person narrative is often a better subject for analysis than a third-person narrative. Begin such an analysis by asking: Who is telling the story? How does the narrator reveal his or her personality? Is the narrator trustworthy? What irony develops because of the narrator's limitations?

Setting comprises physical details of the place and time in which a work unfolds and the social environment of the characters. Setting often has little significance in a story, play, or poem, but at other times it is indispensable. To examine setting, begin by asking some of the following questions: Where and when does the action take place? What relation does setting have to the characters? How long does it take for the events to occur? How do the manners or customs of the social environment affect the characters? How does the physical environment affect the characters?

Symbols are actual objects and places infused with emotional significance that goes beyond their concrete qualities. Symbols do not stand for abstractions, such as *love* or *hate;* instead they hint at or suggest a meaning. Not every work embodies symbols, but if symbols are important in a work you are examining, ask yourself: What do the symbols suggest about a character? How do they relate to the action? How do they support the theme?

Theme is the central idea that emerges from a work. A successful theme comments on the larger human experience, not just on the experiences of individual characters. Theme, therefore, is the general application of the central idea embodied in a literary work. To deal with the theme of a narrative work, begin by asking: What is the work's subject? What does the author seem to be saying about the subject? In what ways do characters, setting, plot, and symbols contribute to the theme?

Sometimes an analytical essay combines several approaches. One such essay is an **explication,** a line-by-line analysis of a short poem or a passage from a long poem, work of fiction, or play. Explications are thorough, detailed examinations that are often concentrated on such elements as the uses of words, rhythm, rhyme, and images. A **critical review** also combines several approaches. Critical reviews deal with book-length works, such as a collection of poems or short stories or a novel, and evaluate the work's strengths and weaknesses.

47b Review the text for evidence.

Once you have identified a general subject for an essay about literature, review the work to find key passages that relate to the subject and that might serve as evidence in your paper.

Incidents, details of setting, character traits, symbols, paraphrases, and summaries of long passages can all serve as evidence. Of course, the most convincing evidence is a direct quotation and your explanation of its meaning as it relates to your subject.

47c Formulate a thesis statement and develop a plan.

No one can examine every aspect of a literary work in a brief essay; consequently, you must decide on a topic by selecting a single aspect of your subject. Then develop a limited thesis statement that announces the topic and expresses your attitude toward it. (See thesis statement, 45j.)

> In "The Chrysanthemums," John Steinbeck portrays a character who senses but cannot understand the need to communicate her deepest feelings.

> "Buffalo Bill's defunct" by e. e. cummings creates an ambiguous image of an American folk hero.

Once you have developed a working thesis statement, you can sift through the evidence you have identified and develop a plan as you would for any essay. (See informal plan, 45i; formal plan, 45k.)

47d Assume that your reader has read the work.

Do not include excessively long quotations or unnecessary summaries merely to familiarize readers with the work. Instead, assume that they have read the work at least once and that your job is to enrich their experience by pointing out elements and patterns that a closer examination uncovers.

47e Write an introduction that presents the thesis statement and supplies background information.

The introduction should include the name of the author, the title of the work, and a clear thesis statement. It should also have enough background information, which might include a brief quotation, to prepare the reader for what follows. (See introduction, 45m.) In an introduction to an analytical essay on Guy de Maupassant's "Moonlight," one student wrote the following:

> Guy de Maupassant's "Moonlight" deals with an awakening. The principal character, Father Marigan, is a self-satisfied woman-hater who believes he understands "God ... His plans, His wishes, His intentions." Marigan's awakening comes when he is seduced by moonlight into realizing, to his dismay, that God's plan includes love between a man and a woman. In this story de Maupasssnt uses setting to reinforce the characterization of Father Marigan and to convey the idea that love is natural and good.

Clearly, this student's analysis will show how setting supports characterization and reflects the theme of the story. But whether you are writing an analysis of setting, theme, characterization, symbols, plot, or point of view, the introduction should always include the author's name, the title of the work, necessary background information, and the thesis statement.

47f Write a discussion consisting of several paragraphs.

Arrange the discussion according to significant ideas. Do not feel bound by the structure of the story, novel, play, or poem you are examining. Your discussion should consist of several paragraphs, each supporting one aspect of the thesis statement and each unified by a fully developed topic sentence.

One way to develop the topic sentence is by combining your comments with a quotation that supports them, as in the following discussion paragraph from an analysis of Flannery O'Connor's "Revelation." (See direct quotations, 28a.)

> O'Connor creates a conflicting portrait of Mrs. Turpin. We see her from the inside and the outside. Throughout the story she professes Christian love and charity, but in her mind she judges others by superficial standards. For example, at night before sleeping she categorizes and judges people by their economic condition:
>
> > On the bottom of the heap were most colored people ... next to them–not above, just away from–were the white trash; then above them were the homeowners, and above them the home-and-land owners, to which she and Claud belonged. Above she and Claud were people with a lot of money and much bigger homes and much more land.

This judgmental vision of Mrs. Turpin ends in confusion when rich blacks who own land and "white trash" who've grown rich don't fit into her scheme, but she solves the problem by mentally consigning everyone--white, black, rich, and poor--to boxcars headed for a gas oven, a grim reference to Nazi Germany and the result of categorical thinking when carried to its limits.

Other paragraphs in the discussion might be developed by accurately summarizing the content of a work as it relates to your point, as the following discussion paragraph from an analysis of *Oedipus Rex* illustrates.

Sophocles uses the imagery of sight and blindness ironically throughout the play. It is blind Tiresias, the prophet of Apollo, who is the god of foresight and insight, who sees more clearly than those who have eyes. Early in the play, Oedipus promises to bring the dark secret of Laius' death to light for all to see, yet he does so while still blind to his own moral faults. After blinding himself near the play's end, Oedipus sees who he really is and what he has done. Ironically, throughout the play, Oedipus prides himself on his clear-sightedness, but by the end he recognizes that this pride has blinded him.

You might also combine very brief quotations from a work and your comments on them, as this discussion paragraph from a critical evaluation of *Serpentine* does.

A minor flaw in the book comes from Thompson's flagrant use of clichés in place of more thoughtful prose. He writes, "It was the dead of winter, 1967, and the prison walls were cold as ice." He refers to Sobhraj's courtroom chicanery as a "bag of tricks." His girlfriend clung to him "like moss on an oak." He tries to pass off their tawdry affair as an "epic romance more poignant than Romeo and Juliet." Trite expressions such as these mar every page and blemish an otherwise captivating work.

47g Write a conclusion.

The conclusion to your analytical essay should briefly summarize your thesis and the major thoughts in your paper, and it should end with your general view of the work. Here is an effective conclusion from an analysis of Flannery O'Connor's "Revelation."

> Clearly, O'Connor's "Revelation" takes a careful reader into the shadowy mind of a bigot who gains awareness through a personal catastrophe. O'Connor seems to be offering a positive message--that is, there is even hope that a bigot such as Mrs. Turpin can learn not to judge others by the weight of their wallets or the color of their skin.

47h Create a precise title.

The title of your essay should be brief and should express the ideas your essay examines. If the title of the work you analyze is included in your essay title, only it should be italicized or put within quotation marks, as appropriate. (See quotation marks, 28b; italics, 37a.)

e. e. cummings's "Buffalo Bill's defunct": The Backside of a Folk Hero

Imagery in Oedipus Rex

Mrs. Turpin's Revelation

47i   Identify your quotations and specific references.

In a brief essay about literature, you might be allowed to omit complete citations for primary sources. If so, you should still identify the location of each quotation and specific reference you make. After the quotation or reference, place the page number or numbers from the original work in parentheses and close the sentence with the end punctuation mark after the last parenthesis. (See parenthetical citations, 49c.)

> Hemingway ends the story on an ironic note: "After all, he said to himself, it's probably only insomnia" (72).

> Near the end of his life we find that Gimpel has achieved peace. He now understands that soon all illusion will be swept away. He believes he will truly see without the confusion of ridicule and deception. He will see what is real (85-86).

47j   Use the present tense of verbs.

The dominant verb tense in an essay about literature—whether fiction, drama, or poetry—should be the present. (See present tense, 11a.)

> In The Executioner's Song Mailer re-creates life as it is lived in the rural West. He evokes people struggling to make a living in gas stations, roadside cafés, movie theaters, small factories, country stores, and on farms. It is a world filled with pickup trucks, six-packs, country music, Monday Night Football, deer hunting, motorcycles, and honky-tonk violence. The city slicker is suspect, and the easy buck is hard to find. The four-wheel-drive Blazer, not the sleek Mercedes, is the status symbol.

47k   Avoid common mistakes in essay writing.

Do not summarize excessively. Summarize enough of a work only to clarify your thought or a point. Summary should always serve a clear purpose.

Do not refer to authors by their first names or as Dr., Prof., Mr., Mrs., Miss, or Ms. After giving an author's full name in the introduction, refer to him or her by last name throughout the rest of the essay.

Do not miscopy a direct quotation. Always recheck any quotation you use to be sure you have copied it accurately.

Do not set off the title of a work with commas when it follows the word book, poem, *or* play.

INCORRECT	In his poem, "Traveling through the Dark," William Stafford reflects on humans' relation to nature.
CORRECT	In his poem "Traveling through the Dark," William Stafford reflects on humans' relation to nature.

Exercise 22

Visit your library and select an anthology of literature that includes fiction, poetry, and drama, such as X. J. Kennedy's *Literature* or Sylvan Barnet, Morton Berman, and William Burto's *An Introduction to Literature.* Browse through the books to find a work that interests you. After reading the work several times, compose a five- to seven-paragraph explication of a brief poem or passage or an analytical examination with character, plot, point of view, setting, symbol, or theme as the subject.

48 Researching a Paper *res*

A research paper is a formal composition based on an investigation of detailed information and other writers' ideas about a topic rather than solely on your own attitudes and experiences. No doubt you have opinions about a number of topics, but unless you have taken many courses or read extensively, you probably do not have an *informed* opinion about a given topic. Writing a research paper offers you the opportunity to develop an informed opinion and to apply your thinking and writing skills to an objective discussion of a topic. Unlike the personal essay, which grows from personal experiences and viewpoints, the research paper grows from an in-depth study and a careful examination of the ideas of other writers.

A research paper is more than a summarized version of what others have said or written, however. Ideally, your research paper represents a synthesis of your own perceptions, attitudes, ideas, and experiences supported by information gained from other sources. In most cases, those sources are materials in your college or community library. You can use these materials to enlarge, to strengthen, to define, or otherwise to complement your own basic views about a subject. No one expects you to solve a major world problem as a result of your research, but if you have done your work seriously and thoroughly, you will gain a broader and more informed view than any one source alone has yet provided.

48a Find and limit a topic suitable for research.

If your instructor has not already given you a specific research assignment, allow yourself time to select an appropriate topic for research. The best way to start your search is by examining your own interests and experiences.

1. Begin with Topics that Interest You.

Your favorite section of the newspaper; the kinds of books, magazines, or films you enjoy; or a particular textbook chapter that excited your curiosity are all strong clues to your real interests. The best ingredients for a successful paper are your own understanding of and enthusiasm for a subject.

2. A Suitable Topic Allows Room for Discussion.

To choose an appropriate research topic, you also must be aware of what your paper can achieve. Since most research papers attempt to add new dimensions or perspectives to a body of ideas already expressed by others, process or how-to papers or those that merely summarize already known information ("the major decisions during John F. Kennedy's presidency") are not good choices. Strictly philosophical subjects or topics based on personal beliefs—"the nature of reality," "Loyalty to one's government comes before loyalty to one's family," "Public nudity should be left to personal choice"—should be avoided because they are based on opinion and often do not require research for objective evidence and do not lend themselves to objective discussion. Look for a topic that allows you to explore areas that still need discussion or review, such as an unsettled and continuing problem or a little-known situation. "Whether the sale of handguns should be controlled in this country," for example, might prove a suitable problem to investigate for a research paper. An examination of home schooling (as in the sample research paper by Jeanne Artoya beginning on p. 429) could also produce an informative, researched discussion.

3. Narrow the Topic to Manageable Size.

The topic of your research paper should allow you to generate enough discussion to fulfill your instructor's requirements about length and about the kinds of sources you should use for your research. A subject that is too narrow, such as "whether the shopping mall provides enough security for Christmas shoppers," or too recent, such as "the hazards of in-line skates," will not work because there will not be enough written for you to build on.

Likewise, some topics may be so large or already have so much written about them—"the events leading up to President Nixon's resignation," for example—that you cannot expect to learn enough in a few weeks' time to write about them convincingly. In such instances, you will need to narrow the focus of your paper, just as you did when developing a thesis or writing the personal essay.

Sometimes reviewing the general sources for a broad subject can help you see particular ways to narrow the approach or to shift the emphasis of a topic. Often the topic itself becomes more refined only after you have begun researching it, and it may not evolve into its final form until the completion of the paper. For instance, if you were to begin with a broad topic, such as "art" or "psychology," you might

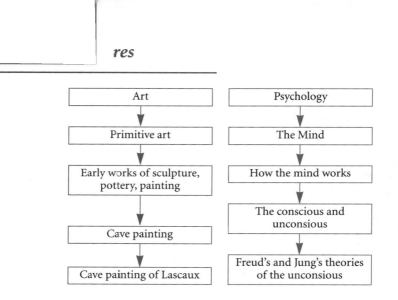

find yourself moving gradually toward a narrower topic in the manner illustrated above.

Narrowing a topic from general to specific is seldom as smooth or orderly as the following illustrations might make the process seem. Usually you will have several false starts, but reading in a general subject area will help you find your way.

Education major Jeanne Artoya, the author of the sample paper, moved quickly from the broad subject of alternative education to home schooling. Yet even as she began reading about this narrower topic, Artoya discovered that there were still numerous aspects to be discussed, too many for a single paper. Finally, she decided that her keenest interest was in one major issue: whether home schooling was a viable alternative to traditional public school education. She liked this subject because it was current and seemed to be something that would become increasingly important in the future. At first Artoya had trouble finding adequate information, but once she became more familiar with the library, she found plenty of material dealing with home schooling and its effectiveness.

Do not rush the essential step of narrowing the topic to something that interests you and that can be easily researched. Careful selection and limitation of the right topic can save you time and work later and can provide an early foundation for a successful finished product.

48b Use the library and other resources.

Use reference books to get an overview of your topic and to evaluate its appropriateness for your assignment. In addition to encyclopedias, dictionaries, almanacs, indexes, guides, atlases, and book reviews, your library's reference section probably contains a large selection of special reference sources, ranging from *The Encyclopedia of Evolution* to the *Guinness Book of Records*.

A complete listing of the hundreds of reference books would, of course, be impractical here. The following is a sampling of the variety of sources available. Survey your own library for the reference books most applicable to your topic. You can also consult Eugene P. Sheehy's *Guide to Reference Books* for a comprehensive catalog of reference books.

GENERAL ENCYCLOPEDIAS

Encyclopedia Americana
The New Encyclopedia Britannica

THE ARTS

Art Books: A Basic Bibliography on the Fine Arts
Encyclopedia of World Art

BUSINESS AND ECONOMICS

Business Index
Business Periodicals Index
Encyclopedia of Computers and Data Processing
The Encyclopedia of Management
Marketing Terms: Definitions, Explanations, and/or Aspects

HISTORY

Dictionary of American History
An Encyclopedia of World History

LITERATURE, THEATER, FILM, AND TELEVISION

Bibliography of American Literature
The Complete Encyclopedia of Television Programs 1949–1972
Contemporary Authors
International Index of Film Periodicals
Macmillan Dictionary of Films and Filmmakers
Play Index
The New York Times Encyclopedia of Television
Short Story Index

MUSIC

Bibliographic Guide to Music
The New Harvard Dictionary of Music
The New Grove Dictionary of Music and Musicians

PHILOSOPHY AND RELIGION

*The Philosopher's Index: An International Index to Philosophical
    Periodicals and Books*
Religion Index One: Periodicals

SOCIAL SCIENCE

Bibliographical Guide to Psychology
Handbook of Social Science Research
Social Science Citation Index

SCIENCES

Applied Science and Technology Index
Biological Abstracts
Environmental Periodicals Bibliography
General Science Index
Index Medicus

UNABRIDGED DICTIONARIES

The Oxford English Dictionary
Webster's Third New International Dictionary of the English
  Language

SPECIAL DICTIONARIES

Dictionary of Contemporary Usage
Dictionary of Modern English Usage
Modern American Usage
The New Roget's Thesaurus of the English Language in
  Dictionary Form

BIOGRAPHICAL REFERENCE

Dictionary of American Biography
Webster's New Biographical Dictionary
Who's Who in America

ATLASES AND GAZETTEERS

Columbia Lippincott Gazetteer of the World
Rand McNally New Cosmopolitan World Atlas

ALMANACS AND YEARBOOKS

Britannica Book of the Year
Facts on File Yearbook
Information Please Almanac
Reader's Digest Almanac and Yearbook
World Almanac and Book of Facts

1. Use the Card Catalog to Find Books on Your Topic.

The best guide to the books available is your library's card catalog. Whether on microfilm or microfiche, on a computer screen, or in the traditional card tray, the library's catalog alphabetically lists and cross-references its holdings by subject, author, and title. Special information given with each entry can supply useful data about a

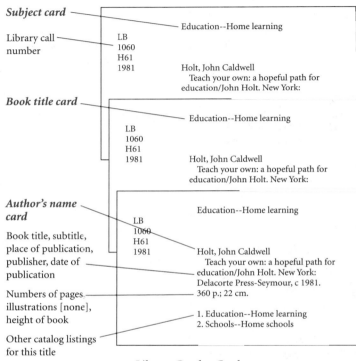

Subject card —

Library call — number

Book title card —

Author's name card

Book title, subtitle, place of publication, publisher, date of publication

Numbers of pages, illustrations [none], height of book

Other catalog listings for this title

Education--Home learning

LB
1060
H61
1981

Holt, John Caldwell
Teach your own: a hopeful path for education/John Holt. New York:

Education--Home learning

LB
1060
H61
1981

Holt, John Caldwell
Teach your own: a hopeful path for education/John Holt. New York:

Education--Home learning

LB
1060
H61
1981

Holt, John Caldwell
Teach your own: a hopeful path for education/John Holt. New York:
Delacorte Press-Seymour, c 1981.
360 p.; 22 cm.

1. Education--Home learning
2. Schools--Home schools

Library Catalog Cards

book's publication date, whether or not it includes illustrations, and its length. You can locate books on your topic by looking under the author, title, or subject heading. (See the card and computer catalog samples, pp. 388–389.) There are two widely used classification systems—the Dewey decimal system and the Library of Congress system. The system a library uses has no effect on your library work; it merely determines the call number of any book.

Type the LINE NUMBER to display titles.
(Next screen key) to see Next screen.
(Prev screen key) to see previous screen.
Press: START key to return to MAIN MENU

.>>
                                        Enter ? for HELP.
Your search: S=EDUCATION HOME
                    Holdings highlighted for:NORTH CAMPUS
Line   #of
  #   titles   ----------------------------SUBJECTS----------------------------
  1   0   Education, Home.
  2   search for Domestic education.

Type the LINE NUMBER to display titles.
(Next screen key) to see Next screen.
(Prev screen key) to see previous screen.
Press: START key to return to MAIN MENU

>>
                                        Enter ? for HELP.
Your search: S=DOMESTIC EDUCATION
      Holdings highlighted for:NORTH CAMPUS
Line
  #   ----------Author----------   ----------------------------Title----------------------------   Date
  1   Ginott, Haim G.   Between parent and child; new solutions to   1965
  2   Hainstock, Elizabeth   Teaching Montessori in the home   1968
  3   Holt, John Caldwell   Teach your own; a hopeful path for educati   1981

Type the LINE NUMBER to display titles.
(Next screen key) to see Next screen.
(Prev screen key) to see previous screen.
Press: START key to return to MAIN MENU

.>>
                                        Enter ? for HELP.

You selected: 3=HOLT, JOHN CALDW TEACH
              Holdings highlighted for: NORTH CAMPUS

AUTHOR(s):   Holt, John Caldwell, 1923-
TITLE(s):   Teach your own : a hopeful path for education / John Holt.
               369 p. : 24 cm.
               Includes index.

PUBLISHER: New York, N.Y. : Delacorte Press/Seymour Lawrence, c1981.
SUBJECT: Domestic Education

CALL NUMBER: LC37 .H66
STATUS: AVAILABLE

Computer Catalog Screens

2. Use Periodicals for More Focused Information about your Topic.

Periodicals are valuable sources of more specific or current information. Many different indexes catalog the various kinds of journals, magazines, newspapers, and other periodicals, and certain guides are more useful to the general researcher than are others. One such source is the *Reader's Guide to Periodical Literature,* which provides a monthly, quarterly, and annual index to the most widely circulated magazines in the United States.

Articles listed in the *Reader's Guide* are cross-referenced under author, title, and subject. Information about each entry is listed in a condensed form explained in the front of every volume of the *Reader's Guide.* On page 391, for example, are entries on "home schooling" and "home education" that Jeanne Artoya used for her research paper.

In addition to magazines, newspaper articles are important contemporary sources for research. While most libraries can store no more than a few nationally circulated or local newspapers, most university and college libraries have copies of several major newspapers on microfilm. Articles are usually listed in a separate index, such as *The New York Times Index,* which lists news articles, first by general subject, then in chronological sequence according to the dates they appeared in the newspaper. Like entries in the *Reader's Guide,* subject headings in *The New York Times Index* are cross-referenced by "see" and "see also" directions. An additional feature is that each entry in *The New York Times Index* describes the length of the article as either short (S), medium (M), or long (L). This feature can help you decide whether the article is likely to yield enough information to make researching it further worthwhile.

Jeanne Artoya looked in *The New York Times Index* under the general subject heading "Home Schooling." As the first sample entry on page 392 shows, a "See also" note referred her to another subject heading, "Education and Schools," where she would find four articles listed chronologically by their dates of appearance—September 23, October 14, and November 4 and 22.

In addition to consulting the *Reader's Guide* and *The New York Times Index* for sources, Artoya wanted to find discussions written for

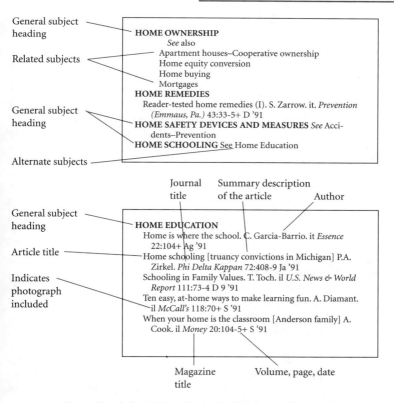

General subject heading → **HOME OWNERSHIP**
 See also
Related subjects →
  Apartment houses–Cooperative ownership
  Home equity conversion
  Home buying
  Mortgages
HOME REMEDIES
 Reader-tested home remedies (I). S. Zarrow. it. *Prevention (Emmaus, Pa.)* 43:33-5+ D '91
General subject heading → **HOME SAFETY DEVICES AND MEASURES** *See* Accidents–Prevention
Alternate subjects → **HOME SCHOOLING** *See* Home Education

Journal title — Summary description of the article — Author

General subject heading → **HOME EDUCATION**
Article title → Home is where the school. C. Garcia-Barrio. it *Essence* 22:104+ Ag '91
Home schooling [truancy convictions in Michigan] P.A. Zirkel. *Phi Delta Kappan* 72:408-9 Ja '91
Schooling in Family Values. T. Toch. il *U.S. News & World Report* 111:73-4 D 9 '91
Indicates photograph included → Ten easy, at-home ways to make learning fun. A. Diamant. il *McCall's* 118:70+ S '91
When your home is the classroom [Anderson family] A. Cook. il *Money* 20:104-5+ S '91

Magazine title — Volume, page, date

From *Reader's Guide to Periodical Literature (1991)*

audiences with more scholarly interest in the subject of home schooling than the general public may have had. She knew that her library contained several reference sources intended for readers interested in researching topics within certain academic disciplines. Such discipline indexes, for example, as *Social Sciences Index, Arts and Humani-*

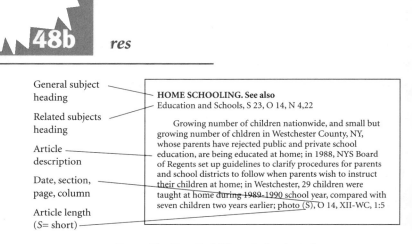

General subject heading

Related subjects heading

Article description

Date, section, page, column

Article length (S= short)

> **HOME SCHOOLING. See also**
> Education and Schools, S 23, O 14, N 4,22
>
> Growing number of children nationwide, and small but growing number of chldren in Westchester County, NY, whose parents have rejected public and private school education, are being educated at home; in 1988, NYS Board of Regents set up guidelines to clarify procedures for parents and school districts to follow when parents wish to instruct their children at home; in Westchester, 29 children were taught at home during 1989-1990 school year, compared with seven children two years earlier; photo (S), O 14, XII-WC, 1:5

From *The New York Times Index (1990)*

ties Index, and *Applied Science and Technology Index* report results of research studies or other scholarly information not generally addressed in popular magazines and newspapers. Thus, because her topic fell within the discipline of education, Artoya consulted *Education Index.* Although she looked first under "Home education," a "See" note directed Artoya to other subject headings, where she eventually found the magazine and journal sources shown in the sample *Education Index* entry opposite.

Besides the *Reader's Guide* and the newspaper and discipline indexes already discussed, most libraries contain a number of other guides to periodical literature on general and specialized subjects. The list that follows is representative of the most common indexes to periodical literature. Investigate your own library's holdings and use such sources to compile your bibliography.

> *Abstracts of Popular Culture*
> *Alternative Press Index*
> *The American Humanities Index*
> *Bibliography and Index of Geology*
> *Biography Index*

Alternate
subject heading   Summary description

Major subject
heading
Home Education *See* Correspondence schools and
courses: Home schooling

Major subject
heading
Home Education

Article
title
An argument for privacy in support of the choice of
home education by parents. D. E. Tompkins. bibl *J
Law Educ* 20:301-23 Summ '91

Jornal title
Debates in education (resolved: there should be
increased state regulation of home schooling.) C. J.
Russo: R. D. Mawdsley. *Curric Rev* 31:3-7 Mar '92

Includes a
bibliograpy
Home is where the class is (home education in Great
Britain) F. Rafferty. il *Times Educ Suppl* 3929:23-4
O 18 '91
Home schooling and the law. M. M. McCarthy. bibl
Educ Horiz 69:176-9 Summ '91
Is anybody home? Home schooling and the library.
J. LaRue and S. Larue. bibl il *Wilson Libr Bull*

Volume, page,
date
66:32-7+ S '91
Learning at home: public library service to home-
schoolers. S. B. Madden. *SLJ* 37:23-5 Jl '91

Contains
illustrations and
photographs
'National curriculum is a dirty word' (profile of K.
Trafford, a home educator in Great Britain) S.
Bayliss. il por *Times Educ Suppl* 3929:24 O 18 '91
Parents as teachers. T. Anderson. *Hispana* 74:426-9
My '91

Article continues
on other pages
Project SHINE: summer home instruction and eval-
uation. P. M. Barbetta and T. E. Heron. bibl *Inter-
vention Sch Clin* 26:276-81 My '91
Social studies in the home school. J. H. Litcher and
S. J. Schmidt. bibl *Soc Educ* 55:239-41+ Ap My '91
Why I teach my children at home. B. Pike. il *Phi
Delta Kappan* 73:564-5 Mr '92

Subtopic heading
History
From pedagogy to ideology: origins and phrases of
home education in the United States. 1970-1990. J.
G. Knowles and others. il *Am J Educ* 100:195-235 F
'92

From *the Education Index (July 1991–June 1992)*

Biological Abstracts
Book Review Digest
Book Review Index
Business Periodicals Index
Cumulative Index to Periodical Literature
Economics Abstracts
Education Index
Humanities Index
Index Medicus
Index to Jewish Periodicals
International Political Science Abstracts
MLA International Bibliography of Books and Articles on the
    Modern Languages and Literatures
The Music Index
Poole's Index to Periodical Literature (1802–1906)
Popular Periodical Index
United States Government Publications

3. Use Computer Databases to Supplement your Library's Resources.

Perhaps your library subscribes to one or more of the numerous computer database services that give users immediate access to a vast library of information on a multitude of subjects. Using such databases, you can peruse a comprehensive bibliography of your subject, read related encyclopedia articles, and find answers to specific factual questions. You can also have all the on-screen information printed so that you can keep a copy and use it when you wish. We suggest, though, that you begin the search for information in your library and turn to computer databases only to fill a gap in the library's resources.

4. Use Primary and Secondary Sources in your Research.

Primary sources are the original materials about which secondary sources are written. They include novels, short stories, plays, poems, letters, journals, government documents, surveys, reports of experiments, interviews, and oral histories. Artoya used a primary source when she included parts of an interview with a professor of child psychology and education at her school. Using primary sources puts you in direct contact with the raw material from which your paper will develop. Through this contact, your own analysis can become an integral part of your research paper.

Secondary sources are written materials about your topic, including books, magazines, newspaper articles, encyclopedia entries, pamphlets, and other works that examine, analyze, or report facts. Artoya used several books, reference works, and articles as secondary sources of information to complete her paper.

48c Gather information and prepare a working bibliography.

When you have decided on a topic, you will be ready to start gathering information about it. Most of your research data will probably come from the reference books, general books, and periodicals available in your college or community library. Systematically investigate each of these three major sources to establish a preliminary bibliography for your paper.

A working bibliography helps you determine whether your chosen topic is researchable in your library. It helps you keep track of the available sources you need to seek. Finally, the working bibliography provides a handy source of information you will need for evaluating your sources during the writing stage, for citing sources in your text, and for completing your list of works cited.

Keep your Working Bibliography on Index Cards.

Keep your working bibliography on 3-by-5-inch index cards, with a separate card for each source you consult. To find the source easily, or for reference if you need the work later, record the library call number in the upper right-hand corner.

Record the information you would need to list the source in your paper's Works Cited section. For a book, this information includes the author's name (or the editor's name followed by "ed."), the title of the book (underlined), the place of publication, the publisher's name, and the year of publication.

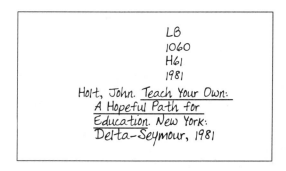

LB
1060
H61
1981
Holt, John. Teach Your Own:
A Hopeful Path for
Education. New York:
Delta-Seymour, 1981

Bibliography Card

For a magazine or journal article, list the author's name, the title of the article (in quotation marks), the title of the magazine or journal (underlined), the volume or issue number if the source is a journal, the date of publication, and the page numbers on which the article appears.

A sample bibliography card for a book with a single author is shown above. Other kinds of sources will require slightly different information. Follow the guide to documentation forms (50a and 50b) to learn what information to record for any source you may need to locate again or to include in your paper's Works Cited list.

Bibliographic formats vary among disciplines. They all, however, have the same intent—to make sure the writer includes the information that a reader needs to find those same sources. Section 50c contains a list of guides for disciplines using documentation styles other than those of MLA or APA.

The forms presented in this text follow the guidelines of the Modern Language Association and the *MLA Handbook* (1995), which it publishes. But before beginning to record bibliographic information, check with your instructor about the format you should follow for your research paper. (American Psychological Association [APA] guidelines are discussed in 50b.) Then carefully follow the handbook, taking care during the final typing of your paper to use the spacing and punctuation shown in the illustrations. Also be sure to notice how bibliographic form—the form you will use in your Works Cited list—differs from in-text citation form. (See parenthetical citations, 49c.)

48d Reading and writing for a tentative thesis and working outline.

When you have set up a working bibliography (usually about fifteen sources for a college paper), you will be ready to examine your research materials more closely. Your first efforts should be directed toward preliminary reading and establishing a tentative thesis and working outline.

Preliminary reading consists of skimming the most promising materials in your bibliography to give yourself an expanded overview of the topic. You should gain a more detailed sense of the scope and complexity of the topic and a familiarity with the kinds of information you will compare and analyze during the research process. Work quickly by using tables of contents and indexes to locate information. At this point, take notes only for general information about the topic. Once you have explored enough material, you will start to form an idea (or sharpen an already existing one) of the central point you want to develop in your paper.

1. Develop a Tentative Thesis Statement.

Begin by developing a tentative thesis statement, no more than one or two sentences, that presents and limits your topic (see 45j). The tentative thesis may actually change during further research or in the writing stage of the paper, but at this point it will add focus and organization to your research. Jeanne Artoya's preliminary reading revealed two major ideas about home schooling: Home schooling is controversial, and it has also generally been successful. She decided to include these ideas in her research paper, so she formulated the following as a *tentative* thesis statement.

Despite the controversy about home schooling's legality and effectiveness, it offers an important and viable alternative form of education.

2. Develop a Working Outline.

Your preliminary reading and your tentative thesis statement should aid you in establishing a working outline for the paper (see 45i and 45k). As with everything you have done so far, the working outline need not be in permanent form; it is an early guide, a flexible blueprint to aid you in organizing your research, arranging your ideas logically, and making sure you have not left out any important aspects of your topic. The working outline may simply state the tentative thesis and then list supporting ideas. Artoya's working outline was roughly organized around the major ideas in her thesis statement and the research materials she found to support it.

After a long battle for acceptance, home schooling has proved to be an increasingly popular and worthwhile form of alternative education.

HISTORY AND LEGALITY

—Once the dominant means of education in America
—During the mid-nineteenth century, education became more formalized and home schooling became suspect.
—By 1918 education and public school attendance were mandatory; home schooling illegal.
—*Pierce* v. *Society of Sisters* (1925) opened the door for legal home schooling.
—Home schooling now essentially legal in every state, though all have requirements

POPULARITY OF HOME SCHOOLING

—200,000 to 300,000 children home-school
—Home-school families increase in numbers each time a state law becomes more liberal about home schooling.

REASONS FOR HOME SCHOOLING

—Used to be for religious reasons, but that's changed
—Represents central debate over who controls a child's education—society or parents?
—Home-school parents feel it's their responsibility to educate their children, not the state's.
—Belief in a child-based curriculum
—Follows ideas of "progressive education"

SUCCESS OF HOME SCHOOLING

—Abraham Lincoln, Douglas MacArthur, Pearl S. Buck, Thomas A. Edison, and others were home-school educated.
—Avoids the negative socialization of public schools
—Home-schooled children outperform peers on national tests.
—Home-schooled children get accepted to colleges and universities—often ahead of their public school peers.
—Colfax family—home-schooled children admitted to Harvard

FAILURE OF PUBLIC SCHOOLS

—Public school methods haven't changed much since the nineteenth century.
—Distrust and disappointment with public schools—e.g., violence, materialism, shabbiness, rigid curriculum
—School districts are too broke to provide necessary educational environment.
—Research shows that children learn best after age twelve.
—Public school curriculum is rigid, lock-step.
—Percentage of high school graduates in U.S. has decreased every year since 1972.
—School violence is up 12 percent nationwide.

HOME SCHOOLING EXPERIENCES

—Curriculums and routines for home schooling vary greatly.
—Visit museums, cook meals, handle banking, raise animals, work part time, travel
—Many parents read and study with children.

CONCERNS ABOUT EFFECTIVENESS

—59 percent of Americans think home schooling is a "bad
thing."
—Many fear children will be too isolated.
—"Socialization" is a central concern.
—All states have laws that regulate home schooling in terms of
curriculum, parent qualifications, and achievement testing.
—Twenty-nine states require standardized or supervised tests
of home schoolers.

Notice that the working outline need not be complete. At this stage,
it is useful in roughly charting the direction the paper may finally take
and in pointing out the research that still needs to be done.

48e Take Effective Notes.

Using Note Cards

Begin the next step in the research process by using note cards to
record information from and about your sources. Although there are
many ways to keep research notes, storing them on cards is the most
practical: cards are more durable than loose slips of paper; they are
more easily organized than entries on notebook pages; and unlike
computer-stored notes, the cards can go with you and are available
for reference anywhere you do research. You will find large 4-by–6-
inch index cards the most practical since they provide plenty of space
for content and are easily distinguished from the smaller 3-by–5-inch
bibliography cards you have been keeping.

Make a habit of using note cards to create consistent and useful
records throughout your research. Start by skimming your sources,
then reading closely those that appear promising. Analyze information and take notes as you proceed. What you select to read and
decide to take notes about should correspond to the major categories
of ideas listed earlier on your working outline (48d). Use these categories to direct your research and as topic headings, written at the top

of the note cards, by which you can easily identify and organize the information you record. Expect to create additional headings for the note cards as your later reading suggests. Use a separate card for each note, even if two notes come under the same heading or from the same source.

Since you will undoubtedly need to document the sources for any note material included in your paper, be sure to record the name of the author and the page numbers for each piece of information you record. The sample summary card on p. 403 demonstrates a basic format for note card information.

Avoiding Plagiarism

Most of your notes will be composed of words and ideas copied directly or adapted from your sources. Whenever you later incorporate into your paper any language, opinions, facts, particular line of reasoning, or explanation from the authors of these sources, you must acknowledge your indebtedness (see MLA Documentation Style, 50a). Failure to give credit for words or ideas you have borrowed from another source is **plagiarism,** a serious breach of academic integrity. Plagiarism occurs, for example, any time you omit quotation marks around language that you borrow directly from a source or when you reword or paraphrase a source's language (see p. 404) without citing the original author and listing the source in your paper's Works Cited section. *Done consciously or not, plagiarism in any form is the same as* stealing, *punishable in most colleges by immediate failure or even dismissal from the school.*

You can avoid plagiarizing by taking careful, accurate notes and using them during the paper's writing stage to ensure the integrity of your documentation. Following these steps will help.

1. Consistently include on each note card the name of the source's author and the page number(s) for any language you copy or adapt and for each piece of information you record (other necessary information about the source is already entered on your bibliography cards).

2. On your note cards and in your paper, put quotation marks around any language you reproduce directly from the source.
3. Cite the source in the text and Works Cited section (see 49c) whenever you include material from the notes in your final paper.
4. Scrupulously recheck your note cards during and after the writing stage to make sure you have used and acknowledged all your sources accurately.

Note-Taking Techniques

Information you store on note cards must be not only accurate but also useful, worth the time you spend writing it down. Using the right recording methods will allow you to tailor notes to your expected needs for the paper and keep you from overrecording information or writing too little because of inefficient note-taking methods. You can ensure the value of your notes and the time you spend on them by practicing four standard techniques for recording information: summarizing, paraphrasing, using quotation, or combining quotation and paraphrase.

Summarizing

Summarizing is a technique for quickly recording information in a condensed form and in your own words and style. Summarize whenever you need only a few facts or statistics from a source and are not concerned about having a larger, more detailed record of its content or an author's perspective. Summarizing is also useful for broadly characterizing the general contents of a source or for registering your own reactions (e.g., "Describes state laws on home schooling. Not as complete as Baker article.").

Convenience and brevity are the keys to effective summarizing. Focus on recording only main points or useful facts, possibly adding a brief note to yourself when doing so seems helpful. Write the notes quickly, without too much concern for your own wording and style. Use synonyms and other wording or symbols to express the information in your own way, but also take care not to distort the meaning of the original. Avoid simply copying words and sentences from the original, since this defeats the purpose of summarizing by taking more time, and it leads easily to plagiarism (see p. 401). If you must retain certain exceptional wording from the source, enclose it in quotation marks. Include the author's name and the page number for the summarized material on your note card in case you want more information later or need to list the source in your paper's Works Cited section.

The following paragraph comes from one of the sources Jeanne Artoya used for her paper on home schooling. The sample note card below the original paragraph shows how Artoya summarized information from it. Notice that the card includes a topic heading to help Artoya locate and organize the note material later.

ORIGINAL

The number of children being educated outside of public or private schools seems likely to increase and to be accompanied by pressure on state legislatures to deregulate home schooling. Several states are considering voucher proposals that would provide public funds for children to attend private schools; the status of home education has not been clarified under such plans.

—Martha M. McCarthy,
"Home Schooling and the Law"

SUMMARIZED NOTE

Legal status of home schooling
   McCarthy, 178

   Home schooling likely to increase. Not clear if it will meet voucher requirements. Note: Brooks says it will—see him again?

Paraphrasing

You **paraphrase** information by clearly restating it in your own words. Paraphrasing is useful when you need to make a source's language or style more understandable and when it needs revision to match the style and flow of your own writing if you later include the material in your paper. Unlike a summary, which condenses original material into its essential meaning, a good paraphrase captures the sense of each part of the source, whether the source is a single sentence or several pages. For this reason, a paraphrase has no typical length, although it is seldom much shorter or longer than its source.

Your goal in paraphrasing is to re-create the entire original in different, clearer language, accurately conveying the source's meaning as well as the attitude of its author. As you interpret the original, remember that the way ideas are stated can change or add to their meaning. Be sure your paraphrase reflects the less evident as well as the obvious aspects of the source's language and style by paying attention to the author's word choice, emphases, qualifications, and overall tone. To serve as a later reminder for yourself and to indicate an author's attitude to your own readers, it is often helpful to include brief phrases that describe the manner in which the source's author relates the original (e.g., "Jenkins argues . . ." or "Henderson concedes that . . . ").

Do not make the mistake of simply rewriting the original by rearranging its parts or integrating its words and sentence structures with your own. (Whether or not you cite the source, this practice amounts to plagiarism, because the reader will assume the paraphrase is composed of your own wording.) Instead, always rewrite the source in your own style and language, taking care to use synonyms and other words that accurately capture the sense of the original. If you feel you must retain certain exceptional wording from the source, enclose it in quotation marks.

The following examples demonstrate the difference between unsuitable paraphrasing and paraphrasing that achieves its purpose. Notice how the first, poor paraphrase incorrectly repeats words and phrases from the source (shown here in italic type).

ORIGINAL

Public schools have, apparently willingly, assumed the role of "holding tanks." Social contact limited strictly to "peers" (defined as everyone of the same chronological age) is a fraud. The world for which we have the responsibility of preparing young people is *not* full of their peers. It is full of people both older and younger, from social strata both higher and lower. What are we teaching about this very real world? Not much.

—Bob Pike,
"Why I Teach My Children at Home"

POOR PARAPHRASE NOTE

Pike says that *public schools* seem too willing to serve *the role of "holding tanks,"* places where the *social contacts* children have are *limited strictly* to their *chronological peers.* This is simply *fraud. We have the responsibility of preparing* children for a world populated by people *younger* as well as *older,* and from different levels of society. What lessons are they learning about the *real world ?* Very few (564).

BETTER PARAPHRASE NOTE

Pike complains that schools seem deliberately to serve as isolated, fraudulent environments in which children socialize only with others their own age. However, the world for which education readies these children is, he insists, populated by people of all ages and from all levels of society. The education we give children about the world beyond the classroom amounts to very little (564).

In contrast to the first paraphrase, the second version effectively rewords the source to avoid unintended plagiarism. In addition, the second paraphrase more accurately conveys the disgruntled attitude of the original author by using such terms as *complains* and *insists* to characterize the way he presents his argument. The first version, in contrast, uses only the much less descriptive word *says,* which communicates nothing of the irritation implied in the source.

Once you have written your paraphrase, compare it with the original to make sure you have not omitted key details or distorted the meaning. Remember also to record the author's name and the page number of the source on your note card so you can properly document the paraphrase when you use it in your paper.

Using Quotation

Take down the precise words of a source when you sense that what is said can be used to strengthen your research paper's discussion. Quote selectively and accurately, with the expectation of giving your reader only enough quoted material to convey and support your ideas. Blend single words, phrases, and sentences directly into your own writing as much as possible to keep your discussion flowing and to maintain your style.

> By arguing that people "don't want more taxes, just fewer criminals ruining their neighborhoods," Philips ignores the question of how we pay for more law enforcement.

Keep in mind that a quotation introduces the voice of another writer. Used excessively, it may suggest that you are depending too heavily on others for ideas. When used sparingly and accurately, however, quotation can bring variety and a sense of immediacy to a discussion.

The following are some of the most effective uses for quotation.

1. Quote from a source to lend authority to what you say. Use the quotation to reinforce your point, not make it for you.

   To do their job right, schools first need more money for teachers, which is why the prestigious 1991 *President's Report on Education* called low teacher salaries "the single greatest roadblock to this nation's quest for educational excellence."

2. Use quotation when summary or paraphrase would sacrifice the accuracy, precision, or eloquence of the original.

The world's largest single radio telescope has "27 receivers moving on Y-shaped railway tracks, with each arm of the Y stretching 20 km."

Americans have historically agreed in principle with Henry David Thoreau, who said, "That government is best which governs least."

3. Use quotation to provide brief examples of language, as when you discuss a literary work or analyze a political speech.

Melville describes the whale as "primal," "preadamic," and "as elemental as the substance it swims in."

4. Use quotation when the original may appear extreme or of questionable veracity.

Linguist Mary Hiller states that "half of the world's 6,000 known languages will disappear in the next fifty years because no children living today speak them."

Remember always to put quotation marks around any quotation and to include documentation of the source, in both your notes and your paper. Failure to provide either of these each time you quote is plagiarism (see p. 401). Be careful also not to distort the original or to quote out of context. Although you must always use the exact language of the original whenever you quote, there are acceptable methods for altering a quotation to blend with the grammar of your own writing or to suit other needs. For example, use ellipses to show that you have omitted material from a quotation (see ellipses, 29a) and place brackets around your own comments when they interrupt the quotation (see brackets, chapter 31).

Combining Quotation and Paraphrase

You can sometimes reduce the amount of information you need to quote by combining quotation with paraphrase. The technique is simple: use quotation when the exact wording of the original is important, and paraphrase any part whose meaning, but not whose

precise language, is worth recording. You must be careful when using quotation and paraphrase together to distinguish quoted material from paraphrasing by means of clearly written quotation marks. Use ellipses and brackets to alter quotations as necessary to maintain sense or to omit unnecessary material. The following example demonstrates how to use quotation and paraphrase to record information on a note card.

> Pike argues that when schools serve more like "holding tanks" and limit student contact only to peers, they are "a fraud." The real world "for which we . . . [prepare children] is *not* full of their peers." It includes "older and younger" people from various social levels. "What are we teaching [children] about this very real world? Not much."

48f Twenty student questions, twenty answers

Research is a complicated activity that raises innumerable questions. The following common questions asked of instructors, with answers that may help your own research.

1. **I want to write a paper arguing against child abuse. I know a lot has been written on the subject. Is that a good choice for a topic?**
   First, who would argue against you in favor of child abuse? That is, are there two sides to the question? A topic like this might lead you into a discussion of morality, which would be too philosophical for a research paper. You would need to concentrate on arguing a thesis about some unsettled issue or problem related to child abuse, such as prevention, laws, or some aspect that needs further investigation.

2. **I have scoured all the reference indexes and the card catalog, but I have found only three sources on my topic. Where do I go next?**
   There are other places to look—pamphlets, other libraries, or some community sources of information. At this point,

though, you may need to reconsider your topic. It might be too recent an idea, and perhaps not much has been written about it. Or it might be so narrow or so broad that it is not identified in any indexes or catalogs. Try to redefine the topic along the lines of other ideas you have seen in sources, or develop another topic entirely.

3. **A book I need for my research is not available in any convenient libraries. Is there any way for me to get the book or find out about it?**

   Yes. You can ask the librarian to get the book through interlibrary loan from another college or university. Or use the *Book Review Digest* or a similar guide to find a comprehensive review of the book. You may find the information you need in the review, which itself will serve as a research source for your paper.

4. **For my paper I want to interview a friend. Is that a good primary source?**

   Use interviews with careful judgment. In most cases the people you choose to interview should be in a position to speak objectively and knowledgeably about the subject. They should also be able to give you insights or information not available in regular, published sources—that is why you have to interview them instead of using the library. If your friend or anyone else fits these broad criteria, use that person as a source to reaffirm or illustrate the information you obtain from more broadly available and recognized authorities.

5. **I couldn't find a date of publication, but I found a copyright date. How do I cite that date?**

   In most cases, the copyright date and date of publication are treated as the same. If both are supplied, give the publication date. If only the copyright date is included, give that date.

6. **My book source was published in three different cities. Which do I cite?**

   Cite the first city or place listed.

7. **Can I use a political rally poster I found on my campus bulletin board as a reference source?**

   Yes. Any item from which you get information is a legitimate source for research.

8. **Out of a total of twelve sources so far, six of my preliminary works cited are from one major magazine. Is that all right?**

   Your list of works cited should be balanced in terms of both the categories of sources you use (books, magazines, and so on) and the specific publications within each category. Any one source or category of source presents a limited point of view. Try to include as many viewpoints as possible, although you do not have to ignore any source.

9. **My paper topic has a long and fascinating history. How much of that history should I include?**

   Include only as much history as is relevant to your thesis or to a current situation. For the most part, keep histories to a minimum, focusing your paper's content on the development and support of your thesis statement.

10. **I need to use a number of technical terms in my paper. What is the best way to make sure my reader understands them?**

    For general college papers, keep technical vocabulary to a minimum. Recast technical terms in familiar wordings whenever possible. Refer, for example, to poikiloterms as "cold-blooded animals." Or use descriptive phrases to define unfamiliar terms: "Such pinnate, featherlike leaves are common to these plants." Finally, ask yourself if the terms are really necessary to convey your point. If not, leave them out.

11. **My paper seems like a paragraph-by-paragraph summary of my sources. Where do my own ideas come in the paper, and how do I express them?**

    Your thesis statement is *your* most important opinion in the paper and should control the organization and presentation of material. Be sure your thesis is truly an argumentative one, and then argue it as you would any idea you believe in and can support with ample evidence. Take time to review both your sources and your own attitude toward what you have learned in your research. Compare, evaluate, define, make concessions, analyze, and comment just as you would in any thorough discussion.

12. **I find little information that needs to be cited in my ten-page paper. Are three or four citations enough for a paper this long?**
Probably not. A lack of citations results from inadequate use of your research data or weak support of your own arguments. Very likely, too, you have not always given credit to your sources as you should. Review the paper's content to be sure that you have offered supportive evidence from your research and that you have properly cited the sources of that evidence.

13. **I remember hearing something about using abbreviations like *ibid., loc. cit.,* and *op. cit.* for subsequent references. What are they for?**
These abbreviations formerly were used for specific kinds of subsequent references. Scholarly groups and universities, however, have generally abandoned them in favor of the simplified method described in this text. (See 50a and 50b.)

14. **One major work I read disagrees with several others on an issue important to my paper. How do I handle this situation?**
Give careful consideration to the authority and evidence of all sources, and base your discussion on what you feel is a fair representation of the case. Provide an explanatory note to inform your readers of the differing opinion and to explain briefly the rationale for your presentation in the paper.

15. **I have a magazine title with no capital letters. Do I write the title that way in my paper?**
Capitalize according to standard practices. Commercial, popular writing often emphasizes visual impact over traditional uses of punctuation. Unless you know that such variations are part of the author's purpose, capitalize and punctuate all titles in accordance with standard rules.

16. **Where can I find sources other than those in my library?**

    Go to public agencies, departments within your school, businesses, local museums, and special-interest groups or societies. Such groups usually have pamphlets or other material available for the public as well as special libraries devoted to their particular activities.

17. **I heard a lecture in one of my classes and took notes on it. Is that a good primary source?**

    Yes. Be sure your notes are accurate. For your paper, cite the lecturer, place, and date, and identify it as a lecture.

18. **After writing the first draft, I can tell that my paper is shorter than the length required by my instructor. What should I do?**

    Check to see that you have supplied ample support for your thesis and that you have discussed all relevant aspects of the topic. Is the issue you are writing about really as simple as you have made it sound? Is your thesis too narrow or obvious to allow much discussion and presentation of evidence? Perhaps you need to broaden your subject. If time allows, ask your instructor to look over the draft with you to see what parts might need fuller treatment.

19. **I have cited six works in my paper, but I want to include in my list of works cited all twelve sources I listed in my working bibliography. Is that right?**

    No. Only the works cited in the text of your paper should appear in your Works Cited. Distinctions are sometimes made between works *cited* and *consulted,* but if you have not used a source for other than common background information, it should not be cited.

20. **How should I refer to an author? Should I use the full name or Dr., Mr., Mrs., Miss, or Ms.?**

    Simply use the full name without titles the first time you refer to an author. Then use only the last name throughout the rest of the paper. If, however, you have more than one author with the same last name in your Works Cited, use the full names throughout the paper.

49 Writing a Research Paper *res*

49a Revise the thesis and outline.

After completing the reading and note taking for your paper, you probably will have changed your concept of the paper's content and organization. At this point you will start to revise your thesis and then your outline. Begin by sorting the note cards by topic and then arrange them in a way that parallels your tentative outline. This process will show whether you have adequate material to support the points in your outline. Once the sorting is completed, evaluate your tentative thesis and working outline with an eye for revision. Then begin to rearrange the note cards and rework the tentative thesis to fit the concept you see emerging from the material you have collected.

After reading and taking notes, Jeanne Artoya decided that her paper needed to focus more strongly on the problems confronting home schooling than on its apparent growing popularity. She also decided that home schooling's early history and later battles for legal acceptance were not the central issues she wanted to discuss in her paper. Artoya's research had shown her that home schooling was actually a great deal more successful than its critics recognized. She revised her tentative thesis to reflect this focus.

TENTATIVE THESIS

After a long battle for acceptance, home schooling has proved to be an increasingly popular and worthwhile form of alternative education.

REVISED THESIS

Despite occasional opposition from local schools and ongoing general concerns over its effectiveness, home schooling offers parents and students a legal, viable, and refreshing path to education in the United States.

After sorting her cards and revising her thesis, Artoya also found that the tentative outline needed substantial revision. To begin, she moved examples of home schooling's popularity, along with general descriptions of home-school curriculum and activities, to the beginning of her paper. She felt this material would make an effective introduction to the paper. Next, Artoya decided that the "failures of public schools" was not a subject she wanted to concentrate on in the paper, so she omitted that section in the final outline. Finally, she moved the section about home schooling's success to the end of the revised outline. In this way, the paper's discussion conformed to the order of ideas expressed in her final thesis statement. Refer back to Artoya's working outline on pp. 398–400. Following are the beginning sections of Artoya's revised outline.

REVISED OUTLINE

Popularity of Home Schooling

—200,000 to 300,000 children home-school
—Home-school families increase in numbers each time a state law becomes more liberal about home schooling.

History and Legality

—Once the dominant means of education in America
—During the mid-nineteenth century, education became more formalized and home schooling became suspect.
—By 1918 education and public school attendance were mandatory; home schooling illegal.
—*Pierce v. Society of Sisters* (1925) opened the door for legal home schooling.
—Home schooling now essentially legal in every state, though all have requirements.

Reasons for Home Schooling

—Used to be for religious reasons, but that's changed
—Represents central debate over who controls a child's education—society or parents?
—Home-school parents feel it's their responsibility to educate their children, not the state's.
—Distrust and disappointment with public schools—e.g., violence, materialism, shabbiness, rigid curriculum
—Research shows that children learn best after age twelve.
—Want a student-based curriculum

Home Schooling Experiences

—Curriculums and routines for home schooling vary greatly.
—Visit museums, cook meals, handle banking, raise animals, work part time, travel

Concerns about Effectiveness

—59 percent of Americans think home schooling is a "bad thing."
—Many fear children will be too isolated.
—"Socialization" is a central concern.
—All states have laws that regulate home schooling in terms of curriculum, parent qualifications, and achievement testing.
—Twenty-nine states require standardized or supervised tests of home schoolers.

Success of Home Schooling

—Avoids the negative socialization of public schools.
—Home-schooled children outperform peers on national tests.
—Home-schooled children get accepted to colleges and universities—often ahead of their public school peers.

Once Artoya completed this stage of the revision process and rranged her notes according to the headings of the revised outline, he was ready to develop the final outline by following the formal utline form. (See final plan for an essay, 49d.) Artoya's formal sentence outline is on p. 431–435, preceding her research paper. If you compare the formal outline to the working and revised outlines, you will see how much more information she included and how she rephrased the sentences for accuracy in the formal outline.

49b Write the first draft.

You can begin writing the paper at any point in the outline, perhaps writing the middle paragraphs before the introductory and concluding paragraphs. Artoya, for instance, began writing her research paper at the point she felt was most interesting: the section dealing with the differing types of activities and curricula—from dairy farming to field biology studies—that home-schooled students enjoy. She then wrote the section dealing with the history of home schooling in the United States. The appropriate introduction occurred to Artoya when she was telling a classmate about the growing numbers of home-schooled children and how their schooling differed from her own. At that point, she had already written major portions of the paper; however, while talking about her subject with a classmate, Artoya discovered a valuable lesson for every research paper writer: talking about your subject with someone else can sometimes provide just the perspective you need to discover how other parts of your research fit together.

49c Acknowledge your sources.

Acknowledging sources for your paper lends it authority and credibility and provides readers with information to locate the sources for themselves. To a large extent, in fact, the value of your paper's content and your own integrity as a writer depend on how accurately and fairly you make use of and credit the ideas you borrow from other writers. (See avoiding plagiarism, pp. 401) As you write the paper and integrate information from your sources into it, follow standard documentation practices to ensure accurate acknowledgment of your sources.

Parenthetical Citations: MLA Documentation Style

Acknowledge sources in your paper by naming them in brief parenthetical citations as explained below and in the examples provided in
"A Documentation Guide" in section 50a. The Modern Language
Association (MLA) recommends that sources be acknowledged within parentheses placed directly in the text. In this system of parenthetical citation, numbered notes, although rarely necessary, serve only to
identify supplementary or explanatory comments. (See p. 424.)

Use parenthetical citations to acknowledge quotations (except for
common sayings or well-known quotations), summaries, paraphrases, the opinions of others, lines of thinking you adopt, and statistics.
In short, use parenthetical citations whenever you borrow information that is not commonly known or believed, especially by people
generally acquainted with your subject. Do not provide parenthetical
citations for facts or common knowledge, such as that hydrocyanic
acid is a colorless, poisonous liquid or that Abraham Lincoln was the
sixteenth president of the United States.

Because a parenthetical citation must always designate a specific
entry alphabetically listed in Works Cited, the information in the citation must clearly direct a reader to that entry. Usually, but not always
(see examples below), the author's last name and a page reference are
enough to identify the source and the specific location from which
you have borrowed material.

> The wings of jetliners built in Europe or the USSR are more
> difficult to inspect and maintain than those built in the U.S.
> because of the way they are manufactured (Seo 28).

Page references never include *p.* or *pp.* If you are referring to several consecutive pages, join the page numbers with a hyphen—for
example: (Seo 78–81). When referring to two or more individual
pages in one citation, use commas to separate them—for example:
(Seo 16, 41, 63). If the work consists of only one page, list the page
number in the Works Cited entry and do not include it in the parenthetical citation: (Birnbaum).

Keep parenthetical citations as concise as possible so that the interruption in your text is minimal. You are required to give only enough information to guide a reader to the specific source you have fully identified in Works Cited. If you have integrated into your text any information that should be included in the parenthetical citation, such as the author's name, you need not include that in the citation.

> Wilson Bryan Key has taken the mystery from subliminal-advertising discussions. He claims to have found subliminal messages in vodka ads (99).

To keep your paper as readable as possible, insert parenthetical citations before a period or comma as close to the borrowed material as possible and outside quotation marks, if you are directly quoting a source.

> In her 1979 essay collection The White Album, Joan Didion sounds confused by random violence and personal terror (15-20), but by 1982 its meaning has become clear to her: "I came to understand, in a way I had not understood before, the exact mechanism of terror" (Salvador 21).

If the borrowed material is set off from the text, the parenthetical citation follows the final punctuation. (See quotation marks, 28a.)

> In contrast to great art works, Oates sees literary criticism as a refined form of communication between writer and reader. She writes,
>
>> If the greatest works of art sometimes strike us as austere and timeless, with their private music, as befits sacred things, criticism is always an entirely human dialogue, a conversation directed toward an audience. (2)

To acquire skill in accurately acknowledging your sources in parenthetical citations, study their use in Jeanne Artoya's paper (49e) and review the following examples, paying close attention to the details of form and punctuation.

Entire Work

At times you may wish to acknowledge an entire work rather than a specific part of the work. In this case, include the author's name in the text rather than in a parenthetical citation. Since the reference is to a work in general, you are not required to cite a page number.

> Peter Brooks's analysis of plot and plotting is established on basic psychoanalytic principles.

Part of an Article or of a Single-Volume Work

When you refer to specific passages or when you quote directly from a work, you must give the relevant page reference in the parenthetical citation.

> Campbell's point is stunningly clear: "Communication is not confined to radios, telephones, and television channels. It occurs in nature, wherever life exists" (67).

> Most people spend more time picking a car than they do a doctor and hospital (Mathisen 63-64), but obviously you can't kick tires in a doctor's office, and if you attempted the equivalent in a hospital--laying your foot into a $600,000 CAT scanner--you would get some very nasty looks indeed.

If another author listed in Works Cited has the same last name as the one you are acknowledging, give the first initial as well as the last name: (L. Sanders 34).

For a work with two or three authors, give all the last names. If, however, there are more than three authors, give one last name followed by et al.: (Scholes et al. 28-29).

If you list more than one work by a single author in Works Cited, give the title or a shortened version after the author's name: (Barthes, Images 12–13).

Multivolume Work

In the parenthetical citation for a multivolume work, include the volume number followed by a colon, a space, and then the page reference: (Kroos 1: 210–15). If you refer to an entire volume in general rather than to specific pages, place a comma after the author's name and include *vol.*: (Kroos, vol. 1). If you place the information in your text, write out *volume* and the numeral: "Kroos's volume 1 covers the first...." Use arabic numerals rather than roman numerals to indicate volume numbers.

> "Feeling-toned complexes" were defined by the early psychiatric community as "failures to react" (Jung 8: 93).

> At first the prose is groping, unsure of its footing, but midway through the work, sharp portraits of avant-garde artists emerge (Nin, vol. 1).

Work Listed by Title

For a work alphabetized by title in your Works Cited, use the title or a shortened version of the title in the parenthetical reference. To make tracing the reference easier for your reader, begin the citation with the word by which the work is alphabetized. If you are acknowledging a one-page article, omit the page reference.

> A debit card, according to MasterCard's president Hogg, "looks like a credit card but works like a check" ("Now It's the No-Credit Card").

> The Planning Commission Handbook clearly states that land development is not the landowner's god-given right, but is a privilege granted by a public agency (31–32).

Work by a Corporate Author

Because the names of corporate authors are often long, identify them in your text and cite the specific page reference in the parenthetical citation. When necessary, you may offer a shortened version of the name in the parenthetical citation.

> The Commission on Post-Secondary Education in California states that remedial education in the University of California and State University systems has dramatically increased (5-10).

Fiction, Poetry, Drama, and the Bible

When citing the Bible and other literary works available in more than one edition, include the appropriate unit—that is, chapter, book, scene, line. In general, use arabic numerals rather than roman numerals in citing volumes or divisions of a work. Roman numerals may be used in citing acts and scenes of a play.

For a novel, give the page number first, a semicolon and space, and then the divisions, using appropriate abbreviations with periods.

> Politics, the undercurrent of the novel, sweeps Julien from one extreme to another. Nowhere is this more evident than in the description of the king's visit to Verrières (Stendhal 115-26; pt. 1, ch. 18).

For extended works of poetry, give the division reference first, followed by the line reference. Use a period with no space to separate the two. Do not give a page reference.

> Antenor described Odysseus's power as a powerful orator: "But when he let the great voice go from his chest, and the words came / drifting down like the winter snows, then no other mortal / man beside could stand up against Odysseus" (Homer 3.221-23).

If the poem is short or not divided into books or cantos, give only the line reference. When acknowledging only line numbers, use *line* or *lines* in the citation, but after you have established that the numbers designate lines, use only numbers.

> "For the Anniversary of My Death" begins with the suggestion that after death the soul starts a journey through time "Like the beam of a lightless star" (Merwin, line 5). The poem ends with Merwin's affirmation of concrete experience, behind which lies the mystery of existence.
>
> > As today writing after three days of rain
> > Hearing the wren sing and the falling cease
> > And bowing not knowing to what. (11-13)

For a play give the act, scene, and line references, using period without spaces to separate the divisions. You may use roman numerals in citing acts and scenes.

> The imagery of futile battle is also found in the "To be, or not to be" soliloquy (Shakespeare 3.1.56-89).

For the Bible give the book title, chapter, and verse, using period to separate the divisions. Within the parenthetical citation (but not in the text itself), you may abbreviate a book title, using a period to end the abbreviation—for example, "Gen." for *Genesis,* "Rev." for *Revelation.*

> In the opening verses of the Book of Job (1.1-5), Job appears to have fulfilled the blessing that God had bestowed on humankind when Adam and Eve were created, "Be fruitful, multiply, fill the earth and conquer it" (Gen. 1.28)

Indirect Sources

Whenever possible, draw your material from an original source, but at times you will need to rely on an indirect source for information. For instance, you may need to use someone's published account of what another person has said. When you do quote or paraphrase from an indirect source, you must indicate in the parenthetical citation that you have done so by putting *qtd. in* ("quoted in") before the acknowledgment of the source, unless, of course, you have clearly indicated in your text that you are relying on an indirect source.

> Poet Michael McClure claims Mailer had a strong belief that he would only be listened to if he were irreverent. When people asked Mailer to moderate his irreverence, he would say, "Hey, I <u>feel</u> irreverence, and there's truth in the irreverence" (qtd. in Manso 281).

Two or More Sources in a Single Parenthetical Citation

To acknowledge more than one source in a single citation, cite each work as you normally would but separate the citations with a semicolon and a space.

> Whenever we open another novel, we embark on an adventure in which we have a chance to become a new person in the sense both that we can assume the imaginary role the writer thrusts at us and that we can reformulate ourselves by discovering what had previously seemed to elude our consciousness (Gibson 265; Iser 294).

When multiple references in a single citation would be too long, acknowledge them in a note instead. (See explanatory notes section that follows.)

Explanatory Notes: MLA Style

Explanatory notes have a limited use in the MLA's system of documentation. Notes are used to offer definitions, provide translations, make comparisons between sources, or generally furnish information not strictly pertinent to the immediate discussion in the text.

Identify notes in your text by numbering them consecutively throughout with superscript (raised) arabic numerals. The numerals correspond to notes appearing either in footnotes at the bottom of the page or on a page titled "Notes" placed at the end of the paper before Works Cited.

> **TEXT REFERENCE**
>
> Once in effect, compulsory education and school attendance laws introduced a seemingly inevitable and perpetual battle between parents and schools over who should control the curriculum.[1]
>
> **NOTE**
>
> [1]Parents and schools continue even today to battle over sex and drug education programs in the school curriculum as well as over sports, dress codes, and even lunch menus. For a discussion of some contemporary cases, see Leo.

49d Complete the final draft.

After you have completed the first draft, put your paper aside for a day or two if possible. This will give you a chance to return to it with a fresh approach. Reread the entire draft carefully several times and at least once aloud to listen for missing transitions or awkward constructions (see 45p–45r). Watch for careless grammar, spelling, or punctuation mistakes. More important, examine the content to see that you have kept to your thesis, provided ample evidence to support the assertions in your topic sentences, and integrated your own views with those of your sources to create a balanced whole. As a last step, check your citations and list of works cited to be sure they are correct in form, content, and punctuation.

Guidelines for Typing the Research Paper

Although formats for research papers vary, the following guidelines are the most common practices for typing the title page, outline (if required), quotations, citations, and Works Cited. Unless otherwise noted, all typing should be double spaced. Additional information is covered in chapter 50.

Title page. Center the title about a third of the way down the page. Do not underline it or put quotation marks around it unless the words would also be underlined or quoted in the paper's text. Ten lines down from the title, center the word *by*. Two lines below *by*, center your name. Ten lines down from your name, type the course title, the instructor's name, and the date, each on a separate line.

Your instructor may prefer that you follow the MLA guidelines, which recommend not using a separate title page. If you are to follow the MLA style, present the identifying information on the first page of the text. Place your name, your instructor's name, the course number and section, and the date on separate double-spaced lines in the upper-left-hand corner of the page, observing the same left-hand margin as the text. Double-space below the date and center your title; then double-space between your title and the first line of the text.

Outline. On a separate page, center the word *Outline* one inch from the top. Two lines below, type the thesis statement, followed by the outline itself. Use standard outline form, with the various topic levels successively indented and numbered with roman or arabic numerals and lowercase or uppercase letters as required. The outline included in Jeanne Artoya's paper begins on p. 431.

Quotations. Indent quotations requiring more than four typed lines ten spaces from the left margin (or one inch), double-spacing throughout (see 28a). Do not put quotation marks around an indented quotation. When quoting two or more paragraphs, indent the first line of each paragraph three additional spaces (or one-fourth inch). The parenthetical citation appears at the end of the indented quotation, following the period or other end mark. Shorter quotations, not indented, should be enclosed in double quotation marks.

Other punctuation marks. Most computer keyboards have bracket keys. On the typewriter, brackets are made with the slash mark (/) and the underscore (raised for the top of the bracket). You can write brackets in neatly by hand with a pen if you wish. For a dash, use either two unspaced hyphens (--) without space on either side or an em dash, if available.

Notes. Starting on a new page, center the word *Notes* one inch from the top, with the first entry two lines below the title. Indent the note number, raised, five spaces from the left margin, leaving one space between the number and the first word of the note. All subsequent lines of the note begin at the left margin. Double-space within each note and between notes.

Works Cited. Type the words *Works Cited* on a new page, centered, one inch from the top. Begin the first alphabetized entry at the left margin two lines below the title. Remember to cite the first author with the last name first; subsequent authors' or editors' names in the same entry are typed in regular order; subsequent lines of an entry are indented five spaces. When you have more than one work by the same author, the name is not repeated; instead, type three hyphens followed by a period. Double-space throughout. Follow periods with only one space.

After you have typed the final version of the paper, carefully read it again for errors in typing. Include, in order, an outline, the text of the paper, the notes, and the list of works cited. Other sections, such as an appendix or glossary, if they are included, precede the notes. When you are satisfied that you have written and typed the paper in a manner that fulfills your own goals and the requirements of your instructor, make a photocopy to keep for yourself and present the original copy to your instructor.

49e Examining a sample research paper.

Jeanne Artoya's research paper, which follows, illustrates the advice given in this chapter. She followed the style for citations and list of works cited given in the *MLA Handbook*. The comments accompanying the paper identify specific points about the research paper format as well as some of the decisions Artoya made while writing.

1. Title page format: Artoya centered all the lines of the title page. She began by typing the title of her paper a third of the way down from the top. About ten lines below the title, she typed *by*, skipped two lines, and typed her name. Ten lines below her name, she typed information her instructor requested: course title, instructor's name, and the date, all double spaced.

1.

Home Schooling: Education Gains an Option

by
Jeanne Artoya

English 101
Professor Melinda Cather
December 12, 1992

2. Outline format: Artoya placed her final outline, which many instructors ask students to include with the research paper, on the page after the title page. You can leave the outline pages unnumbered or number them with small roman numerals. If you number the outline pages, omit the number on the first page and number the second page *ii*. Center the heading *Outline* an inch below the top of the page.

3. Two double-spaced lines below the heading *Outline,* type the final thesis statement, as Artoya did, so that the instructor can see how the parts relate to the thesis.

4. Although some instructors request topic outlines, which are written in phrases without periods following them, Artoya's instructor requested a sentence outline.

5. The main divisions of the outline (indicated by capital roman numerals) refer to the main divisions of the paper, and all subdivisions refer to their respective main divisions.

2. | Outline

3. | Thesis: Despite occasional opposition from local schools and
ongoing general concerns over its effectiveness, home schooling offers parents and students a legal, viable, and refreshing
path to education in America.

4. | I. Home schooling is a widely practiced educational alterna-
tive in the United States.

     A. As many as 200,000 to 300,000 children may be learn-
ing through individualized curricula at home.

     B. Many parents view home schooling as an important
alternative to public schooling.

5. | II. Home schools are not new to American education.

     A. Home schooling was the earliest form of education in
the United States.

     B. Home schooling became less popular after the Civil War.

        1. Americans wanted to strengthen democracy
through public education.

        2. Compulsory education and school attendance laws
made home schooling legally suspect.

     C. Since then, court decisions and change of public atti-
tude have reestablished home schooling's legitimacy.

        1. <u>Pierce v. Society of Sisters</u> (1925) reestablished the
legal basis for home schooling in this country.

        2. Ex-President Reagan publicly reaffirmed parents'
responsibility for educating their children as a
"primary right, duty."

        3. Though all states have requirements, home school-
ing is now legal in virtually every state.

III. Arguments about home schooling are rooted in funda-
mental beliefs about education and the way children
learn.
   A. Parents and schools historically have been at odds
      about who has authority over a child's education.
   B. Home schooling encourages learning that is highly
      varied and individualized rather than uniform.
IV. Parents home-school their children for a variety of rea-
sons.
   A. As in the past, a majority of families home-school to
      protect religious teachings and values.
   B. Most home-school parents regard their children's
      education as their own–not society's–primary responsi-
      bility.
   C. Others embrace progressive education philosophies
      that conflict with public education.
      1. They feel that public schools emphasize conformity
         in learning and values.
      2. Many want a student-based curriculum in which
         students learn or enter school when they feel ready
         to do so.
V. Critics are concerned about the effectiveness of home
schooling.
   A. The greatest concern is over the issue of socialization.
      1. Many fear home-schooled children are too isolated
         from their peers and others.
      2. Home-school advocates counter that public schools
         provide only the worst kind of socialization.

B. Many also distrust the value of home-school instruction.

   1. Parent-teachers are often not trained or highly educated themselves.

   2. As a result of such concerns, states have instituted regulations governing home schools.

VI. Despite these concerns, home schooling continues to prove successful.

A. Home-schooled children have more positive socialization attitudes than do their public school peers.

B. They outperform public school students on national tests.

C. Their acceptance rate at colleges and universities is good.

VII. Home schooling has an undeniably important role in this nation's educational future.

6. To begin, Artoya offers a statistical example to introduce the paper's subject and immediately capture the reader's attention.

7. Include specific titles when citing authors listed with multiple works in the paper's Works Cited section.

8. To further engage the reader, Artoya provides several examples that distinguish home-school education from traditional classroom learning.

9. Quotation marks here indicate that Artoya uses the word *class* ironically.

10. Artoya's second paragraph defines her subject and provides the background leading to the thesis statement.

11. The quotation implies the opposition home schooling faces and sets the stage for the discussion of home schooling's effectiveness. The parenthetical note cites the source for the quotation.

12. A citation of a source having two authors must include each author's last name. Note that no comma separates the second author's name and the page number.

Home Schooling

Although their numbers escape exact count, it is likely
6. that from 200,000 to 300,000 American children (Lines,
7. "Home" 211) will not be showing up for school next year--at
least not at the kinds of schools most of us know. Rather than
attending the public or private institutions in which the majority of this country's young are educated, these students will be
8. going to school right in their own homes. Most of them will
have one or both parents as teachers, and they will follow a
curriculum liberally suited to their individual interests and
learning styles. Like other children going to school, these students will read books and do homework, and some will even
9. have "class" at regular times of the day. For most of them, however, learning will occur naturally, almost unconsciously, in the
course of their completing daily household responsibilities or
gaining firsthand experiences in their communities and else-
where.
10. These students are the products of home schooling, an
alternative form of education in which children are taught at
home rather than in the public or private school systems and
in which the curriculum is specifically shaped around their
individual interests and needs. Although still considered "a
11. fringe element in education" (Lee), home schooling is a long-
standing grass-roots movement with a swelling increase of
popularity since the 1960s and 1970s. Once primarily an alternative for parents wishing to base their children's education
upon religious principles rather than the secular values taught
12. in public schools (LaRue and LaRue 35), home schooling today

13. Having used the first two paragraphs to introduce the subject and engage the reader, Artoya concludes this second paragraph with the thesis statement.

14. Artoya uses the next three paragraphs to trace the history of home schooling in the United States. She explains the cultural roots of home schooling, as well as the origin of some opposition to it.

15. A citation of a source having three authors must include each author's last name.

16. The dash here effectively interrupts the sentence to clarify the motives behind instituting compulsory education laws.

appeals to a broad spectrum of Americans disenchanted with and distrustful of public education generally. Faced with over-crowded, underfunded schools, failing curricula, and the increasingly dangerous conditions of today's public schools, thousands of American parents and their children have

13. turned their hopes for education toward home. Despite occasional opposition from local schools and ongoing general concerns over its effectiveness, home schooling offers parents and students a legal, viable, and refreshing path to education in America.

14. Though unfamiliar to most of us, home schools are not new to the American education scene. In fact, during colonial times and continuing until the latter part of the nineteenth century, home schooling was the predominant form of education in the United States. Before the Civil War, education was not universal, compulsory, or tax supported. Parents assumed the primary responsibility for educating their children (Rakestraw and Rakestraw 68). By the mid-nineteenth century, however, public attitudes about education changed, and formalized public schooling was emphasized as necessary for "Americanizing" Native Americans and immigrants, as well as for

15. improving undesirable conditions emanating from and among the lower classes of society (Knowles, Marlow, and Muchmore 201).

16. By 1918 compulsory education--with the ostensibly worthy goals of preserving democracy, improving the country economically, and equalizing opportunity among races and classes of people (Rakestraw and Rakestraw 69)--became the law of the land. Home schooling, once the single most widely practiced

17. Underline court cases when they are named in the paper's text.

18. Artoya uses direct quotation to preserve the authority and effectiveness of the source language. Integrated into Artoya's sentence structure, too, is the fact that home schooling is today a legal alternative to public education.

19. In note 1, Artoya provides examples to illustrate her point further and directs the reader to a fuller discussion in one of the sources listed in the Works Cited section. (See Notes, p. 459.)

form of education in this country, was rendered illegal by the requirements of nationwide compulsory education and mandatory school attendance laws. Although opposed to these laws, home-school practitioners had no recourse from them until **17.** 1925, when the Supreme Court ruled in <u>Pierce v. Society of Sisters</u> that parents could provide private education for their children (McCarthy 177). The decision opened the door for home education's return to legitimacy in this country.

Thereafter the outcome of numerous state-by-state court decisions regarding the status of home schooling revolved around home schools meeting court requirements for providing "education" or constituting an actual "school" (McCarthy 177). By 1984, when ex-President Ronald Reagan publicly stated **18.** that "the primary right, duty, and responsibility of educating children belongs to parents," he was affirming this nation's recognition of parents' rights to teach their children at home (Rakestraw and Rakestraw 71). Although still subject to close scrutiny and regulation (Cain), home schooling is today legal in virtually every state (Pedersen and O'Mara 79).

Despite its statutory acceptance, the philosophical underpinnings of home schooling remain fundamentally opposed to the concepts embodied in compulsory education laws. Once in effect, these laws introduced a seemingly inevitable and perpetual battle between parents and schools over who should con- **19.** trol the curriculum.[1] Dissatisfied with when, what, and how their children have come to be taught in the public schools, today's home-school parents have withdrawn from the battle, however, by opting for home education.

20. Indent a quotation longer than four lines ten spaces (or one inch) from the left margin. Introduce the quotation formally with a colon following a complete main clause. Do not put quotation marks around the indented block of material. Cite the source parenthetically, one space after the final period.

Representing a wide spectrum of social and political philosophies (Knowles, Marlow, and Muchmore 197), parents who teach their children at home do so for a variety of reasons. As in the past, a majority of families continue to home-school for religious reasons, amounting mainly to dissatisfaction with the secular, humanistic values that dominate public school instruction (McCarthy 176). At the same time, however, an increasing number also choose to home-school because they disagree with the basic assumptions of public education. A primary belief on the part of home-school parents is that they--not public institutions--have the primary responsibility for raising and educating their children. Bolstered by the opinion of education experts that parents serve as the principal motivation for children to learn (Wlodkowski and Jaynes 15), home-school supporters believe that teaching their own children should be a priority for all parents:

20.

> Public schools should serve as an educational safety net: a path to literacy for those families who cannot provide that path themselves. As for the rest of us--at what point did the size of our houses (and the size of the monthly mortgage payment) supplant the responsibility of raising our children? (LaRue and LaRue 37)[2]

Home-school parents elect to teach their children at home not only because they accept doing so as a primary responsibility, but also because they do not believe the public schools are-- or can be--effective. In their view, the public school curricula are too institutionalized to meet the diverse needs of children as individuals. The majority of home-school parents embrace

21. Artoya uses a colon here to introduce examples of other education reformers.

22. Use a semicolon between multiple sources cited parenthetically in the text.

23. Here Artoya effectively weaves a quoted phrase into her own sentence to introduce a longer block of quotation.

the philosophies of educational reformers such as Francis W. Parker, the nineteenth-century founder of the liberal, progressive education movement in this country, as well as his more modern counterparts: John Dewey, Maria Montessori, John Holt, and others who advocate education centered upon the individual interests and readiness of the learner rather than the expectations of a prescribed and rigid curriculum (Pedersen and O'Mara 51; Knowles, Marlow, and Muchmore 204).

In following such philosophies, home-school parents believe public school curricula ignore the most fundamental truth of the educational process--that is, that all children do not learn at the same rate. They find that as public classroom teaching gives in to institutional as well as community pressures for academic advancement, the primary curriculum is "pushed down into kindergarten and the kindergarten curriculum into prekindergarten" (Charlesworth 569) without regard for students' readiness for learning. In doing so, public schools perpetuate what home-school supporters see as a "blind and valueless conformity" to an impractical curriculum:

> We do not expect our children to walk at the same age. We admit that some children speak before others. We recognize that most boys mature more slowly than do girls. Yet, in our public school system, we expect every child to go to school at the same age and move in lock-step from grade to grade at the beginning of an utterly arbitrary school year. (LaRue and LaRue 36)

Advocates also argue that once freed from the artificial, sometimes wholly arbitrary schedules and rules that other

24. These general examples further illustrate the kind of educational opportunities offered by home schooling. They effectively conclude with a description of a specific case.

25. Artoya uses parentheses to show that her remark is intended to have only slight significance.

children endure, home-schooled children enjoy educations focused upon their own interests and abilities rather than on a prescribed curriculum. Home-school curricula, in fact, are as

24.   varied as their students' interests. Some learn baking, animal husbandry, or basic accounting by assuming practical, "real-life" responsibilities at home, for example. Others may visit a local museum or spend the day interviewing one of their town's oldest inhabitants as part of a history lesson. To study mathematics, home-schooled students may help a neighbor design and build a storage shed, or they may learn fractions by mixing recipes for the meals they prepare in the family kitchen. To acquire a foreign language, these students might work part time in a place where customers or co-workers speak Spanish, French, or Vietnamese more often than English. Others may travel, as sixteen-year-old Brittany Barker did when she studied biology and nature art by traveling across Canada for eight weeks with a nature writer and water-colorist and his field-biologist wife (Pedersen and O'Mara 203).

Backed by extensive research showing that children learn best when they begin formal schooling after the age of twelve, many home-school parents teach their children at home until they are ready to enter junior high school (Pedersen and O'Mara 23-25). In some cases, home-school parents, working in cooperation with local schools, may allow their children to enter, withdraw, and reenter the public education system as learning needs develop and change (Knowles, Marlow, and Muchmore 216).

5.   Statutory tolerance and the (occasionally grudging) coop-eration of school districts, however, should not imply that home

26. Use numerals for percentages.

27. Artoya uses quotation marks here to indicate that quotation marks appeared in the source.

28. Describing her source in the text rather than parenthetically allows Artoya to describe the source's qualifications and lends authority to the quotation.

schooling has necessarily won the acceptance of the general

26. public. In a 1988 Gallop Opinion Poll, for example, 59 percent
of those responding viewed home schooling as a "bad thing"

27. (Rakestraw and Rakestraw 73). Threatened by a practice at
odds with the familiar institutions they have created and continue to support through tax dollars, most people distrust
home schooling and deem its practitioners suspect. Critics fear
that home schooling overly isolates children, leaving them prey
to parents who may wrongfully indoctrinate or mistreat them
or who might simply use home schooling as an excuse to avoid
employment (Rakestraw and Rakestraw 72; Redder 30).

Nothing has raised concern about home schooling, however, as much as the question of its social effect on children.
Opponents of home schooling worry that children educated at
home may be deprived of appropriate social development
because of inadequate interaction with their peers. According

8. to Dr. Ronald Lee, professor of child psychology and education
at Granger State University, peer interaction and social development are not necessarily a guaranteed product of home
schooling:

> To develop socially, children need the give-and-take
> experiences that learning and playing with other
> children provide, and they need friendships with
> others outside their families. With home schooling,
> there's no guarantee they'll get very much of either.
> I'm not saying these things cannot happen with
> home schooling. What I'm saying is, they may not
> always happen. A lot depends on the parents and
> whether or not they recognize the need for their

29. No page number is given for a personal interview. The source for the quotation has been given in the text above.

30. Cite the author of a signed encyclopedia article by last name.

31. Artoya uses brackets here to indicate that she has added the enclosed content to the original.

32. The double quotation marks appeared in the original. No quotation marks should appear around the indented quotation as a whole.

33. Here Artoya quotes from two sources consecutively to illustrate the positions of those finding fault with public schools.

29.   children having adequate opportunities for peer
         interaction.

       In the sense of preparing children to live and work pro-
ductively with others by instilling in them the values and
social behavior of the community, socialization has long been
30.   accepted as the fundamental purpose of education (White).
Home-school parents acknowledge that children need socialization, but they reject the idea that public schools can provide the
right kind. "In all but a very few of the schools I have taught in,
visited, or know anything about," said leading home-school
1.   advocate John Holt in 1981, "the social life of the children is
mean-spirited, competitive, status-seeking, [and] snobbish" (44-
45). Others agree, arguing that modern public schools can
expose children only to a limited and mostly negative type of
socialization:

2.   Public schools have, apparently willingly, assumed the
              role of "holding tanks." Social contact limited strictly
              to "peers" (defined as everyone of the same chrono-
              logical age) is a fraud. The world for which we have
              the responsibility of preparing young people is not
              full of their peers. It is full of people both older and
              younger, from a social strata both higher and lower.
              What are we teaching children about this world? Not
              much. (Pike 564)

              Today there are children who are ashamed to go to
              school because they do not have the right labels on
              their clothes. There are children who have children of
              their own. There are children who join gangs, who

34. The raised note number appears after punctuation marks such as the period and the comma.

35. The use of academic abbreviations, such as *cf.* ("compare" keep parenthetical content brief. Cite no page number if the sourc material appears on a single page only, as here with the reference t Taylor.

36. Use a hyphen to separate multiple pages.

commit crimes, who kill people--all in order to "fit in."
This too is "socialization." (LaRue and LaRue 36)

Such conditions, all too prevalent in today's public
schools,[3] are all the evidence most home-school parents need
to feel justified in teaching their children at home. If that were
not enough, considerable research shows that home-schooled
children possess demonstrably higher levels of self-esteem and
positive socialization attitudes than do their public-school
peers. For example, a majority (77 percent) of home-schooled
students score higher than the national average on self-concept tests (Taylor; cf. Lines, "An Overview" 512). Research has
also shown that more than half of home-schoolers spend 20 to
30 hours a month in organized community activities; 40 percent spend more than 30 hours each month with peers outside
their families (Wartes 43-45).

The concern of those distrustful of home schooling has
also extended to questioning the validity of its academic
instruction. Critics express doubts, for example, about the abilities of parents to teach and evaluate their children effectively
within the usually unstructured environment of the home
school (Lee). As a result of such concerns, most states have
enacted laws requiring teacher certification, achievement testing, and record keeping for home schools (Rakestraw and
Rakestraw 72), and twenty-nine now require home-schooled
students either to take standardized tests or to complete supervised state forms of assessment (McCarthy 178).

Whether because of or despite such requirements, how
ever, home schooling continues to prove highly successful in

37. The abbreviated phrase *qtd. in* here shows the source ◂
Artoya's indirect quotation.

preparing students academically. Statewide tests in Tennessee, New York, Washington, and Alabama, for example, show that home-schooled children consistently perform higher than the national average on the Stanford Achievement Test, and the Alaskan Department of Education found that home-educated students taking other standardized tests outperformed their classroom counterparts from both Alaska and California (Rakestraw and Rakestraw 73).

Though their acceptance of home-schooled students is still cautious, colleges and universities are also increasing their recognition of home education's value. Home-schooled students--some as young as twelve or thirteen years old and often lacking high school diplomas--have been admitted to and graduated from four-year institutions all over the nation, including such schools as Harvard and Radcliffe Colleges, the University of Texas at San Antonio, Michigan State University, and Brigham Young University (Pedersen and O'Mara 214-15).

Hand in hand with the compulsory public education that first displaced it and today accounts for a great part of its impetus, home schooling has again gained a credible place in American education. Its current success and historical persistence suggest that home schooling has an undeniably important role in this nation's educational future. And as more communities and parents answer ex-President Bush's calls to "break the mold" and "reinvent the American school" (qtd. in "Revolution" 53), it will undoubtedly be viewed as an increasingly proven and necessary alternative to current forms of public education. Certainly home schooling is not for every family, nor will it necessarily benefit every child. In its best

tradition, however, it will persist, as it does today, not only in affirming the role parents have in educating their children but also in unlocking the unique capacities for learning within every individual.

38. Artoya begins the commentary notes on a new page and centers the title *Notes* one inch from the top.

39. Raised numbers identify each note. Indent the first line of each note five spaces. Separate the note from the number by one space.

40. Artoya uses note 2 to clarify and elaborate briefly on her comments in the text. She cites the source for her remarks here parenthetically, just as she would in the text of the paper.

41. Use *see* to refer to sources listed in Works Cited.

Notes

38.

39.   [1] Parents and schools continue even today to battle over sex and drug education programs in the school, as well as over sports, dress codes, and even lunch menus. For a discussion of some contemporary cases, see Leo.

40.   [2] Home-school supporters do not expect mothers to stop having careers in order to stay home with the children. Rather, its advocates insist that home schooling is a family affair involving the shared, active participation of everyone--including mothers as well as fathers, sisters, brothers, grandparents, aunts, and uncles (see LaRue and LaRue 136-37).

41.   [3] For discussion of the negative conditions existing in today's public schools, see Redder 143-56.

42. Artoya's list of works cited begins on a new page, with the title *Works Cited* centered one inch from the top. Double-space to the first entry. List the entries in alphabetical order by the authors' last names.

43. List second and succeeding edition numbers of books as shown.

44. For works with three authors, list each author, but reverse only the first author's name.

45. Place article titles in quotation marks, and underline the title of the periodical. For a journal with continuous pagination throughout each volume, give the volume number, year in parentheses, colon, and page number(s) of the article as shown here.

46. For a journal that paginates each issue in a volume separately (i.e., starting every issue with page 1), give the volume number followed by a period and the issue number, as shown here. Indicate discontinuous pages with a semicolon.

47. For an interview, give the name of the interviewee, the kind of interview (e.g., personal, telephone, taped), and the inverted date of the interview.

48. For a weekly magazine, list the full date inverting the day and abbreviating the month.

49. The ending information on this entry shows that Artoya used a data base information service (ERIC, or Educational Resources Information Center) to obtain the source article. Include such pertinent identifying information for any entry provided by a computer or information service ("Online.") and the date.

50. Use three unspaced hyphens in place of the author's name to list the second and succeeding works by the same author. Follow the hyphens with a period. List the entries in chronological order.

51. Use the abbreviation *Ed.* for "Edited by." Give the state (abbreviated) if the city of publication is not well known.

Works Cited

Cain, Robert. "Courts Approve of Home Teaching." New York
    Times 14 Oct. 1991, late ed., sec. 2: 1.

Charlesworth, Rosalind. Understanding Child Development: For
    Adults Who Work with Young Children. 3rd ed. New York:
    Delmar, 1992.

Holt, John. Teach Your Own: A Hopeful Path for Education. New
    York: Seymour-Delacorte, 1981.

Knowles, J. Gary, Stacey E. Marlow, and James A. Muchmore.
    "From Pedagogy to Ideology: Origins and Phases of Home
    Education in the United States, 1970-1990." American
    Journal of Education 100 (1992): 196-235.

LaRue, James, and Suzanne LaRue. "Is Anybody Home? Home
    Schooling and the Library." Wilson Library Bulletin 66.3
    (1991): 32-37; 136-37.

Lee, Ronald. Personal interview. 2 Dec. 1992.

Leo, John. "Schools to Parents: Keep Out." U.S. News & World
    Report 5 Oct. 1992: 33.

Lines, Patricia M. "An Overview of Home Instruction." Phi Delta
    Kappan 68 (1987): 510-17. ERIC. Online. 1 Dec. 1992.

---. "Home Instruction: Characteristics, Size and Growth." Home
    Schooling: Political, Historical, and Pedagogical Perspec-
    tives. Ed. Jane Van Galen and Mary A. Pitman. Norwood,
    NJ: Ablex, 1991.

McCarthy, Martha M. "Home Schooling and the Law."
    Educational Horizons 69 (1991): 176-79.

Pedersen, Anne, and Peggy O'Mara, eds. Schooling at Home:
    Parents, Kids, and Learning. Sante Fe: Muir, 1991.

52. Identify the work as a dissertation, and give the university and year. Abbreviate the title of *Dissertation Abstracts International;* give volume number, year, and entry number and letter as shown here. Abbreviate *university* as *U.*

53. List the author of a signed encyclopedia article by last name.

54. Use shortened forms for publishers' names.

Pike, Bob. "Why I Teach My Children at Home." <u>Phi Delta Kappan</u> 73 (1992): 564-65.

Rakestraw, Jennie F., and Donald A. Rakestraw. "Home Schooling: A Question of Quality, an Issue of Rights." <u>Educational Forum</u> 55 (1990): 67-77.

Redder, John. <u>American Schools: Too Little Too Often</u>. New York: Young, 1992.

"A Revolution Hoping for a Miracle." <u>Time</u> 29 Apr. 1991: 52-53.

52. Taylor, John W. "Self-Concept in Home Schooling Children." Diss. Andrews U, 1987. <u>DAI</u> 47 (1987): 2809A.

Wartes, Jon. "The Washington Home School Project: Quantitative Measures for Informing Policy Decisions." <u>Education and Urban Society</u> 21 (1988): 42-51.

53. White, Leslie A. "Culture." <u>Encyclopedia Britannica: Macropedia</u>. 1988 ed.

54. Wlodkowski, Raymond J., and Judith H. Jaynes. <u>Eager to Learn: Helping Children Become Motivated and Love Learning</u>. San Francisco: Jossey. 1991.

50 A Documentation Guide *doc*

50a Guide to MLA *Works Cited* and parenthetical note forms

Examples of the MLA *Works Cited* and parenthetical note forms (if different from the standard style detailed in 49c) follow this list of sample resources.

General Books

1. A Book with One Author
2. Two Books with the Same Author
3. A Book with Two or Three Authors
4. A Book with More Than Three Authors
5. A Book with a Corporate Author
6. A Book with a Later Edition
7. A Book in More Than One Volume
8. A Book Reprinted or Republished by a Different Publisher
9. A Book in a Series
10. A Book with an Editor
11. A Book with Two Editors
12. A Book with an Author and an Editor
13. A Book with an Introduction, Foreword, or Afterword
14. A Book That Has Been Translated
15. A Book That Includes a Reference to Another Work
16. A Selection from an Anthology, Collection, or Critical Edition
17. A Book with a Title in Its Title
18. A Book with a Publisher's Imprint
19. An Anonymous Book

Periodicals

20. An Unsigned Article in a Magazine
21. A Signed Article in a Magazine

General Books

1. A Book with One Author

    Norris, William. The Unsafe Sky: The Unvarnished Truth about Air Safety. New York: Norton, 1981.

2. Two Books with the Same Author

    Panati, Charles. The Browser's Book of Beginnings: Origins of Everything under (and Including) the Sun. Boston: Houghton, 1984.

    ---. Extraordinary Origins of Everyday Things. New York: Harper-Collins, 1987.

    [Note that the author's name is given only the first time. For al subsequent entries by the same author, three unseparated hyphens are used where the name would appear.]

3. A Book with Two or Three Authors

    Boeck, Wilhelm, and Jaime Sabartes. Picasso. New York: Abrams, 1971.

    McCrum, Robert, William Cran, and Robert McNeil. The Story of English. New York: Viking, 1986.

4. A Book with More Than Three Authors

    Young, Ralph A., et al. Personal Finance Companies and Their Credit Practices. New York: Nat. Bur. of Econ. Res., 1940.

    [If not commonly known by its initials or acronym, shorten th publisher's name so the reader will still be able to identify it.]

5. A Book with a Corporate Author

    Reader's Digest Association. Family Word Finder. New York: Reader's Digest, 1975.

6. A Book with a Later Edition

Meyers, L. M., and Richard L. Hoffman. <u>The Roots of Modern English</u>. 2nd ed. Boston: Little, 1979.

> [Use standard abbreviations for the edition numbers: 2nd, 3rd, 4th; Rev. ed.]

7. A Book in More Than One Volume

Holroyd, Michael. <u>Lytton Strachey: A Critical Biography</u>. Vol. 1. New York: Holt, 1967.

8. A Book Reprinted or Republished by a Different Publisher

Redhall, Frederick. <u>London Towers</u>. 1949. New York: Boswich, 1974.

9. A Book in a Series

Amos, William H. <u>Wildlife of the Rivers</u>. Wildlife Habitat Ser. New York: Abrams, 1981.

10. A Book with an Editor

Newhall, Beaumont, ed. <u>Photography: Essays and Images</u>. New York: Museum of Modern Art, 1980.

11. A Book with Two Editors

Pluto, Terry, and Jeffrey Neuman, eds. <u>A Baseball Winter: The Off-season of the Summer Game</u>. New York: MacMillan, 1986.

12. A Book with an Author and an Editor

WORKS CITED FORM

Whitman, Walt. <u>Leaves of Grass</u>. Ed. Emory Holloway. New York: Doubleday, 1926.

PARENTHETICAL NOTE   (Whitman 140)

> [Use these forms when the work of the book's author is your subject. Entries focusing on the work of the editor would appear as below.]

WORKS CITED FORM

Holloway, Emory, ed. <u>Leaves of Grass</u>. By Walt Whitman. New

York: Doubleday, 1926.

PARENTHETICAL NOTE   (Holloway vii)

> [The small roman numerals indicate page numbers that precede those of the text, as for introductions or forewords.]

13. A Book with an Introduction, Foreword, or Afterword

WORKS CITED FORM

Mays, Willie, Foreword. <u>How to Coach, Manage & Play Little</u>

<u>League Baseball</u>. By Charles Einstein. New York: Fireside,

1968.

PARENTHETICAL NOTE   (Mays 5)

> [Use these forms when your focus is on the writer of the introduction, foreword, or afterword rather than on the author of the book.]

14. A Book That Has Been Translated

Massoun, Jeffrey Moussaieff, trans. <u>The Complete Letters of Sig-</u>

<u>mund Freud</u>. Cambridge: Belknap-Harvard UP, 1985.

15. A Book That Includes a Reference to Another Work

WORKS CITED FORM

Manso, Peter. <u>Mailer: His Life and Times</u>. New York: Simon, 1985.

PARENTHETICAL NOTE   (qtd. in Manso 103)

> [See the discussion of "Indirect Sources," p. 423. The citation there identifies McClure as the source of the quotation, but Manso's book, which quoted McClure, is listed in *Works Cited*.

16. A Selection from an Anthology, Collection, or Critical Edition

West, Rebecca. "The Nature of Will." Hamlet: <u>An Authoritative Text</u>. Ed. Cyrus Hoy. New York: Norton, 1963. 256–66.

[Although the title of the play *Hamlet* would ordinarily be underlined, names of works that appear as part of other works' titles are not underlined. Notice that the page numbers for West's essay are indicated since the citation focuses on her work rather than on Hoy's book.]

17. A Book with a Title in Its Title

Jass, William. <u>Consciousness and Consent in Shakespeare's</u> Macbeth. New York: Denning, 1939.

[If the title of the work included in the source title is normally underlined, do not underline it here. Do underline all other parts of the title of the source containing or discussing the work.]

Unger, Raymond. <u>Frost's "Stopping by Woods on a Snowy Evening" and the Lure of Beauty</u>. Boston: Mangeri, 1990.

[If the title of the work included in the source title normally appears within quotation marks, retain the marks and also underline the complete title, as shown here.]

18. A Book with a Publisher's Imprint

Carver, Raymond. <u>Where I'm Calling From</u>. New York: Vintage-Random, 1989.

[When a work has been reprinted by a division of a publisher, list the division first, joined by a hyphen to the name of the main publisher.]

9. An Anonymous Book

<u>The Times Atlas of the World</u>. 7th ed. New York: New York Times, 1985.

[If the work cited has no author's name on the title page, begin the entry with the title and alphabetize by the first word other than an indefinite or a definite article.]

Periodicals

20. An Unsigned Article in a Magazine

    "Four Exercises Women Do Too Many Of." <u>Self</u> Sept. 1988:

    174–77.

21. A Signed Article in a Magazine

    Cunningham, Kim. "U.S. Davis Cuppers Set to Conquer." <u>World</u>

    <u>Tennis</u> Oct. 1988: 68–69.

22. An Article in a Journal with Continuous Pagination in Each Volume

    Gordon, J. M. "Ideal Solar Concentrators for Photoelectrochemi-

    cal Cells." <u>Solar Energy</u> 40 (1988): 391–95.

    > [*Continuous pagination* means that a publication numbers it
    > pages continuously through an entire volume composed of sev
    > eral issues. For instance, if the first issue in a volume ends o
    > page 85, then the second issue will begin on page 86.]

23. An Article in a Journal with Separate Pagination in Each Issue

    Bagley, Bruce M. "Colombia and the War on Drugs." <u>Foreign</u>

    <u>Affairs</u> 37.1 (1988): 70–92.

    > [*Separate pagination* means that a publication numbers its page
    > separately for each issue of a volume, always beginning with pag
    > 1.
    >
    > Most of these types of publications will have an issue number a
    > well as a volume number. In this example, *67* is the volume num
    > ber and *1* is the issue number.]

24. An Unsigned Newspaper Article

    "Air Travel Less Safe Now, Most Americans Believe." <u>Orange</u>

    <u>County Register</u> 11 Aug. 1988: A10.

25. A Signed Newspaper Article

Malnic, Eric. "Jet Engine, Wing Flaps under Study." <u>Los Angeles</u>
<u>Times</u> 2 Sept. 1988, sec. I: 1+.

> [The plus sign is used here to indicate that the article continues
> on other, not necessarily continuous, pages.]

26. A Letter to the Editor

Masters, Mark. Letter. <u>The Futurist</u> Sept.–Oct. 1988: 2.

27. An Unsigned Editorial

"Magic Words for Colleges." Editorial. <u>Los Angeles Times</u> 3 May
1985, sec. B: 6.

28. A Signed Editorial

Birnbaum, Norman. "The Center Holds." Editorial. <u>Nation</u> 1 June
1985: 660–61.

Encyclopedias

29. An Unsigned Article from an Encyclopedia

"Cancer." <u>Encyclopedia Brittanica: Micropedia</u> 1988 ed.

> [Volume and page numbers are not required for an article
> appearing alphabetically in an encyclopedia.]

30. A Signed Article from an Encyclopedia

Pepper, Eleanor. "Interior Design." <u>Encyclopedia Americana</u> 1987
ed.

> [Encyclopedia articles are sometimes signed with only the
> author's initials, which are usually identified in the index or the
> front of the volume.]

Other Sources

31. An Unsigned Pamphlet

<u>Herbert Hoover: The Uncommon Man</u>. Washington: Hoover Pres.
    Lib., 1974.

32. A Signed Pamphlet

Lobsenz, Norman M. <u>Grandparents Today</u>. New York: Publ. Aff.
    Comm., 1987.

33. A Government Publication

WORKS CITED FORM

United States. Committee on Government Operations. <u>Near Miss</u>
    <u>es and Air Traffic Control Issues in Chicago</u>. 100th Cong.
    Washington: GPO, 1988.

> [Begin with the name of the government, then the agency spon
> soring the material. Include, if relevant, the Congress und
> which the material was printed. GPO is the standard abbrevi
> tion for Government Printing Office, the agency responsible f
> printing most U.S. government materials.]

PARENTHETICAL NOTE   (U.S. Committee on Government Opera
tions 44–47)

> [To avoid lengthy parenthetical notes, it is usually best to nan
> corporate and government authors in the text: "According to ti
> U.S. Committee on Government Operations . . . ."]

34. A Published Conference Proceeding

Stone, Linda, and Mary Shrire, eds. <u>Proceedings of the Fourth</u>
    <u>Oregon Conference on Euthanasia</u>. 22 Nov. 1990. Portland
    U of Portland P.

35. An Unpublished Dissertation

> Better, Shirley Jean. "Black Working Women: Role Perception,
> Role Strain, and Life Satisfaction." Diss. U of California, Los
> Angeles, 1987.

36. An Unpublished Dissertation Listed in *Dissertation Abstracts* or *Dissertation Abstracts International*

> Better, Shirley Jean. "Black Working Women: Role Perception,
> Role Strain, and Life Satisfaction." Diss. U of California, Los
> Angeles, 1987. DAI 49 (1988): 344A.

7. Information from CD-ROM and Other Databases

> Benta, Harriette. "Japanese-American Internees." New York
> Times 1 April 1995, late ed.: C3. New York Times Ondisc. CD-
> ROM. UMI-Proquest. May 1995.

> > [Provide the information as you would for an article or a book.
> > Then add the title of the database, the publication medium, the
> > name of the vendor if available, and the electronic publication date.]

8. Information from an Online Source

> Lines, Patricia. "An Overview of Home Instruction." Phi Delta
> Kappan 68 (1987): 510–17. ERIC. Online. 1 Dec. 1992.

> > [Cite a source obtained through a database or information ser-
> > vice as you would normally, but include identifying technical
> > information after the end of the entry.]

9. A Film or Videotape

> Roll Over. Dir. Alan J. Pakula. IPC Films, 1981.

> > [Begin with the film title, followed by the director, distributor,
> > and year of release.]

> Rocky IV. Videocassette. Dir. Sylvester Stallone. New United
> Artists, 1986.

[After the title, insert the word *videocassette,* followed by the director, distributor, and year of release.]

40. A Television or Radio Program

Good Morning America. ABC. KABC, Los Angeles. 4 Oct. 1985.

[After the title, include the network, local station, city, and date of broadcast.]

41. A Biblical Citation

The Bible.

[The King James version of the Bible is usually assumed, but let your reader know fuller details about the source if you quote extensively (e.g., The Bible. Standard Revised Version). Titles of sacred writings, such as the Bible, the Koran, the Talmud, the Upanishads, and so on, are not underlined or placed within quotation marks.]

42. A Poem

Dante. The Inferno. Trans. John Ciardi. New York: NAL, 1954.

Roethke, Theodore. "Elegy," The Far Field. New York: Doubleday, 1964. 46–47.

43. A Play

Brecht, Bertold. Galileo. Trans. Charles Laughton. New York: Grove, 1966.

Shakespeare, William. Hamlet. Shakespeare: The Complete Works. Ed. G. B. Harrison. New York: Harcourt, 1968. 341–77.

44. A Performance of a Play

Hay Fever. By Noel Coward. Dir. Robert Fryer. Ahmanson Theater, Los Angeles. 8 Apr. 1983.

[In addition to the basic information, also give the theater, city, and date of the performance.]

45. A Musical or Audio Recording

Eliot, T. S. <u>The Waste Land and Other Poems</u>. Caedmon, 1971.

> [After naming the manufacturer—Caedmon in this example—include the year of issue.]

46. A Work of Art

Renoir, Pierre-Auguste. <u>Gabriel and Jean</u>. Museum of Fine Arts,

Boston.

> [For a work of art located in a museum or private collection, give the artist's name, title of work, and location.]

Renoir, Pierre-Auguste. <u>Gabriel and Jean</u>. Museum of Fine Arts,

Boston. <u>The Impressionists: A Retrospective</u>. Ed. Martha

Kapos. New York: Levin, 1991. 317.

> [For a work reproduced in another work, such as a book, give the title, author's or editor's name, and publication data after listing the work.]

47. An Interview

Seymour, Carolyn. Personal interview. 7 Aug. 1988.

48. A Personal Letter

Cardan, Richard. Letter to the author. 14 Dec. 1991.

49. A Lecture or an Address

Ruiz, Armando. Lecture. El Camino College, Torrance, CA, 2 Oct.

1985.

Kubler-Ross, Elisabeth. "Life, Death, and Transition." Church of

Religious Science. Huntington Beach, CA. 28 June 1985.

> [Include the title of the lecture if you know it; if you do not know the title, use a descriptive label.]

50. A Cartoon

Martin, Henry. Cartoon. <u>New Yorker</u> 12 Sept. 1988: 42.

50b APA documentation style

The American Psychological Association (APA) style of documentation is frequently used in courses in psychology and other social sciences. Although all documentation styles require essentially the same information, each has its own conventions of arrangement, punctuation, and abbreviation.

Parenthetical Citations: APA Style

The APA parenthetical style cites the last name of the author and the date of publication, separated by a comma. For some citations, these two items of information are the only ones necessary, but page references should be added when you present a direct quotation or refer to specific information rather than general concepts. Notice the following examples.

> AUTHOR AND DATE ONLY
>
> More than half of home-schooled children spend 20 to 30 hours a month in organized community activities, while 40 percent spend more than 30 hours each month with peers outside their families (Wartes, 1988).

> DATE ONLY
>
> Wartes (1988) has shown that more than half of home-schooled children spend 20 to 30 hours a month in organized community activities, while 40 percent spend more than 30 hours each month with peers outside their families.

> AUTHOR, DATE, AND PAGE
>
> Some people try to apologize for our schools' failure to create literate society by arguing, for example, that they have "to pay

due regard to the demands of both local and national accultur-
ation" (Hirsch, 1987, p. 25).

[For direct quotations, include the page number. Use "p." for *page* and
"pp." for *pages*.]

Although still subject to close scrutiny and regulation, home
schooling is today legal in virtually every state (Pederson &
O'Mara, 1991, p. 37).

[Join the names of multiple authors with an ampersand: &.]

The majority of home-school parents embrace the philosophies
of educational reformers such as Francis W. Parker as well as
his more modern counterparts (Knowles, Marlow, & Muchmore, 1992; Pederson & O'Mara, 1991).

[For more than one source, list them in alphabetical order by the first
authors' names, and separate the citations by a semicolon.]

References: APA Style

In APA style, the works cited are listed at the end of the paper in a section titled "References." As you study the following examples of APA
reference listings, notice carefully the order in which information is
given, the use of punctuation and capitalization, and spacing between
items.

Only the most frequently encountered situations are illustrated
here. For a comprehensive guide, consult the *Publication Manual of
the American Psychological Association.* 4th ed. Washington: APA,
1994.

Guide to APA Reference and Parenthetical Note Forms

Examples of APA *reference* and parenthetical note forms follow this
list of sample resources.

doc

APA Style for Books

1. A Book with One Author

Lopez, B. (1986). <u>Arctic dreams: Imagination and desire in a northern landscape</u>. New York: Scribner's.

> [Indent the first line 5 spaces; begin additional lines at the left margin. Use the first initial only for the author's first name. Enclose the year in parentheses, followed by a period. Only the first word of the title and subtitle is capitalized; other words are lowercase unless they are proper nouns.]

2. A Book with More Than One Author

Peters, T.J., & Waterman, R.H. (1982). <u>In search of excellence: Lessons from America's best-run companies</u>. New York: HarperCollins.

> [List all authors and invert all authors' names. Use & for *and*.]

3. A Book in More Than One Volume

Shell, S. (1985). <u>A brief history of drugs and their use</u> (Vol. 2). New York: Corbin.

4. A Book with an Editor

Newhall, B. (Ed.). (1980). <u>Photography: Essays and images</u>. New York: Museum of Modern Art.

> [This form focuses on the editor's work.]

APA Style for Periodicals

5. A Signed Article in a Periodical

Cunningham, K. (1988, October). U.S. Davis Cuppers set to conquer. <u>World Tennis</u>, 168–69.

> [Spell out the month, and repeat all numbers for inclusive pages.]

Bagley, B. M. Colombia and the war on drugs. <u>Foreign Affairs</u>, <u>67</u> (1), 70–92.

> [Underline the volume number and, if applicable, put the issue number in parentheses. A comma precedes both the volume number and the page numbers.]

6. An Unsigned Article in a Periodical

Four exercises women do too many of. (1988, September). <u>Self</u>, pp. 174–77.

APA Style for Encyclopedias

7. An Unsigned Article from an Encyclopedia

Cancer. (1988). <u>Encyclopedia Brittanica: Micropedia</u>. (Vol. 2, pp. 301–309). Chicago: Encyclopedia Britannica.

30c CBE and other documentation styles

Documentation styles different from MLA and APA styles are used in the natural and applied sciences. In these styles, each in-text (or parenthetical) citation is a number, which is the reason these documentation styles are frequently called the "number-system style." The number in the in-text citation always corresponds to a full citation in the list of sources located at the end of the research project. The citations in the reference include the name of the author(s), title, and other publication information.

The requirements for arranging and punctuating citations vary among these documentation styles. You must, therefore, be sure which style your science instructor wants you to follow. Sources fo common style manuals you might need to use are as follows:

> American Chemical Society: *Handbook for Authors of Papers i the American Chemical Society Publications.*
> American Institute of Physics: *Style Manual for Guidance in th Preparation of Papers.*
> American Mathematical Society: *A Manual for Authors c Mathematical Papers.*
> Council of Biology Editors: *CBE Style Manual.*

Of the number-system documentation styles, the one most com monly used in undergraduate research is one advocated by the Counc of Biology Editors (CBE). Besides a system similar to APA's author ye system, CBE documentation style offers writers two number-syster choices:

1. Sources are alphabetized and numbered in the reference section
2. Sources are numbered in the reference section as they appear i the text.

In-Text Citations

Whether the alphabetized or sequential numbering system is use the numbers placed in an in-text citation correspond to the numb of the source listed in the reference section. The numbers themselv placed within the text, can be enclosed in parentheses or brackets can be raised above the line (you must, of course, follow one pr scribed style consistently throughout your paper—in other words, not use brackets for some citations and parentheses for others). F example, the source of the following excerpt would be the third ite listed in the numbered reference section.

> The unique scent of a spring meadow, for example, may
> appear to come from a single source when in reality it comes

from a multitude of fragrances mingling in the air and stirred
together by breezes (3).

f you need to document a specific reference, the page number or
umbers (using *p.* to indicate one page and *pp.* to indicate more than
ne page), follow the number assigned to the source.

In some animals the sense of smell functions as an early
warning system. "Even in slumbering felines, the nose can
catch a whiff of danger and rouse the beast to action" (5, p. 23).
In other animals, however, especially those that have been long
domesticated, the sense of smell is not so acute and may have
diminished to the point at which they can barely use it to find
their dinner bowls (5, pp. 25-27).

u can refer to more than one source in a single in-text citation, and
you need to cite a source already cited in your paper, refer to it by its
iginal number.

The human nose fails miserably from disuse (3, 5). Early
human hunters could smell an animal downwind before the
eye ever picked it out of the brush, and Native American war-
riors could smell a nearby enemy before they heard a war cry
(3, 6).

ferences

le the reference section Literature Cited, References Cited, or Ref-
nces. Center the title at the top of the page. When listing your
rces, follow these general guidelines.

1. Arrange the sources either alphabetically or sequentially as they
   appear in the text.
2. Number each source.

3. Neither underline nor place quotation marks around titles.
4. As a general guideline, capitalize only the first word in the titl
   except proper nouns. For example: The urban coyotes of Lo
   Angeles.
5. Begin with the author's last name. In place of an author's firs
   name, use initials. If the source has multiple authors, separat
   their names with a semicolon.
6. The title of the source follows the author's name and ends wit
   a period.
7. For books, the city of publication follows the title and end
   with a colon. The publisher follows and ends with a semicolo
   which is followed by the year of publication, and the enti
   entry is closed with a period.
8. For journal articles, the name of the journal follows the title
   the source. The volume number follows the name of the per
   odical and ends with a colon, which is followed by the pa
   numbers, a semicolon, and the year of publication; the enti
   entry is closed with a period. A journal title may be abbrevia
   ed, unless it is composed of a single word.
9. For popular magazine articles, the name of the magazine fo
   lowed by a period comes after the title of the article. The date
   publication, (year, month, and day) follows the magazine ti
   and ends with a colon, which is immediately followed by t
   page number. The entire entry is closed with a period.

Use the following sequentially arranged References Cited page a
guide to help you create your own reference section.

Sample Reference List

References Cited

POPULAR MAGAZINE   1. Carnack, V. Carried on the wind. Nature.
                          1983 Dec. 15:102.

JOURNAL ARTICLE   2. Deem, A. W.; Thorp, F. Toxic algae in Col-
                          orado. J. Am. Vet. Med. Assoc. 95:542;198

OOK	3. Ackerman, D. A natural history of the senses. New York: Random House; 1991.
ORPORATE AUTHOR	4. Council for Science and Society. Companion animals in society. London: Oxford University Press; 1988.
ULTIPLE BOOK UTHORS	5. Rivlin, R.; Gravelle, K. Deciphering the senses: the expanding world of human perception. New York: Simon & Schuster; 1984.
OOK WITH AN DITOR	6. Allen, J. W. T., ed. The customs of the Swahili people. Berkeley and Los Angeles: University of California Press; 1981.
ANDARD WORKS TH EDITORS GIN WITH TITLE	7. Dictionary of genetics. 3d ed. King, R. C. & Stansfield, W. D., eds. London: Oxford University Press; 1985.
	8. Annual review of cell biology. Pallade, G. E. Palo Alto, CA: Annual Reviews; 1987.

When typing your References Cited page, double-space through-
t and begin the second and subsequent lines of that entry directly
der the first letter of the first line, not under the numeral. If your
)ject requires citations more complicated than these basic exam-
s, you should check the *CBE Style Manual* for more detailed infor-
tion.

Glossaries

Glossary of Usage

Glossary of Grammatical Terms

Glossary of Usage

The entries in this glossary are words and phrases that frequent
cause problems for inexperienced writers. Based on recent editions
dictionaries and usage guides, the suggestions for standard writte
English included in this glossary represent current practice amor
experienced writers. You should avoid using words and phras
labeled *nonstandard,* and use entries labeled *colloquial* sparingly ar
with care. They are used primarily in informal speech and writir
and, therefore, are usually inappropriate in college and business wri
ing.

"Diction" offers guidelines for selecting appropriate words and phra
es in your writing, and this glossary makes specific recommend
tions. It is necessarily brief, so you should keep a good dictionary
your side when writing and refer to it when you question the appr
priateness of a word or phrase you wish to use.

a, an Use *a* before a consonant sound, *an* before a vowel sound.

a history	a university	a one o'clock meeting	a C
an hour	an undertow	an orphan	an F

aggravate *Aggravate* means "make worse." In writing it should not be used
its colloquial meaning of "irritate" or "annoy."

agree to, agree with *Agree to* means "consent to" a plan or proposal. *Ag*
with means "be in accord with" a person or group.

ain't Nonstandard for *am not* or *aren't*.

all right *All right* is always two words. *Alright* is a misspelling.

all together, altogether *All together* means "in a group," "gathered in
place," or "in unison." *Altogether* means "wholly" or "completely." *They m*
the jungle trek all together *rather than in small groups. I did not* altoge
approve of the plan.

allusion, illusion An *allusion* is a reference to something. An *illusion*
deceptive appearance. *Dr. Conn fills his lectures with classical* allusions*. Des*
the hard facts, she clings to her illusion *of true love.*

a lot *A lot* is always written as two words. *Alot* is a common misspelling.

among, between *Among* is used to refer to three or more people or things. *Between* is used with two people or things. *Half the treasure was divided between the captain and the ship's owner, the other half among the crew.* Sometimes *between* is used with more than two if the relationship concerns individual members of the group with each other. *The treaty between the five countries guarantees access to deep water ports.*

amount, number *Amount* refers to a quantity of something that cannot be counted. *Number* refers to things that can be counted. *A large number of saltwater fish requires an aquarium that holds a tremendous amount of water.*

an See *a, an.*

and etc. *Et cetera* (etc.) means "and so forth"; *and etc.*, therefore, is redundant.

and/or A legalism that many people consider awkward in college and business writing.

anxious, eager *Anxious* means "nervous" or "worried." *Eager* means "enthusiastically anticipating something." *I am eager to start the trip across the desert but anxious about the weather.*

anyone, any one *Anyone* means "any person at all." *Any one* refers to a particular person or thing in a group. Similar definitions apply to *everyone, every one, someone, some one.* *Anyone with the price of membership can join. Any one of the seniors might have started the brawl.*

anyplace Colloquial for *anywhere.*

anyways, anywheres Nonstandard for *anyway* and *anywhere.*

as Avoid using *as* for *because, since, while, whether,* and *who.* *Because* [not *as*] the firm is almost bankrupt, buying a computer is out of the question. We doubt whether [not *as*] they can continue.

as, like See *like, as, as if, as though.*

awful An overused word for *bad, shocking, ugly.* Colloquially, *awful* substitutes for intensifiers meaning "very" or "extremely."

awhile, a while *Awhile* is an adverb. *A while* is an article and a noun. *Awhile,* therefore, can modify a verb but cannot serve as an object of a preposition. *After six hours on the road, they rested awhile. After six hours on the road, they rested for a while.*

bad, badly *Bad* is an adjective and should be used in formal writing to mod ify nouns and as a predicate adjective after linking verbs. *Badly* should b used only as an adverb. *The doctor felt <u>bad.</u> The tenor sang <u>badly.</u>*

being as, being that Colloquial for *because.* <u>*Because*</u> [not <u>*Being that*</u>] *the su has risen each morning of your life, you may expect it to rise tomorrow.*

beside, besides *Beside* means "next to." *Besides* means "except" and "in addi tion." *The older sister stood <u>beside</u> her father. <u>Besides</u> one stranger, only relative were on the bus.*

between See *among, between.*

bring, take Use *bring* to carry something from a farther place to a neare one. Use *take* to carry something from a nearer place to a farther one. *<u>Tak</u> these pages to the printer and <u>bring</u> me yesterday's batch.*

bunch *Bunch* should not be used to refer to a crowd or group of people o things. Reserve it to refer to things that grow fastened together, such as grap and bananas.

burst, bursted, bust, busted The verb *burst* means "fly apart," and its princ pal parts are *burst, burst, burst.* The past tense *bursted* is nonstandard. *Bu and busted* are considered slang and so are inappropriate in college or bus ness writing.

can, may *Can* indicates ability, and *may* indicates permission. Colloquial *can* is used in both senses. *If I <u>may</u> use the car, I believe I <u>can</u> reach the sto before it closes.*

center around *Center on* is more accurate than *center around.*

climactic, climatic *Climactic* refers to a climax. *Climatic* refers to climate.

compare to, compare with *Compare to* means "regard as similar." *Compa with* means "examine for similarities or differences." *The boy <u>compared</u> father's bald head <u>to</u> an egg. The investigator <u>compared</u> the facts of the Rinem case <u>with</u> the facts of the Billings incident.*

continual, continuous *Continual* means "often repeated." *Continuous* mea "unceasing" or "without a break." *My afternoons are <u>continually</u> interrupted telephone calls. The waves lap <u>continuously</u> at the shore.*

convince, persuade Careful writers use *convince* when someone changes or her opinion. They use *persuade* when someone is moved to take action. *T attorney <u>convinced</u> several students that capital punishment is immoral. T attorney <u>persuaded</u> several students to demonstrate against capital punishmen*

ould of Nonstandard for *could have.*

redible, creditable, credulous *Credible* means "believable." *Creditable* means "praiseworthy." *Credulous* means "inclined to believe just about any-thing." *Hitchcock's fantastic stories are hardly <u>credible</u>; nevertheless, as a director e gets <u>creditable</u> performances from his actors regardless of whether the audience s <u>credulous</u>.*

riteria, data, phenomena *Criteria* is the plural form of *criterion.* Careful riters use *criteria* only in the plural sense. *The <u>criteria were</u> so ill phrased that hey were hard to apply.* *Data* and *phenomena* are plurals of *datum* and *phe-omenon,* respectively. They should be treated as plural forms. *New <u>data sug-est</u> the drug is harmful. Today's unexplainable <u>phenomena are</u> tomorrow's* *ientific explanations.*

ata See *criteria, data, phenomena.*

eal Colloquial and overused for *bargain, transaction,* or *business transac-on.*

iffer from, differ with *Differ from* means "be unlike." *Differ with* means isagree."

ifferent from, different than *Different from* is idiomatic and widely accept-. *Different than* is acceptable when it precedes a clause. *An elephant is <u>diffent</u> om a mastodon. Paris was <u>different than</u> I had expected.*

sinterested, uninterested *Disinterested* means "impartial." *Uninterested* eans "bored" or "indifferent."

n't *Don't* is a contraction of *do not* and should not be used for *does not,* ose contraction is *doesn't. Although the performance <u>doesn't</u> begin for an* ur, I still <u>don't</u> think Bernice will be ready.*

e to Many people object to the use of *due to* as a preposition that means ecause of" or "owing to." *The class was canceled <u>because of</u> [not <u>due to</u>] low rollment. Due to* is acceptable when used as a subject complement. In this sition it usually follows a form of *be. His unpredictable behavior is <u>due to</u>* ohol.*

ger See *anxious, eager.*

thused Colloquial for "showing enthusiasm." The preferred adjective is *husiastic.*

. See *and etc.*

everyday, every day *Everyday* is an adjective meaning "used daily" or "common" and is always written as a single word. *These are my <u>everyday</u> shoes. Every day* is composed of the noun *day* and the adjective *every* and is always written as two words. *I leave campus <u>every day</u> at 3:00 p.m.*

everyone, every one See *anyone, any one.*

everywheres Nonstandard for *everywhere.*

every which way Colloquial for *in every direction* or *in disorder.*

expect Colloquial when used to mean "suppose" or "believe." *I <u>suppose</u> [not <u>expect</u>] the Reynolds clan is still squabbling about the settlement of the will.*

explicit, implicit *Explicit* means "expressed directly or precisely." *Implicit* means "expressed indirectly or suggested." *The threat was <u>explicit</u>—"I'll break your nose!" Although his voice was gentle, his body carried an <u>implicit</u> threat.*

farther, further *Farther* refers to actual distance. *Further* refers to additional time, amount, or other abstract matters. *I cannot walk any <u>farther</u>. <u>Further</u> encouragement is useless.*

fewer, less *Fewer* refers to items that can be counted. *Less* refers to a collective quantity that cannot be counted. *The marsh has <u>fewer</u> ducks living in it, but also has <u>less</u> water to support them.*

finalize Avoid using *finalize* for the verb *complete.*

former, latter *Former* refers to the first named of two things or people. *Latter* refers to the second of two named. *First* and *last* are used to refer to items in a series of three or more. *Gina and Jose are very successful; the <u>former</u> is a dentist, the <u>latter</u> a poet. Jogging, biking, and swimming require tremendous endurance; the <u>last</u> requires the most.*

further See *farther, further.*

get A common verb used in many colloquial and slang expressions. *Get with her prattling gets me,* and the like. Using *get* in such ways is inappropriate college and business writing.

goes Nonstandard when used instead of *says* or *said* to introduce a quotation. It should not be used to indicate speech. *He <u>said</u> [not <u>goes</u>], "Leave me alone."*

good, well *Good* is an adjective; *well* is an adverb. *Dr. Hunato is a <u>good</u> golfer. She strokes the ball <u>well</u>. Well* should be used to refer to health. *You look <u>well</u> [not <u>good</u>]. Are you feeling <u>well</u> [not <u>good</u>]?*

had ought, hadn't ought Nonstandard for *ought* and *ought not.*

half *Half a* or *a half* is appropriate, but *a half a* is redundant. *We drank half a [not a half a] gallon of soda.*

herself, himself See *myself, herself, himself, itself, yourself.*

hisself Nonstandard for *himself.*

hopefully *Hopefully* means "with hope." *They prayed hopefully for the blizzard to stop. Hopefully* is used colloquially to mean "it is hoped" in place of *I hope;* however, *I hope* is preferred in college and business writing. *I hope [rather than Hopefully] the blizzard will stop.*

illusion See *allusion, illusion.*

implicit See *explicit, implicit.*

imply, infer *Imply* means "suggest." *Infer* means "conclude." *Irving implied that he had studied for the quiz, but I inferred that he was unprepared.*

in, into *In* indicates a location or position. *Into* indicates movement or change. *Beata is in the study with a clairvoyant, who is in a trance. I must go to Murkwood, but I don't want to fall into danger. Into* has also come colloquially to mean "interested in" or "involved in" something, which is an inappropriate use in college and business writing. *My brother is interested in [not into] restoring Victorian houses.*

individual, party, person *Individual* should be used to refer to a single human being when expressing that person's unique qualities. *Each individual has a right to pursue his or her interests within the law.* When not emphasizing unique qualities, use *person. A romantic person will love the Austrian countryside.* Except in legal documents, use *party* to refer to a group. *Who is the missing person [not party]?*

infer See *imply, infer.*

in regards to Nonstandard for *in regard to* or *regarding.*

into See *in, into.*

irregardless Nonstandard for *regardless.*

is because See *reason is because.*

is when, is where A common predication error in sentences that define. *"Bandwagon" is a propaganda device by which [not is when or is where] advertisers urge consumers to become one of the millions buying their products.*

kind, sort, type These are singular words and take singular modifiers and verbs. *This kind of butterfly is rare in North America.* When referring to more than one thing, *kind*, *sort*, and *type* must be made plural and then take plural modifiers and verbs. *These kinds of butterflies are rare in North America.*

kind of, sort of Colloquial when used to mean *somewhat* or *rather*. *The picnic was rather [not sort of] dull.*

lay See *lie, lay.*

learn, teach *Learn* means "acquire knowledge." *Teach* means "dispense knowledge." *I must teach [not learn] the children better manners.*

leave, let *Leave* means "go away." *Let* means "allow" or "permit." *Let [not leave] me finish the job. The firm should have let [not left] her resign.*

less See *fewer, less.*

let See *leave, let.*

liable See *likely, liable.*

lie, lay These verbs are often confused. *Lie* means "recline," and *lay* means "place." In part, they seem to be confusing because the past tense of *lie* is the same as the present tense of *lay.*

lie ("recline")	*lay* ("place")
lie	lay
lay	laid
lain	laid
lying	laying

Lay (meaning "place") is also a transitive verb and as such takes an object. *Don't forget to lay the book on my desk. Today I laid the tile, and tomorrow I'll be laying the carpet. Lie* (meaning "recline") is intransitive and as such never takes an object. *The book lay on my desk for weeks. I can't waste time lying in bed; I've lain there long enough.*

like, as, as if, as though *Like* is a preposition and introduces a prepositional phrase. *As, as if,* and *as though* usually function as subordinating conjunctions and introduce dependent clauses. In college and business writing, do not use *like* as a subordinating conjunction. *The sky looks as if [not like] the end of the world is near.*

like, such as When introducing a representative series, use *such as*. To make irect comparison with an example, use *like*. *The 1980s produced some power-ul hitters in tennis, <u>such as</u> Borg, Connors, and McEnroe, but I want to play a ame of strategy <u>like</u> Vilas.*

kely, liable *Likely* is used to express probability. *Liable* is used to express esponsibility or obligation. *She is <u>likely</u> to finish the project before the week-nd. Mr. Wert is <u>liable</u> for his son's destructive behavior.*

ts, lots of Colloquial for *a great deal, much,* or *plenty.*

ay See *can, may.*

ay be, maybe *May be* is a verb phrase, and *maybe* is an adverb meaning erhaps."

ay of Nonstandard for *may have.*

edia, medium *Media* is the plural form of *medium*. Use plural modifiers d plural verbs with *media*. *<u>These kinds</u> of mass <u>media</u>—television, radio, wspapers—<u>influence</u> our emotional attitudes.*

ight of Nonstandard for *might have.*

ost Colloquial when used for *almost.*

ust of Nonstandard for *must have.*

yself, herself, himself, itself, yourself These and other *-self* pronouns are exive or intensive—that is, they refer to or intensify a noun or another noun in a sentence. *The family members disagree among <u>themselves</u>, but I self know how the inheritance should be divided.* Colloquially these pro-uns often are used in place of personal pronouns in prepositional phrases. is use is inappropriate in college and business writing. *None of the team ept <u>you</u> [not <u>yourself</u>] has learned to rappel.*

way Nonstandard for *no.*

where near Colloquial for *not nearly*. *Brytan's game is <u>not nearly</u> [not vhere near] as good as Schrup's.*

wheres Nonstandard for *nowhere.*

nber See *amount, number.*

, O.K., okay All are acceptable spellings, but avoid using them in college business writing.

ty See *individual, party, person.*

people, persons *People* refers to a collective mass and emphasizes faceless anonymity. *Persons* refers to individuals who make up the group and emphasizes separate identity. *People surged into the convention hall. Several persons angrily denounced the membership's reluctance to act.*

percent, percentage Both *percent* and *percentage* refer to numbers and should be used only in actual references to statistics. Avoid using them to replace the word *part.* *The major part [not percent] of my trouble is caused by mismanagement.* *Percent* is always preceded by a number (*60 percent; 45 percent*), and *percentage* follows an adjective (*a major percentage*). In formal writing *percent* should always be written out (not %).

person See *individual, party, person.*

persons See *people, persons.*

persuade See *convince, persuade.*

phenomena, phenomenon See *criteria, data, phenomena.*

plus Nonstandard for *moreover.* *Nguyen Enterprises has a fine economic future; moreover [not plus], it offers young executives many tax-free perquisites.*

raise, rise Two commonly confused verbs. *Raise (raising, raised, raised),* meaning "force something to move upward," is a transitive verb and takes a direct object. *Rise (rising, rose, risen),* meaning "go up," is an intransitive verb. When the subject of a verb is being forced to move upward, use a form of *raise.* *Increasing the interest rate will raise monthly mortgage payments.* When the subject of a verb is itself moving upward, use a form of *rise.* *Unsteadily the ailing man rose from the chair.*

real, really *Real* is an adjective; *really* is an adverb. *The linebacker was really [not real] tough to block.*

reason is because Use *that* instead of *because* in the phrase *reason is because* or rewrite the sentence. *The reason the MG stalled is that [not is because] oil had leaked from the crankcase.*

respectfully, respectively *Respectfully* means "with respect" or "showing respect." *Respectively* means "each in the order given." *He respectfully expressed his opposition to the plan.* The Collector, The Optimist's Daughter, *and* The Human Comedy *were written by John Fowles, Eudora Welty, and William Saroyan, respectively.*

rise See *raise, rise.*

says, said   See *goes*.

sensual, sensuous   *Sensual* refers to pleasures of the body, especially sexual pleasures. *Sensuous* refers to pleasures perceived by the senses. *The poet's sensual desires led him to create the <u>sensuous</u> images readers find in his work.*

set, sit   Two commonly confused verbs. *Set (setting, set, set),* meaning "put or place," is a transitive verb and takes a direct object. *Sit (sitting, sat, sat),* meaning "be seated," is an intransitive verb. When you mean "put something down," use a form of *set. Ralph <u>set</u> the paint beyond the child's reach.* When you refer to being seated, use a form of *sit. Don't <u>sit</u> in the wet paint.*

shall, will   *Shall,* which was once used to form the simple future tense in the first person, has been replaced by *will. I <u>will</u> deal with him later.* In first-person questions that request an opinion, *shall* is the correct form to use. *<u>Shall</u> I march? <u>Shall</u> we strike?*

should, would   Use *should* when expressing a condition or obligation. Use *would* when expressing a wish or customary action. *If they <u>should</u> appear, you must be prepared to battle. He <u>would</u> nap each afternoon when he was on vacation.*

should of   Nonstandard for *should have*.

sit   See *set, sit*.

someone   See *anyone, any one*.

sort   See *kind, sort, type*.

sort of   See *kind of, sort of*.

such as   See *like, such as*.

sure   Colloquial when used as an adverb for *surely* or *certainly. Barnett <u>surely</u> [not <u>sure</u>] was correct in his cost estimate.*

sure and, sure to, try and, try to   *Sure to* and *try to* are the preferred forms. *<u>Try to</u> [not <u>try and</u>] attend.*

than, then   *Than* functions as a conjunctive used in comparisons, *then* as an adverb indicating time. *I would rather be in class <u>than</u> [not <u>then</u>] at work.*

that, which   *That* always introduces a restrictive clause. *Which* may introduce a restrictive clause or a nonrestrictive clause. Many writers prefer to use *which* to introduce only nonrestrictive clauses. *This is the class <u>that</u> requires six outside reports. This class, <u>which</u> requires six outside reports, meets once a week.*

theirselves Nonstandard for *themselves.*

then See *than, then.*

try and, try to See *sure and, sure to, try and, try to.*

uninterested See *disinterested, uninterested.*

use to, suppose to Sometimes carelessly written for *used to* and *supposed to*

wait for, wait on *Wait for* means "await." *Wait on* means "serve."

ways Use *way* when referring to distance. *The trout stream is only a little w* [not *ways*] *from here.*

well See *good, well.*

which See *that, which.*

which, who Never use *which* to refer to people. Use *who* or *that* to refer people and *which* or *that* to refer to things.

who, whom Use the relative pronoun *who* to refer to subjects and subj complements; use the relative pronoun *whom* to refer to the object of t verb or preposition. *The award was given to the person who deserved it. T award was given to whom?*

will See *shall, will.*

would See *should, would.*

yourself See *myself, herself, himself, itself, yourself.*

Glossary of Grammatical Terms

absolute phrase A phrase that modifies a whole clause or sentence rather than a single word and is not joined to the rest of the sentence by a connector. It consists of a noun and a participle: *Hands trembling, she opened the envelope. Our original plan looks best, all things considered.* See *phrase;* also 3f, 23h.

abstract noun See *noun.*

active voice See *voice.*

adjective A word used to modify a noun or pronoun. It tells what kind, how many, or which one: *Careless drivers must attend seven hours of that class.* A **predicate adjective** follows a linking verb and describes the subject of the sentence: *The speaker was nervous.* See also 2i.

adjective clause A dependent clause that modifies a noun or a pronoun. See *clause.*

adjective phrase Any phrase that modifies a noun or pronoun. See *phrase.*

adverb A word used to modify a verb, an adjective, another adverb, or a whole phrase, clause, or sentence. Adverbs tell how, when, where, or to what extent. *He speaks hurriedly.* [*Hurriedly* modifies *speaks* by telling how.] *She is never ambitious.* [*Never* modifies *ambitious* by telling when.] *Our dog wanders everywhere.* [*Everywhere* modifies *wanders* by telling where.] *He is quite easily confused.* [*Quite* modifies *easily* by telling to what extent.] See also

adverb clause A dependent clause that modifies a verb, an adjective, another adverb, or a whole clause. See *clause.*

adverbial conjunction See *conjunctive adverb.*

adverb phrase Any phrase used as an adverb. See *phrase.*

agreement The correspondence in person, number, and gender between two words. A verb must agree with its subject in person and number. A pronoun must agree with its antecedent in person, number, and gender. A demonstrative adjective (*this, that, these, those*) must agree with its noun in number. See *gender, person, number;* also 8, 9.

antecedent The word or group of words that a pronoun refers to. *When she graduated, she immediately took a job in New York.* [*Stacy* is the antecedent of the pronoun *she.*] See also 9.

appositive A noun or group of words used as a noun, placed next to a nou or pronoun to explain, describe, or identify it: *The lawyer, a Harvard grad ate, easily won her first case.* Most appositives are nonrestrictive and are set c with commas. See also 3b, 23c.

article *The* is a definite article. *A* and *an* are indefinite articles. Articles a classed as adjectives. See also 1d.

auxiliary verb See *helping verb.*

case The form of nouns and pronouns classified according to how th function in a sentence. English has three cases: the **subjective** to indicate t subject of a verb or a subject complement; the **objective** to indicate the obj of a verb, verbal, or preposition; and the **possessive** to indicate ownersh Nouns and most pronouns change form only in the possessive case (*cat dral's, everyone's*). All other uses require only the plain form (*cathedral, eve one*). The personal pronouns *I, we, he, she,* and *they* and the relative interrogative pronoun *who* have three case forms. The personal pronouns ; and *it* have a separate possessive form. See also 10, especially p. 57.

clause A group of words that has a subject and a predicate. A **main (in pendent) clause** forms a grammatically complete sentence: *He ran all the to the station.* Main clauses can be joined to other main clauses with coo nating conjunctions, conjunctive adverbs, or semicolons. (See 1g, 1 **Dependent (subordinate) clauses** are not sentences and must be joined main clause to form a grammatically complete sentence: *Although he tired, he ran all the way to the station.* Dependent clauses function as ad tives, adverbs, and nouns. See also 4.

collective noun See *noun.*

comma splice An error occurring when main clauses are joined only comma: *Last summer we went camping, everyone laughed at my inabili pitch a tent.* See also 4a and 7.

common noun See *noun.*

comparative degree See *comparison.*

comparison Adjectives and adverbs have three forms: the **positive de** which only describes [*large*]; the **comparative degree,** which compares things [*larger*]; and the **superlative degree,** which compares three or things [*largest*]. See also 14e.

complement A word or group of words that completes the meaning of a subject, an object, or a verb. Complements function as **direct objects, indirect objects, predicate adjectives,** and **predicate nominatives:** *The manager opened the <u>door</u>* [direct object]. *Please send <u>me</u> a letter* [indirect object]. *The <u>sea</u> was <u>calm</u>* [predicate adjective]. *Her father is an <u>accountant</u>* [predicate nominative]. See also 2g–2j.

complete predicate See *predicate.*

complete sentence See *sentence.*

complete subject See *subject.*

compound Words or groups of words of two or more parts functioning as a unit. **Compound words:** *brother-in-law, lifeguard.* **Compound constructions:** *Betty and Joe* [compound subject] *flew to Chicago. The children giggled and blushed* [compound predicate]. See also 2e–2f.

compound-complex sentence See *sentence.*

compound predicate See *compound.*

compound sentence See *sentence.*

compound subject See *compound.*

concrete noun See *noun.*

conjunction A word that connects and shows the relation between words, phrases, and clauses. **Coordinating conjunctions** (*and, but, or, nor, yet, for, so*) connect items of equal grammatical rank: *The beauty of the scenery and the friendliness of the people make British Columbia an attractive tourist spot.* **Correlative conjunctions** (*either . . . or, not only . . . but also,* and so on) are used in pairs: *You may choose <u>either</u> the vase <u>or</u> the picture.* **Subordinating conjunctions** (*when, while, if, although, because,* and so on) introduce dependent clauses and connect them to main clauses: *The carnival activity began after the sun went down.* See also 1g.

conjunctive adverb An adverb used to connect two main clauses: *Susan practiced faithfully; <u>therefore</u>, she improved rapidly.* See also 1g.

coordinating conjunction See *conjunction.*

correlative conjunction See *conjunction.*

count/noncount noun Count nouns are nouns which may be used in singular or plural form (e.g., *textbook, textbooks; assignment, assignment* Noncount nouns may be used in singular form only (e.g., *advice, homewor* See list of noncount nouns on pp. 93.

dangling modifier A modifying phrase or clause that does not sensibly connect to any word in a sentence. See also 17h.

degree See *comparison*.

demonstrative pronoun See *pronoun*.

dependent clause See *clause*.

direct address A noun or pronoun used parenthetically to indicate the person or group spoken to: *I believe, <u>friends</u>, that we will win this election.*

direct discourse The presentation of the exact words, spoken or written another: *Steven asked, "<u>Where have you been?</u>"* **Indirect discourse** reports words of another in paraphrase or summary form: *Steven wanted to kr <u>where we had been</u>.* See also 19e.

direct object See *object*.

double negative Two negative words used in the same construction: *I d<u></u> have <u>no</u> reason to stay home.* Double negatives are nonstandard English. sentence must be revised: *I <u>didn't</u> have <u>any</u> reason to stay home* or *I had no son to stay home.*

elliptical construction A construction in which one or more words are o ted but understood. *Bob types faster than Margaret [types].* See also 10e, 2C

expletive The word *there, here,* or *it* followed by a form of the verb *be* used to begin a construction in which the subject follows the verb: *<u>It is</u> ea spend money foolishly.* [*To spend money foolishly* is the subject of *is.*] See 8h.

finite verb A verb that makes an assertion about a subject. A finite verb function as the main (or only) verb in a sentence: *On weekends I <u>work</u> i garden.* Gerunds, infinitives, and participles are nonfinite verbs and ca function as main verbs in a sentence. See *verbal*.

fragment See *sentence fragment*.

fused sentence An error occurring when main clauses are joined with coordinating conjunction or semicolon: *We traveled to Georgia it was a trip.* See also 7.

future perfect tense See *tense*.

future tense See *tense*.

gender The classification of nouns and pronouns as masculine (*man, he*), feminine (*woman, she*), or neuter (*house, it*). See also *agreement; 9.*

genitive case Same as possessive case. See *case*.

gerund A verbal ending in *-ing* that functions as a noun. The form of the gerund is the same as that of the present participle. Gerunds may have objects, complements, or modifiers. *Cigarette <u>smoking</u> is dangerous to your health.* [The gerund *smoking* is the subject of the sentence. *Cigarette* modifies the gerund. *Dangerous* is a predicate adjective complementing the gerund.] See also *verbal; 3e.*

gerund phrase See *phrase*.

helping verb A verb used with a main verb to form a verb phrase: *Sarah <u>was</u> living in San Francisco at that time.* See also *1c, 11.*

imperative See *mood*.

indefinite pronoun See *pronoun*.

independent clause Same as main clause. See *clause*.

indicative See *mood*.

indirect discourse See *direct discourse*.

indirect object See *object*.

infinitive The plain form of a verb, as listed in the dictionary; it usually appears in combination with *to* to form a verbal that functions as a noun, an adjective, or an adverb. Infinitives may have objects, complements, or modifiers. *He promised <u>to mow</u> the lawn.* [The infinitive phrase *to mow the lawn* functions as a noun, the direct object of the verb *promised*. *Lawn* is the direct object of the infinitive *to mow*.] See also *verbal; 3c.*

infinitive phrase See *phrase*.

intensive pronoun See *pronoun*.

interjection A word expressing surprise or strong emotion: <u>*Oh*</u>, *here he comes!* See also *1h.*

interrogative pronoun See *pronoun*.

intransitive verb See *verb*.

irregular verb A verb that does not form its past and past participle ~~adding~~ -*d* or -*ed* to the infinitive form: *fly, flew, flown; sink, sank, sunk*. S~~also 11.~~

linking verb See *verb*.

main clause See *clause*.

misplaced modifier A modifier positioned incorrectly in a sentence. See al~~17.~~

modifier An adjective, an adverb, or a word, phrase, or clause used as ~~adjective or adverb to limit or qualify another word or group of words.~~

mood The form of a verb indicating a writer's (or speaker's) intent in a se~~tence.~~ The **indicative mood** is used for questions and statements of fact~~opinion:~~ *John is a good student.* The **imperative mood** indicates a comma~~or direction:~~ *Be a good student.* The **subjunctive mood** expresses doubt~~condition contrary to fact, or a wish:~~ *I wish I were a good student.* See also

nominative case Same as subjective case. See *case*.

nonrestrictive element A modifier that is not essential to the meaning ~~main clause.~~ Nonrestrictive elements are set off by commas: *Mr. Perkins, v* *retired from the grocery business last summer, is a noted rose grower.* See ~~23c.~~

noun A word that names a person, place, thing, or idea. **Proper nouns** na~~particular people,~~ places, or things: *James Joyce, Chicago, Fenway P* **Common nouns** name general classes: *athlete, singer, hotel.* **Abstract no** ~~name~~ intangible qualities: *loyalty, grace, devotion.* **Concrete nouns** name ~~gible things:~~ *desk, snow, glasses.* **Collective nouns** name groups: *team, sqt* ~~committee.~~ See also 1a.

noun clause A dependent clause that functions as a subject, an object, ~~complement.~~ See *clause*.

number The indication of singular or plural in the forms of nouns ~~toys),~~ pronouns (*I, we*), demonstrative adjectives (*this, these*), and verbs (~~eat).~~ See also *agreement*; 8, 9.

object A word, phrase, or clause that receives the action of or is affected ~~transitive verb,~~ a verbal, or a preposition. A **direct object** receives the actic~~a transitive verb or verbal and answers the question:~~ What? or Whom?:

...ade <u>money</u> tutoring neighborhood <u>children</u>. [*Money* is the direct object of the ...ansitive verb *make,* answering the question What? *Children* is the direct ...bject of the verbal *tutoring,* answering the question Whom?] An **indirect ...bject** indicates to whom or for whom an action is done: *I gave <u>David</u> five dol-* ...rs. [*David* is the indirect object of the verb *gave. Dollars* is the direct object.] ...n **object of a preposition** is the noun that a preposition relates to the rest of ...sentence: *Joan sat by the <u>door</u> of the <u>church</u>.* [*Door* is the object of the preposi-...on *by; church* is the object of the preposition *of.*] See also 2g–2h, 3a.

...jective case See *case.*

...renthetical expression A word, phrase, or clause that interrupts the ...ought of a sentence. See also 23d, 27a, 30a.

...rticipial phrase See *phrase.*

...rticiple A verbal that functions as an adjective, an adverb, or a part of a ...rb phrase. **Present participles** end in *-ing.* **Past participles** of regular verbs ...d in *-d* or *-ed: The light from the <u>floating</u> candles created grotesque shapes on ...* dark walls. [The present participle *floating* is used as an adjective modify-...g *candles.*] *He ran <u>screaming</u> down the street.* [The present participle *scream-*...g is used as an adverb modifying *ran.*] *The thief had <u>taken</u> her favorite ...celet.* [The past participle *taken* is used as part of the verb phrase *had tak-*...] See also *verbal;* 3d.

...ticle Another name for the preposition or adverb portion of a phrasal ...b. See *phrasal verb.*

...ts of speech The classification of words on the basis of their use in a sen-...ce. The parts of speech are nouns, pronouns, verbs, adjectives, adverbs, ...positions, conjunctions, and interjections. Each part of speech is defined ... separate entry in the glossary. See also 1.

...sive voice See *voice.*

...t participle See *participle.*

...t perfect tense See *tense.*

...t tense See *tense.*

...fect tenses See *tense.*

...son The form of pronouns and verbs used to indicate the speaker (first ...on—*I am*), the one spoken to (second person—*you are*), or the one spo-...about (third person—*she is*). See also *agreement;* 8, 9.

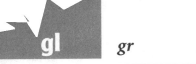

personal pronoun See *pronoun.*

phrasal verb Two-word or three-word verb consisting of a verb form plus preposition or adverb (e.g., *look over, put up with*).

phrase A group of words lacking a subject or a predicate or both and used as a single part of speech. A **verb phrase** consists of more than one verb: *has been talking, was swimming.* It functions as a predicate for clauses and sentences: *The professor <u>has been lecturing</u> for more than an hour.* A **prepositional phrase** consists of a preposition, its object, and any modifiers: *under the house, after the party.* It functions as an adjective, adverb, or noun: *She wandered <u>to the elm grove beyond the fence</u>.* [*To the elm grove* is used as an adverb modifying *wandered; beyond the fence* is used as an adjective modifying *grove.*] An **infinitive phrase** consists of an infinitive, its object, and any modifiers: *to hear the peaceful music, to learn I had been selected.* It functions as a noun, adjective, or adverb: *<u>To see her again</u> was a pleasure.* [*To see her again* is used as a noun, the subject of the sentence.] A **participial phrase** consists of a participle, its object, and any modifiers: *studying all night, glancing through the album.* It functions as an adjective or adverb: *The man <u>jogging around the track</u> is my brother.* [*Jogging around the track* is used as an adjective modifying *man.*] A **gerund phrase** consists of a gerund, its object, and any modifiers. Like participial phrases, gerund phrases use the *-ing* ending of the verb: *watching the birds, hoping for rain.* Therefore, they can be distinguished from participial phrases only in the context of a sentence. Gerund phrases function as nouns. *<u>Jogging around the track</u> is good exercise.* [*Jogging around the track* is used as a noun, the subject of the sentence.] An **absolute phrase** consists of a noun and usually a participle. It modifies a whole clause or sentence. *<u>The election being over</u>, the loser pledged support to the winner.* See also 3.

positive degree See *comparison.*

possessive case See *case.*

predicate The part of a sentence that tells what the subject did or how it was acted on. A predicate must have a finite verb. The **simple predicate** is the verb and its helping verb(s). The **complete predicate** is the simple predicate plus any modifiers, objects, and complements. *This play should set an attendance record in New York.* [*Should set* is the simple predicate.] See *finite verb;* also 2d.

predicate adjective See *adjective; complement.*

predicate nominative See *complement.*

reposition A word that shows the relation of a noun or a pronoun (the bject of the preposition) to some other word in the sentence. See also *object; hrase;* 1f.

repositional phrase See *phrase.*

resent participle See *participle.*

resent perfect tense See *tense.*

resent tense See *tense.*

rincipal parts The present, present participle, past, and past participle of a rb: *look, looking, looked, looked.* See also 11.

ogressive tense See *tense.*

onoun A word that takes the place of a noun. Words that function as pro-uns are classified as follows. **Personal pronouns:** *I, you, he, she, it, we, they* d their possessive forms, *my, mine, your, yours, his, her, hers, its, our, ours, eir, theirs.* **Reflexive pronouns:** *myself, yourself, himself, herself, itself, our-ves, yourselves, themselves,* which are also sometimes used as **intensive pro-uns,** as in *I myself saw it.* **Relative pronouns:** *who, whom, that, which, ose.* **Interrogative pronouns:** *who, which, whom, whose, what.* **monstrative pronouns:** *this, that, these, those.* **Indefinite pronouns:** *all, h, few, several, nobody,* and so on. See also 1b.

oper adjective An adjective derived from a proper noun: *French perfume, wellian nightmare.* See also 34f.

oper noun See *noun.*

otation See *direct discourse.*

lexive pronoun See *pronoun.*

ular verb A verb that forms its past and past participle by adding *-d* or to the infinitive form: *wander, wandered, wandered; scheme, schemed, emed.* See also 11.

ative pronoun See *pronoun.*

trictive element A modifier that defines or identifies the noun it modifies i is therefore essential to the meaning of the main clause. Restrictive ele-nts are not set off by commas. *All students who have successfully completed y units may apply for upper-division standing.* See also 23c and 24f.

run-on sentence See *fused sentence.*

sentence A group of words that contains a subject and a predicate and is no introduced by a subordinating conjunction. Sentences are classified accord ing to their structure. A **simple sentence** has one main clause: *Maria fe asleep.* A **compound sentence** has two or more clauses: *Maria tried to sta awake, but she fell asleep.* A **complex sentence** has one main clause and least one dependent clause: *When Maria lay down to rest, she fell asleep.* **compound-complex sentence** has two or more main clauses and at least or dependent clause: *Maria tried to stay awake because she wanted to study, bi she fell asleep.* Sentences may also be classified according to their purpose. **declarative sentence** makes a statement: *I am going home.* An **imperativ sentence** gives a command or makes a request: *Go home now.* An **interrog tive sentence** asks a question: *Are you going home?* An **explanatory senten** expresses strong feeling: *We're going home!* See also 5.

sentence fragment A portion of a sentence punctuated as though it were sentence: *Suddenly appearing on the horizon.* See also 6.

simple predicate See *predicate.*

simple sentence See *sentence.*

simple subject See *subject.*

simple tenses See *tense.*

squinting modifier A modifier placed so it may refer to either a word p ceding it or a word following it. See also 17b.

subject The part of a sentence that acts, is acted upon, or is described. T **simple subject** is the essential word or group of words of the **complete su ject.** The complete subject is the simple subject plus its modifiers. *A te stately gentleman appeared at the door.* [*Gentleman* is the simple subject. *tall, stately gentleman* is the complete subject.] See also 2a, 2c.

subject complement See *complement.*

subjective case See *case.*

subjunctive See *mood.*

subordinate clause Same as dependent clause. See *clause.*

subordinating conjunction See *conjunction.*

superlative degree See *comparison.*

tense The form of a verb and its helping verbs that expresses the verb's relation to time. The **simple tenses** are **present** (*I laugh, you choose*), **past** (*I laughed, you chose*), and **future** (*I will laugh, you will choose*). The **perfect tenses** indicate completed action: **present perfect** (*I have laughed, you have chosen*), **past perfect** (*I had laughed, you had chosen*), and **future perfect** (*I will have laughed, you will have chosen*). The **progressive tense** indicates continuing action (*I am laughing, you are choosing*). See also 11.

transitive verb See *verb.*

verb A word or group of words expressing action or a state of being. A **transitive verb** expresses action that has an object: *She <u>painted</u> a picture.* An **intransitive verb** expresses action that does not have an object: *The artist <u>failed</u>.* A **linking verb** expresses a state of being or a condition. It links the subject of a sentence with a complement that identifies or describes the subject: *Their laughter <u>was</u> maddening.* A verb may be transitive in one sentence and intransitive in another: *She <u>paints</u> pictures* [transitive]; *She <u>paints</u> well* [intransitive]. See also tense, 1c, 11; mood, 12; voice, 13.

verbal Also called *nonfinite verb.* A form of a verb used as a noun, an adjective, or an adverb. Gerunds, infinitives, and participles are verbals. Verbals may take objects, complements, and modifiers. A verbal cannot function as the main verb of a sentence. See also *gerund; infinitive; participle; phrase,* 3.

verb phrase See *phrase.*

voice The form of a transitive verb that indicates whether the subject acts (**active voice**) or is acted upon (**passive voice**). Active voice: *Donita <u>wrote</u> a fine research paper.* Passive voice: *A fine research paper <u>was written</u> by Donita.* See also 13.

Text Credits

would like to thank the following authors and publishers for permission to reproduce material from their works. Page numbers in parentheses preceding th credit line refer to the text page on which the material appears.

. 140-141) Mark Schorer, excerpt from *Sinclair Lewis: An American Life.* iversity of Minnesota Pamphlets on American Writers, #27. Copyright © 1963 the University of Minnesota. Reprinted by permission.

185) "The Love Song of J. Alfred Prufrock" by T. S. Eliot. Reprinted by permission of Harcourt Brace Publishers.

202) The lines from "Anyone Lived in a Pretty How Town" are reprinted from *nplete Poems: 1904–1962* by E.E. Cummings, edited by George J. Firmage, by mission of Liveright Publishing Corporation. Copyright © 1940, 1968, 1991 by Trustees for the E.E. Cummings Trust.

. 268-269) William G. Carleton, "Take Your College in Stride." *Vital Speeches of Day,* March 1947.

271–273) Robert Tilling, "A Volcanologist's Perspective." *Geo,* August 1980. rinted by permission of the author.

. 277–278) N. Scott Momaday, "The Way to Rainy Mountain. Copyright © 9 by The University of New Mexico Press. First published in *The Reporter,* 26 lary 1967.

. 281-282) John F. Wilson and Carroll C. Arnold, *Public Speaking as a Liberal* Allyn & Bacon, Inc., 1964, 1974.

283) Rachel Carson, *Silent Spring.* Copyright © 1962 by Rachel L. Carson. rinted by permission of Houghton Mifflin Company and Frances Collin, rary Executor.

:86) Lester del Rey, *The Mysterious Sky.* Reprinted by permission of the author the author's agents, Scott Meredith Literary Agency, Inc., 845 Third Avenue, / York, New York 10022.

:89) Victor B. Cline, "How TV Violence Damages Your Children." Copyright © 5, Meredith Corporation. All Rights Reserved. Reprinted from *Ladies' Home* nal magazine.

Index